D1526240

Soldiers of Fortune

SOLDIERS
OF FORTUNE

The Story of the Mamlukes

Sir John Glubb

STEIN AND DAY/*Publishers*/New York

First published in 1973
Copyright © 1973 by John B. Glubb
Library of Congress Catalog Card No. 73-80841
All rights reserved
Printed in the United States of America
Stein and Day/*Publishers*/Scarborough House, Briarcliff Manor, N.Y. 10510
ISBN 0-8128-1611-0

To prepare for the future, examine the present. To understand the present, study the past.

WILLIAM ARTHUR WARD

States, peoples and individuals are established upon their own particular definite principle, which has systematised reality in the entire compass of their surroundings. Yet are they the unconscious tools and organs of the world spirit . . . justice and virtue, wrong, force and crime, talents and their results, small and great passions, innocence and guilt. The splendours of individuals, national life, independence, the fortune and misfortune of states and individuals have in the sphere of conscious reality their definite meaning and value . . . To the nation . . . is assigned the accomplishment of it . . . In the history of the world, this nation is for a given epoch dominant, although it can make an epoch but once . . . The special history of a world historic nation contains the unfolding of its principle from its undeveloped infancy up to the time when . . . it presses in upon universal history. It contains, moreover, the period of decline and destruction, the rise of a higher principle . . . thus indicates to world history the rise of another nation. From that time onwards the first nation has lost absolute interest . . . but is, after all, only a recipient and has no indwelling vitality and freshness . . . Perhaps it loses its independence, perhaps continues to drag itself on.

HEGEL, Philosophy of Right

Preface

I HAVE referred on several past occasions to the extraordinarily narrow prejudices which, for many centuries, have governed the teaching of history in the West. One of the deepest of these prejudices has been the omission of the history of the Muslim nations from the syllabuses of schools and universities. This omission was doubtless based on the hatreds bred in the long wars between the Muslims and the Christian West, from the rise of Islam in the seventh century to the dominance of Europe in the seventeenth—a thousand years of struggle for power.

Today, perhaps, some people are ready to admit that true history is the history of the human race and that the great Muslim nations of the past contributed generously to the culture of the West today. But prejudices imbibed for so many centuries die hard. Historical works on Greece, Rome and Europe continue to increase on our bookshelves, but works on the past history of Muslim nations are few and far between.

One of the chief victims of our prejudices has been the Mamluke Empire, which was one of the Greatest Powers from 1250 to 1517. Few people in Britain have ever even heard of the Mamlukes, and those who have normally connect them with Napoleon Bonaparte and the Battle of the Pyramids in 1798. During the summer and autumn of 1972, millions of people formed long queues all day down the street outside the British Museum to view the treasures of Tutankhamun, a Pharaoh who died more than 3,300 years ago. The study of Egyptian history under the Pharaohs, whose rule ended in 341 B.C., is respectable in the West, but the history of the Mamluke Empire, which ended only 455—not 2,313—years ago and which closely affected the rise of modern Europe, is not taught in our schools or universities.

Nevertheless, apart from national or religious prejudices, the story of the Mamlukes is of great interest. The extraordinary nature of their institutions, the recruitment of a ruling class by the purchase of young boys from the Russian steppes, for example, is unique in history. The fact that, with so exotic a system, they built one of the world's great empires, which lasted longer than the British Empire, might well cause us to re-think many ideas which we accept as axiomatic.

To me, however, an additional interest is provided by the fact that they provide us with a clear, well-documented history of the rise and fall of an empire, including a great many factors which we can scarcely fail to recognise as existing before our eyes today in the countries of the West. Refusal, through national or religious prejudice, to study the history of certain nations of the past deprives us of the case-histories of many peoples from whom we might derive guidance in our own problems.

Author's Note

I DO not claim to be a scholar. My life was spent in active, largely outdoor occupations until I was fifty-nine, an age at which professional scholars are beginning to think of retirement.

Having begun my serious studies at an age when most professors are thinking of leaving off, I cannot aspire to compete with them. If I have any excuse for writing on Middle East history, it is that I lived intimately among all classes of the people there, for almost all my working life. The fact that I am not a professional scholar may indeed be an advantage, for it means that I am on the intellectual level of the man in the street. My object, as a result, is to convey to the general public some impression of the past history, the culture and the way of life of the peoples of the Eastern Mediterranean, North Africa and Western Asia.

The peoples of these countries now travel freely to Europe and North America and the English-speaking peoples visit Middle Eastern countries in their thousands every year. I venture to submit, therefore, that it is high time that the general public in the West acquired at least some knowledge of their neighbours, the Arabic-speaking peoples of Western Asia and North Africa. If I can in any way contribute to their mutual sympathy, respect and understanding, my humble efforts will have been amply rewarded.

ARABIC TRANSLITERATION

The letters of the Arabic alphabet differ from those of the languages of the West, presenting a problem to those who wish to transcribe Arabic names into English characters. Innumerable systems of transliteration exist. I have endeavoured to write Arabic names in such a manner that the English reader will be able to pronounce them, although he does not know Arabic. When confronted with these names, I therefore ask the reader to pronounce them as if they were English.

Where the emphatic syllable is in doubt, I have placed an accent over it, the first time the name is mentioned. If the name occurs again, I have not repeated the accent. There are no accents of this kind in Arabic.

ARABIC NAMES

The ordinary Arab name consists of the name of the man and that of his father, like John son of Thomas. The word for son is *ibn*, giving the form Ahmad ibn Hasan. Very often the word *ibn* combined with that of an ancestor becomes a family name, which is borne by all the old man's descendants. Such is, of course, the origin of many English names, like Johnson, Jameson or Williamson. Thus many Arabic family names take the form of Ibn Hasan, Ibn Khaldun, Ibn Saoud.

Unfortunately, during the period of the Mamlukes, prominent persons also made use of complicated titles. The two commonest forms which appear in this book are the religious name and the throne-name. Religious names, sometimes prefixed to personal names, take the form of Shems-al-Deen, Sun of the Religion, Saif-al-Deen, Sword of the Religion, and many others.

The throne-name was assumed by a sultan, a khalif or a prince, when he came to the throne. Such assumed titles might be Al-Malik-al-Ashraf, the most noble king, Al-Malik-al-Mansoor, the victorious king, and so on. In Arabic, *malik* means a king and the article is repeated, The-King-the-Victorious, preceding the personal name— e.g. The-King-the-Victorious Hasan. As this makes names wearisomely long, I have often omitted the first *Al* and sometimes also the word *Malik*. Thus the above title would be shortened to Al-Mansoor Hasan, the Victorious Hasan. I have connected the words of the throne-name with hyphens, though there are no hyphens in Arabic.

MAMLUKES

In various places in previous works, I have spelt this word mamlooks. Readers, however, have pointed out that -look is pronounced in English like cook, took or book. The correct sound here is -luke as in the English personal name Luke. In the present work, therefore, I have written mamluke. Where I have used quotations, I have left the original author's spelling unchanged. The form mamaluke is incorrect. Mamluke has only two syllables.

SOURCES

I have followed the same procedure as in some of my previous books, which is to take the principal narrative from Arabic historians, who were witnesses of many of the events which they record. The principal of these, in the present instance, were Ibn al Athír, Maqrízi, Ibn

Taghri Birdi and Ibn Iyás. I have in each case used the Arabic text, but have also taken advantage of translations into European languages where they exist, notably Quatremère, Wiet, and Gaudefroye-Desmonbynes in French, and William Popper in English.

I have used the minor Arabic historians to amplify the main narrative, such as Abulfeda, Ibn Abdul Dhahir, Al Dhahabi, Qalqashandi, Nuwairi, Umari and others.

There are very few English books on the Mamlukes. The only two dealing with the period as a whole are Stanley Lane-Poole, *History of Egypt in the Middle Ages*, and Sir William Muir, *The Mameluke Slave Dynasty of Egypt*. Among modern works in English dealing with certain aspects of the period are A. N. Poliak, *Feudalism in Egypt, Syria, Palestine and Lebanon*, and the various treatises of David Ayalon, such as *Gunpowder and Firearms in the Mamluk Kingdom*, *Studies in the Structure of the Mamluk Army*, *The Circassians in the Mamluk Kingdom* and others.

A short bibliography will be found at the end of the book.

ACKNOWLEDGMENTS

I would like once again to express my gratitude to the Library of the School of Oriental and African Studies in the University of London, and to the Public Library of Tunbridge Wells. I am deeply indebted to Mrs. Barbara Ranger and to Mrs. Norma Williams for typing and re-typing the text. Whenever I changed my mind (which was often), they patiently typed all over again the same pages which they had already done over *ad nauseam*. They must hate the Mamlukes now almost as much as Hulagu did.

Contents

List of Maps

List of Genealogical Trees

List of Illustrations

I

Historical Background

History shows but very few cases in which the course of great events was foreseen by those who launched them. Far from being the result of deliberate and cool calculation, the campaigns seem to have started as raids . . . The movement acquired momentum as the warriors passed from victory to victory . . . The Arabians burst forth upon an unsuspecting world as members of a national theocracy. It was Arabianism and not Muhammadanism that triumphed first. Not until the second and third centuries of the Moslem era did the bulk of the people in Syria, Mesopotamia and Persia profess the religion of Muhammad. Between the military conquest of these regions and their religious conversion, a long period intervened.

PHILIP HITTI, *History of the Arabs*

In spite of all this tumult the Ayoubid régime meant a period of prosperity for Egypt and Syria, even after Saladin's death. Its attention was devoted to agriculture, which could be maintained at its peak only through persistent tending of the irrigation system, no less than to commerce. The enmity with the Christians did not prevent it from concluding a series of trade agreements with European states.

CARL BROCKELMANN, *History of the Islamic Peoples*

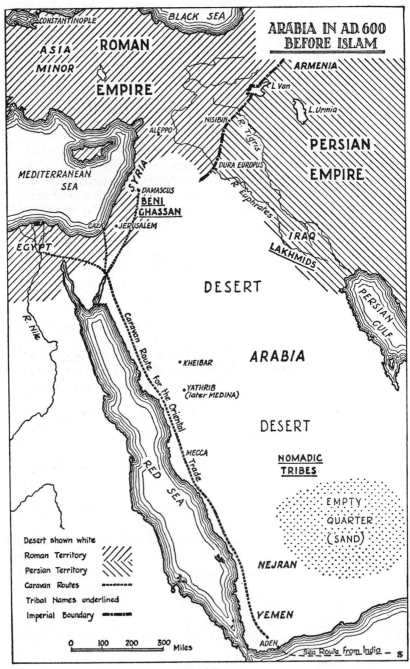

ARÁBIA IN A.D. 600
BEFORE ISLAM

CONSTANTINOPLE · BLACK SEA · ASIA MINOR · ROMAN EMPIRE · ARMENIA · L. Van · L. Urmia · ALEPPO · NISIBIN · R. Tigris · DURA EUROPUS · PERSIAN EMPIRE · MEDITERRANEAN SEA · SYRIA · DAMASCUS · BENI GHASSAN · R. Euphrates · GAZA · JERUSALEM · IRAQ · LAKHMIDS · EGYPT · R. Nile · Caravan Route for the Oriental · DESERT · PERSIAN GULF · KHEIBAR · ARABIA · YATHRIB (later MEDINA) · DESERT · MECCA · NOMADIC TRIBES · RED SEA · Trade · EMPTY QUARTER (SAND) · NEJRAN · YEMEN · ADEN · Sea Route from India

Desert shown white
Roman Territory
Persian Territory
Caravan Routes
Tribal Names underlined
Imperial Boundary

0   100   200   300 Miles

MAP 1

I

IN the seventh century A.D., the Western world, from India to
the Mediterranean, was divided between two great empires,
Byzantium, or the Eastern Roman Empire, and Persia, which
included Iraq, Iran and Afghanistan. It is a human tragedy that,
where two outstanding Great Powers exist, they cannot be satisfied
with what each possesses, but, out of greed or fear, must always be
fighting or intriguing. Byzantium and Persia continued for centuries
to wage endless hot or cold war against each other. From 602 to 628,
they were engaged in a murderous war, after which peace was concluded on the basis of the pre-war frontiers of 602, but both empires
were bankrupt and exhausted.

Meanwhile, in 570, a boy called Muhammad had been born in
Mecca in Arabia, a desert peninsula which neither of the Great
Powers had bothered to annex. Muhammad began to preach in 613,
and when he died in 632 his influence had spread all over Arabia. He
claimed to preach the original faith of the Patriarch Abraham, from
which the Jews had wandered. Jesus had come to rectify the errors
of Judaism, but the Christians had subsequently deviated from the
teachings of Christ. He, Muhammad, had been sent to restore the
true religion once more to its primitive purity.

So great was the enthusiasm of the Arabs that, in 633, the year
after the Prophet's death, they broke out of their desert peninsula
and simultaneously attacked both the Great Powers, exhausted by
their recent twenty-six years of war. Within eighty years, the Persian
Empire had been obliterated and the Arabs had invaded India. On
the north, they had reached the Caucasus and the Byzantines had
been driven west of the Taurus. Sweeping across North Africa and
over the Straits of Gibraltar, they had conquered Spain and invaded
France.[1]

Medina, an oasis in Arabia, was the first capital of the world's
greatest empire. But a more central capital was essential to so vast an
area and, in 661, the government moved to Damascus. Muhammad
had left no son and a family of his cousins, the Umaiyids, became his
khalifs,[2] and ruled over the empire from the Atlantic to China.

In 750, however, the Umaiyids were evicted by a rival group of
cousins, the Abbásids, who built a new imperial capital at Baghdad.

[1] Map 2, page 22.
[2] Khalif merely means successor. The word is sometimes spelt Caliph, a Greek form.

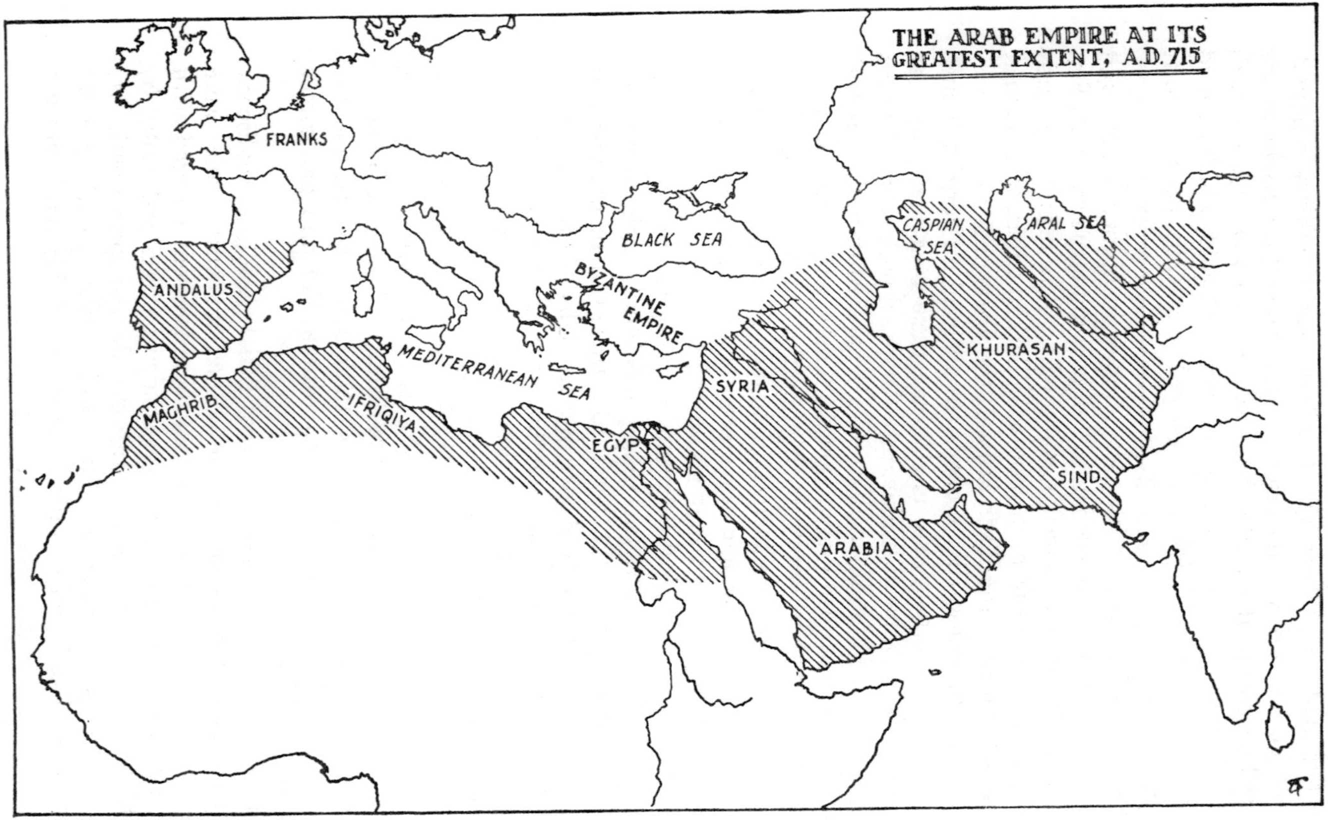

THE ARAB EMPIRE AT ITS
GREATEST EXTENT, A.D. 715

ARAL SEA

CASPIAN SEA

KHURASAN

SIND

ARABIA

SYRIA

BLACK SEA

BYZANTINE EMPIRE

EGYPT

MEDITERRANEAN SEA

FRANKS

ANDALUS

MAGHRIB

IFRIQIYA

MAP 2

The Umaiyid Age, 661 to 750, had been one of military conquest, that of the Abbasids was the era of wealth and culture. Baghdad was the richest city in the world. Men and women were covered with gold and jewels, their weapons were inlaid with gold, which covered also their saddles and bridles, and the pillars and roof beams of their houses.

But, as has happened with every empire in history, wealth and power resulted in decadence and a dislike of military service. At first the Abbasids enlisted mercenaries from East Persia, but afterwards they engaged soldiers from the nomadic Turkish tribes, who roamed the steppes north of the Black Sea and the Caspian.[3]

These tough and warlike nomads almost lived on horseback, and displayed extraordinary skill in shooting their bows and arrows at full gallop. The Abbasid khalifs were delighted with them, for they seemed to be almost invincible. The Khalif Mutasim (832–842) maintained a great army of mercenary Turks, with which he completely defeated the Byzantines. Mutasim was a man of dominant personality, to whom his mercenaries were devoted. All unawares, he had inaugurated the age of mercenaries, which was to endure a thousand years and give rise to great empires.

But while Mutasim had commanded his great mercenary army with ease, his two successors, Wáthiq and Mutawakkil, were weaklings. The rude Turkish soldiers regarded them with scant respect. In 861, the Khalif Mutawakkil was murdered by his palace guards. They had no intention of changing the form of government, nor were they idealists, democrats or revolutionaries. They had merely become involved in a palace quarrel.

The khalif had nominated his eldest son, Muntasir, as his successor, but had subsequently become infatuated with a Greek concubine. This young woman persuaded him to disinherit his eldest son and to nominate her son Mutazz as his heir. Indignant at the treatment of Muntasir, the Turkish guards killed Mutawakkil and proclaimed Muntasir khalif.

It is impossible for us, in our drab industrial world, to visualise the glamour of the Khalifs of Baghdad. Their immense armies were dressed in bright-coloured uniforms, their weapons covered with gold. Their palaces, with courtyards shaded by trees and cooled by splashing fountains, were paved with marble and spread with rare carpets. This state of affairs was accepted by contemporaries as right and natural. The khalif was the ruler of the world, and it did not occur to them that it would ever be otherwise.

[3] Map 9, page 52.

When the deed was done, however, the mercenaries gradually realised what had happened. A handful of Turks had killed the ruler of the world, and had appointed another, and they could do it again. Unintentionally, they had become the power behind the throne.

From 847 to 974, Baghdad was in endless confusion. The power was held by the commanders of the Turkish mercenaries, who, in a hundred and twenty-seven years, made and unmade fourteen khalifs. Of these fourteen, six were murdered, three were deposed, blinded and died in prison, and only five died a natural death.

But the mercenaries did not rule the empire. For nearly two hundred and fifty years, the empire had been held together by the glorious figure of the Prince of the Faithful, a member of the Prophet's family. When the provinces realised that the khalif had become the puppet of his barbarian mercenaries, they broke away and each pursued its own interests, leaving only central Iraq to the khalifs and their mercenaries.

*　　*　　*

The first crudity of Turkish military rule was gradually modified. In the second and third generation, the army commanders spoke Arabic and began to absorb Arab culture and religion. In 868, Ahmad ibn Tulun (pronounced Tuloon), a Turkish officer thirty-three years of age, was sent from Baghdad to be the governor of Egypt. A Turk by race, he was an authority on Arabic literature and theology. Ibn Tulun invaded and annexed Syria, made himself an independent ruler and defeated the Byzantine Emperor near Tarsus in 883.

Throughout the period of Abbasid glory in Baghdad (750–861), the priceless oriental trade from India and China to Byzantium and Europe had passed up the Persian Gulf and through Baghdad to northern Syria. But the administration of Ibn Tulun in Egypt was so just and conditions in Iraq were so chaotic, that the merchants who handled the oriental trade decided to switch their route from the Persian Gulf to the Red Sea and Egypt. This was the beginning of the rise of Egypt and the decline of Iraq.

In Arab imperial days, Egypt had been a secondary province, the successive capitals being Medina, Damascus and Baghdad. But with effect from the reign of Ibn Tulun (868–884), Egypt became the principal emporium for the eastern trade, growing richer and richer, while Iraq became poorer and more chaotic. In 905, Egypt and Syria were reunited with Iraq, but the trade route continued to go

THE DYNASTIES OF THE KHALIFS
(The Family of the Prophet Muhammad)

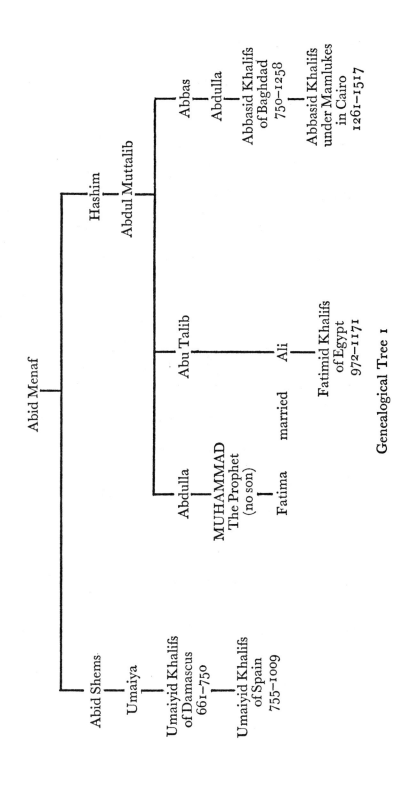

Genealogical Tree 1

up the Red Sea and across Egypt, providing the wealth which was to
enable Egypt herself to play an imperial rôle.

* * *

The Dailamites were tribesmen living at the southern end of the
Caspian. In 913, emerging from their mountains, they overran
western Persia. In 945, they took Baghdad. Their chiefs, known as
the Buwaihids, ruled Baghdad and West Persia from 945 to 1055.

These catastrophes provided an opportunity for a third branch of
the Prophet's family to make a bid for power. The descendants of Ali
and his wife Fátima, daughter of the Prophet, had claimed the
khalifate ever since 656. Those Muslims who supported their claim
were called the Shia, or the Party. The majority, who opposed their
claims, were known as Sunnis. Now that the Abbasids had lost their
power, the Aliids made a bid for the khalifate.[4]

On 15th January, 910, their leader seized Qairawan, in the area
we now call Tunisia. Assuming the name of Ubaidullah[5] and the
title of the Mehedi, he conquered North Africa as far west as the
Atlantic and founded the Fátimid dynasty, who based their claim on
their descent from Fátima, the Prophet's daughter. But the Mehedi[6]
was not content with the rule of North Africa. In August 969, a
Fatimid army occupied Egypt, subsequently moving into Syria also.
In July 972, the new Fatamid Khalif, Muizz, made his state entry
into Egypt, where a new city had been founded in his honour on the
edge of the old city of Fustat. He called it Al Qáhira, but we call it
Cairo. Thus in 972, three hundred and forty years after the Prophet's
death, his family were divided into three mutually jealous dynasties,
an Umaiyid in Spain, a Fatimid in Egypt and an Abbasid in Iraq.

* * *

The Turkish mercenaries in Iraq, though now Arabicised, were
not cut off from their relatives, the nomads of the steppes, who often
received news of the wealth and splendour of their emigrants. Their
relationship may be compared to that of the poorer people of Ireland
in the nineteenth century to their relatives who had gone to America.
In bad years, many of them abandoned their hard nomadic life and
sought their fortunes in the New World of Iraq, Syria and Egypt.

In 1055, however, a powerful nomadic tribal group invaded the

[4] Genealogical Tree 1, page 25.　　　　[5] Little servant of God.
[6] Mehedi, in English often spelt Mahdi, was the Muslim Messiah, a prophet who would
one day rule the world in peace.

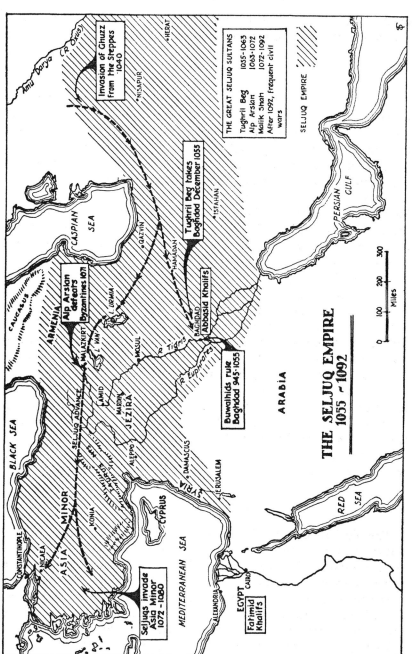

Invasion of Ghuzz
from the Steppes
1040

THE GREAT SELJUQ SULTANS

Tughril Beg   1055-1063
Alp Arslan   1063-1072
Malik Shah   1072-1092
After 1092, frequent civil
wars

SELJUQ EMPIRE

Tughril Beg takes
Baghdad December 1055

Abbasid Khalifs

Alp Arslan
defeats
Byzantines 1071

Buwaihids rule
Baghdad 945-1055

Seljuqs invade
Asia Minor
1072-1080

Fatimid
Khalifs

THE SELJUQ EMPIRE
1055 ~ 1092

MAP 3

Arab countries. They were known as the Ghuzz, and were led by a chief called Tughril Beg, of the Seljuq family. In December 1055, Tughril Beg took Baghdad,[7] which, it will be remembered, had been held since 945, by a Persian Shiite family, the Buwaihids.

The position of the Abbasids in Baghdad was actually improved by the advent of the Seljuqs. The Buwaihids, as Shiites, had refused to recognise the Abbasids as khalifs. But Tughril Beg had become a Sunni Muslim and treated them with veneration. It is true that the Seljuqs, like the Buwaihids, themselves ruled the country without consulting the khalif. But at least the latter was now treated with respect as the spiritual head of the Muslim world.

As has happened with other barbarians in history, the first three generations of Seljuqs made splendid rulers. Neither Tughril Beg, nor his son, Alp Arslan, could read or write. But they were great fighters and, being men of simple minds unwarped by laws and traditions, they administered justice with common sense, without fear or favour.

For four hundred and thirty-eight years (633–1071), the eastern boundary of the Byzantine Empire had lain roughly along the Taurus Mountains from the Mediterranean to Armenia. In 1071, however, the Seljuqs, under Alp Arslan, completely defeated the Byzantines at Malazkirt and, following hotly on their heels, had overrun all Asia Minor and reached the Bosphorus opposite Constantinople. When Alp Arslan died in 1072, he was succeeded by his son, Malik Shah.

A junior branch of the family set up an independent Seljuq dynasty in Asia Minor, with its capital at Nicaea, only fifty miles from Constantinople. The remainder of the empire followed Malik Shah.[8] Meanwhile the Seljuqs had driven the Fatimids out of Syria,[9] and confined them to Egypt.[10]

Tughril Beg and Alp Arslan had been illiterate but Malik Shah had been educated as a prince. He was especially interested in astronomy and established a great observatory in Persia, of which Umar Khayyam was in charge. Famous in the West as a poet, he was primarily a mathematician. The reign of Malik Shah was of short duration, yet was something of a golden age, for this enlightened prince ruled with moderation and justice. He died in November 1092.

The glory of the Seljuq Empire ended with his death. He left four sons, the eldest of whom was twelve years old. Civil war broke out immediately between rival war-lords, each claiming to support one

---

[7] Map 3, page 27.   [8] Genealogical Tree 2, opposite.
[9] The word Syria is used as a geographical term and includes the present states of Syria, Lebanon, Israel and Jordan.
[10] Map 3, page 27.

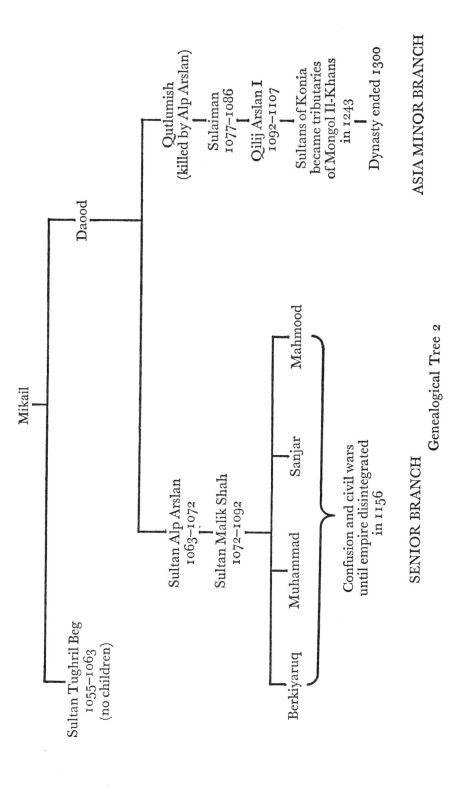

Mikail

Sultan Tughril Beg
1055–1063
(no children)

Daood

Sultan Alp Arslan
1063–1072

Sultan Malik Shah
1072–1092

Berkiyaruq   Muhammad   Sanjar   Mahmood

Confusion and civil wars
until empire disintegrated
in 1156

SENIOR BRANCH

Qutlumish
(killed by Alp Arslan)

Sulaiman
1077–1086

Qilij Arslan I
1092–1107

Sultans of Konia
became tributaries
of Mongol Il-Khans
in 1243

Dynasty ended 1300

ASIA MINOR BRANCH

Genealogical Tree 2

of the sons, but actually seeking power for himself. The junior branch
of the Seljuq family, however, retained their independent state in
Asia Minor.

* * *

The shattering defeat suffered by the Byzantines at Malazkirt, and
the arrival of the Seljuqs on the Bosphorus, had alarmed the courts
of Europe. Today and for many centuries past, Western pride has
concealed the fact that Europe, for three hundred and eighty years
(712 to 1092), had lived in fear of a Muslim conquest of Europe, just
as Asia and Africa lived in fear of European conquest, from 1700 to
1950. The distortion of history to flatter national vanity makes the
process of human development incomprehensible.

Throughout the four centuries of Muslim domination, the easy
route for the invasion of Europe had been blocked by the Byzantine
Empire and especially by the fortress of Constantinople. The Arabs
had invaded the West through Spain, and later, at various times,
had occupied the south of France, the Balearics, Sicily, southern
Italy, Crete and other points in southern Europe. But their lines of
communication by these routes had been too long to enable them to
assert the maximum effort there. The arrival of the Seljuqs opposite Constantinople, therefore, created alarm, lest they cross into
Europe.

The omission from history books of all mention of the centuries of
Muslim dominance leaves us at a loss to explain the Crusades.
Assuming the West to have always been strong, we try to explain the
Crusades as an early example of Western imperialism. The Byzantine
Emperor Alexius visualised the Crusades as a rescue operation to
save the eastern bastion of Europe.

There were in the West at that time no consolidated national
states as we know them, nor were there national armies. When the
Pope appealed for help to save the eastern Christians, four barons
volunteered:

(1) Godfrey de Bouillon, Duke of Lotharingia (roughly modern
    Belgium) and Lorraine.
(2) Bohemond, Duke of Apulia, a Norman who had conquered a
    dukedom in southern Italy.
(3) Raymond de Saint Gilles, Count of Toulouse and Marquis of
    Provence, in the south of France.
(4) Robert, Duke of Normandy, eldest son of William the Con-
    queror.

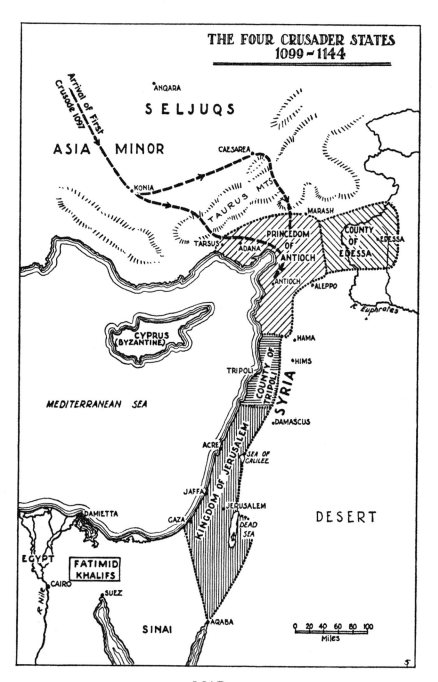

THE FOUR CRUSADER STATES
1099~1144

Arrival of First
Crusade 1097

ANQARA

SELJUQS

ASIA MINOR

CAESAREA

KONIA

TAURUS MTS

MARASH

COUNTY OF EDESSA

EDESSA

TARSUS

ADANA

PRINCEDOM OF ANTIOCH

ANTIOCH

ALEPPO

R. Euphrates

CYPRUS (BYZANTINE)

HAMA

HIMS

TRIPOLI

COUNTY OF TRIPOLI

SYRIA

MEDITERRANEAN SEA

DAMASCUS

ACRE

SEA OF GALILEE

KINGDOM OF JERUSALEM

JAFFA

JERUSALEM

DAMIETTA

GAZA

Mts DEAD SEA

DESERT

EGYPT

FATIMID KHALIFS

R. Nile

CAIRO

SUEZ

SINAI

AQABA

0 20 40 60 80 100
Miles

MAP 4

The strategy proposed by the Emperor Alexius was to recover Asia Minor, giving him room to manœuvre before a Muslim army could again reach the Bosphorus. But the barons were illiterate, ignorant of geography, had no maps, and would not listen to Alexius. Jerusalem was a name familiar to them through the Gospels and they conceived the emotional idea of freeing the Holy City from the Muslims. They accordingly burst through Asia Minor, defeating the junior branch of the Seljuqs on the way, and took Jerusalem on 15th July, 1099. The Seljuqs closed over their communications in Asia Minor and cut them off from Europe.

When Jerusalem was taken, the jealous barons quarrelled. Godfrey de Bouillon became King of Jerusalem, though he refused the title. Bohemond made himself Prince of Antioch, Raymond de Saint Gilles became Count of Tripoli and Robert of Normandy returned to France. Baldwin of Boulogne, the brother of Godfrey, carved out a small state for himself and assumed the title of Count of Edessa. Thus the Crusaders formed four small independent states, not a single united kingdom.

The Crusaders were fortunate in that the Seljuq Sultan Malik Shah had died in 1092, and that they arrived in Syria in 1097, when the Seljuq Empire was torn by civil wars. Had Malik Shah been still alive, it is unlikely that they would ever have entered Syria.

Meanwhile, with the collapse of Seljuq imperial authority, Turkish war-lords had seized power in Aleppo, Amid, Mosul and Damascus, who, as jealous of each other as were the Crusader barons, were unable to oppose a single front to the invaders.

In 1127, however, Zengi, the son of a Turkish slave of Malik Shah, became Lord of Mosul. Within three years, he had annexed Nisibin, Harran, Mardin and Aleppo from their respective Turkish lords, and built up a single state from Aleppo to east of Mosul.[11]

In 1137 and again in 1139, the Byzantine Emperor John Comnenus intervened in Syria and halted Zengi's advance, but in 1144 the latter took Edessa, and the Crusader states were reduced to three. On 14th September, 1146, however, Zengi was assassinated. His son, Noor-al-Deen (Light of the Religion) Mahmood, succeeded him in Aleppo and, in 1159, took Damascus. The Crusaders and Noor-al-Deen were about equally matched. The Fatimid khalifs in Egypt had played but little part in the conflict, though their country had grown immensely rich on its monopoly of the oriental trade.

Both Noor-al-Deen and the Crusaders realised that whichever of them could seize the wealth of Egypt would be able to outmatch the other. In January 1169, however, an army sent by Noor-al-Deen

[11] Map 5, page 35.

THE AYOUBIDS

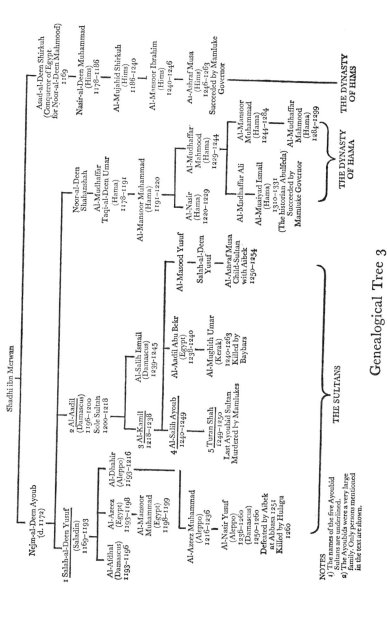

Genealogical Tree 3

occupied Cairo. This army was commanded by a Kurdish mercenary called Shirkuh, who had on his staff a young nephew whose name was Salah-al-Deen (Benefit of the Religion), but is known to us as Saladin.

Shortly afterwards, in March 1169, Shirkuh died in Cairo and Saladin seized command. In September 1171 he declared the abolition of the Fatimid khalifate and seized the immense wealth of Egypt. On 15th May, 1174, Saladin's master and employer, Noor-al-Deen, died in Aleppo, leaving an eleven-year-old son. Saladin marched into Syria with an army of Turkish and Kurdish mercenaries, paid and equipped with the wealth of Egypt. In ten years of fighting, he unified a great empire extending from the Western Desert of Egypt to Erbil, east of Mosul.

The Crusaders were now at his mercy. On 4th July, 1187, he destroyed their army at Hattin and on 2nd October, 1187, he took Jerusalem. By the summer of 1188, nothing was left of the Kingdom of Jerusalem but the fortress of Tyre.

The fall of Jerusalem was a shock to the West, and, on 20th April, 1191, Philippe Auguste, King of France, landed at Acre, followed, on 8th June, by Richard, Cœur-de-Lion, King of England. In a year's fighting, Richard reconquered the whole coastal plain from Jaffa to Tyre, both inclusive, but he failed to take Jerusalem. The capital of the Kingdom of Jerusalem was established at Acre. The County of Tripoli and the Princedom of Antioch were still intact, and had not been conquered by the Muslims. Richard sailed for home on 9th October, 1192, and Saladin died in Damascus on 3rd March, 1193.

Saladin, originally a Kurdish mercenary, established a dynasty of sultans. His brother, Malik-al-Aadil (the Just King) became the ruler of his empire and was followed by his son, Malik-al-Kamil,[12] (the Perfect King), who reigned from 1218 to 1238. He, in his turn, was followed by his son Malik-al-Salih (The Good King)[13] Ayoub.

The dynasty of Saladin's family was called the Ayoubids. It produced three splendid rulers, Saladin, Malik-al-Aadil and Malik-al-Kamil. Cultured, courteous, just and religious, they set an example of tolerance and enlightenment to all their contemporaries, in east and west. Against them, successive Crusades from the West endeavoured to recover Jerusalem, but the Ayoubids weathered all the storms.

[12] Genealogical Tree 3, page 33.

[13] It was an ancient custom that each khalif and sovereign, on his accession, assumed a "throne-name" which he used before his personal name. Khalifs' throne-names took the form of "Trusting-in-God", "Supported-by-God" and so on. Lay rulers assumed throne-names based on the word king, such as "The Just King", "The Victorious King", "The Beloved King".

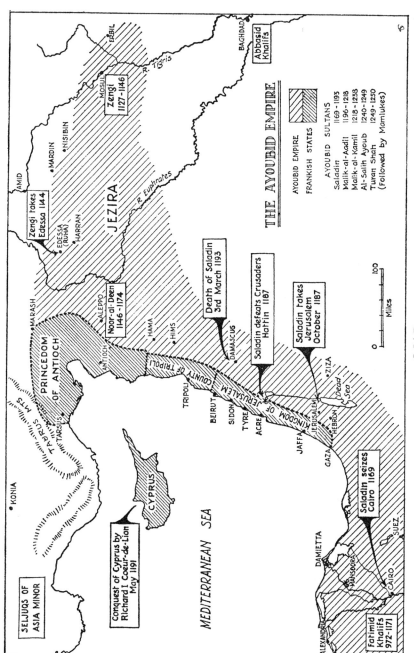

THE AYOUBID EMPIRE

AYOUBID EMPIRE

FRANKISH STATES

AYOUBID SULTANS
Saladin   1169 - 1195
Malik-al-Aadil   1196 - 1218
Malik-al-Kamil   1218 - 1238
Al-Salih Ayoub   1240 - 1249
Turan Shah   1249 - 1250
(Followed by Mamlukes)

Abbasid Khalifs

Zengi 1127 - 1146

Zengi takes Edessa 1144

JEZIRA

R. Tigris

R. Euphrates

BAGHDAD

ERBIL

MOSUL

NISIBIN

MARDIN

AMID

EDESSA (RUHA)

HARRAN

Noor-al-Deen 1146 - 1174

Death of Saladin 3rd March 1193

Saladin defeats Crusaders Hattin 1187

Saladin takes Jerusalem October 1187

MARASH

PRINCEDOM OF ANTIOCH

TAURUS MTS.

ALEPPO

HAMA

HIMS

DAMASCUS

TARSUS

ANTIOCH

COUNTY OF TRIPOLI

TRIPOLI

BEIRUT

SIDON

TYRE

ACRE

KINGDOM OF JERUSALEM

JERUSALEM

HEBRON

JAFFA

GAZA

Dead Sea

ZIZA

Saladin seizes Cairo 1169

SELJUQS OF ASIA MINOR

KONIA

CYPRUS

Conquest of Cyprus by Richard I Coeur-de-Lion May 1191

MEDITERRANEAN SEA

DAMIETTA

ALEXANDRIA

MANSOORA

CAIRO

SUEZ

Fatimid Khalifs 972 - 1171

0   100
Miles

MAP 5

*   *   *

Malik-al-Salih Ayoub, the son of an Abyssinian slave girl, was a
devoted and energetic ruler, but he failed to achieve the stature of
the three previous Ayoubid sultans, in so far as culture, courtesy and
piety were concerned. Many of his relatives, his brother, his uncle
and his cousins refused to accept his authority. He assumed power
in Cairo on 19th June, 1240.

The Crusaders were as divided as the Ayoubids. The Templars
supported Malik-al-Salih Ismail, the uncle of Malik-al-Salih Ayoub,[14]
and marched with him on Egypt, but were defeated near Gaza. The
Hospitallers took the part of Al-Salih Ayoub.[15] On 2nd October,
1245, he took Damascus and reconstituted the Ayoubid Empire,
from Egypt to the Jezira.

In 1247, however, the Ayoubid Princes of Hama and Aleppo
rebelled, Al-Salih Ayoub toiled back to Syria and in 1248 laid siege
to Hama. But early in 1249 news was received that a new Crusade
was about to land in Egypt. Patching up a hasty truce with his
captious cousins, Al-Salih Ayoub hastened back to Egypt.

*   *   *

Saladin's army had consisted of many categories. Some, including
his own bodyguard of five hundred, dressed in yellow tunics, were
mamlukes, as explained below. Some were Kurdish mercenaries, like
himself, voluntarily enlisted. Others were Turkish or Arab volunteers, or bedouin nomads from the desert.

The word *mamluke* in Arabic is a past participle meaning owned.
The word *malik*—a king—is the same root, meaning owner or king.
The use of Turks as mercenaries had been introduced four hundred
years before by the Khalif Mutasim, as already stated. (In the same
way, Germans and Swiss were employed for several centuries as
mercenaries in Europe.) When, therefore, a Middle Eastern ruler
wished to increase his army, he sent to recruit from the tribes of the
steppes.

The Mamluke[16] system was merely a modification of the common

---

[14] Genealogical Tree 3, page 33.

[15] Throne-names being long, the words Al-Malik are often omitted. Similarly the first
article al.

[16] The word *mamluke* literally means a soldier, who has been recruited by purchase.
Yet when such persons established an empire, the word Mamluke became virtually a
national designation. I have spelt Mamluke with a capital M when referring to their
empire, or as a collective for them as a ruling community. When, however, the status of

system of hiring foreign mercenaries. A special class of merchants followed this trade. Visiting the nomads of the steppes, they bought boys (and sometimes girls as slaves or wives) from their parents. The boys were usually from ten to twelve years of age. The merchants returned with their young charges and sold them in Syria or Egypt to rulers or ameers.

Merely to call such boys "slaves" in English creates a wrong impression. The boys came freely and were not tied up or chained together. Members of one of the hardiest races in the world, they could probably have escaped if they had wished. It seems probable, therefore, that Egypt appeared to the poor nomads of the north an earthly paradise, its streets paved with gold. The boys were doubtless perfect natural riders, and their purchasers in Syria and Egypt trained them in strict discipline and in weapon training.

When they were competent in the use of bow, lance, sword and mace on horseback and were old enough to fight in battle, they were freed by their owner, and given weapons, armour and horses. But in the Arab countries, a freedman was thought to be under a moral obligation to remain as the loyal retainer of his patron, with whom he lived in intimacy, whose meals he shared and to protect whom he must give his life. This devotion to the man who had brought him up and freed him was an obligation of honour on which the whole Mamluke system was founded.

His honourable obligation to serve, however, was limited to the patron who had freed him. Some of this attachment might or might not be given to his son. But it included no loyalty to the state, the constitution or the army as a whole. Once his patron was dead, the mamluke was free to take service where he wished, or to abandon soldiering and go into business or farming. But he would not be bound to die in the service of his new employer, as he had been in the case of his patron.

*   *   *

Malik-al-Salih Ayoub found his throne precarious, faced not only with the enemy Crusaders, but also with his jealous relatives. To strengthen his position, he bought young boys from the steppes, most of them from the Qipchaq tribe of Turks, whose country had been overrun by the Mongols. It does not seem that Al-Salih Ayoub's

military slave, as opposed to their owners, is intended, I have used a small m—for example, "the sultan was followed by his mamlukes".

However, I have used a capital to designate the Royal Mamlukes as a military unit, as one would write the Brigade of Guards.

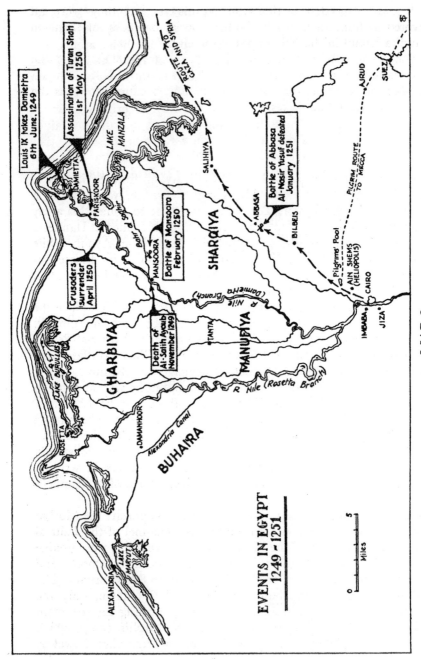

EVENTS IN EGYPT
1249 – 1251

MAP 6

Louis IX takes Damietta 6th June, 1249

Assassination of Turan Shah 1st May, 1250

Crusaders surrender April 1250

Battle of Mansoora February 1250

Death of Al-Salih Ayyub November 1249

Battle of Abbasa Al-Nasir Yusuf defeated January 1251

ROUTE TO SYRIA
GAZA

DAMIETTA

FARISKOOR

Bahr el Saghir

LAKE MANZALA

SALIHIYA

ABBASA

BILBEIS

MANSOORA

R. Nile (Damietta Branch)

SHARQIYA

PILGRIM ROUTE TO MECCA

Pilgrims' Pool

AIN SHEMS (HELIOPOLIS)

CAIRO

IMBABA

JIZA

ARUD

SUEZ

GHARBIYA

TANTA

MANUFIYA

R. Nile (Rosetta Branch)

DAMANHOOR

Alexandria Canal

BUHAIRA

Lake BURULLUS

ROSETTA

Lake MARYUT

ALEXANDRIA

0 Miles 5

bodyguard exceeded a thousand mamlukes, but they were all devoted to him. In Cairo he built a special barracks for them on Raudha Island in the Nile opposite the city.[17]

The word *bahr*[18] in Arabic properly means the sea, but the Egyptians often speak of their belovéd Nile as Bahr al Nil. Living on an island in the Nile, the new mamluke unit became known as the Bahris, or River Mamlukes.

*   *   *

The news which brought back Al-Salih Ayoub from Syria was to the effect that Saint Louis IX, King of France, was leading a Crusade to invade Egypt. The sultan had time to collect his army and to reach Mansoora[19] in April 1249. Louis IX landed at Damietta on 5th June and took the town the next day. Sultan Ayoub, while still in Syria, had been suffering from tuberculosis. The disease was now in an advanced stage and he was confined to his bed, but still showed a heroic and tireless energy.

A great army was concentrated at Mansoora, to which place the dying sultan's tent had been moved, guarded by his own regiment, the Bahris. Devotedly nursed by his favourite wife, Spray-of-Pearls, he died in her arms on 23rd November, 1249. Two days later, the Crusaders advanced from Damietta to engage the Muslims.

Al-Salih Ayoub had one son, Turan Shah, but he was far away in the Jezira, and could not arrive for two or three months. Left alone in their tent with her dead husband in the tense atmosphere of an impending major battle, this heroic woman concealed the sultan's death and assumed command in his name. Officers constantly reported to the royal tent, and received their orders in writing, ostensibly signed by the sultan, whose signature one of her eunuchs had learned to forge.

On 21st December, 1249, the Franks camped opposite the Muslim army, the two being separated only by the channel of the Bahr al Saghir, a distributary of the Nile, which the Crusaders were unable to cross. Eventually, however, they found a ford at Salamoon, and their army began to cross on the night of 7th to 8th February. The ford was deep and the banks slippery and, by dawn, only the advanced guard was across. These, without waiting for the main body, galloped wildly away and charged the Muslim camp, which was taken completely by surprise. The Bahri Mamlukes, however,

---

[17] Map 14, page 72.   [18] Pronounced with two syllables "bahher".
[19] Map 7, page 40.

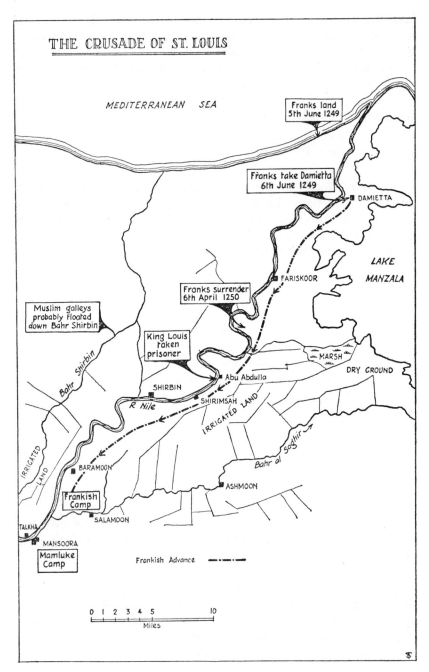

THE CRUSADE OF ST. LOUIS

MEDITERRANEAN SEA

Franks land
5th June 1249

Franks take Damietta
6th June 1249

DAMIETTA

FARISKOOR

LAKE
MANZALA

Franks surrender
6th April 1250

Muslim galleys
probably floated
down Bahr Shirbin

King Louis
taken
prisoner

MARSH

DRY GROUND

Bahr Shirbin

Abu Abdulla

SHIRBIN

R Nile

SHIRIMSAH

IRRIGATED LAND

IRRIGATED LAND

Bahr al Soghir

BARAMOON

ASHMOON

Frankish
Camp

TALKHA

SALAMOON

MANSOORA

Mamluke
Camp

Frankish Advance   — · — · —

0 1 2 3 4 5   10
Miles

MAP 7

soon counter-attacked, the Crusader advanced guard was exterminated, and when the main body crossed the stream, they found themselves confronted by the whole Muslim army.

On 11th February, another desperate battle was fought south of the Bahr al Saghir, but without any decisive result. Eventually the Crusaders' communications with Damietta were cut, and, weak with hunger and dysentery, they began to withdraw on 5th April, but next day they were overrun by the pursuing Muslims and were obliged to surrender.

Meanwhile, on 28th February, 1250, the young Turan Shah had arrived in the camp. Only then did Spray-of-Pearls admit the sultan's death. Al-Salih Ayoub had refused to nominate Turan Shah as his successor and his reluctance now proved justified. The young man behaved with youthful folly. He had brought some profligate young men with him from Syria, to whom he gave military ranks senior to the veteran commanders of the army, boasting of his intention to dismiss the latter. He had quarrelled with Spray-of-Pearls, who had kept the throne for him. Every night he indulged in drunken revels with his boon companions.

On 1st May, 1250, while Turan Shah was resting at Fariskoor, Baybars, the officer who had led the Bahri counter-attack at Mansoora, entered his tent and ran the sultan through with his sword. The alarm was given, and the sultan shouted that a Bahri Mamluke had tried to kill him. When they heard this, the Bahris realised that, if the sultan lived, they would be executed, and they quickly advanced on his tent. Turan Shah escaped them, ran down to the river and waded into the water, but was overtaken and killed. Thus in folly and ignominy ended the imperial dynasty of the great Saladin.

For several days the Muslim army was in a state of anarchy, the mamlukes demanding the massacre of the Crusader prisoners. Eventually, however, they agreed to accept a million gold dinars as ransom. On 7th May, 1250, Louis IX and the remnants of his army set sail from Damietta for Acre.

SUMMARY OF BACKGROUND HISTORY

A.D. 600 to 1250

Great War between Byzantium and Persia   602–628

Muhammad
    Born   570
    Began to preach   613
    Died   632
In control of all Arabia
The Arabs conquer an empire from the
    Atlantic to China   633–712

Dynasties of Arab Khalifs
    The Umaiyads (capital Damascus)   661–750
    The Abbasids (capital Baghdad)
    (a) As active rulers   750–861
    (b) As puppets of various military dictators 861–1055
    (c) As religious leaders   1055–1258
    The Fatimids (Cairo)   Over Africa and
        Egypt   910–1171

The Seljuq Empire
    Main Empire (Asia Minor to Indian
        Border)   1055–1092
    Seljuq Kingdom of Asia Minor   1077–1300
    Main Empire (in civil wars)   1092–1156

The Ayoubid Empire (Egypt and Syria)
    Saladin   1169–1193
    Al-Azeez (Egypt only)   1193–1198
    Al-Aadil (whole empire)   1200–1218
    Al-Kamil   1218–1238
    Al-Salih Ayoub   1240–1249
    Turan Shah   1249–1250

The Crusader States
    Kingdom of Jerusalem established 1099
    Jerusalem lost. Capital moved to Acre 1187–1291
    Princedom of Antioch   1098–1268
    County of Tripoli   1099–1289
    County of Edessa   1098–1144

II

"O God, Give Us Victory!"

In their policy of securing foreign slaves as a body-guard the Ayoubids followed the precedent established by the caliphs of Baghdad, with the same eventual results. The bondmen of yesterday became the army commanders of today and the sultans of tomorrow.

PHILIP HITTI, *History of the Arabs*

The Ayoubids had introduced . . . a feudal system that dominated Egypt . . . for six hundred years and vitally affected the social conditions, arts, literature and material aspect of Cairo . . . Slavery in the East is no disgrace; on the contrary, the relationship ranks far above mere hired service. The slave is regarded almost as a son.

STANLEY LANE-POOLE, *The Story of Cairo*

Though the dynasty founded by the great Saladin had given place to the Mamluks, a form of government than which in theory none could be worse, Egypt from 1260 to 1341, enjoyed not only widespread power and prestige, but also a high degree of prosperity. This was mainly due to three things. Sultans Baybars, Qalaun and Malik-al-Nasir were exceedingly capable rulers. Secondly, the bureaucratic administration which Egypt had inherited was the most efficient which existed in the Middle Ages. Thirdly, Egypt enjoyed almost a monopoly of the Indian trade.

H. A. R. GIBB, *Introduction to Ibn Batuta* (abbreviated)

WILD were the rejoicings in Cairo, when news arrived of the departure of the Franks.[1] The Mamlukes were Turkish nomads, among whom women took more part in public affairs than they did among Muslims. They enthusiastically proclaimed Spray-of-Pearls to be Queen of Egypt, for her courage had shown her worthy to rule. Unfortunately, as a young slave girl, she had been sent as a present by the Abbasid Khalif Mustasim to the Ayoubid Sultan Al-Salih Ayoub, who had fallen in love with her and married her.

The Khalif Mustasim, a petty man soon to come to a bad end, was outraged by the idea of his slave girl becoming a queen and wrote haughtily to Cairo, "The Prophet said, 'Unhappy is the nation governed by a woman'—If you have no men, I will send you one." The khalif still enjoyed religious prestige and it was consequently thought wise to appoint a male ruler. This was done by marrying Spray-of-Pearls to the commander-in-chief, the Ameer Aibek, who was proclaimed sultan with the throne-name of Malik-al-Muizz Aibek. At the same time, a six-year-old great-grandson of Sultan Al-Kamil, called Malik-al-Ashraf Musa, was proclaimed joint-sultan with Aibek to give the new régime a (slight) air of Ayoubid legitimacy.[2]

MALIK-AL-MUIZZ AIBEK

The Syrian Ayoubids, however, refused to recognise this Mamluke arrangement and the ruler of Aleppo, the Ayoubid Malik-al-Nasir Yusuf left Damascus with an army to invade Egypt. At the beginning of January 1251, a battle was fought at Abbasa, near Cairo. The situation was confused. The loyalty of mamlukes, as we have seen, was to their patrons, not to the country, the army or their fellow Turks. Thus though both armies were composed of mamlukes, some were fighting for their Ayoubid patrons, others were attracted by the idea of a Mamluke régime.

---

[1] The Arabs called the Byzantines Roum (Romans), but all other Europeans Franks, without distinguishing French, English, Germans or Italians. Similarly, Europeans called all the Middle East Muslim Peoples Saracens, without distinguishing Arabs, Kurds or Turks.

[2] For a complete list of Mamluke sultans, see Appendix, page 459.

When the action began, the left wings of both armies drove back the right wings of their opponents, the centres of both armies standing firm. A party of Al-Nasir Yusuf's troops having gone over to the enemy, however, the prince lost heart and took to flight, leaving the victory to the Mamlukes of Egypt.

The Mamluke ameers in Egypt had already proclaimed Malik-al-Muizz Aibek, the commander-in-chief, to be sultan. The streets of Cairo were decorated and Aibek rode through the city in state, the ghashiya[3] being carried before him.

The body of Malik-al-Salih Ayoub was carried with great pomp to a splendid mausoleum built for it in Cairo, the people weeping and mourning their dead sultan, for they were all deeply loyal to the Ayoubids. The Mamluke seizure of power was not in any sense a popular revolution. The new rulers were nervous and a number of ameers were imprisoned without trial, suspected of favouring the Ayoubids.

When Malik-al-Nasir Yusuf, the ruler of Aleppo, had been defeated outside Cairo, a number of Ayoubid princes and Mamluke ameers had been taken prisoners. Aibek treated the former with respect but several Mamluke officers were beheaded. The Mamluke ameers already arrested for Ayoubid sympathies were quietly strangled in prison.

Although the Ayoubids had built up their armies principally of Turkish mamlukes, they had left the administration of their empire to the highly cultured Syrians and Egyptians, who had already constituted a skilled civil service for six hundred years. Many of these, judges and administrators, attained to high rank and honour and accumulated great wealth. It was a pattern, originating under the Ayoubids, which was to last throughout the Mamluke period—the army consisted of Mamlukes, the civil government of Syrians and Egyptians.

It will be remembered that the Ayoubid Prince of Damascus, Malik-al-Salih Ismail, had, in 1244, disputed the throne of the empire with his nephew, Al-Salih Ayoub.[4] This Ismail had returned with Al-Nasir Yusuf and had been taken prisoner at Abbasa. Led through the streets of Cairo with the other prisoners, to confinement in the Citadel, he had passed the mausoleum of Malik-al-Salih Ayoub. The Bahri Mamlukes, who had been raised by Ayoub, surged round the prisoner Ismail, calling to their dead sultan in his tomb,

---

[3] The ghashiya had originally been a saddlecloth. Covered with gold embroidery, it was carried before sovereigns as an emblem of royalty. The Seljuqs had used it in Baghdad, possibly also the Ayoubids (Quatremère).

[4] Page 36.

"Look, my lord, look! O where are your eyes? See here is your enemy Ismail, whom we have captured."

This incident illustrates the simple-minded and honourable devotion of the mamlukes to the patron who had brought them up and freed them. We are tempted to consider the Battle of Abbasa as a contest between the Ayoubids and the Mamlukes for control of Egypt, as, in one sense, it was. Yet here we see the Bahri Mamlukes, the corps d'élite of the army of the Egyptian régime, paying tribute, not to Aibek their commander in the battle, but to their dead Ayoubid master, Al-Salih Ayoub.

*   *   *

When Malik-al-Nasir Yusuf returned to Damascus after his defeat at Abbasa, he reigned as King of Syria. In Cairo, meanwhile, the Bahri or River Mamlukes were becoming increasingly arrogant. In addition to their loyalty to their patron, mamlukes were bound together by loyalty to their comrades, who were called *Khushdashiya*. All the mamlukes freed by the same patron adopted his throne-name as a cognomen. Thus those trained and freed by Malik-al-Salih Ayoub were called Salihis, and constituted a closely knit brotherhood.

Sultan Aibek, however, was not a Salihi. He had been freed by an ameer called the Turkmani and his cognomen was thus Aibek al Turkmani, though after winning his freedom he had served under Al-Salih Ayoub. He was, therefore, not a barrack-comrade of the Salihis, who constituted the great majority of the River Mamlukes. The Ameer Aqtai, who enjoyed the unwavering loyalty of his barrack-comrades, was their commander, and thus constituted a possible rival to Aibek.

In the spring of 1252, a delegate sent by the Abbasid Khalif Mustasim negotiated an agreement between the Mamlukes in Egypt and Al-Nasir Yusuf, the Ayoubid King of Syria. Egypt and Palestine were given to the Mamlukes and the remainder of Syria to the Ayoubids.[5]

In Cairo, the Bahri Mamlukes were behaving with increasing arrogance, creating disorders, robbing peaceful citizens and abducting young women. So disgraceful were their outrages, according to the good Maqrizi,[6] that if the King of the Franks had taken Cairo his men could not have behaved worse. They were even suspected of plotting to murder Aibek and make Aqtai sultan.

[5] Map 8, page 48.   [6] Maqrizi, *Kitab al Sulook*.

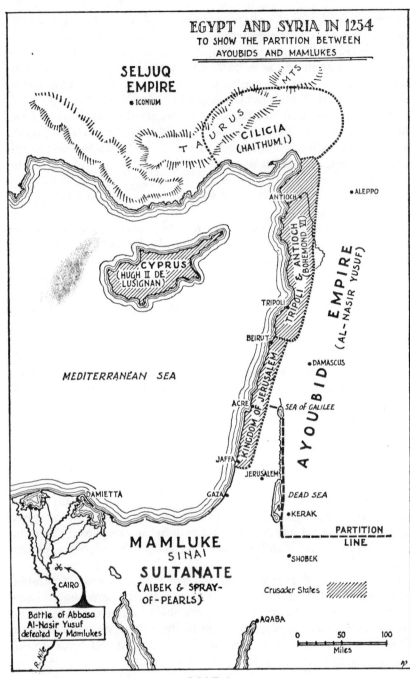

EGYPT AND SYRIA IN 1254
TO SHOW THE PARTITION BETWEEN
AYOUBIDS AND MAMLUKES

SELJUQ
EMPIRE
● ICONIUM

TAURUS MTS

T A U R U S

CILICIA
(HAITHUM. I)

● ALEPPO

ANTIOCH ●

ANTIOCH & TRIPOLI (BOHEMOND VI)

A Y O U B I D   E M P I R E
(AL-NASIR YUSUF)

CYPRUS
(HUGH II DE
LUSIGNAN)

TRIPOLI

BEIRUT

MEDITERRANEAN   SEA

● DAMASCUS

JERUSALEM KINGDOM OF

ACRE

SEA of GALILEE

JAFFA

JERUSALEM

DEAD SEA

DAMIETTA

GAZA

● KERAK

PARTITION
LINE

MAMLUKE
SINAI
SULTANATE
(AIBEK & SPRAY-
OF-PEARLS)

●SHOBEK

Crusader States

CAIRO

Battle of Abbasa
Al-Nasir Yusuf
defeated by Mamlukes

R. Nile

● AQABA

0   50   100
Miles

MAP 8

In 1253, the tribes south of Cairo rebelled. Aqtai and the Bahris were sent against them and defeated them in a fierce battle, massacring all the men and carrying off the women and children. "The Arab tribes of Egypt," says Maqrizi, "never recovered from this defeat and lost all power and influence."[7] Their chief, Ibn Thaalib, wrote to beg an amnesty from Aibek, who replied in cordial terms.

As a result, the chiefs rode in to discuss terms with the sultan, who was camped near Bilbeis. No sooner had they dismounted in front of Aibek's tent, than they were surrounded and their throats cut. Orders were then given to double the taxes previously imposed on the tribes. Among the Mongols, and perhaps also among the nomadic Turks, treachery and deception were regarded as laudable military qualities, in contrast to the early Arab conquerors, for Muhammad had insisted that faith must always be kept, even with enemies. The Mamlukes, as we shall see, always dealt harshly with tribes, an attitude subsequently inherited by the Ottomans and by certain local governments today.

Meanwhile Aqtai held his own court, received petitions, wrote to the Ayoubid King of Syria and behaved as if he, not Aibek, were head of the state. The River Mamlukes, the backbone of the army, obeyed Aqtai alone, took no notice of Aibek and raided the public baths in use by women, carrying off the fair bathers by force.

Aibek had had enough. One day in 1254, he invited Aqtai to visit him in the Citadel for a conference. Aqtai arrived, but as he walked down the corridor to Aibek's room, he was attacked by three Mamlukes, who ran him through with their swords. The three murderers were led by an officer called Qutuz, whom Aibek had made his deputy.

When news leaked out that Aqtai had been seized, seven hundred River Mamlukes mounted and rode up to the Citadel, led by three officers, Baybars al Bunduqdari, Qalaoon al Elfi and Sonqor al Ashqar, names soon to become famous. Imagining that Aqtai had merely been arrested, they loudly demanded his release. While they were still shouting, the severed head of Aqtai came flying over the ramparts and fell at their feet. The River Mamlukes were completely taken aback and quickly dispersed. Many left Cairo the same night.

Next morning, Aibek ordered the arrest of all River Mamlukes, some being executed and some held in prison. Their wealth, their houses, their wives and children were all seized, immense riches being found in the house of Aqtai. When the fugitive Bahris reached Gaza, they sent a letter to the Ayoubid King of Syria, Al-Nasir Yusuf,

[7] The word "Arab" at this time meant nomads, not an ethnic group. The Egyptian tribes were of mixed Arab, Berber and Nubian origin

offering to enter his service. Receiving an affirmative reply, they enlisted in his forces in Damascus.

It will be remembered that when Aibek first assumed power in Egypt, a six-year-old boy, Al-Ashraf Musa, was also made joint-sultan. In 1254, however, after the murder of Aqtai, Aibek felt him-self master of the situation and sent the Ayoubid child to live in exile with the Greek Emperor, Theodore II Lascaris.

In 1256, a new mediator from the Khalif Mustasim came to negotiate between Aibek and Al-Nasir Yusuf, the King of Syria. A clause in a new agreement stipulated that Al-Nasir Yusuf would not employ the Bahri Mamlukes. The latter, accordingly, enlisted under Malik-al-Mughith Umar, the independent Ayoubid Prince of Kerak.[8]

Aibek also sent emissaries to ask the hand of the daughter of Malik-al-Mansoor, the Ayoubid Prince of Hama. The same delega-tion was to go on to Mosul to request the hand of the daughter of Bedr-al-Deen Lulu, a former mamluke of the family of Zengi, who had succeeded his patrons as Lord of Mosul. The rulers of the various cities were now partly Turkish commanders, formerly mamlukes, and partly Ayoubid princes. The newly independent Mamlukes of Egypt thought themselves the social equals of either.

The political marriage between Aibek and Spray-of-Pearls had not been a happy one. A condition of the agreement had been that Aibek divorce his wife by whom he had a son. Spray-of-Pearls had ruled Egypt as queen before the marriage and believed herself still to be such. Aibek regarded himself as sole sultan. In general, Aibek assumed command of the army, but Spray-of-Pearls still directed the civil government. She was, however, much incensed to hear that Aibek had sent to court other wives.

A further source of friction was Aibek's harsh treatment of the River Mamlukes, who were devoted to Spray-of-Pearls. To revenge herself, she wrote to Al-Nasir Yusuf, King of Syria, offering to murder Aibek, after which she would marry the king and thereby reunite Egypt and Syria. Another cause of quarrel was that Spray-of-Pearls had hidden the treasure of her late husband, Al-Salih Ayoub, and refused to reveal the hiding place to Aibek.

One day, Aibek had been playing polo. Returning hot and tired to the Citadel, he went straight to the bath, where Spray-of-Pearls had posted five of her servants. These, after a brief struggle, strangled Aibek in the bathroom. Suddenly everything was in panic. The supporters of Spray-of-Pearls invited the Ameer Izz-al-Deen Halebi to be sultan. Aibek's party demanded the elevation of Ali, Aibek's son by his first wife.

[8] Genealogical Tree 3, page 33.

Aibek's mamlukes were victorious, proclaimed Ali the son of Aibek to be sultan and seized and imprisoned Spray-of-Pearls, who was then handed over to Aibek's first wife, whom she had compelled him to divorce. Mad with jealousy, the mother of Ali with her slave girls beat Spray-of-Pearls to death with their clogs. Her body, clad only in a vest and drawers, was thrown over the battlements of the Citadel into the moat, where it lay for several days until someone removed it for burial.

Capable and beautiful, she must be one of very few women in history who commanded an army in a major battle, as she did against Louis IX, King of France. She had been devoted to her husband, Al-Salih Ayoub, but she was also jealous and vindictive. She spent her last hours grinding up her pearls and jewellery to prevent any other woman ever wearing them. Her rivals were no less vindictive, for they killed forty of her eunuchs by halving them at the waist, harmless creatures who constituted no danger to those in power.

Aibek was sixty years old when he was murdered and had reigned for six years. He was a prudent leader, brave in battle, but addicted to bloodshed. Maqrizi reports that he put many innocent persons to death to inspire fear. He introduced numerous new taxes, a process in which he was ably seconded by his wazeer, the head of the civil administration, Sharaf-al-Deen ibn Saeed al Faizi. As already explained, under the Mamlukes, as under the Ayoubids, the civil service was in the hands of Syrians and Egyptians.

At this period, virtually none of the Turkish Mamlukes knew Arabic, their official language being Turkish, which was unknown to their subjects. It is of interest to note that a qadhi, or judge, Zain-al-Deen ibn Zubair, was chosen as deputy wazeer, because he knew Turkish and thus could converse with the Mamlukes.

* * *

MALIK-AL-MANSOOR ALI IBN AIBEK

On 20th March, 1257, the Ameer Ali, the son of Aibek, was proclaimed sultan by the Mamluke ameers of Aibek's party. As he was only fifteen years old, the Ameer Qutuz, who had been Aibek's deputy, was appointed regent. Sharaf-al-Deen Faizi remained as wazeer.

Shortly afterwards, two Mamluke ameers are alleged to have

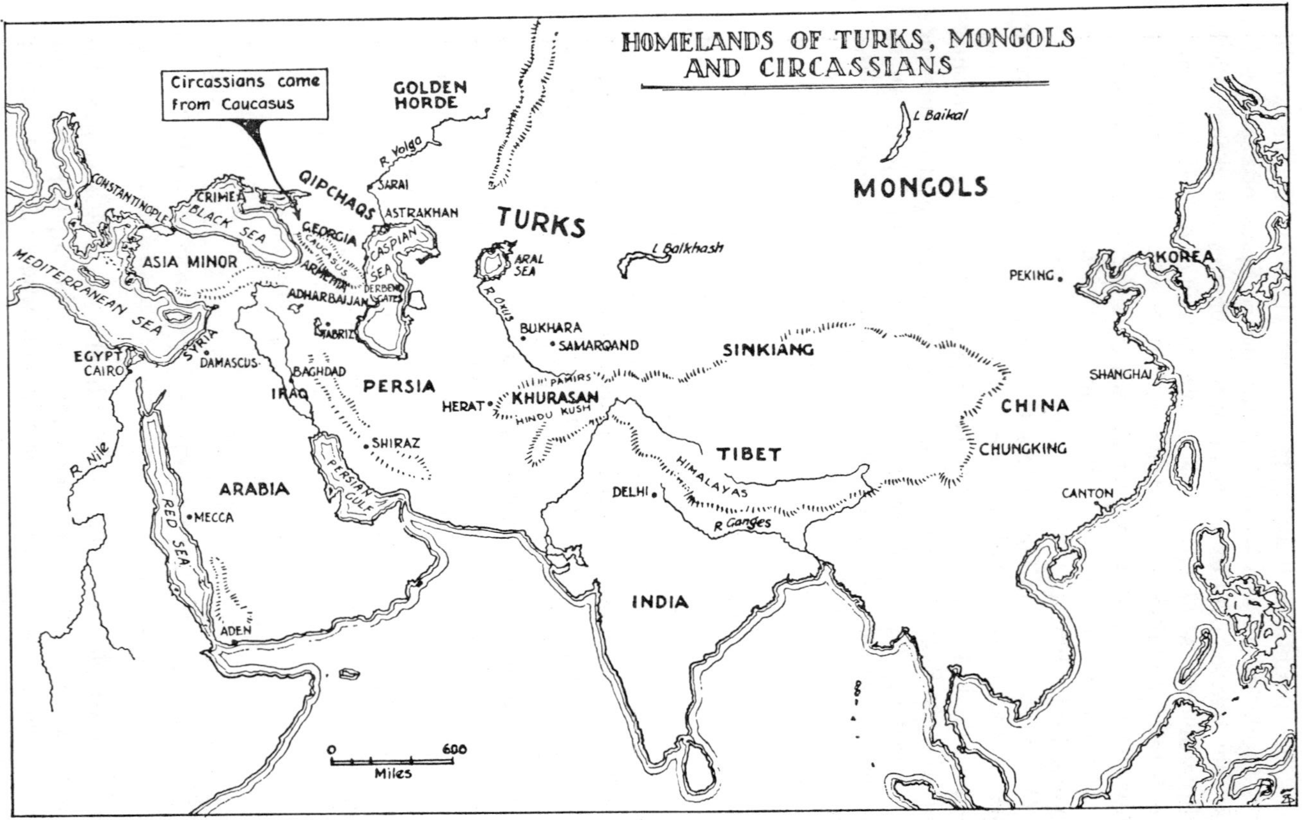

HOMELANDS OF TURKS, MONGOLS AND CIRCASSIANS

MONGOLS

TURKS

Circassians come from Caucasus

MAP 9

KOREA
SHANGHAI
CANTON
PEKING
CHINA
CHUNGKING
L. Baikal
SINKIANG
TIBET
L. Balkhash
HIMALAYAS
R. Ganges
DELHI
INDIA
BUKHARA
SAMARQAND
PAMIRS
ARAL SEA
KHURASAN
HINDU KUSH
R. OXUS
HERAT
PERSIA
SHIRAZ
GOLDEN HORDE
R. VOLGA
SARAI
ASTRAKHAN
QIPCHAQS
CASPIAN SEA
GEORGIA
ARMENIA
CAUCASUS
ADHARBAIJAN
TABRIZ
TAKRIT
BAGHDAD
IRAQ
PERSIAN GULF
ADEN
CRIMEA
BLACK SEA
CONSTANTINOPLE
ASIA MINOR
DAMASCUS
MEDITERRANEAN SEA
EGYPT
CAIRO
R. NILE
ARABIA
MECCA
RED SEA

600
Miles
0

reported that they had heard the wazeer say that the country could not be ruled by a child. The mother of Ali sent some men who strangled him. As in the days of Spray-of-Pearls, the presence of a lady in the palace giving orders without reference to the regent must have increased the complications of this situation of blood-stained anarchy.

Meanwhile a number of River Mamlukes, who had been with the Seljuq ruler of Asia Minor, attempted to return to Cairo, but were driven out again, the Ameer Qalaoon, a leader of the party, being taken prisoner. The Bahris were obviously still unwelcome as long as the Aibek party were in power, under Qutuz, his former deputy. As a result, the remainder, under Baybars al Bunduqdari, joined the Prince of Kerak, Al-Mughith Umar. Soon afterwards, the Ameer Qalaoon escaped from prison and joined his barrack-comrades in Kerak.

*　　*　　*

We must here give a brief account of the coming of the Mongols, who were natives of the Asian steppes like the Turks, but were even more savage. Their habitat was south of Lake Baikal and east of the Turks.[9] In 1206, a tribal council had elected Jenghis Khan to be chief of the Mongols. He spent the years from 1211 to 1216 raiding China.

In 1219, he left Mongolia for the West. The Seljuq Empire had disintegrated and the petty rulers who had succeeded to it were unable to resist. Jenghis Khan spent the years 1220 to 1225 in reducing Persia to an uninhabited desert. The method he employed was always the same. His army drove with it herds of men taken as prisoners. On reaching a defended city, the prisoners were used to work the siege engines, fill in the ditch and climb up the breaches. When the city was taken, all the people were collected on a plain outside. The women were raped, then all the inhabitants were butchered, regardless of age or sex. The city was then looted, demolished and razed to the ground. By this means, all Persia was depopulated. Jenghis Khan died cn 18th August, 1227, at the age of sixty-six.

His eldest son, Juji, inherited the steppes north of the Black Sea and the Caspian, hitherto inhabited by the Qipchaq Turks. His third son, Ogotai, remained as Great Khan in Mongolia, and devoted himself to the completion of the conquest of China. Other Mongol

[9] Map 9, opposite.

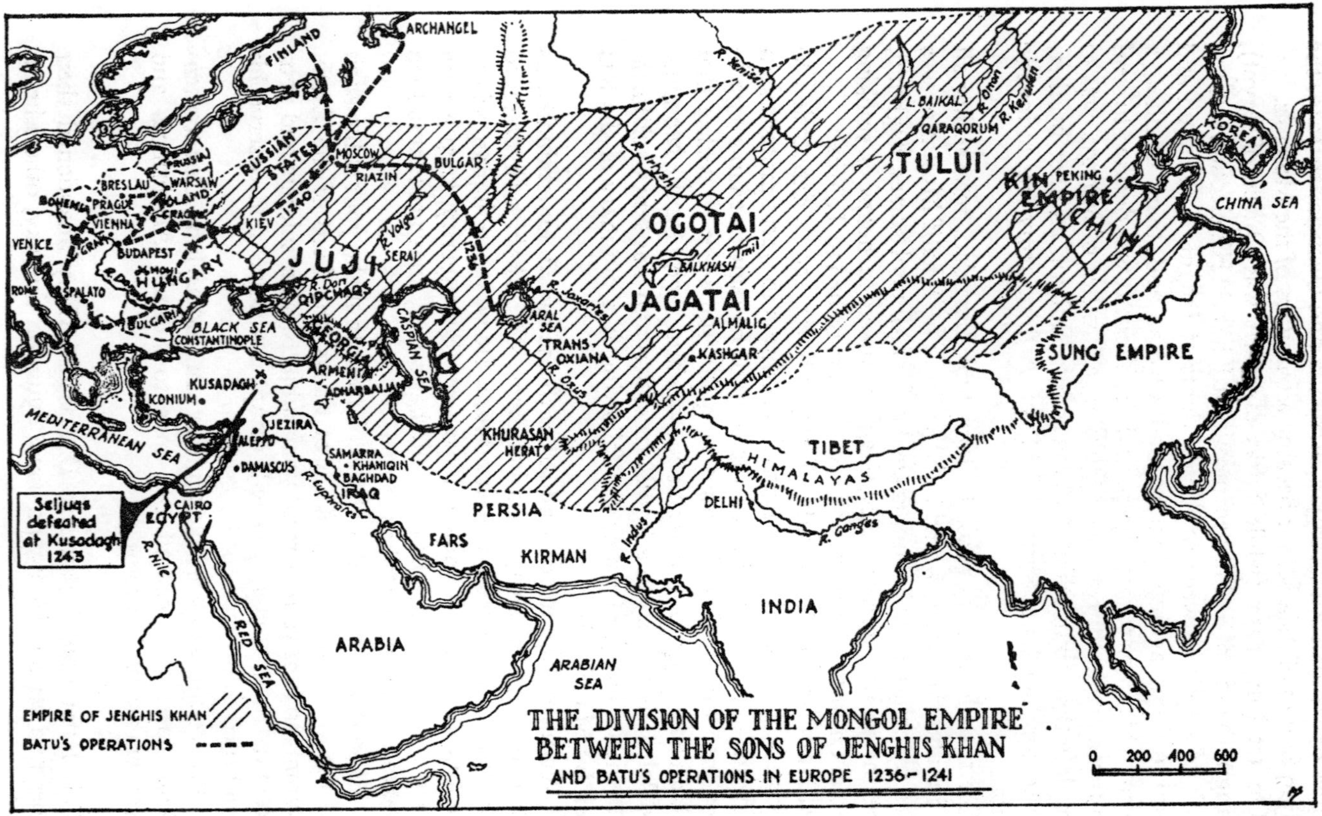

THE DIVISION OF THE MONGOL EMPIRE
BETWEEN THE SONS OF JENGHIS KHAN
AND BATU'S OPERATIONS IN EUROPE 1236–1241

MAP 10

EMPIRE OF JENGHIS KHAN
BATU'S OPERATIONS

0   200   400   600

KOREA
CHINA SEA
KIN (PEKING) EMPIRE
CHINA
SUNG EMPIRE
TULUI
L. BAIKAL
R. Onon
QARAQORUM
R. Kerulan
R. Selenga
OGOTAI
JAGATAI
R. Yenisei
R. Irtish
L. Balkash
Imil
ALMALIG
KASHGAR
TIBET
HIMALAYAS
R. Ganges
INDIA
DELHI
ARABIAN SEA
KIRMAN
FARS
PERSIA
KHURASAN
HERAT
TRANS OXIANA
R. Oxus
ARAL SEA
R. Syr
CASPIAN SEA
1256
JUJI
QIPCHAQ
SERAI
R. Volga
R. Don
R. Ural
RUSSIAN
BULGAR
MOSCOW
RIAZIN
ARCHANGEL
FINLAND
KIEV
GEORGIA
ARMENIA
KHANIQIN
SAMARRA
BAGHDAD
IRAQ
R. Tigris
R. Euphrates
JEZIRA
ALEPPO
DAMASCUS
RED SEA
ARABIA
EGYPT
CAIRO
R. Nile
MEDITERRANEAN SEA
KONIUM
KUSADAGH
CONSTANTINOPLE
BLACK SEA
SPALATO
ROME
VENICE
ZARA
HUNGARY
BUDAPEST
VIENNA
BOHEMIA
PRAGUE
POLAND
WARSAW
BRESLAU
BULGARIA

Seljuqs defeated
at Kusadagh
1243

armies devastated Adharbaijan, Armenia and Georgia. In 1243, the Seljuq Sultan of Asia Minor became a tributary of the Mongols.

On 1st July, 1251 (while Spray-of-Pearls was Queen of Egypt), Mangu, the son of Tului, became Great Khan.[10] His election was the result of a split between the descendants of Jenghis Khan: Juji and Tului uniting against Jagatai and Ogotai and their families, a schism which was to save Egypt and the West. It was decided to send out three armies of conquest. Qubilai, a brother of Mangu, was to complete the subjugation of China, while Hulagu, another brother, was to conquer Iraq, Syria and Egypt. A third army was to invade India.

On 13th February, 1258, Hulagu took Baghdad, massacring all the inhabitants, man, woman and child. The Khalif Mustasim was killed by being trampled under the hoofs of Mongol horses. Baghdad, once the world's greatest city,[11] was reduced to heaps of smoking rubble. On 20th February, 1258, Hulagu marched to Tabriz.

Al-Nasir Yusuf, the Ayoubid King of Syria, sent a deputation to Hulagu in Tabriz laden with gifts. In addition to warm protestations of friendship, Yusuf requested the help of Hulagu to enable him to reconquer Egypt. The Ayoubid king did not seem to realise that Hulagu had come to conquer both Syria and Egypt for the Mongols. The delegation received a hostile reception and was sent back forthwith with a letter, of which the following is a summary of the text given by Maqrizi:[12]

We have conquered Baghdad with the sword, exterminated its defenders and destroyed its buildings. The khalif well deserved the death to which we sentenced him. He was an evil man, whose reputation was well known. If you are in prosperity, keep it with care. How many men have slept in happiness, unaware that sudden death was about to strike them.

As soon as you read my letter, hasten to make your submission to the Great Khan, the King of Kings, the Lord of the Earth. Submit to him your person, your subjects, your soldiers and your wealth. In so doing, you will escape his anger and deserve his kindness.

Where can you flee? No fugitive can find asylum. Our tremendous power has caused the lions to submit. All princes and wazeers are subject to us.

This letter spread panic in Damascus. Many abandoned their homes and set out for Egypt, some dying on the way, others being

[10] Genealogical Trees 4 and 5, pages 58 and 78.
[11] Map 11, page 56.   [12] Maqrizi, *Kitab al Sulook*.

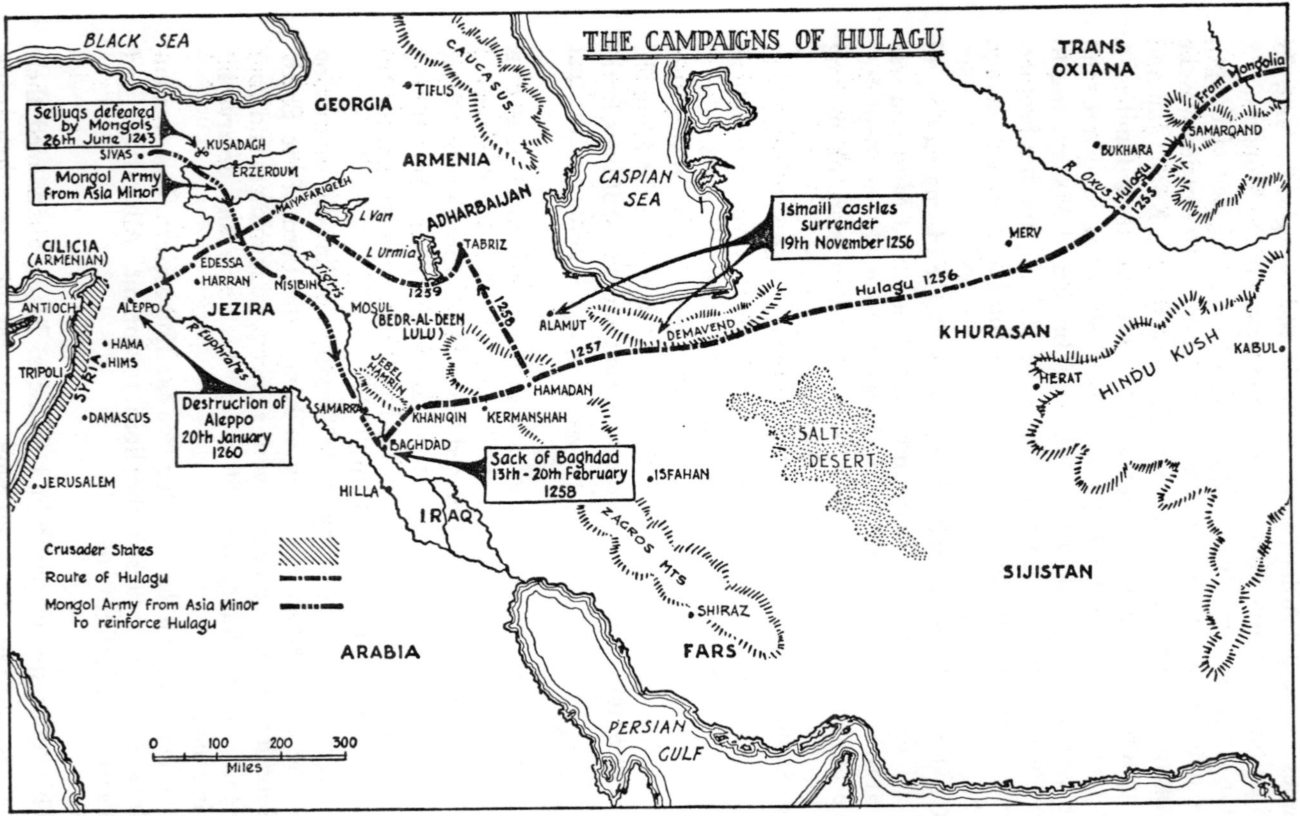

THE CAMPAIGNS OF HULAGU

Crusader States

Route of Hulagu

Mongol Army from Asia Minor
to reinforce Hulagu

Seljuqs defeated by Mongols
26th June 1243

Mongol Army from Asia Minor

Destruction of Aleppo
20th January 1260

Ismaili castles surrender
19th November 1256

Sack of Baghdad
13th-20th February 1258

BLACK SEA

GEORGIA

ARMENIA

CILICIA (ARMENIAN)

ANTIOCH

TRIPOLI

DAMASCUS

JERUSALEM

HIMS

HAMA

ALEPPO

EDESSA

HARRAN

JEZIRA

R. Euphrates

NISIBIN

MAYAFARIQIN

ERZERUM

SIVAS

KUSADAGH

CAUCASUS

TIFLIS

L. Van

L. Urmia

TABRIZ

ADHARBAIJAN

MOSUL (BEDR-AL-DEM LULU)

R. Tigris

JEBEL HAMRIN

KHANIQIN

BAGHDAD

SAMARRA

HILLA

IRAQ

ARABIA

1258

1259

1257

ALAMUT

CASPIAN SEA

DEMAVEND

HAMADAN

KERMANSHAH

ISFAHAN

ZAGROS MTS

SHIRAZ

FARS

PERSIAN GULF

SALT DESERT

KHURASAN

MERV

R. Oxus

1255

BUKHARA

SAMARQAND

Mongolia

TRANS OXIANA

HINDU KUSH

KABUL

HERAT

SIJISTAN

Hulagu 1256

Miles

0   100   200   300

MAP II

stripped by robbers. Al-Nasir Yusuf sent a deputation to Cairo to ask help of the Mamlukes. Meanwhile the Tatars[13] were reported to be crossing the Euphrates.

When Yusuf's letter reached Cairo, Qutuz called a meeting of Mamluke ameers and of the Egyptian chief qadhi or judge. The latter was asked whether the wealth of the public could be seized to pay for such a war. With some courage he replied that wealth could be seized, if the Mamlukes first spent all their own riches but not otherwise. It is of interest to note that the Mamlukes accepted the Egyptian qadhi's ruling.

No decision was taken regarding the despatch of troops to Damascus, but Qutuz pointed out that a soldier-sultan, not a child, was needed in such a crisis. Ali, the son of Aibek, passed his time in play. It was his mother who gave orders in his name. The ameers, however, protested vigorously and Qutuz, fearing their anger, adopted a moderate tone. The Tatars, he said, were marching on the country and it was vital to have a single leader. "As soon as the enemy is defeated," he said, "you will be free to elect whom you like to be sultan." After the meeting, he spoke privately to several ameers and overt opposition ceased. He was then recognised as sultan, and set himself, with all his energy, to prepare for war. He sent an ambiguous but conciliatory letter to the Syrian King, Al-Nasir Yusuf.

MALIK-AL-MUDHAFFAR QUTUZ

Meanwhile Hulagu, having taken Harran by assault, crossed the Euphrates and, in December 1259, camped beneath the walls of Aleppo. According to Maqrizi,[14] the Mongols took seven days to capture Aleppo. They then spent five more days, killing, looting and raping. The streets were soon covered with corpses, which the Tatars trampled under the feet of their horses. The citadel resisted for nearly a month, but was taken in January 1260. The enemy then painstakingly razed every building to the ground and cut down all the trees, leaving only a dusty plain and mounds of rubble. A hundred thousand women and children were driven off as slaves.

Al-Nasir Yusuf at first spoke of resisting Hulagu, but his continual vacillation undermined the morale of the army. When an officer advised him to submit, Baybars, the River Mamluke, protested with the utmost vehemence, walked out in a rage and left for Egypt.

---

[13] The Arab historians used the words Tatars and Mongols as synonyms. Tatars is correct, not Tartars.

[14] Maqrizi, *Kitab al Sulook*.

THE MONGOL KHAQANS

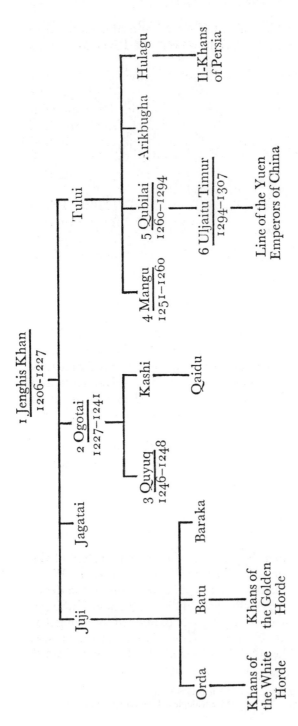

NOTES

1) The names of the Khaqans are underlined.

2) There were interregna between Ogotai and Quyuq, and between Quyuq and Mangu.

3) The Ogotai clan never recognised the descendants of Tului as Khaqans. Qaidu passed his life making war against Qubilai.

4) When Qubilai became Khaqan, his own brother Arikbugha rebelled but was defeated.

5) There was in fact no supreme Khaqan after Qubilai. Each branch of the family thereafter governed its own appanage independently.

6) Ogotai was nominated by Jenghis Khan in 1227 but was not elected by the quriltai till 1229.

Genealogical Tree 4

Qalaoon, another River Mamluke, left Kerak and also returned to Cairo. Although Aibek's party were in power, the River Mamlukes rallied to the cause.

In Damascus, the army began to disintegrate owing to the king's vacillation. When news came of the destruction of Aleppo, the people of Damascus gave way to unrestrained panic. The king, with a few officers, left for Gaza, leaving Syria to its fate. Great crowds of people stood at the city gates trying to hire transport, seven hundred silver pieces being asked for one camel. Those unable to hire pack animals scattered over the countryside in wild terror, as if the Day of Judgment had come upon them, says Maqrizi.

Of the other Ayoubid princes, Malik-al-Ashraf[15] Musa, Prince of Hims, joined Hulagu. Malik-al-Mansoor[16] Muhammad, Prince of Hama, took his women and children and left for Egypt. The people of Hims and Hama fled on foot to the Lebanese mountains. From Damascus, one of the qadhis of the city, Muhi-al-Deen Zeki, went to Hulagu, was well received and returned on 14th February, 1260, with a decree from the Mongol prince, promising an amnesty. On 1st March, 1260, the Mongol army entered Damascus, led by a commander called Kitbugha, beside whom rode Bohemond VI, Prince of Antioch, and Haithum I, Christian Armenian King of Cilicia. Nobody was molested, the Damascenes scarcely believing that they were still alive. The amnesty, however, covered only Damascus and the Mongols spread southwards like a swarm of locusts as far as Gaza, Hebron and Ziza, killing, raping and looting to their hearts' content.[17]

Qutuz was alarmed at the idea of an Ayoubid king in Cairo and Al-Nasir Yusuf turned eastward to Amman, where he was seized, handed over to Hulagu and beheaded.

*   *   *

When a Great Khan died, it had been the ancient custom of the Mongol tribes to collect in one place and elect a successor. When Hulagu was preparing to march on Egypt, news came of the death of the Great Khan Mangu. Leaving part of his army under Kitbugha to hold Syria, Hulagu took the rest of his troops and left for Mongolia, perhaps hoping himself to be elected Great Khan. If so, he was disappointed, for his brother Qubilai was elected before he arrived.[18]

---

[15] Most Noble King.　　[16] Victorious King.
[17] Map 5, page 35.　　[18] Genealogical Tree 4, page 58.

* * *

Meanwhile four ambassadors from Hulagu had brought a letter to Cairo. Its contents may be summarised as follows:

From the King of Kings of the East and the West, the Great Khan.

Qutuz is a mamluke, who fled to escape our swords . . . You should think of what happened to other countries . . . and submit your fate to us. We are not moved by tears or touched by lamentations. We have conquered vast areas, massacring all the people. You cannot escape from the terror of our armies. Only those who beg our protection will be safe.

Hasten your reply before the fire of war is kindled . . . You will suffer the most terrible catastrophes, your countries will become deserts . . . and we will kill your children and your old men together.

This letter had been written before Hulagu had heard of the death of the Great Khan Mangu.

Qutuz collected the Mamluke ameers and read the letter to them. Having now heard of the departure of Hulagu, all were in favour of fighting. The four ambassadors were accordingly halved at the waist and their heads nailed up on the Zuwaila Gate of Cairo.

Orders were issued for the mobilisation of the Mamluke army, and a few days later the troops camped at Salihiya, north-east of Cairo. Summoning the ameers to a council, Qutuz proposed an advance against the Mongols, but met with strong opposition, several ameers stating obstinately that they would not march. All were ready to defend Egypt but not to march against the Tatars in Syria.

Qutuz was furious. "Ameers of the Muslims," he shouted, "for a long time now you have been devouring the treasures of this country, and now you refuse to march. Right! I am going to march! Those who are faithful can go with me, the rest can return home. The guilt for the fate of the women of Islam will rest on those who refuse to fight."

Before summoning the council, Qutuz had obtained private oaths of loyalty from several ameers. These now offered to accompany him, the remainder being shamed into following their example. The Ameer Baybars the Bunduqdari, was given command of the advanced guard, and the Mamluke army advanced up the coastal plain

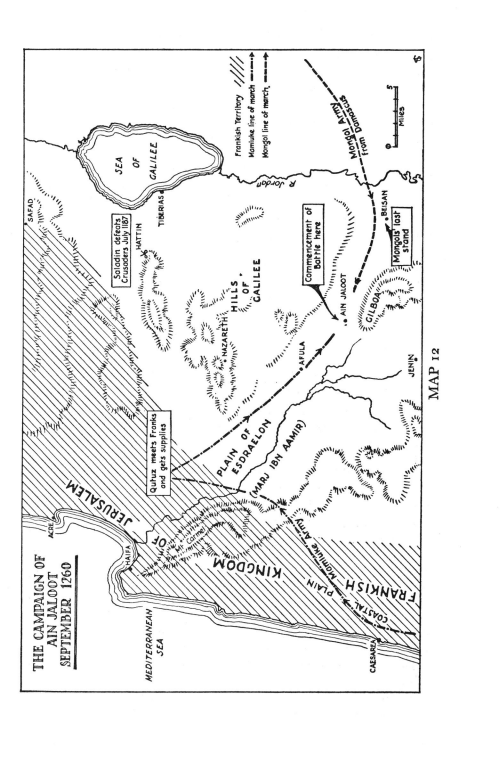

THE CAMPAIGN OF
AIN JALOOT
SEPTEMBER 1260

MEDITERRANEAN
SEA

ACRE

HAIFA

Mt. Carmel

COASTAL PLAIN

CAESAREA

KINGDOM OF JERUSALEM

FRANKISH

PLAIN OF ESDRAELON
(MARJ IBN AAMIR)

AFULA

JENIN

Mamluke Army

Qutuz meets Franks
and gets supplies

NAZARETH

HILLS
OF
GALILEE

HATTIN

Saladin defeats
Crusaders July 1187

TIBERIAS

SEA
OF
GALILEE

R. Jordan

Commencement of
Battle here

AIN JALOOT

GILBOA

BEISAN

Mongols' last
Stand

Mongol Army
from Damascus

SAFAD

Frankish Territory

Mamluke line of march

Mongol line of march

Miles
5

MAP 12

towards Acre, the capital of the Kingdom of Jerusalem, which had
declared for the Mamlukes, although Tripoli and Antioch had submitted to the Mongols.

The Franks of Acre offered to march with the sultan, who, however, rejected their armed help, but accepted supplies for his army.
The Franks then swore to him to remain neutral. Before moving
forward to battle, Qutuz called another council of ameers, at which
he delivered a powerful and moving appeal. He reminded them of the
massacres, the rapings, the ruin and desolation which had overtaken
so many countries at the hands of these unspeakable heathen. The
only course was to stand up like men and fight, and put an end to the
abominable outrages of the Tatars.

Many of these ruthless soldiers of fortune shed tears, swearing to
drive the heathen from Syria. Baybars then moved out with the
advanced guard, the main body following with colours flying and
rolling drums.

*   *   *

Kitbugha, the Mongol commander, had been left with the un-
enviable task of defending Syria with inadequate forces. The
Nestorian Christian Church, pronounced heretical by the Orthodox
Byzantines in the fifth century, had moved to Iraq and had carried
its missionary work far into Central Asia. Hulagu's favourite wife
was a Nestorian Christian, as was also Kitbugha, the Tatar commander in Syria.

As soon as Kitbugha heard of the advance of Qutuz, he marched
south from Damascus, crossed the Jordan and advanced up the
Plain of Esdraelon—in Arabic Marj Ibn Aamir—past Beisan.[19] He
knew he was outnumbered, but he believed that Tatars were always
invincible.

On the morning of 3rd September, 1260, soon after sunrise, as they
were approaching Ain Jaloot (the Spring of Goliath), the Mamluke
advanced guard sighted the Mongol scouts. Coming from the west,
the Plain of Esdraelon, seven miles wide at Afula, narrows to only
some three miles wide at Ain Jaloot. On the south rises the steep
slope of the biblical Mount Gilboa, on the north the rolling hills of
Galilee. The long plain falls sharply to the Jordan, so that the
Mamlukes were riding downhill, the Mongols uphill. From the
Mamluke ranks, the loud and continuous roll of drums filled the air.

Kitbugha charged with so much fury that the Mamluke advanced
guard was swept aside and their left flank overrun. But the Mamlukes

[19] Map 12, page 61.

did not panic, as did most armies at the first Mongol charge. The centre and the right flank stood firm, and soon the disparity of numbers began to tell. With the Mamlukes working round their flanks, the Tatars fought back savagely. The indefatigable Kitbugha galloped right and left, encouraging his men and launching new counter-charges.

At this decisive moment, Qutuz himself rode out in front of the Mamluke army, took off his helmet so that all could recognise him, and roared in stentorian tones, "O Muslims! O Muslims! O Muslims!" Then surrounded by his escort and followed by the rest of the army, he plunged recklessly into the Mongol ranks. The impetus of the charge was irresistible and the Tatars were swept off the field.

The gallant Kitbugha, his horse killed under him, was taken prisoner, led before Qutuz and decapitated.[20] The Mongols were now in flight, with the Mamlukes galloping at their heels, shooting, thrusting and slashing. Baybars had fought side-by-side with Qutuz in the heart of the mêlée.

At Beisan, the Mongols turned to fight and a desperate hand-to-hand battle was renewed. Qutuz once more took the lead, shouting, "O God, give us victory!" his mighty voice being heard all over the field. The Mongols finally collapsed, the survivors taking to flight, while Qutuz dismounted and offered up a prayer of two prostrations in gratitude for victory. Kitbugha's severed head was sent post-haste to Cairo, as proof of the Mongol defeat.

When news of the battle reached Damascus, the Mongols hastily set out for the north, the country people chasing them and cutting off their stragglers.

Two days after the battle, Qutuz camped near Tiberias, whence he wrote the official despatch announcing the victory. The Damascenes gave themselves up to wild rejoicings, but soon turned on the local Christians, whom they accused of associating with the Mongols. The houses of Christians were looted and two churches were wrecked. The houses of Jews, and of Muslims accused of helping the enemy, were also sacked, until the local militia intervened. The city meanwhile looked as if it had been plundered by a hostile army.

NOTABLE DATES

Departure of Louis IX from Damietta	7th May, 1250
Spray-of-Pearls Queen of Egypt	May, 1250

[20] Maqrizi, on the other hand, says that he was killed in Qutuz's charge.

Malik-al-Muizz Aibek and Spray-of-Pearls rule
    Egypt   1250–1257
Malik-al-Nasir Yusuf, King of Syria   1250–1260
Murder of Aqtai by Aibek and dispersion of the
    River Mamlukes   1254
Murder of Aibek and of Spray-of-Pearls   1257
Elevation of Malik-al-Mansoor Ali, son of
    Aibek   20th March, 1257
Destruction of Baghdad by Hulagu   13th February, 1258
Qutuz becomes Sultan   1259
Destruction of Aleppo   January, 1260
Death of Great Khan Mangu   1260
Entry of Kitbugha into Damascus   1st March, 1260
Battle of Ain Jaloot   3rd September, 1260

PERSONALITIES

EGYPT
Spray-of-Pearls
Malik-al-Muizz Aibek al Turkmani
Malik-al-Mansoor Ali, son of Aibek
Malik-al-Mudhaffar Qutuz

Mongols
Jenghis Khan
Great Khan Mangu
Hulagu, son of Tului
Great Khan Qubilai
Kitbugha, Mongol commander in Syria

Ayoubids
Malik-al-Salih Ayoub, Ruler of the Ayoubid Empire
Malik-al-Salih Ismail. Rebelled against Ayoub
Malik-al-Nasir Yusuf, King of Syria
Malik-al-Mansoor Muhammad, Prince of Hama
Malik-al-Ashraf Musa, Prince of Hims
Malik-al-Mughith Umar, Prince of Kerak

III

Death of a Khalif

We must at least give the Mamluks their due as a splendid soldiery. Four times they had to meet the most formidable of all possible invasions, the repeated advance of the Mongol hordes.

STANLEY LANE-POOLE, *The Story of Cairo*

It is only recently that European history has begun to understand that the successes of the Mongol army . . . were won by consummate strategy and were not due to a mere overwhelming superiority of numbers.

J. B. BURY, *Notes on Gibbon's Decline and Fall of the Roman Empire*

A most spectacular event of Baybars' reign was his inauguration of a new series of Abbasid caliphs, who carried the name but none of the authority of the office.

PHILIP HITTI, *History of the Arabs*

Whoever serves his country well has no need of ancestors.

VOLTAIRE

In consolidating their power, the Mamluks had to think of facing the Crusaders . . . The conflicts with the Latins took the shape of concentrated and vehement Mamluk attacks against weakening Crusader defences . . . The attacks were ruthless and the destruction they left in their wake, especially in the coastal towns, paralysed the area for generations.

NICOLA A. ZIADEH, *Damascus under the Mamluks*

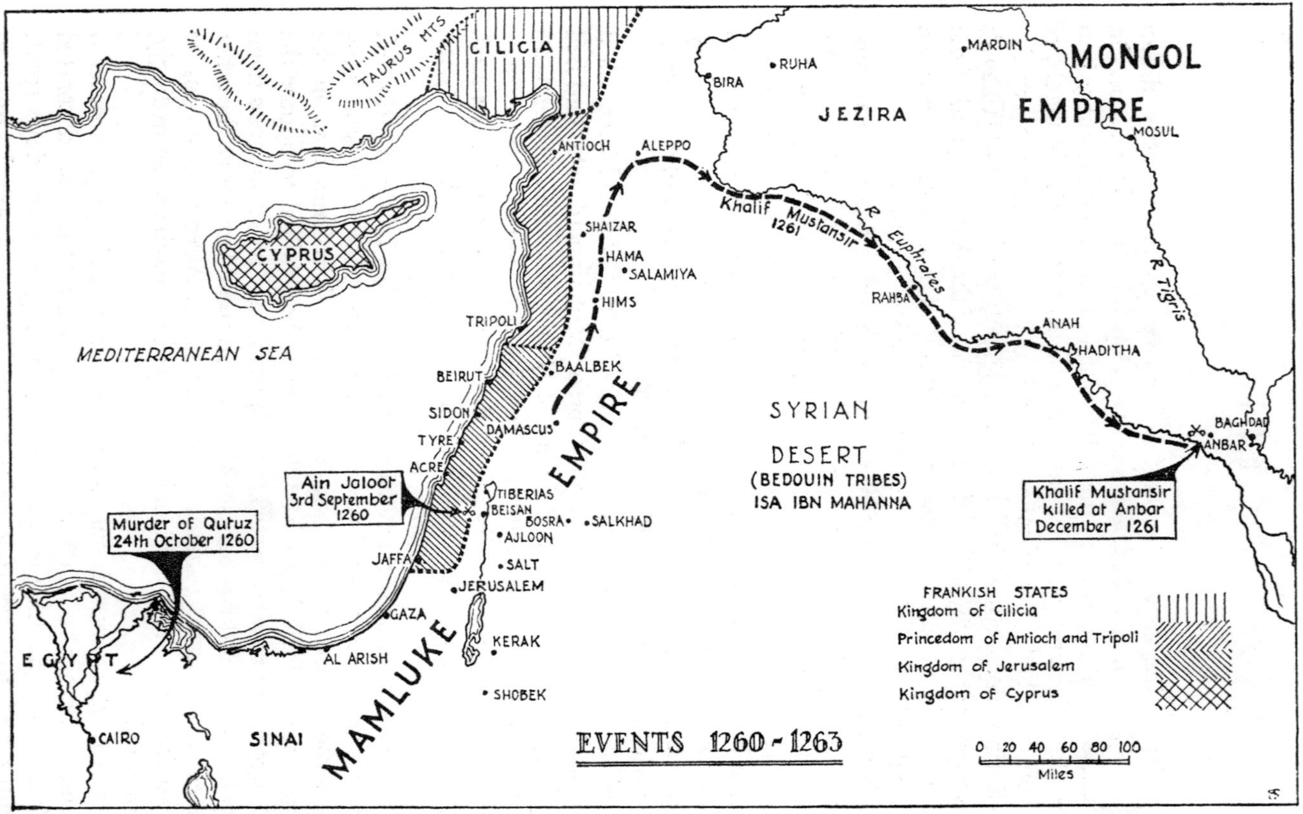

MONGOL
EMPIRE

• MOSUL

R Tigris

• MARDIN

JEZIRA

BAGHDAD
• ANBAR

HADITHA

ANAH

R Euphrates

RAHBA

Khalif Mustansir killed at Anbar
December 1261

• RUHA

Khalif Mustansir 1261

• BIRA

SYRIAN
DESERT
(BEDOUIN TRIBES)
ISA IBN MAHANNA

FRANKISH STATES
Kingdom of Cilicia
Princedom of Antioch and Tripoli
Kingdom of Jerusalem
Kingdom of Cyprus

0 20 40 60 80 100
Miles

ALEPPO

CILICIA

• SHAIZAR
• HAMA
• SALAMIYA
• HIMS

ANTIOCH

BAALBEK

EMPIRE

TRIPOLI

TAURUS MTS

DAMASCUS
• SALKHAD
• BOSRA
TIBERIAS
BEISAN • AJLOON
• SALT
JERUSALEM
• KERAK

• SHOBEK

BEIRUT
SIDON
TYRE
ACRE

Ain Jaloof
3rd September
1260

JAFFA

GAZA

MAMLUKE

MEDITERRANEAN SEA

CYPRUS

AL ARISH

Murder of Qutuz
24th October 1260

SINAI

E G Y P T

• CAIRO

EVENTS 1260~1263

MAP 13

ON 8th September, 1260, five days after the Battle of Ain Jaloot, Qutuz and his army camped outside Damascus. On 10th September, the sultan made a triumphant entry into the city. The energetic Baybars was sent to pursue the Mongols, of whom he killed great numbers. Mamluke columns visited every city in Syria as far north as the Euphrates. The ultimate effect of Hulagu's invasion, of the cowardice of Al-Nasir Yusuf the Ayoubid, and of the courage of Qutuz, was to end Ayoubid rule of Syria and to constitute a single Mamluke Empire, from Egypt to the Euphrates.

Qutuz gave a number of landed fiefs in Syria to Mamluke ameers. Baybars, who had led the advanced guard and had fought hand-to-hand beside Qutuz, had asked for the governorship of Aleppo but had been refused. The post was given to an ameer Ala-al-Deen, the son of Bedr-al-Deen Lulu, the Lord of Mosul, whose daughter Aibek had courted. Ala-al-Deen was the son of a slave of the Seljuqs and was not a Mamluke at all. The Mamlukes had rallied to resist the Mongols, but now old feuds revived.

Most of the Ayoubid princes scattered over Syria had been killed by the Mongols, but Malik-al-Mansoor Muhammad, who had fled to Egypt, was reinstated as Prince of Hama, where his descendants remained till the fourteenth century. Malik-al-Ashraf Musa, Prince of Hims, who had actually joined the Mongols, was also reinstated. Isa ibn Mahanna, paramount chief of the bedouins in the Syrian desert, was given the town of Salamiya as a fief.

On 5th October, thirty-two days after the battle, Qutuz left Damascus for Cairo with the army. An atmosphere of tension hung over the ameers. Qutuz had been Aibek's right-hand man in the suppression of the River Mamlukes, who had rallied to oppose the Mongols, but now suspected that Qutuz would try to suppress them again. Qutuz and Baybars stood head and shoulders above the other ameers in courage, initiative and leadership. Already belonging to rival factions, they could not exist together. Baybars, accordingly, concerted a plot.

When the army was only a few miles from Cairo, Qutuz ordered camp to be pitched for a day's hunting, while Cairo was decorated for a victory march the next day. Returning from the day's sport, Qutuz and Baybars rode side-by-side. The latter asked Qutuz to give him a girl captured from the Mongols, to which the sultan readily agreed. Baybars thanked him warmly, seizing his hand as if to kiss it.

It was the signal agreed between him and the conspirators. The Ameer Bektout drew his sword and ran it into the sultan's neck. The Ameer Anis seized Qutuz and dragged him from his horse, while the Ameer Bahadur finished him with an arrow at short range. It was 24th October, 1260.

The ameers hastened to gather in the royal tent, and one of them cried, "Which of you killed Qutuz?" "I did," Baybars replied. "My Lord," answered the first, "sit in his place on the sultan's seat." The ameers then pressed forward, and each in turn did homage and took the oath of loyalty.

Qutuz had reigned only eleven and a half months. He was sometimes hard and cruel, but his courage and will were outstanding. It was his forcefulness which drove the hesitating ameers into battle, and it was he in person who led them to victory. He saved Syria and Egypt from the devastation which had destroyed Persia, and from which that country has still not recovered. If Egypt had suffered the fate of Baghdad, the world would be a different place today. To have turned back the wave of Mongol destruction by his sole will-power and courage should surely entitle him to a niche in the Hall of Fame.

*   *   *

BAYBARS AL BUNDUQDARI

Realising that he would not be secure in power until he had occupied the Citadel of Cairo, Baybars rode off at once, accompanied by the officers who supported him, and entered the Citadel quietly at night, thereby making sure of the keys of power.

Orders had already been given to decorate Cairo for the triumphal entry of Qutuz. The orders had been carried out with delight, so immense was the popular joy at the defeat of the Tatars. But at dawn, criers were sent through the streets, calling, "Pray for God's mercy on Malik-al-Mudhaffar Qutuz. Pray for the long life of your Sultan Baybars." Many people were alarmed by the elevation of Baybars, remembering the outrages perpetrated by the River Mamlukes in the days of Aibek.

Baybars was by origin a Qipchaq Turk. Brought as a boy to Syria, he had been bought and trained by the Ameer Aidekeen the Bunduqdar. Bunduq, in the Arabic of those days, meant a crossbow, so this officer may have had the task of carrying the sultan's cross-bow, or he may have been a technician in crossbows. When Sultan Al-Salih Ayoub formed the Bahris, or River Mamlukes, he bought Baybars from his owner. He soon attracted attention, for he was a big man, with a strong personality, a born leader and of fearless courage. He was freed by Al-Salih Ayoub, and thus became a Salihi. It was he who had led the Mamluke counter-attack against Louis IX and his Crusaders at Mansoora. He was the Bahri Mamluke who attempted to assassinate Turan Shah on 1st May, 1250, and who had played so prominent a rôle in the campaign of Ain Jaloot. In a moment of crisis, Baybars always took charge. As he had blue eyes, his ethnic origin was doubtless mixed. He was to be the real founder of the Mamluke Empire, which, after him, was to be held by Bahris or their descendants for a hundred and twenty-one years.

*   *   *

Before leaving for the war, Qutuz had imposed a number of new taxes in order to pay for the campaign. On the first day of his reign, Baybars abolished all these additional taxes. Then, seating himself in the Hall of Audience, he received the oaths of loyalty of the army.

All the provinces accepted the new sultan, except for the Viceroy of Damascus, Sanjar al Halebi, an associate of Qutuz, who had appointed him. Chagrined by the murder of his chief, he felt it dis-honourable to swear loyalty to his assassin. He accordingly de-nounced Baybars, assumed the throne-name of Malik-al-Mujahid,[1] and accepted the oaths of loyalty of his subordinates to himself. A few days later, he rode in state through the streets of Damascus, bearing the emblems of royalty. He then set to work to repair the citadel of Damascus, damaged by the Mongols.

Baybars' coup d'état had produced the same effect as we so con-stantly see in military seizures of power today. If one army officer can seize power, others think they can do the same. The people of Damascus, not yet resigned to be subordinate to Egypt, worked joy-fully at the repair of the fortifications.

Geography created a problem in the Middle East still unsolved today. The three cities of Cairo, Damascus and Baghdad lie each in the middle of a rich area, but separated from each other by hundreds of miles of desert, and inevitably regarding one another with jealousy, a factor which was at least partly responsible for the joyful support of Sanjar by the Damascenes.

Meanwhile, in Aleppo, the Mamluke ameers had driven out

[1] The Diligent King.

1 A street in Fustat or Old Cairo. Even as early as A.D. 1000, some
of the houses were six or seven storeys high.

Ala-al-Deen, the son of Lulu, and had chosen for their governor
Husam-al-Deen[2] Lajeen. Most of the ameers in Aleppo were former

[2] Sword of the Religion.

mamlukes of the Ayoubid Princes of Aleppo, Al-Azeez Muhammad (1216–1236) or of his son Al-Nasir Yusuf (1236–1260).[3] All were, therefore, barrack-comrades, bound to one another. Husam-al-Deen Lajeen, however, did not ally himself to Sanjar, the Viceroy of Damascus, but professed allegiance to Baybars. Such were some of the problems created by the Mamluke system with its lack of loyalty to the state, but its honourable devotion to the mamlukes' original patrons and to their barrack-comrades.

Lajeen had been jokandar, or warden of his polo-sticks, to the Prince of Aleppo, an honorary court title like that of gentleman of the bedchamber at a European court. The Mamlukes were passionate polo-players and sultans, kings and ameers played frequently. In 1261, a force of six thousand Tatars raided across the Euphrates, reaching the vicinity of Hims, but they were virtually exterminated by the Ayoubid Princes of Hims and Hama, and by Zámil ibn Mahanna, one of the chiefs of the bedouins of the Syrian desert.

On 12th January, 1261, Baybars rode in state through the streets of Cairo with the emblems of royalty. Before him went the ghashiya or golden saddlecloth, while over his head was carried the yellow silk parasol, surmounted by a gold and silver bird, which had been introduced by the Fatimids. It is notable that, for such inaugural ceremonies, the Mamlukes had taken over the traditional dress of the Abbasid Khalifs of Baghdad. On his head, the new sultan wore a large black turban, from which two black ribbons hung down his back. His voluminous black robes were without gold embroidery or ornamentation. At his side hung an antique Arab sword, supported by a sash over his right shoulder. This sword was alleged to have belonged to Umar ibn al Khattab, the second successor of the Prophet.

It is significant that the clothing worn by the Mamluke sultans on state occasions was purely traditional Arab costume, with nothing of Turkish origin. This fact suggests that the Mamlukes were not merely arrogant foreign conquerors, but that they respected the ancient culture and traditions of their subjects.

The procession left the Chain Gate of the Citadel, passed through the Zuwaila Gate, up the Grand Avenue and out by the Victory Gate. Baybars on horseback was preceded by the ameers on foot, by a large force of Mamlukes and by a band of drums and trumpets. The streets had been gaily decorated, and handfuls of gold and silver were rained upon the sultan. On his return to the Citadel, a grand levée was held and robes of honour were distributed to the principal Egyptian officials and to the Mamluke ameers. Thereafter, Baybars

[3] Genealogical Tree 3, page 33.

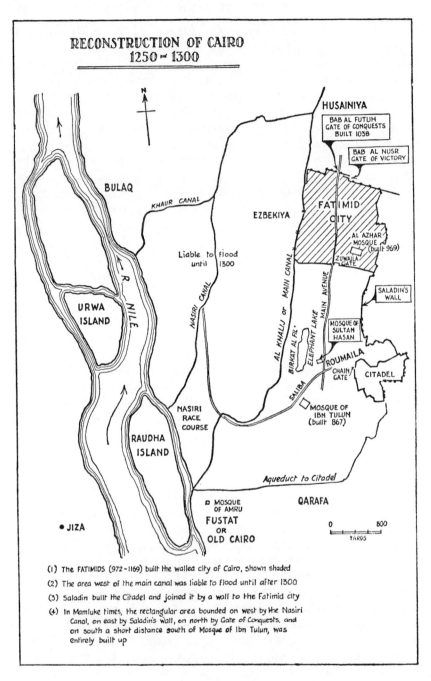

RECONSTRUCTION OF CAIRO
1250 ~ 1300

N

HUSAINIYA

BAB AL FUTUH
GATE OF CONQUESTS
BUILT 1038

BAB AL NUSR
GATE OF VICTORY

BULAQ

KHAUR CANAL

EZBEKIYA

FATIMID
CITY

AL AZHAR
MOSQUE
(built 969)

ZUWAILA
GATE

Liable to flood
until 1300

NASIRI CANAL

URWA
ISLAND

AL KHALIJ or MAIN CANAL

BIRKAT AL FIL

ELEPHANT LAKE

MAIN AVENUE

SALADIN'S
WALL

MOSQUE OF
SULTAN
HASAN

ROUMAILA

SALIBA

CHAIN
GATE

CITADEL

NASIRI
RACE
COURSE

MOSQUE OF
IBN TULUN
(built 867)

RAUDHA
ISLAND

Aqueduct to Citadel

QARAFA

MOSQUE
OF AMRU

• JIZA

FUSTAT
OR
OLD CAIRO

0   800
YARDS

(1) The FATIMIDS (972–1169) built the walled city of Cairo, shown shaded

(2) The area west of the main canal was liable to flood until after 1300

(3) Saladin built the Citadel and joined it by a wall to the Fatimid city

(4) In Mamluke times, the rectangular area bounded on west by the Nasiri
Canal, on east by Saladin's wall, on north by Gate of Conquests, and
on south a short distance south of Mosque of Ibn Tulun, was
entirely built up

MAP 14

often rode ceremonially from the Citadel to play polo, surrounded by ameers and preceded by a band.

Meanwhile Baybars sent an emissary to Damascus with a large sum of money to win over supporters from Sanjar al Halebi. A numerous group of ameers and mamlukes left the city, proclaiming their loyalty to Baybars. Sanjar gave chase but was defeated and wounded, taken prisoner and sent to Cairo. Peace being thus established, Baybars set to work with immense energy. In Egypt, dykes and bridges were constructed and the walls of Rosetta and Damietta strengthened. In Syria, all the fortresses damaged by the Mongols were repaired and their ditches re-dug, including Damascus, Salt, Ajloon, Salkhad, Bosra, Baalbek and Shaizar. Mamluke garrisons were posted, and reserves of rations and ammunition laid in.[4]

The cultivators, impoverished by the Mongol invasion, were given grain for seed. Relays of post horses were placed along the main roads, so that despatches could reach Damascus in four days from Cairo. Mails reached Cairo twice a week from all the cities of the empire.

The fleet had been neglected since the death of the Ayoubid Sultan Malik-al-Salih Ayoub. Baybars restored it to a strength of nearly forty war-galleys, as it had been under the Ayoubids. The sultan himself visited the naval arsenal and drew up its standing orders.

Baybars, having received a report of a plot to assassinate him, ordered the arrest of a number of ameers. The wazeer, the head of the civil government, an Egyptian called Ibn Zubair, was dismissed and replaced by Baha-al-Deen Ali. As already indicated, the Mamlukes constituted the army, the civil and judicial administrations being staffed by Syrians and Egyptians. In March 1261, a force was sent to seize Shobek, which belonged to the independent Ayoubid Prince of Kerak, Malik-al-Mughith Umar. Baybars was unwilling to allow the survival of independent princes. Those of Hims and Hama had done homage to him.

* * *

In 1261, a report came from Damascus stating that an individual had arrived from the eastern desert claiming to be a member of the Abbasid family of Baghdad and uncle of the Khalif Mustasim, killed by the Mongols. He had lived for two years in hiding with the nomads of the desert. Baybars ordered that he be shown the highest

[4] Map 12, page 61.

respect and sent to Cairo with a staff of chamberlains and a large escort.

When the cortège drew near to Cairo, the sultan rode out to meet it, accompanied by the wazeer, the chief qadhi, the ameers, the notables of Cairo and a large body of troops. The Jews and the Christians also joined in the formal welcome, the Jews bearing before them the Torah—the Pentateuch—the Christians preceded by a copy of the Gospels.

The Abbasid prince, accompanied by Baybars, reached the Gate of Victory, the whole procession passing down Grand Avenue, through the Zuwaila Gate to the Citadel. Four days later, a formal levée was held in the Citadel, in honour of the Abbasid. The chief qadhi, the judges, the lawyers, the religious shaikhs, the ameers and the city notables, obtained an audience of the prince. The sultan sat modestly beside his guest, without any insignia of royalty. A eunuch from Baghdad, some Arabs from Iraq and the bedouins with whom he had crossed the desert, certified that the visitor was Ahmad, son of the Khalif Dháhir, the Prince of the Faithful. The chief qadhi drew up a legal document, stating that he had been recognised as the new khalif, Al Mustansir Billah, Prince of the Faithful.

Baybars himself did homage to the new khalif, promising to govern justly. Then all those present filed past, pledging loyalty to the Prince of the Faithful. Finally, the doors were flung wide, and the whole population was allowed to file past and pay homage.

On Friday, the khalif preached in the mosque, subsequently held a levée of his own, bestowed robes of honour on the notables and the ameers, and himself led a grand procession through the city. "These," writes Maqrizi, "were days of real popular rejoicing and jubilation."

Preparations were then set on foot to enable the khalif to return to his capital in Baghdad. The first step was to raise an army, then to choose a staff, a wazeer, a treasurer and secretaries. Weapons were issued, equipment, standards, drums and rations. A hundred mamlukes formed a bodyguard, with pages, surgeons and religious teachers.

When all was ready, the sultan and the khalif set off together for Damascus. Baybars originally meant to send ten thousand horsemen to establish the khalif on his throne in Baghdad. But Maqrizi suggests that, in Damascus, one of the sons of Lulu of Mosul whispered to Baybars that a strong khalif might become a rival to the sultan in Cairo. As a result, Baybars sent the unhappy khalif to conquer Baghdad with only three hundred horsemen. At Rahba[5] he was

[5] Map 13, page 66.

joined by a bedouin chief with four hundred tribesmen. Sixty Mamlukes from Mosul and thirty from Hama made up about eight hundred horsemen, with which to challenge the Mongol Empire. On the Euphrates, he collected a few Turkmans and marched down the river, through Anah and Haditha, to Anbar. The Mongol commander in Baghdad, Karabugha, hearing of the khalif's march, had moved out to Anbar, where he massacred the inhabitants, although they were his own subjects. This was a frequent practice on the part of the Mongols, who found it more enjoyable to live by plunder than by collecting taxes.

The khalif, whose courage exceeded his wisdom, advanced against the enemy and charged them, sword in hand. The Arabs and Turkmans fled, and the khalif and his escort were surrounded and killed. Another alleged Abbasid, who had taken refuge in Egypt, escaped with fifty men. The khalif's body was never found. This incident took place at the end of November or in early December 1261.

The whole of this affair is mysterious. Why did Baybars give Ahmad, son of the Khalif Dhahir, so dazzling a reception? The feasting, parades, decorations and robes of honour were on an unprecedented scale. The sultan did homage to the khalif whom he had created. The whole affair is said to have cost Baybars more than a million gold dinars. Did he think the khalif would be an ally against the Mongols? Was he jealous of the khalif, whom he himself had made so conspicuous?

To send the khalif to capture Baghdad with only a handful of tribesmen was obviously absurd. But why did the khalif agree to go with so tiny a force?

*   *   *

We have seen that Hulagu had abandoned Syria and hurried back to Mongolia when he heard of the death of the Great Khan Mangu. When, however, he learned that his brother Qubilai had been made Great Khan, he returned to Tabriz. He sent his allegiance to Qubilai, who was in Peking, and the latter replied, delegating Hulagu to rule Persia, and giving him the title of Il-Khan. The Ogotai and Jagatai clans rejected the election of Qubilai.[6]

The descendants of Juji were now established north of the Caucasus from the Volga to Hungary and north to Moscow, with Sarai[7] on the lower Volga as their capital. They assumed the titles of the Golden and the White Hordes.[8]

---

[6] Genealogical Tree 4, page 58.   [7] Map 10, page 54.

[8] The anglicised form "horde" is derived from the Turkish *urdu*, a camp. The Urdu language was the camp jargon, evolved by mixed mercenary armies.

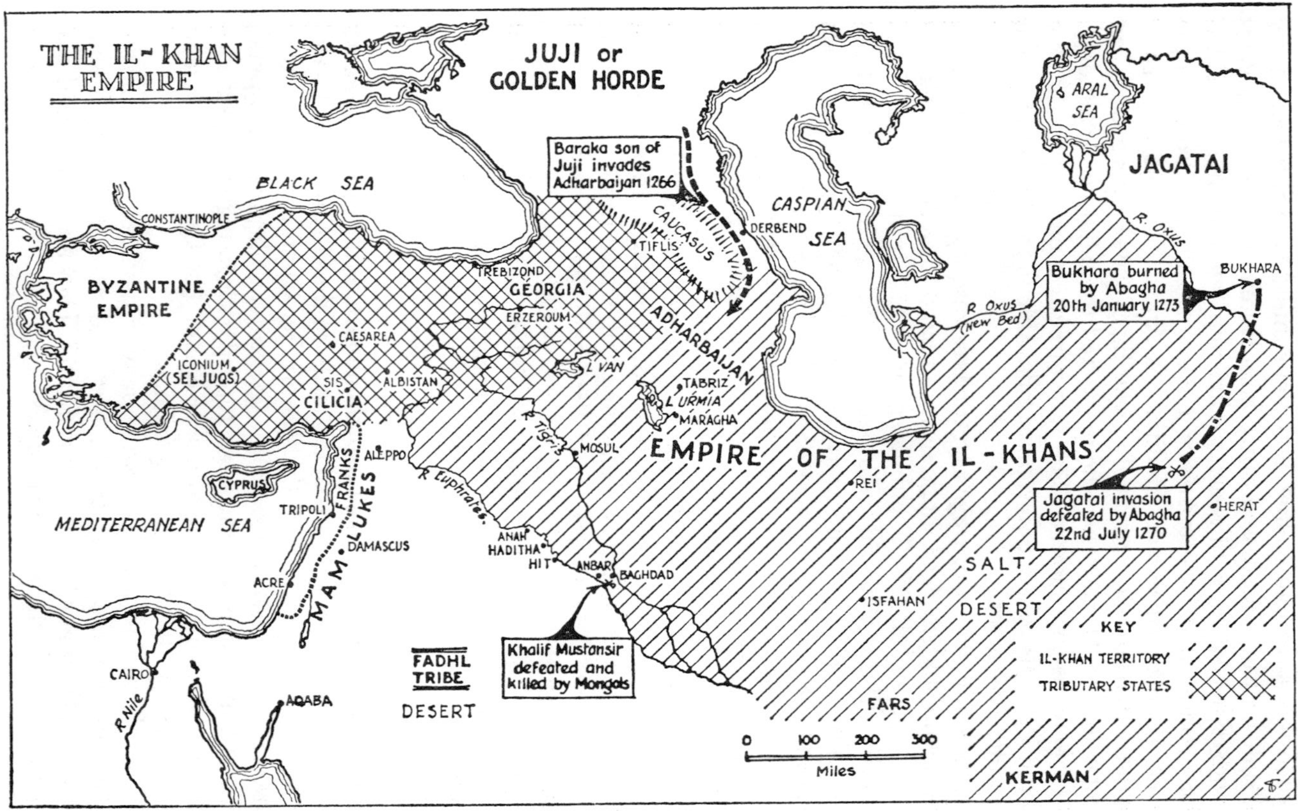

THE IL-KHAN EMPIRE

JUJI or GOLDEN HORDE

JAGATAI

ARAL SEA

Baraka son of Juji invades Adharbaijan 1266

Bukhara burned by Abagha 20th January 1273

BUKHARA

R. Oxus

R. Oxus (New Bed)

R. Oxus (New Bed)

Jagatai invasion defeated by Abagha 22nd July 1270

• HERAT

CASPIAN SEA

DERBEND

CAUCASUS

TIFLIS

ADHARBAIJAN

TABRIZ
L. URMIA
MARAGHA

EMPIRE OF THE IL-KHANS

SALT DESERT

• REI
• ISFAHAN

FARS

KEY

IL-KHAN TERRITORY
TRIBUTARY STATES

KERMAN

BLACK SEA

GEORGIA

TREBIZOND

ERZERUM

L. VAN

MOSUL

TIGRIS

ANBAR
HADITHA
HIT
BAGHDAD

Khalif Mustansir defeated and killed by Mongols

CAESAREA

ALBISTAN

SIS
CILICIA

ICONIUM (SELJUQS)

BYZANTINE EMPIRE

CONSTANTINOPLE

FRANKS

ALEPPO

DAMASCUS

Euphrates

FADHL TRIBE

DESERT

MAMLUKES

TRIPOLI

ACRE

CYPRUS

MEDITERRANEAN SEA

AQABA

CAIRO

R. NILE

0   100   200   300
Miles

MAP 15

Hulagu proceeded to consolidate his personal empire. He annexed Mosul, extended his rule over southern Persia, and over Cilicia. The last Seljuqs of Asia Minor were glad to become his vassals. His dominions extended from the Oxus to within a hundred and fifty miles of Constantinople.[9] He died at Maragha, south of Tabriz, on 8th February, 1265, and was succeeded by his son Abagha.

From 1256 to 1266, Baraka, the third son of Juji, was ruler of the Mongols north of the Caucasus, and was converted to Islam. In 1262, Baybars wrote to him as a fellow Muslim, inviting him to attack his cousin Hulagu, the arch-enemy of Islam, who had killed the khalif of Baghdad. Baraka actually did so shortly before his death. These Mongol feuds reduced the danger of another invasion of Syria.

* * *

In the spring of 1262, Baybars raided the territory of the Prince of Antioch, who had assisted the Mongols. He returned laden with loot, having burned the crops which were ripe for harvest. The Franks begged for peace, which the sultan ultimately granted.

In Damascus, Baybars summoned the tribal chiefs and made each one responsible for law and order in his territory. Isa ibn Mahanna, the principal nomadic chief of the Syrian desert, was given the title of Ameer of the Arabs, that is, of nomads. He held Salamiya as a fief. Baybars, by the strength of his own personality, was now complete master of the situation.

* * *

We have seen that another Abbasid had escaped from the Battle of Anbar. Abu al Abbas Ahmad returned to Cairo, where he was recognised as khalif, with the throne-name of Al-Hákim-bi-amr-Illah, "the Ruler by God's command". He was given apartments in the Citadel, but Baybars decided that it was unwise to have two personalities in one country and placed Hakim virtually under house arrest.

* * *

A brief explanation regarding the ranks of Mamluke ameers may here be useful. The government was divided into two distinct classes, "men of the pen" and "men of the sword", civil servants and

[9] Map 15, opposite.

THE IL-KHANS OF PERSIA

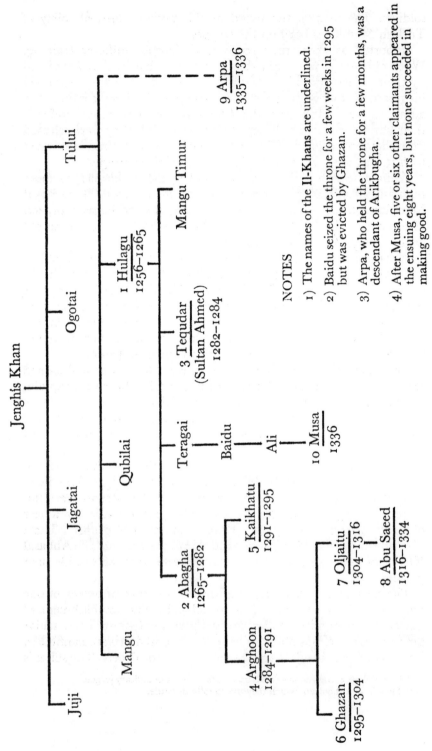

NOTES

1) The names of the Il-Khans are underlined.

2) Baidu seized the throne for a few weeks in 1295 but was evicted by Ghazan.

3) Arpa, who held the throne for a few months, was a descendant of Arikbugha.

4) After Musa, five or six other claimants appeared in the ensuing eight years, but none succeeded in making good.

Genealogical Tree 5

soldiers. The men of the sword at this period consisted solely of Turkish Mamlukes born on the steppes.

Imported as boys, they received a rigorous military training. When old enough to bear arms and engage in battle, they were freed by their owners and given horses and weapons, but they remained his retainers, though they were his social equals. They continued to admit an honourable loyalty to him and also to his other retainers, their barrack-comrades. When their patron died, they were released from their obligation to his family, though they sometimes continued with it, but they retained their loyalty to their comrades.

While ameers had their own mamlukes, the sultan had far more than anyone else, his power depending on the number. These Royal Mamlukes, being directly under the sultan, enjoyed better prospects of promotion than did ameers' mamlukes, who were, to use an old expression, "gentlemen's gentlemen".

When the sultan wished to promote an efficient soldier to officer rank, he was given a commission and the rank of "an ameer of ten", corresponding, let us say, to a lieutenant. He was obliged to maintain ten mamlukes of his own, and was given a small fief of government land, on the income from which he had to live and maintain his ten mamlukes. In the event of war, the officer and his ten men served in the army, providing their own horses, weapons and supplies.

Next above an ameer of ten was an ameer of forty, who maintained forty trained mamlukes. We may compare this officer to a captain. At this stage, he was allowed to have a *tablkhana*,[10] a small military band, consisting of drums, and possibly also cymbals, oboes and trumpets. The essential component was the drums, which were used in battle.

Bertrand de la Brocquière, who travelled in Egypt in the fourteenth century, states of the Mamlukes, "Ils ont un tabolcan dont ils se servent pour se réunir dans les batailles".[11] The drums were not merely a military ritual, but played a vital part in battle. An ameer of forty was consequently often called "an ameer of drums". There was, however, an ancient ceremonial side to the custom. The Abbasid Khalifs of Baghdad had a band of drums and trumpets outside their palaces.

The next rank above ameer of drums was that of ameer of one hundred, whom we may liken to colonels. The establishment of ameers of one hundred under Baybars was twenty-four. These senior ameers were each supposed to have one hundred private mamlukes. They had larger bands than those of the ameers of forty. The sultan's

[10] One of those extraordinary words used in the Mamluke military jargon.
[11] They have a tabolcan, which they use to rally in battle.

own band was larger still, and was commanded by a band-master.[12] The drums were presumably side-drums or kettle-drums, for they were beaten on horseback.

Ameers of one hundred are often described as "commanders of one thousand". The one hundred were the ameer's personal retainers, always under arms. In war time, when the reserves were mobilised, the ameer commanded a thousand troopers.[13] All real Mamluke units were mounted. They had no infantry and disliked fighting on foot.

In peace time, the sultan and all ameers of a hundred were entitled to have their bands play outside their houses at sunset. History does not explain what happened if several ameers lived next door to one another in the same street, for in Egypt all ameers seem to have had houses in Cairo. The resulting evening cacophony must have been trying for civilian neighbours.

The new khalif, Hakim, is alleged to have made a set of large drums from ox-hides, such as the Abbasid khalifs formerly maintained in Baghdad. According to Maqrizi, the sound produced was both loud and unpleasant. As the khalif had apartments near the sultan in the Citadel, the latter was presumably obliged to endure the unpleasant noise—all the more annoying as the khalif's drums were bigger than the sultan's. Perhaps this was one of Hakim's indiscretions, which resulted in his spending much of his life under house arrest.

Reasonably enough, the right to beat drums was a military privilege. In 1418, when the Mamlukes were beginning to decline, Maqrizi tells of an Egyptian wazeer, Bedr-al-Deen Hasan, who was granted the right to beat drums at sunset. Maqrizi, though himself a Syrio-Egyptian, was shocked. "Never before this", he writes, "had the right to beat drums before his house been granted to a man of the pen."

*   *   *

In 1262, the Ameer Saif-al-Deen Kerzi returned from the court of the Emperor of the Franks, bringing a letter for the sultan. It is not clear who this monarch can have been. The German Empire was in some confusion, the nominal emperor being Conradin, an infant and the last of the Hohenstaufens. The last Latin Emperor of Constantinople, Baldwin II, had been driven out in 1261, and a Greek Emperor, Michael VIII Palaeologus, reigned in his stead.

The latter sent an ambassador to Baybars, asking him to send a

---

[12] Khalil al Dhahiri.   [13] The reserves are referred to again below.

Melkite Patriarch to Constantinople. The Christians of Syria and Egypt were Melkites, those of Greece being Orthodox. Baybars sent a patriarch, accompanied by the Ameer Akoosh as his ambassador. The Byzantine Emperor showed him a mosque which he had built for Muslim visitors. As has occurred before and since, the Christians and the Muslims of the Middle East felt nearer to one another than the former did to the Christians of the West. We must not imagine that, in 1262, Europe was the more civilised area. On the contrary, the Mamluke Empire was stronger, more wealthy and more civilised than any Western nation.

In 1262, a Mamluke column again ravaged the territory of Antioch, the Franks shutting themselves in the city and offering no resistance. The Muslims then suddenly swooped down upon Sidon and took it by assault, all the population being killed or taken prisoners. The Franks were so weak and divided that they could offer no resistance.

In 1262, also, Baraka Khan, of the Golden Horde, fought a battle with Hulagu, who was defeated. Two hundred of Baraka's men came on into Syria, reaching Cairo in November 1262, where they were cordially welcomed. Most of them accepted Islam and joined the River Mamlukes, showing how ready both Mongols and Turks were to receive one another, though apparently bitter enemies. Whatever they fought for, it certainly was not "race", which we consider all-important.

The country ruled by Baraka, from the Volga to the Caucasus, was the homeland of the Qipchaq Turks, the tribe in which Baybars was born. Its rulers were now the Mongol Golden Horde, but most of the people were still Qipchaqs.

At the end of 1262, a Mamluke column from Aleppo raided the Armenian Christian Kingdom of Cilicia, and brought back many prisoners, who were all sent to Cairo, where they were cut in half at the waist. The Mamlukes, steppe nomads like the Mongols, could be as cruel and sadistic as they.

Yet the Mamluke Empire was entirely different from that of the Mongols, who had come to Persia with the intention of exterminating the population and obliterate their towns and cities, at that time more civilised than any part of Europe. They pitched their tents and grazed their flocks over land formerly covered with towns, gardens and crops.

The Mongols refused to operate a system of taxation, preferring to live by plundering their own subjects. Themselves illiterate, they depended on the surviving Persians for any administration. Rasheed-al-Deen, a cultured Persian, author and historian, tells how he was

made wazeer by the Il-Khan. When called to an interview with the
khan, he was obliged to remain on his knees throughout the audience.
At meals, he stood behind the khan's chair. If the latter were in a
good mood, he might sometimes throw the prime minister a piece of
food. As a result, the Mongols were ill-served by their Persian
officials, the Treasury was always empty and the army was never
paid.

Turks, on the other hand, had served for four hundred years in the
Arab Empire, and had absorbed their religion and culture. The
Mamlukes, it is true, were boys born on the steppes like the Mongols,
but in Syria and Egypt they found older Turks familiar with Arab
culture. They were immediately subjected to military discipline, and,
by the time they had grown up, were absorbed into an ancient
cultural heritage.

While reserving the military profession for themselves, they appreciated the value of trade, agriculture, wealth, administration and
justice. These departments were left to the Syrians and Egyptians,
who could thereby rise to high rank and great wealth. The Mamluke
Empire consequently was extremely rich, while the Mongol rulers of
Persia were constantly bankrupt.

*   *   *

On 19th February, 1263, Baybars left Cairo for Syria. At Al Arish,
he halted for a big day of hunting. Three thousand men were sent to
form a great circle in the desert, and then to drive an immense
quantity of game slowly forwards to the sultan's shooting party.

At Gaza, he found waiting for him the mother of Malik-al-
Mughith Umar, Prince of Kerak and a great-grandson of Sultan Al-
Aadil, the brother of Saladin.[14] We do not know what passed between
the sultan and the lady, but she returned to Kerak laden with gifts,
and bearing a letter for her son. No sooner did she arrive home and
deliver the letter than the prince set out to visit Baybars, who was
camped at Beisan.

The sultan rode out in state to meet his guest and they returned to
the royal camp together. No sooner did they reach the royal tent
than Al-Mughith Umar was arrested, sent immediately to Cairo and
executed shortly afterwards. Before a considerable assembly in his
tent, Baybars produced letters from the prince to the Mongols,
allegedly stolen by the sultan's agents. It is difficult to avoid the
impression that the sultan decoyed Al-Mughith Umar into his
power by creating the impression in conversation with his mother, or

[14] Genealogical Tree 3, page 33.

in the letter, that the prince would not be molested if he visited Baybars.

*   *   *

The sultan and his army now camped on the territory of Acre, drove off the flocks of the Franks and devastated their crops and gardens. It is true that a truce was in force, but the sultan made the excuse that the Crusaders had already broken it. This indeed is quite possible, for the Franks were in internal dissolution. If one party made a truce, another party might break it.

The original leaders of the Crusades had divided the lands they conquered into feudal fiefs in return for military service, but now they no longer held enough land to pay an army. As a result, the Frankish states were now defended by orders of knights, like the Templars or the Hospitallers, who were paid with money raised in Europe. The knights were, therefore, independent of the local Frankish rulers and were bitterly jealous of one another. Thus if the Templars made a truce, the Hospitallers broke it, and vice versa.

It is, indeed, extraordinary how often a nation in decline destroys itself by the increasing bitterness of its internal feuds. How many Western politicians today jeopardise the safety of their own countries in order to embarrass their party rivals?

For three days, Baybars closed in on Acre, cutting down all fruit trees and destroying the church of Nazareth. Then he withdrew to Jerusalem. It is permissible to wonder why he did not destroy the Franks once and for all. Did he wish to appear as the Muslim hero fighting the Christians? Did he fear that if the Christians disappeared, the Muslims would fight each other?

From Jerusalem, Baybars marched to Kerak, which he besieged. Eventually Othman, the son of Al-Mughith Umar, surrendered and a Mamluke garrison was placed in the fortress. Kerak had been built by the Crusaders and had never been taken by assault. Most of its inhabitants were Christians and many still are.

On 28th May, 1263, the sultan, returning from this expedition, made a state entry into Cairo, which had been gaily decorated. The Viceroy of Egypt in the sultan's absence, the Ameer Saif-al-Deen Rasheedi, was immediately arrested. Baybars had taken the precaution of posting spies in the viceroy's entourage. These had reported that Rasheedi had written to warn Al-Mughith Umar not to visit the sultan.

Such incidents help us to understand Mamluke mentality. They were proud of their community and of the extraordinary manner in

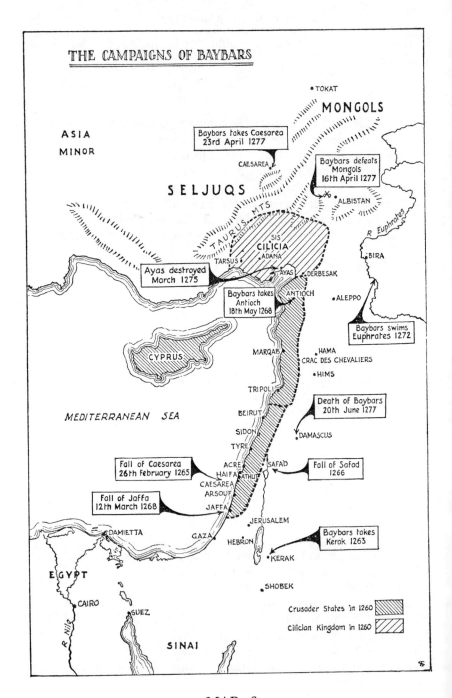

THE CAMPAIGNS OF BAYBARS

• TOKAT

MONGOLS

ASIA
MINOR

Baybars takes Caesarea
23rd April 1277

CAESAREA

Baybars defeats
Mongols
16th April 1277

SELJUQS

• ALBISTAN

R. Euphrates

TAURUS MTS

SIS
CILICIA

• BIRA

TARSUS • ADANA

Ayas destroyed
March 1275

AYAS • DERBESAK

Baybars takes
Antioch
18th May 1268

ANTIOCH

• ALEPPO

Baybars swims
Euphrates 1272

MARQAB

• HAMA
CRAC DES CHEVALIERS

CYPRUS

• HIMS

TRIPOLI

MEDITERRANEAN   SEA

BEIRUT

Death of Baybars
20th June 1277

SIDON

TYRE

• DAMASCUS

Fall of Caesarea
26th February 1265

ACRE
HAIFA ATHLIT
CAESAREA
ARSOUF

SAFAD

Fall of Safad
1266

Fall of Jaffa
12th March 1268

JAFFA

• JERUSALEM

Baybars takes
Kerak 1263

GAZA
HEBRON •

DAMIETTA

EGYPT

• KERAK

• SHOBEK

CAIRO

SUEZ

Crusader States in 1260

Cilician Kingdom in 1260

R. NILE

SINAI

MAP 16

which they, poor, ignorant tribal boys, had risen to be emperors and princes. But each had achieved his wealth and glory by trampling on his fellows. In the struggles between Mamlukes to reach the top, no holds were barred. Their incredible riches and magnificence were the reward of endless vigilance directed, not against the enemy, but against their Mamluke rivals.

* * *

In the summer of 1263, a delegation came from Baraka Khan, announcing that the Mongol Golden Horde had been converted to Islam. They were splendidly entertained and returned laden with gifts and a sixty-five-page letter from Baybars. The party, together with a Mamluke embassy, returned by sea to Constantinople and across the Black Sea to the Crimea. Thence the ambassadors rode for twenty days over the interminable steppes, dotted with tents and grazing flocks until they reached the residence of Baraka Khan, at Itil on the Volga.

They were carefully drilled in Mongol court etiquette, which necessitated their kneeling on both knees during their audience with the khan. They were received in a huge tent of white felt, lined with silk and tapestries and embroidered with pearls and precious stones. The khan, suffering from gout, was leaning on a cushion and beside him sat one of his wives, Tagtagai Khatun.

Baraka Khan had a coarse face and a scanty beard, his hair being gathered in plaits behind his head. He was dressed in a robe of Chinese silk and wore red velvet boots. The Mamluke envoys were invited to stand on the khan's right, where they were served with kumiss,[15] honey, meat and fish. The next day they were entertained to lunch in her tent by the khan's senior wife, Jijek Khatun.

Shortly afterwards, a party of thirteen hundred Mongols arrived in Cairo, and later two more groups, wishing to serve under Baybars, an event which seems to suggest that the sultan's reputation had spread far afield.

In the autumn of 1263, the sultan wrote to the Prince of Shiraz,[16] urging him to make war on Hulagu. The Arab bedouin tribe of Khafaja, west of the Euphrates, were also asked to harass the Mongols. These activities prove that fear of Hulagu was the basis of Mamluke foreign policy at this period.

[15] Fermented mare's milk.   [16] Map 26, page 302.

*   *   *

We are inclined nowadays to believe that, before the inventions of modern science, everything in the world moved with a slowness which to us would be unbearable. It is, therefore, of interest to know that Baybars was able to receive messages from any part of the empire almost as rapidly as could be done by modern telegram. The carrier pigeon system was highly organised. Pigeons flew in relays, each pigeon flying only one stage, and that normally the one on which he always worked. The use of pigeons was not new—it was already in use under the Abbasid khalifs of Baghdad five hundred years earlier —but Baybars had devoted much effort to perfecting its efficiency.

Pigeons, it was believed, were more devoted to their mates than other birds. Only male pigeons were used to carry letters. The female was kept in the homing loft, when her husband was taken away to a staging post. As soon as he had received his letter, his only idea was to rejoin his wife. No sooner had he landed in his home loft than his letter was immediately taken off him and attached to another pigeon, whose wife was one stage further down the line. Pigeons were never released at night, or in rain or when hungry, lest they land on the way to eat and be shot or caught.

When the sultan was on the march or out hunting, pigeons were carried with him to enable him to send a telegram whenever he wished. When a carrier pigeon arrived in the Citadel of Cairo, the regulations were that the sultan must be informed immediately. If he was asleep, he was woken. If he was at dinner, he rose from table. If he were playing polo, the game was stopped. Every minute might make a difference in dealing with a frontier situation, a battle or a political crisis.

Ensuring the good order of the pigeon post was one of the principal anxieties of the sultan's chancellory. A special type of thin paper was used for writing the messages. The letter was fastened under the wing, not to the leg, as it was thus protected from the weather. In the lofts, the pigeons were fed on broad beans, which were issued on a regulation scale, laying down the weight for every hundred pigeons held on the strength. State-owned pigeons were branded on the foot or beak. Registers of state carrier pigeons were carefully kept, show-ing their genealogy, the price of purchase, their medical history and all the incidents of their lives. A fast pigeon with a good pedigree might be worth as much as seven hundred gold dinars.

Ibn Abdul Dhahir wrote a book on carrier pigeons. He says that there were normally some nineteen hundred pigeons in the pigeon loft in the Citadel in Cairo, the central point for communications in the empire. In each of the pigeon stations along the main routes of the empire, and especially in all frontier posts, there might be several hundred pigeons. Mules were stationed at each pigeon relay point to transport the pigeons back to their outposts when they had flown in with a message.

Nuwairi tells a story that the Fatimid Khalif Azeez one day felt a desire to eat fresh cherries of a kind grown in Antioch. The order was sent by pigeon to Baalbek. From there, six hundred pigeons were released, each with one cherry in a silk bag tied to each leg. Three days after expressing his desire in Cairo, the Khalif Azeez was served a large bowl containing twelve hundred fresh cherries from Lebanon, specially despatched by air mail.[17]

NOTABLE DATES

Battle of Ain Jaloot	3rd September, 1260
Assassination of Qutuz	24th October, 1260
Elevation of Baybars	25th October, 1260
Death of the Khalif Mustansir at Anbar	December, 1261
Kidnapping of Al-Mughith Umar	March, 1263
Baybars' raid on the Kingdom of Jerusalem (Acre)	April, 1263
Embassy to Baraka Khan	Summer, 1263

PERSONALITIES

Mamlukes
Sultan Baybars al Bunduqdari
Sanjar al Halebi, Viceroy of Damascus, Pretender to the Sultanate

Mongols
Hulagu, the Il-Khan
Abagha, the Il-Khan, son of Hulagu
Mangu, the Great Khan, elder brother of Hulagu
Qubilai, elected Great Khan after Mangu
Baraka Khan, Prince of the Golden Horde

[17] Quatremère, *Histoire des Sultans Mamlouks.*

IV

The Muslim Hero

Hero-worship exists, has existed and will forever exist, universally among mankind.

THOMAS CARLYLE, *Sartor Resartus*

Baybars the Great—a blue-eyed Turk from Kipchak afflicted by a cataract which caused him to fetch only £20 in the slave market—had the courage and zeal of a second Saladin. A great soldier and a consummate if perfidious diplomatist, Baybars was also an able and laborious administrator. Under him the land was quietly, if not quite godly governed . . . His government was enlightened, just and strict . . . Sometimes over fifty despatches were dictated, signed and sealed late in the night, after a fatiguing march. It was no wonder that such a man was adored by the people, who thought him the ideal of a gallant and generous soldier-king.

STANLEY LANE-POOLE, *The Story of Cairo*

Great men are the guide-posts and landmarks in the state.

EDMUND BURKE

There is properly no history, only biography.

EMERSON, *Essays*

Baybars defended himself against his enemies with extraordinary valour, but frequently by astute and guileful diplomacy as well . . . He must be accredited with the fact that, in Egypt alone, the even course of cultural development was not interrupted by the Mongol invasion . . . But as it turned out, Baybars was an extremely able ruler.

CARL BROCKELMANN, *History of the Islamic Peoples*

IN 1263, died Malik-al-Ashraf Musa, the Ayoubid Prince of Hims, the great-great-grandson of Shirkuh, the uncle of Saladin.[1] As he left no son, a Mamluke ameer was appointed. This left the Prince of Hama as the only surviving Ayoubid ruler.

The Nile failed to rise this year, and famine prevailed in Cairo. Baybars ordered the government grain reserves to be released but sold only to the poor at a fixed price and in small quantities, to prevent speculators buying at the cheap price. The poor were so many, however, that the sultan ordered all senior officials and ameers to feed a number of them at their own expense. Even common soldiers were ordered each to keep one or two destitutes alive, the sultan himself feeding several thousand daily. Some undertook special tasks. The wazeer supported all the blind people in Cairo, the commander-in-chief all poor Turkmans.

Maqrizi, with an unnecessary sneer, says that "the sultan acted thus in order to win all hearts". But it was remarkable that he wished to win the hearts of poor Egyptians, who had no power to oppose him.

On 23rd July, 1264, a report arrived that the Greek Emperor, Michael VIII Palaeologos, had stopped a Mamluke delegation going to Baraka Khan of the Golden Horde. An embassy from Hulagu was in Constantinople, and might have objected to its passage. Fear of Hulagu alarmed all his neighbours.

Immigrants continued to arrive in Syria from Il-Khan territory, where the Mongols still oppressed the people. The superior justice available in the Mamluke Empire is shown by the case of the Master-of-the-Horse, an ameer of one hundred, who accidentally killed a Cairo shopkeeper. The ameer was so frightened that he gave the relatives of the deceased a large sum of money to say that the man had died a natural death.

The ameer then begged the Ameer Qalaoon, a barrack-comrade, to make it right with the sultan. Baybars was furious but could not proceed, because the next-of-kin insisted that the man died of an illness. If a Mongol killed a Persian, by contrast, no questions were asked.

On 10th August, 1264, Malik-al-Saeed Baraka, Baybars' eldest son, was proclaimed heir-apparent and rode in state through the

[1] Genealogical Tree, 3, page 33.

city. On the 14th, the qadhis, lawyers, civil officials and ameers were summoned to the palace and an Act of Succession drawn up. Thus the judges and officials, who were Egyptians, played a prominent part in these royal ceremonies.

Heredity was foreign to the Mamluke system, for all had arrived as boy slaves without family. But it was thought necessary to provide an heir, to prevent immediate civil disturbances in the event of the sudden death of the sultan. The problem of the succession was never satisfactorily solved.

On 26th August, 1264, a review of the army was held. Each ameer, in his armour, rode past in front of his unit, while the sultan stood at the saluting base. It took several hours for the whole army to march past, several people dying of heat stroke in the crowd. Military sports followed. Targets were put up, consisting of balls on the tops of poles. Competitors had to ride at full gallop, shooting arrows at the targets. The sultan himself, a splendid horseman and a well-trained soldier, galloped round the course, hitting the targets with unerring aim.

Then came popular sports lasting many days, the distribution of prizes and robes of honour ending the events. Not only was the army rewarded, but the Egyptian wazeer, qadhis, civil officials and members of leading families also received robes of honour. The foreign ambassadors were impressed by the Mamluke army, which was a regular professional service at a time when other sovereigns used only feudal levies.

On 5th September, 1264, the sultan gave a banquet in honour of Baraka, who cannot have enjoyed it much, as he was circumcised immediately after the meal. Many sons of ameers were circumcised on the same occasion.

On 26th December, 1264, news came that the Mongols were besieging Bira on the Euphrates. On 11th January, Baybars left Gaza by forced marches, but when he approached Bira the Mongols raised the siege and vanished. The sultan then announced a hunting trip in the woods of Samaria, but when he arrived there, all hands were told to cut down trees and make siege engines.

At midnight on 26th February, 1265, the army suddenly marched and surprised the Frankish town of Caesarea at dawn, capturing it by an immediate assault. The citadel resisted until 5th March, but then surrendered also. The whole place[2] was then completely demolished, stone by stone, Baybars wielding a pickaxe with his men.

On 16th March, Haifa was taken, the garrison escaping by sea.

[2] Map 16, page 84.

Athlit was then destroyed, even the trees being cut down. Several Frankish landowners rode into camp to submit and the sultan confirmed them in the ownership of their estates. Siege was then laid to Arsouf. "The sultan himself worked feverishly, sometimes digging the earth, sometimes dragging up the siege engines, sometimes carrying up stones, in order, by his personal example, to stimulate the enthusiasm of others."

On 18th April, 1265, Arsouf surrendered and was demolished. Then the whole area from Arsouf to Haifa was surveyed, and divided into fiefs, which were given to sixty ameers who had shared in the campaign. The title deeds were drawn up by the chief qadhi of Damascus and a Treasury official.

The army camp was full of qadhis and religious teachers, and neither alcohol nor any immoral acts were allowed. From the field, orders were sent to Cairo to close all liquor shops. The whole army was fired with enthusiasm, and no duty, however arduous, was ever shirked. As Baybars drank alcohol in private, his strictly religious pose was doubtless intended to fire the spirit of the troops.

On 31st May, 1265, the sultan made a triumphal entry into Cairo, amid great popular rejoicings. Baybars the Bunduqdari was now the hero and the father of his people. One night, completely disguised, he walked down the city and visited a number of houses of ill-fame, and saw an ameer behaving in an indecent manner with a woman. Next morning, watchmen, officials and owners of immoral establishments were arrested. Was Baybars a man of simple piety or was he playing the part of the Muslim hero?

The Sunni or orthodox division of Islam is divided into four religious schools, the Shafii, the Hanafi, the Malaki and the Hanbali. They differ in small points of law rather than in religion, but in the thirteenth century the law courts administered only religious law. Consequently, if a litigant came before a qadhi of a school different from his own, certain points of law might be strange to him. To ensure equal justice for all, Baybars introduced the innovation of appointing four chief qadhis in Cairo and in Damascus, one from each school, where formerly there had been only one chief qadhi.

It so happened that the first four chief qadhis appointed in Damascus all bore the name of Shems-al-Deen, Sun of the Religion. A local wit produced the following rhyme:

> In Damascus our qadhis are henceforward four,
> All are suns—but we're still in the dark as before.
> This puzzle leaves us in a most sorry plight,
> We have four brilliant suns, but we live in the night.

In April 1266, the army marched to Hebron, whence columns were sent out to ravage all Crusader territory as far north as Tripoli. Acre begged in vain for peace. The detachments then suddenly concentrated and laid siege to Safad, on 14th June, 1266. An immediate bombardment by mangonels was opened and continued for fourteen days, the engineers throwing liquid fire. An assault was then launched, but, after eighteen hours, the weary attackers began to slip away. Baybars was furious and went round rousing officers and men with blows and shouts. "What!" he yelled. "When the Muslims are in danger, you decide to take a rest! Get up!" The drums rolled, the men pulled on their equipment and the attack was resumed.

At length the Franks asked for terms and Baybars promised them freedom if they came out unarmed. They duly came out of the fortress, but next morning the sultan ordered that all be killed in cold blood, on the grounds that arms were found on some of them when searched. If this were true, the weapons thus discovered could only have been small knives hidden in their clothing. The affair has an unsavoury taste, like the arrest of Malik-al-Mughith Umar. The garrison had been Templars.

When all was over, Baybars paraded the troops and apologised for his harshness. "From now onwards we shall be friends," he added. Thus ended the campaign of 1266.

In 1267, the sultan invaded the Armenian Christian Kingdom of Cilicia, carrying fire and sword as far west as Tarsus,[3] and annexing the southern frontier area, including the fortress of Derbesak.

In Damascus, he ordered the construction of the Piebald Palace, in a garden on the banks of the river outside the city. Its name originated from the fact that it was built of alternate black and white stones. In the interior, "the floors and walls were covered with many-coloured marbles and ornamented with gold, azure and mosaic". Thus did Baybars, born in a poor tent on the steppes, imitate the glories of the Umaiyids and the Abbasids. The winter was spent, once again, suppressing the use of wine and hashish, and the activities of the immoral houses of Cairo.

In March 1268, Jaffa was taken by assault and razed to the ground, though the marble found in houses and churches was torn out and sent to Cairo. The army then moved slowly northwards to Hims, where the sultan appeared solely preoccupied with the prohibition of the sale of alcohol.

Then suddenly, by forced marches, he appeared outside Antioch, before the Franks knew that he had left Hims. An immediate assault was launched and, after four days' fierce fighting, the Muslims scaled

[3] Map 16, page 84.

the walls and entered the city. Everyone in Antioch was killed, except the garrison of the citadel who were taken prisoners.

The Counts of Tripoli had become extinct in 1187, with the death of Raymond III, who bequeathed the County to Bohemond IV, Prince of Antioch. In 1268, his grandson, Bohemond VI of Antioch and Tripoli, was living in the latter town. The first he knew of the fall of Antioch was a mocking letter from Baybars, jeering at him for his defeat. Baybars was a lion among men, but he was not a gentleman. How different were his sarcastic insults from the courtesy of Saladin who, after a hot day of battle outside Jaffa, sent cold drinks and fresh fruit to Richard Cœur-de-Lion.

Antioch had been an extremely rich city, principally engaged in the export of oriental goods to Europe. The loot consisted of gold, jewels, textiles, embroideries and articles of luxury. Such was the discipline of the Mamluke army that all plunder was handed in and was distributed to officers and men by the sultan himself. The women and children were likewise equally divided. So many were the female captives that a young girl could be bought for a few pence. From Antioch, Baybars wrote to Haithum, the Armenian King of Cilicia, demanding the surrender of further frontier fortresses.

A truce of ten years was concluded with the Franks of Acre, who retained Haifa and three villages. At Sidon, a narrow coastal plain was left to the Franks, but the mountains overlooking the town were handed over to the Muslims. Nuwairi[4] tells us that Baybars asked a war contribution of a million dinars from Damascus, which the city refused to pay. Eventually the Damascenes paid four hundred thousand in cash, and two hundred thousand each year for three years. The sultan pointed out that the Mamlukes alone had saved the city from the Mongols.

An ambassador from Abagha,[5] the son of Hulagu, came to Baybars in Damascus, with a letter of which the following is a summary. "King Abagha has conquered the whole world. Those who resisted him met a violent death. If you mount to the skies, you cannot escape us. Your best course is to make peace with us." Maqrizi says that the ambassador had orders to say to Baybars in public, "Thou who art a slave who wast sold in Sivas, how darest thou brave the sovereign of the whole world?" Unfortunately Maqrizi does not report the sultan's reply.

*　　*　　*

[4] Nuwairi, *Nihaya al Arab.*
[5] The second syllable is short. The pronunciation is nearer Abgha.

Baybars took great trouble to conceal his intended movements. One day in 1268, when in camp outside Jaffa, he feigned illness in his tent. To senior officers who visited him, he seemed to be in great pain. After dark, he slipped out and rode with four men to Cairo, covering three hundred and sixty miles in three days. Each man rode one horse and led another. He remained three days unrecognised in the city.

On the fifth day, he appeared unescorted on the cavalry parade ground, to see if the troops were carrying out their training. On the eighth day after his disappearance from Jaffa, he left Cairo, riding back post haste.

During his absence, an ameer who was in the secret described the sultan's symptoms to the doctors, who mixed the medicines which the ameer took back into the tent. Thirteen days after his departure, Baybars slipped back into his tent, disguised as a courier carrying a mailbag. Next morning, he received the ameers, saying that he had been very ill, but was now better. During his absence the staff had worked normally and all the correspondence was up to date.

In the same year, the sultan went on pilgrimage, leaving ostensibly to hunt in Kerak. The chamberlain, who knew the secret, sent him a letter to ask if he could go with him, but Baybars ordered that his tongue be cut out. It is easy to see why no one gossiped about the sultan's plans. In Mecca he mixed in the crowds and prayed in the mosque without an escort.

After the pilgrimage, he rode to Kerak dressed as an Arab and arrived unannounced. After one night's sleep, he left for Damascus, no one in Cairo knowing where he was. The Viceroy of Damascus summoned his officers to warn them that he had heard a rumour that the sultan might be coming. At that moment an officer rushed in to say that Baybars had been seen, alone and on foot, in the city square. After taking some food in the viceroy's house, he vanished again. When the ameers and the notables arrived in their best clothes to pay their respects, the sultan had disappeared.

News of his approach preceded him to Aleppo, and a ceremonial parade was drawn up to receive him, but when a single horseman rode up in casual clothes, no one on parade recognised him. After inspecting the defences, he left again and rode back through Damascus and Jerusalem to Egypt.

When in residence in Cairo, he continued his rigorous policy of enforcing public morals, and closing all wine shops. All prostitutes were imprisoned "until husbands could be found for them".

His other occupation in Cairo was his favourite exercise, shooting with a bow on horseback. At midday, he would daily ride down to the

training field, and would remain until evening on horseback, prac-
tising lance, sword and mace and shooting his arrows at full gallop,
thereby encouraging all ranks of the army to concentrate on their
weapon-training.

The sultan continued his policy of piecemeal raids on the Frankish
States, possibly because he was anxious not to provoke another
crusade from the West. In 1270, St. Louis IX, King of France, was
actually preparing a new crusade, but, when it came, he attacked
Tunis, dying himself beneath the walls of the town. The same year,
the Muslims took the famous *Crac des Chevaliers* (Husn al Akrad)
which was held by the Hospitallers.[6]

In the spring of 1271, Baybars appeared to be about to attack
Tripoli, when he heard that Prince Edward of Cornwall, later King
Edward I of England, had landed at Acre. Baybars immediately
made a ten-year truce with Tripoli. Prince Edward had only three
hundred knights, but he wrote to Abagha, who sent ten thousand
Mongols. They reached Aleppo in October 1271. The Jagatai
Mongols, however, attacked Abagha in East Persia, and he was
obliged to withdraw his men from Aleppo.

The affair showed the sultan that Crusades from the West, co-
operating with the Mongols, were still possible. Perhaps as a result,
the sultan also signed a ten-year truce with Hugh III of Cyprus,
titular King of Jerusalem, on 22nd May, 1272, Prince Edward
being present. On 16th June, 1272, an attempt was made to assassinate Prince Edward, possibly at the instigation of Baybars. Princess
Eleanor, his wife, sucked the poison from the dagger-wound into
her own mouth.

The government of Syria was in the hands of viceroys, each of
whom had considerable delegated powers and corresponded direct
with the sultan. The largest province was that of Damascus, the
viceroy of which had official precedence over the others, but no
authority over them. Next in importance was the Viceroy of Aleppo,
while, at various times, Hims, Hama, Gaza and, later, Safad and
Tripoli, were also governed separately by viceroys, directly under
Cairo.

The division of geographical Syria into numerous viceroyalties
was to prevent a general rebellion. Each viceroy had a court, model-
led on that of the sultan, with a chief secretary, chamberlains, a
master of the horse and other court officials. As a further precaution,
the officers commanding the citadels of Damascus and Aleppo were
also directly under the sultan, and independent of the viceroys.
A viceroy of Egypt was also appointed when the sultan was absent.

[6] Map 16, page 84.

The frequent absences of Baybars, when no one knew where he was, prove his absolute supremacy. How many heads of state today in Asia or Africa could vanish from the scene without fear of a coup d'état? The sultan's disappearances bore witness to the efficiency of the whole machine, for in his absence everything continued as usual.

* * *

In the autumn of 1272, a Tatar force advanced to the Euphrates, but Baybars himself swam the Euphrates at the head of the cavalry and chased it away. In the same year, the governor of Aswan led an expedition into Nubia, while another force strengthened the authority of the government as far west as Barka (Cyrenaica), Baybars being at the time in Syria.[7] The sultan's energy had galvanised the whole empire. In Cairo, this year, the sultan swam the Nile both ways wearing his breastplate.

The Ismailis, a sect of Shiite Muslims, had for many years held nine great castles in the mountains of Syria between Marqab and Hama. Baybars set himself slowly to undermine their strength, taking over their castles one by one, until by 1273, they had lost their power. These were the famous *hashashin*, who were supposed to smoke hashish, or hemp, before committing a murder, a practice which originated the English word "assassin".

In March 1275, Baybars again invaded Armenian Cilicia, occupying the capital, Sis, and destroying the port of Ayas. The Mamlukes had an economic object in destroying Ayas, Antioch, Tripoli and Acre, ports which exported oriental goods to Europe. Their objective was to channel all eastern commerce up the Red Sea and across Egypt for re-export from Alexandria.

Baybars, returning from Cilicia, camped at Antioch, where the immense plunder was collected. The sultan distributed it all, every soldier receiving something, while Baybars kept nothing for himself. Cilicia seemed to be utterly ruined.

Trouble was brewing meanwhile in the Seljuq territory in Asia Minor, now reduced to a tributary province of the Il-Khan. Qilij Arslan IV, the Seljuq ruler, was denounced to the Mongols by his own wazeer, who secured his execution. The wazeer, Mueen-al-Deen Sulaiman, commonly called Perwana, ambitious to wield sole power, raised to the throne a three-year-old child, Kai Khosrou III, son of the late ruler. Perwana is alleged to have invited Baybars to conquer Asia Minor and, on 9th July, 1276, the sultan reached

[7] Map 18, page 129.

Damascus. Here he received a number of Seljuq officers come to complain against Perwana and requesting Baybars to occupy their country. However, after visiting Aleppo, he returned to winter in Cairo, accompanied by the Seljuq ameers.

During the winter, banquets were held in Cairo, and mock battles and military exercises. Those successful in the military games received prizes, robes of honour or horses from the sultan's stable. "The sultan himself, in full armour, gave a brilliant display with the lance, exciting universal admiration and winning all hearts."

Maqrizi was a Syrian, domiciled in Egypt. He wrote long after the death of Baybars, when flattery was unnecessary, yet his account is full of praise and affection for the great sultan. After the games, robes of honour were presented to all Mamluke ameers, officials and judges, the latter two categories being, of course, Egyptians. A great banquet was then held, for which thousands of sheep were slaughtered. The same night, the heir-apparent, Malik-al-Saeed Baraka, consummated his marriage to the daughter of the Ameer Qalaoon.

* * *

In February 1277, the sultan left Cairo, accompanied by the Seljuq ameers, to invade Asia Minor. On 16th April, 1277, Baybars defeated a mixed Seljuq-Mongol army at Albistan.[8] The country was mountainous and the Mongols fought on foot.

The Seljuq wazeer, Perwana, took the child ruler and fled to Tokat, four days' march north of Caesarea. The Mamluke army found the crossing of the Taurus extremely difficult. The mountains were formed of high peaks and sheer walls of rock.[9] Heavy rain fell continuously and every stream was a torrent. The people were mostly Turks and Muslims and welcomed the Mamlukes, for they had no love for their Mongol masters.

All the people of Caesarea, the Seljuq capital, including even the women and children, came out to meet the Muslim hero. On 23rd April, 1277, Sultan Baybars made his state entry into Caesarea, seated himself on the Seljuq throne and gave audience to the notables and dignitaries. A magnificent banquet was served, and largesse was scattered in the streets.

But reports now arrived that the Il-Khan Abagha was advancing with the whole Mongol army. Baybars could not risk being cut off in these tangled mountains, and withdrew to Albistan. Seeing the battlefield still strewn with corpses, he ordered the burial of the

---

[8] Map 16, page 84.   [9] Nuwairi, *Nihaya al Arab*.

Mamluke dead excepting only a few, but left the Mongol dead exposed. Then he retreated across the mountains to Antioch. Here he was visited by the Qaraman Ameer, the head of an ambitious Turkish family of whom we shall hear more. Arab and Turkman chiefs and local notables flocked to do homage to the heroic sultan.

When Abagha reached Albistan, he noted the great numbers of dead Mongols and the few Mamluke bodies on the battlefield. In his rage, he ordered his army to plunder Caesarea and the surrounding country, massacring all Muslims, of whom Maqrizi claims that two hundred thousand persons were killed, in the ensuing seventeen days.

Apart from the military glory, the campaign was useless. Baybars could not have left a force in Asia Minor strong enough to hold it against the whole Mongol army. The only result was the ruin of Caesarea and the end of the last shadow of Seljuq independence. On 9th June, 1277, the sultan left Antioch for Damascus.

On 18th June, a reception was held in Damascus at which *kumiss*, the fermented mares' milk of the steppes, was served to guests, although Baybars had frequently forbidden the consumption of alcohol by the public. The sultan was at the height of his glory and perhaps drank too much. Returning to the Piebald Palace, he felt ill and vomited next morning. On the third day, he suffered intense abdominal pain and in the evening of 20th June, 1277, he breathed his last.

Several other accounts of his death exist.[10] An astrologer is alleged to have warned the sultan that, in 1277, a king would die of poison in Damascus. A certain minor Ayoubid prince, Malik-al-Qahir[11] Abdul Malik, had accompanied the sultan on the campaign and had distinguished himself by outstanding bravery. Baybars, accustomed to monopolise public applause, was moved to jealousy by the universal praise bestowed on Malik-al-Qahir.

The idea occurred to him to fulfil the astrologer's prophecy and at the same time rid himself of the man of whom he was jealous, by poisoning Malik-al-Qahir. He accordingly took a phial of poison to the reception. Pouring two cups of kumiss, he emptied the phial into one of them and called the prince to join him for a drink. Accidentally, he gave his guest the wrong cup and drank the poisoned one himself. The truth, however, cannot now be established.

*   *   *

---

[10] See for example, Qutb-al-Deen Joumini, in Quatremère, *Histoire des Sultans Mamlouks.*
[11] Conquering King.

Baybars was only fifty years old when he died. He was tall, with a sallow complexion but with blue eyes, of which one had a white speck. He had a powerful voice and was recklessly brave in battle. Full of initiative, quick to take decisions, he was constantly driven by a restless energy, and was intensely feared by the Mamluke ameers, themselves a rough crew.

But he was not only a soldier. He was devoted to public works, built mosques and colleges, enlarged irrigation canals and dug new ones, constructed roads and bridges, fortified Alexandria and revived the fleet, building forty war-galleys. His administration was wise and just, but taxation was heavy. His army is alleged to have been four times as large as that of the Ayoubid sultans. An Egyptian, Taj-al-Deen ibn Henna, was his wazeer and devised new ways to raise money, including doubling the poll-tax on Jews and Christians. It is only fair to add that his army struck such fear into the Mongols that there were no invasions of Syria during his reign.

Outwardly religious, he left many charitable endowments. He forbade the sale of alcohol and hashish, and closed all taverns and brothels. His pastimes were horsemanship, archery, polo and hunting, while his nights were devoted to office work, not to women. If a courier arrived with letters at daybreak, he received the replies three hours later without fail.[12]

According to Maqrizi, who is weak on military matters, Baybars maintained twelve thousand regular Mamlukes, four thousand each in Cairo, Damascus and Aleppo. His policy and his strategy were based on fear of the Mongols, especially as long as Hulagu was alive. The statement that he had twelve thousand Royal Mamlukes is probably correct, but does not include the reserves or local contingents, which are discussed later.

Baybars may at times seem to us cruel and arbitrary, but we must not make the mistake of comparing Mamluke rule to conditions in our countries today. Such things and worse were common practice in Western Europe in the thirteenth century. Torture was used in England four hundred years after Baybars, and was practised in Europe during the Second World War.

It cannot be denied that he was sometimes treacherous, as in his arrest of Malik-al-Mughith Umar and the massacre of the garrison of Safad. He sent a compromising letter to an Armenian ecclesiastic and arranged for it to be intercepted by the Mongol governor.[13]

E. W. Lane tells us that, in the 1820s, the romance of Baybars was still recited by poets in the streets of Cairo to the Egyptian public,

[12] Stanley Lane-Poole, *A History of Egypt in the Middle Ages*.
[13] Ibid.

although he was a Mamluke, one of their alleged oppressors. Like Alexander the Great and Haroon al Rasheed, Baybars the Bunduq-dari became a legendary hero.[14]

The sultan's body was carried back to Cairo in a litter, the public being informed that he was ill. His death was only announced when the army was back in the Citadel. "To sum up," concludes Maqrizi, "Baybars was one of the best sovereigns who ever reigned over the Muslims." We are, indeed, forced to admit that he was a giant among men.

AL-MALIK-AL-SAEED BARAKA IBN BAYBARS

As soon as the body of Baybars reached the Citadel on 30th July, 1277, the ameers and officials took the oath to Baraka. In the course of the next few weeks, however, the boy-sultan surrounded himself with young mamlukes, and government business fell into confusion. The Ameer Ak Sonkor al Farekani, a man of prudence and experience, was made regent. But Baraka's young companions persuaded him to order the regent's arrest and execution.

The council of ameers then appointed the Ameer Sonkor al Mudhaffari as regent. He had been a mamluke of Malik-al-Mudhaffar[15] Qutuz, and consequently was dismissed by Baraka, who continued to imprison senior officers.

Eventually all the ameers and their mamlukes marched up to the palace and crowded into the Hall of Audience. Their spokesman addressed the boy-sultan as follows: "You have alienated the loyalty of all hearts. You have treated the most prominent ameers as enemies. You must either abandon this attitude, or there will be a clash between us." Baraka was alarmed, swore that he was not hostile to the ameers and a reconciliation was patched up.

In March 1278, Sultan Baraka left Cairo and arrived in Damascus on 20th April. Yielding to the pressure of his young friends, the two most influential ameers, Qalaoon al Elfi and Bedr-al-Deen Baisari, were sent with a column to raid Cilicia. Both were aware that they were being exiled from court on the advice of the sultan's young friends, who were spending large sums of money leading lives of pleasure.

Some months later, the sultan sent a young intimate of his to the

[14] E. W. Lane, *Manners and Customs of the Modern Egyptians.*
[15] The Arabic *dh* is a single letter called *dhad*. Arabs are called *"al natiqun bil dhad"*—speakers with *dhad*—because non-Arabs cannot pronounce it. Others, including Egyptians, Turks and Persians change it into *z*. I have used *dh*, but many transliterations use *z*, e.g. Al-Muzaffar.

Viceroy of Damascus, with an order to pay him a thousand dinars, but the viceroy demurred. The indignant courtiers urged the sultan to dismiss the viceroy.

In May 1279, the army was returning from its northern campaign. The sultan's boon companions persuaded him to order the arrest of the army commanders, Qalaoon and Baisari, but the viceroy sent to warn them. As a result, they camped with the army outside the city, and sent for the young courtiers who had insulted the viceroy. The sultan refused to allow them to go, and Qalaoon and Baisari announced that they were in revolt. Sultan Baraka was afraid and his mother went out to the camp and implored the ameers to obey her son, but met with a firm refusal.

The rebel ameers at the head of the army then marched for Cairo, whereupon the sultan collected what troops he could and pursued his own army. On reaching Bilbeis, the sultan's troops deserted him and returned to Damascus, but he was able to slip into the Citadel unperceived. But soon, finding themselves blockaded in the Citadel, his own mamlukes deserted him. Standing on one of the towers of the Citadel, the sultan himself called out to ask the ameers their terms. The ameers replied that he must abdicate and live in Kerak.

Baraka had no alternative but to comply. Legal documents were drawn up and oaths exchanged. On 18th August, 1279, Malik-al-Saeed Baraka left Cairo under escort for Kerak. He had reigned for two years and nineteen days, which he had spent in frivolity. The revolt had been bloodless, for no one was willing to fight for such a sultan.

NOTABLE DATES

Capture of Caesarea (in Palestine)	5th March, 1265
Capture of Arsouf	18th April, 1265
Siege and capture of Safad	June, 1266
Invasion of Cilicia	1267
Capture of Antioch	18th May, 1268
Prince Edward of Cornwall lands at Acre	12th May, 1271
Ten-year truce signed with Hugh III, King of Jerusalem	22nd May, 1272
Invasion of Cilicia. Ayas destroyed	March, 1275
Battle of Albistan	16th April, 1277
Death of Baybars	20th June, 1277
Elevation of Malik-al-Saeed Baraka ibn Baybars	30th July, 1277
Abdication of Sultan Baraka	18th August, 1279

PERSONALITIES

Mamlukes
Malik-al-Dhahir Baybars, the Bunduqdari
His son, Malik-al-Saeed Baraka
The Ameer Qalaoon

Mongols
Hulagu Khan
His son, Abagha Khan
Baraka Khan, Chief of the Golden Horde

Michael VIII Palaeologus, Byzantine Emperor

V

The Great Day of Hims

No sooner had Qalawun established himself in power than the Mongol Il-Khans of Persia began to threaten his Syrian domain. The scheme did not materialise. Abaqa's army . . . was badly defeated in 1280 at Hims. Qalawun won distinction in other fields. His hospital . . . is the most famous of his buildings. It comprised several wards for segregating various diseases . . . and was provided with laboratories, a dispensary, baths, kitchens and store rooms. The chief of its medical staff gave instruction in a properly equipped lecture-room.

PHILIP HITTI, *History of the Arabs*

Abaqa took advantage of a revolution in Egypt to invade Syria and a great battle was fought near Hims . . . The Egyptians remained masters of the field; in the pursuit which ensued the Mongol losses were heavy.

P. M. SYKES, *A History of Persia*

These were honoured in their generations and were the glory of the times.

Ecclesiasticus XLIV, 7

To be prepared for war is one of the most effectual means of preserving peace.

GEORGE WASHINGTON, Speech to both Houses of Congress, 8th January, 1790

V

THE Mamlukes were a ruthless crew, who were inured to lives full of danger and hardship. The sultan at their head was one of the world's greatest monarchs, feared by the Mongol khans, and solicited by the German Emperor. The King of France with his disorderly feudal levies was no match for him. The Mamlukes were proud of their status. Their system of the survival of the bravest, the most cunning and the most ruthless, ensured that their sultan was always the most capable ruler of his time or, if he was not, his reign was brief.

What could a youth brought up in a palace do in such company? The ameers only gave their loyalty to a man whom they knew to be stronger, tougher and more ruthless than themselves, a man who had climbed to the top over their backs—a man, in a word, of whom they were afraid.

*   *   *

No sooner had Baraka left for Kerak, than the ameers offered the sultanate to the leader of the revolt, the Ameer Qalaoon. Claiming that he had not led the rebellion through personal ambition, he refused the honour, suggesting that another of Baybars' sons be chosen. Qalaoon was a shrewd politician. Malik-al-Dhahir Baybars, though dead, still dominated the scene. Nearly all the senior ameers and governors of provinces were Dhahiris, former mamlukes of Baybars, who might have affirmed their loyalty to his family— Qalaoon's modest refusal gained universal praise.

Salámish, the second son of Baybars, a child seven years old, was proclaimed sultan with the throne-name of Malik-al-Aadil, the Just King.

AL-MALIK-AL-AADIL SALAMISH

Qalaoon was appointed atabek or commander-in-chief. In view of the sultan's youth, Qalaoon was also made controller of the civil government. The Ameer Sonkor al Ashqar was made Viceroy of Damascus. Meanwhile, Qalaoon began quietly to remove or arrest those ameers who might oppose him and also to reduce the Dhahiris' monopoly of power. He brought back many Salihis, his own barrack-comrades, when, as young men, they had been mamlukes of the last Ayoubid Sultan, Malik-al-Salih Ayoub.

At length, on 27th November, 1279, Qalaoon called a council of ameers of one hundred. "You are all aware," he said, "that a man of mature age and experience is essential to the proper government of this empire." The ameers saw the point and voted unanimously to depose Salamish, and the boy was sent to join his brother in Kerak. He had reigned for a hundred days which he had spent in the nursery.

AL-MALIK-AL-MANSOOR QALAOON AL-ELFI AL-SALIHI AL-ALAI

Qalaoon, like Baybars, was a Qipchaq Turk. When brought to Egypt as a child, he was bought by the Ameer Ala-al-Deen Ak Sonkor, for the high price of a thousand gold dinars—hence his nickname of Al Elfi, "the thousander". Al Alai was a reference to the name of his purchaser, who had been a mamluke of Sultan Al Aadil, the brother of Saladin. On the death of Ala-al-Deen, he was bought by Al-Salih Ayoub, who was then raising the Bahris, or River Mamlukes.

He, like Baybars, fled from Egypt when Aibek suppressed the Bahris, but returned and served under Qutuz, when Hulagu invaded Syria. He was proclaimed sultan on 4th December, 1279, under the throne-name of Malik-al-Mansoor, the Victorious King. He ordered that the words Al Salihi be written under his name whenever he signed a document, a token of his devotion to his Ayoubid master, who had died thirty years before.

His first action was to abolish the unjust wheel tax, and also a special tax on Christians, instituted eighteen years previously. It is noticeable, in passing, that Egypt had a regular system of taxes. In most of Europe and in the Mongol Empire, no specific taxes existed. Money was squeezed from the public when possible. However, the worst of the Mamluke system was that each tax was sold to a tax-farmer, who paid a fixed sum to the government and extracted what he could from the public.

The news of Qalaoon's elevation reached Damascus in two days and seven hours from Cairo, a distance of some five hundred miles, showing the high efficiency of the postal system. Qalaoon addressed a personal letter to Sonkor al Ashqar, the Viceroy of Damascus, in which he modestly reported his elevation in the words, "the inhabitants of this kingdom have unanimously submitted to the mamluke". Malik-al-Mansoor Muhammad, the last ruling Ayoubid and Prince

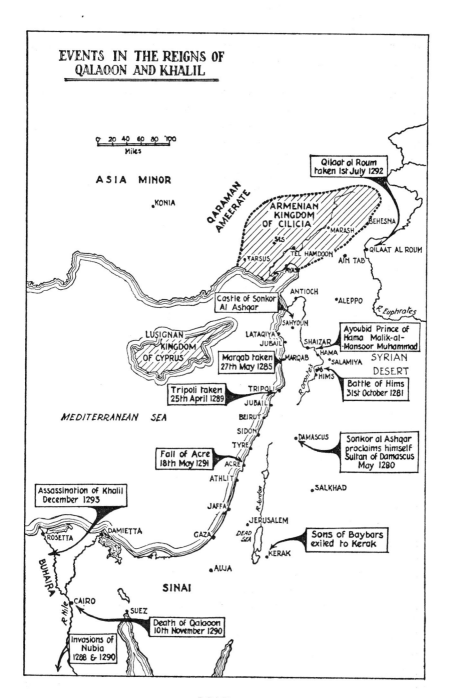

EVENTS IN THE REIGNS OF
QALAOON AND KHALIL

Qilaat al Roum
taken 1st July 1292

ASIA MINOR

KONIA

QARAMAN AMEERATE

ARMENIAN KINGDOM OF CILICIA

BEHESNA

MARASH

Sis

TARSUS

TEL HAMDOON

AYAS

QILAAT AL ROUM

AIN TAB

ANTIOCH

ALEPPO

R. Euphrates

Castle of Sonkor Al Ashqar

SAHYOUN

LATAQIYA
JUBAIL

SHAIZAR

Ayoubid Prince of
Hama Malik-al-
Mansoor Muhammad

LUSIGNAN KINGDOM OF CYPRUS

Marqab taken
27th May 1285

MARQAB

HAMA
SALAMIYA
HIMS

SYRIAN DESERT

Tripoli taken
25th April 1289

TRIPOLI
JUBAIL

Battle of Hims
31st October 1281

MEDITERRANEAN SEA

BEIRUT
SIDON
TYRE

DAMASCUS

Sonkor al Ashqar
proclaims himself
Sultan of Damascus
May 1280

Fall of Acre
18th May 1291

ACRE
ATHLIT

Assassination of Khalil
December 1293

JAFFA

SALKHAD

ROSETTA

DAMIETTA

GAZA

JERUSALEM

DEAD SEA

Sons of Baybars
exiled to Kerak

BUHAIRA

AUJA

KERAK

R. Jordan

SINAI

CAIRO

R. Nile

SUEZ

Death of Qalaoon
10th November 1290

Invasions of
Nubia
1288 & 1290

MAP 17

of Hama, arrived in Cairo to affirm his loyalty. On 24th March, 1280, Baraka, the son of Baybars, was killed, allegedly playing polo, but scandal whispered that he had been poisoned.

Sonkor al Ashqar, the Viceroy of Damascus, however, collected the ameers in that city, told them that Qalaoon had been murdered, made them swear allegiance to himself, and then rode in state through the city with the symbols of royalty. Sonkor had many friends in Cairo, and even the public seemed to be against Qalaoon, calling rude remarks to his officers in the streets.

On 3rd May, 1280, Sonkor, who had taken the name of Malik-al-Kamil, the Perfect King, rode in state to the Damascus polo-ground, preceded by the ameers wearing robes of honour. Qalaoon wrote to Sonkor, pointing out the unscrupulous nature of his action, while many ameers also wrote from Egypt, begging him not to create sedition. Sonkor received the sultan's messenger politely, but continued in his revolt. A force sent by him to seize Gaza was defeated. He then redoubled his efforts, summoning troops from Hama and Aleppo, and calling in Isa ibn Mahanna, the chief of the bedouin tribes.

Qalaoon had no alternative but to send an army and a battle was fought a few miles south of Damascus, on 21st June, 1280. Sonkor fought with desperate courage, but most of his troops deserted him, and he was obliged to escape at a gallop. He reached the castle of Rahba on the Euphrates, whence he wrote to the Il-Khan Abagha, the son of Hulagu, urging him to invade Syria. Then turning back to the west, he established himself in the castle of Sahyoun in the Lebanon, and in the fortified town of Shaizar on the Al Aasi River, better known in the West as the Orontes.

We have already noted that the Mamlukes treated the Egyptians and the Syrians reasonably well, in comparison with other contemporary rulers. It was their desperate rivalries among themselves which frequently caused civil wars or foreign invasion, as was to be the case with Sonkor al Ashqar. The rumoured coming of the Mongols spread panic in Syria, the people of Aleppo abandoning their homes and fleeing to Damascus. Their arrival spread terror there also, many Damascenes setting out post-haste for Egypt.

Three months after the defeat of Sonkor al Ashqar outside Damascus, reports reached Cairo that the Tatars were advancing. Their army was commanded by Mangu Timur, a younger son of Hulagu, and brother of the reigning Il-Khan Abagha. The Mamlukes concentrated beneath the walls of Hama, and wrote to Sonkor to join them against the common enemy. He sent some troops, but did not come in person. It will be remembered that it was he who had invited the Il-Khan to come.

On 20th October, 1280, the Tatars reached Ain Tab, seventy-five miles north of Aleppo. Thence they occupied Aleppo itself, the garrison and the population having alike taken to flight. They remained two days in Aleppo, massacring all they could find, and burning the city to the ground. Then, loaded with every form of loot, they re-crossed the Euphrates and withdrew.

*   *   *

On 25th October, 1280, Qalaoon's son, Ali, was recognised as his successor. Immediately afterwards, the sultan, at the head of the army, left to fight the Mongols. It will be remembered that Qalaoon himself had secured the deposition of Salamish on the grounds that a child sultan was absurd. Nevertheless, an acknowledged heir was useful during a sultan's life, if he had to be absent from Cairo. The presence of a legitimate heir might prove an obstacle to a coup d'état by an ambitious ameer.

When Qalaoon reached Gaza, a report was received that the Mongols had retired after destroying Aleppo. After camping six weeks at Gaza, the army returned to Cairo. Shortly afterwards, Isa ibn Mahanna, chief of the Al Fadhl tribe and paramount shaikh of the nomads of the Syrian desert, arrived in Cairo. He had supported Sonkor al Ashqar and came to seek pardon. The sultan rode out to meet him, received him with honour and loaded him with gifts.

The eastern bedouins caused anxiety to the Mamluke sultans by wandering in the no-man's-land between the Mamluke and Mongol Empires, maintaining a considerable degree of independence, for to them Mongols and Mamlukes were alike foreigners. If either side treated them harshly, they could transfer their allegiance to the other. Qalaoon, threatened by more Tatar invasions, was anxious to secure the loyalty of the bedouins.

In April 1281, the sultan again left with the army for Syria. In Palestine, he signed a truce with the Knights of St. John (the Hospitallers). It was to last for ten years, ten months, ten days and ten hours. Later he signed a similar truce with Bohemond VII, who, since his loss of Antioch, was Count of Tripoli only. Facing a major Mongol attack, the sultan wished to prevent the Franks from joining the invaders.

A few days afterwards, Qalaoon received a report that a number of Baybars' mamlukes were to murder him the next day, when the army was fording the Jordan. A similar warning was sent to him by the Franks of Acre, anxious to win his goodwill.

Collecting all the ameers, he openly accused their leader, Kounduk al Dhahiri, of treasonable correspondence with the Franks, and of plotting to murder him. Taken unawares, the conspirators were speechless. Kounduk was beheaded and thirty-three ameers were arrested. Two ameers and some three hundred mamlukes escaped on horseback and joined Sonkor al Ashqar at Sahyoun. All the conspirators were Dhahiris, former mamlukes of Malik-al-Dhahir Baybars, still loyal to their patron and his sons.

On 11th May, 1281, the sultan made a state entry into Damascus. The streets were decorated and the day was a public holiday. Qalaoon had with him an army of fifty or sixty thousand men. The sultan also signed a decree giving Sonkor al Ashqar a large principality, extending from Lataqiya to Antioch, presumably to prevent him from joining the Mongol invaders.

When the sultan was still in Damascus, intelligence reports were received that Mangu Timur, the brother of Il-Khan Abagha, was preparing to invade Syria with eighty thousand men. He was expected to arrive about October 1281. Qalaoon set to work to call up all the contingents who were under an obligation to report in time of war.

The Murra Arabs came from the desert west of the Euphrates, with four hundred well-mounted horsemen, wearing helmets and breastplates and carrying swords and lances. They were followed by their slaves on camels, leading spare horses. With them was a young woman, seated in a camel litter, whose duty it was to sing and recite poetry in battle, to encourage the warriors. Such girls, known as *amriya*, often accompanied the bedouin men to war. Behind the fighting men came the whole tribe, with the women, the baggage camels and the flocks.

Other contingents came in from Malik-al-Masood Khidhr, a younger son of Baybars, who lived in Kerak, from the Ayoubid Prince of Hama, from Isa ibn Mahanna and the nomads of the Syrian desert, and from the Turkman tribes north of Aleppo. Terror and rumour reigned all over Syria.

On 27th October, 1281, Sultan Qalaoon camped outside Hims with his whole army. Even Sonkor al Ashqar came to join the Muslims. The whole population of Damascus collected in the mosques to implore God's protection from the Tatars. The copy of the Qoran, alleged to have belonged to the third khalif, Othman, was carried in procession, many people weeping and crying to God for help.

Meanwhile Mangu Timur had left Hama and was moving on Hims. His army consisted of fifty thousand Mongols and thirty thousand Georgians and Armenian Cilicians, both of whom were

Mongol tributaries. When the Tatars left Hama, they obliged the governor to release a pigeon with the following message: "The enemy numbers eighty thousand. Tell the sultan to strengthen the left wing of the Mamluke army." This message was presumably a ruse, for the main Mongol attack was directed against the right wing.

On 31st October, 1281, Qalaoon rose early and marshalled his army. On his right, he placed Malik-al-Mansoor Muhammad, Ayoubid Prince of Hama, and a number of Mamluke ameers. In front of the right wing were the Arabs, Isa ibn Mahanna and the Murra tribe. On the left was Sonkor al Ashqar and, in front of him, the Turkmans. In the centre was the sultan, with four thousand Royal Mamlukes, the élite of the army, and various other units. Qalaoon, with a personal escort of two hundred men, took post on a small hill from which he could overlook the battlefield.

Soon the Mongol units began to appear. Maqrizi says that they were twice as numerous as the Mamlukes, but this does not agree with most of the other numbers recorded. The Mongols fell with great fury on the Mamluke right wing, which fought back fiercely, repulsing the charge and driving the Tatar left flank back on their centre.

But meanwhile the Mongol right had completely routed the Mamluke left, where Sonkor al Ashqar was posted. The fugitives reached Hims with the enemy hot on their heels. The gates were hastily closed, but the Tatars made havoc outside the walls, massacring man, woman and child. The fleeing Mamlukes went on to Damascus, some even going as far as Gaza, everywhere proclaiming that all was lost, and spreading panic all over the country.

On the battlefield, the Mamluke right flank had defeated the Tatar left, penetrating almost to their centre, which had begun to advance against Qalaoon's position. The sultan gave orders for the drums to keep beating to rally stragglers. Isa ibn Mahanna rode up with his bedouin horsemen. Officers of the sultan's staff rode out to gather up and re-form broken units and fugitives.

At this critical moment, a senior Mamluke ameer, Azdemir al Haj, galloped across to the Tatars with a few men, calling out that they were deserters and wished to speak to Mangu Timur. When led up to the prince, he suddenly attacked him, wounding and unhorsing him. Horrified at the fall of their commander, the Mongol officers and guards dismounted and ran to his aid.

Seeing confusion in the enemy centre, or perhaps knowing what Azdemir was going to do, the Muslims hastily charged. Mangu Timur, wounded and suffering from shock, was hurried off the field. The Mamlukes pressed on and the whole Mongol army broke and fled, half of them making for Salamiya, the others following the direct road to Aleppo.

Meanwhile the victorious Tatar right wing was still amusing itself killing and looting outside Hims. Eventually they turned back to see how the battle had gone. Qalaoon had remained on his hill with about a thousand men and had just given orders to case the colours and cease beating the drums. The remainder of the Mamluke army had ridden in pursuit of the fleeing enemy.

Suddenly a large force of Tatars appeared from the south— their victorious right wing returning from Hims. Fortunately the drums were silent, and the Mongols rode past without noticing the sultan's little detachment. When they had passed, Qalaoon and his thousand men charged into their rear, scattering them in a wild flight.

It was now sunset, the battle had lasted all day and victory was complete, though the Mamlukes were utterly exhausted. Qalaoon returned to his camp and sat down to write letters to all parts of the empire announcing the victory. Fearing that his camp might be overrun, he had divided up his treasure, and made each of his personal mamlukes wear a belt packed with gold coins.

The Mongols lost more men during their flight than in the battle, great numbers being killed both by the troops and by the population. Many hid in the undergrowth on the banks of the Euphrates, but the brushwood was set on fire and most of them died in the flames. The Ameer Azdemir al Haj, who had wounded Mangu Timur, had been immediately killed by his guards. The victory had been largely due to his bravery.

The day after the battle, a carrier pigeon brought news of the victory to Damascus. The people, hitherto terrorstruck, went mad with joy, the streets were quickly decorated and the bands played. But at midnight the fugitives from the Muslim left flank began to arrive, announcing that all was lost. Panic seized the Damascenes once more, and terrified crowds poured out of the city gates in disorderly flight. At dawn, however, a courier galloped up, post-haste from the army, and announced a splendid victory, just as the mueddhins were singing the call to morning prayers.

Meanwhile, however, carrier pigeons had arrived in Cairo from various towns through which the fugitives had passed, announcing a military disaster. The people of Egypt gave themselves to prayer, and every mosque was packed with worshippers imploring help. This final terror, however, lasted only a few hours, until perfumed pigeons landed in Cairo, with the glorious tidings of the total defeat of the Mongols. The Mamlukes customarily sprayed with perfume pigeons bearing good news. The drums were beaten and Cairo, Fustat and the Citadel were gaily decorated.

The Ameer Torontai, with the troops pursuing the Mongols, captured a horseman carrying a haversack containing the secret papers of Mangu Timur. Among them were letters from Sonkor al Ashqar, urging Mangu Timur to occupy Damascus and promising to help him. The flight of the Mamluke left wing, where Sonkor was posted, was thereby perhaps explained. The letters were taken to Qalaoon, who burned them without showing them to anyone. He then met Sonkor in Hims and renewed his pledge to him, allowing him to return to his castle at Sahyoun. This incident is a striking tribute to the wisdom of Qalaoon. How many men, with the incriminating letters in their hands, would have instantly arrested Sonkor, and divided the empire into rival parties in the very hour of victory?

While Mangu Timur was marching on Hims, his brother, Il-Khan Abagha, was laying siege to Rahba on the Euphrates. On hearing of his brother's defeat, he raised the siege, retiring to Baghdad and thence to Hamadan.[1] Mangu Timur established himself at Jazira ibn Umar, north of Mosul.

On 7th November, 1281, Qalaoon made a triumphal entry into Damascus. The day was a joyous, but also a solemn, holiday. The public abandoned themselves to rejoicing, and poets celebrated the occasion in a great number of verses.

On 13th December, 1281, the sultan reached the Cairo Citadel, having ridden on ahead of the army. A column was sent to march through Cairo, where immense crowds had collected in holiday mood. Included in the procession was a large number of Tatar prisoners, their drums torn and their colours, the staffs broken, dragged along behind them in the dust.

Four days later, in the Hall of Audience, the sultan received an embassy from the King of the Yemen, Yusuf ibn Rasool, and presented it with a number of horses and suits of armour taken from the Mongols. An embassy came also from the Byzantine Emperor, Michael VIII Palaeologus, with a draft treaty already signed by him. Shortly afterwards a number of ameers were quietly arrested and put in prison. They were the traitors whose names had been found with that of Sonkor al Ashqar in Mangu Timur's papers. Although Qalaoon had avoided civil war by burning the incriminating letters, he nevertheless, without publicity, gradually disposed of the traitors.

The treachery of Sonkor al Ashqar tempts us to say that the

[1] Map 11, page 56.

Mamlukes were faithless mercenaries, seeking only their personal gain and ready to betray any cause which they engaged to serve. But when we consider the case of Azdemir al Haj, who rode into the centre of the Mongol army and unhorsed Mangu Timur, thereby giving victory to the Muslims, we are obliged to modify our generalisation. He must have known that he could not possibly survive his exploit. Here then we see a Mamluke ameer deliberately giving his life to win victory for his side.

What impelled him to do this? Was it Mamluke esprit de corps, or was he a sincere Muslim, anxious to earn the crown of martyrdom fighting the pagans? The Mamlukes, in fact, like any other community, contained good and bad, greedy and generous, traitors and heroes.

The same year, there died in Damascus the Ameer Aibek al Shujai, at the age of eighty-five. He had been a great man in his time and Baybars trusted him entirely. A deeply religious man, he was full of kindness and gentleness, though he could be stern with criminals. Throughout his service, he had enjoyed the confidence of every sultan. When too old to serve, he renounced his fief and the rank of ameer and lived in seclusion in Damascus till his death. Here is another type of Mamluke. Unfortunately, then as now, it was the ambitious, the unscrupulous and the violent who obtained the publicity.

According to our modern ideas of nationalism, the Mamlukes were foreign tyrants. In fact, however, it was to religion, not to race, that people gave their allegiance in the thirteenth century. In this light, the Mamlukes were heroes who defended Islam from the pagan Mongols. There was a sound basis for loyalty to the Mamlukes, in some ways ideal partners for the Egyptians and Syrians, who were never successful as soldiers. They were, however, cultured, intellectual, and civilised, which the Mamlukes were not.

The desert Arabs were ethnically of a race different from the Egyptians or the Syrians. They also were uncultured, though not savages, but they were good fighters and were always called upon by the Mamlukes in war. At all periods of history, people tend to assume their circumstances to be normal and natural, though, of course, needing improvement. Thus Maqrizi, a Syrian living in Egypt, never, in his bulky volumes, suggests that Mamluke control of Egypt should cease, though he freely criticises individuals, the high cost of living, the excessive taxes and other problems.

In another direction, also, the Mamlukes were the complement of the Egyptians. The former did the fighting, but left administration, justice, religion and education to the local populations, who were intellectually well ahead, not only of the Mamlukes, but also of the peoples of Europe. We must note also the popular enthusiasm which often greeted the sultans when they rode through a city.

It is unfortunate that most Europeans who have written about the Mamlukes have done so in connection with Napoleon's invasion of Egypt in 1798, two hundred and eighty-one years after the collapse of the Mamluke Empire.

* * *

In November 1282, the Sharif of Mecca took an oath of loyalty to the sultan, promising at the same time to drape the Kaaba, the Holy of Holies in Mecca, with the embroidered covering made in Egypt. This covering, known as the kiswa, is renewed every year. The right to supply it has, on various occasions, become a question of political prestige, and still is today. Henceforward the Hejaz enjoyed local autonomy within the Mamluke Empire.

* * *

Abagha died some weeks after the Battle of Hims, and was succeeded by his brother, Tequdar. In December 1282, an embassy arrived from him to inform Qalaoon of his conversion to Islam and of his assumption of the title of Sultan Ahmed. In a long letter, the new Il-Khan stated that his council had decided to continue the conquest of the world, sending out such vast numbers of invincible troops that all the peoples of the earth froze with terror.

But since he had become a Muslim, he had decided to leave the Muslims in peace. Even when he caught a Mamluke spy, he had returned him instead of executing him. "It is God who leads men in the right path," he concluded piously.[2]

Qalaoon's reply was even longer. Referring to the vast Mongol armies, the sultan remarks drily that it is as well that the khan had decided not to send them. If it should come to fighting, he added, it was God who gave the victory. The Mongol ambassadors received many handsome gifts, but were prevented from communicating with the public.

Soon afterwards, Qalaoon's son, Ali, was married to Princess Mankebek, daughter of the Ameer Noukiah, a Mongol in the sultan's service. A splendid wedding was arranged with torchlight illuminations, a lavish expenditure on perfumes and a great banquet. Once

[2] The letter is much condensed. The full text is in Quatremère, *Histoire des Sultans Mamlouks.*

again we are surprised that the sultan's son should marry a Mongol princess, a few weeks after the Battle of Hims. Qalaoon had also married a woman from the Mongol colony in Cairo. We must remember, however, that all Mamlukes were brought up on the steppes, where Mongols and Turks were now intermixed.

Perhaps, also, the nameless Mamlukes felt a snobbish admiration for the Mongol aristocracy, whose régime was based on heredity and on the royalty of the descendants of Jenghis Khan—the Golden Family. In the same way, the upstart Napoleon was to marry the daughter of the Austrian Emperor, whom he had defeated.

*   *   *

The Christian King of Georgia decided this year to make a pilgrimage to Jerusalem. His country was a tributary of the Il-Khan Empire, and his troops had fought in the Mongol army at the Battle of Hims. Afraid of Mamluke hostility, he decided to travel in disguise with only one companion. It is a high tribute to Qalaoon's intelligence system that, even in so distant a country, he knew not only the king's plan but had a detailed description of both men. The king was forty years old, had a scar on his neck, a pale complexion, narrow forehead, black eyes and a gold ring on his right hand.

The two pilgrims were identified as soon as they crossed the frontier, but nothing was done to alarm them. Unknown to them, they were shadowed all the way to Jerusalem, the sultan being kept constantly informed of their movements. They were arrested in Jerusalem, sent to Cairo and imprisoned in the Citadel. We rarely imagine that Middle Eastern governments could have been so efficient, seven hundred years ago.

*   *   *

It is surprising to us that the Mamluke court was governed by an elaborate ritual and etiquette, which was rigidly observed. Much of the ritual was inherited from the Arab khalifs, perhaps before them from the Persians and the Byzantines, and reached the Mamlukes through the Seljuqs and the Ayoubids. Somewhat unexpectedly, however, the Mamlukes, nomads from the northern steppes, attached great importance to the ritual formalities of the court, and indeed did all they could to render them more dazzling and magnificent.

Robes of honour played an important part in the Mamluke system of government. The presentation of robes of honour was a sign of the royal favour, marked the promotion of the recipient to higher rank, or government approval of the services of a military commander returning from a victorious campaign. In the field of diplomacy, the emissary of a foreign ruler was invested with a robe of honour as a sign of respect for his master. The presentation was made at a formal ceremony in the Citadel. In the event of the investiture of an especially distinguished ameer or official, the recipient sometimes rode down from the Citadel to his home in a formal procession, wearing his robes of honour and surrounded by an escort of other distinguished persons in formal dress.

Mamluke subjects who were eligible to be invested with robes of honour were of three categories:

(1) Men of the sword, Mamlukes proper, imported as boys.
(2) Men of the pen, civil servants and government officials, who, of course, were Egyptians or Syrians.
(3) Men of religion. In the Middle East, as in mediaeval Europe, men trained in religion normally received the best education. As a result, such persons were often used by the government as civil officials, though trained as qadhis and qualified in Islamic law. But some were dedicated to purely religious activities.

The types of robes to which each category was entitled, and each rank within that category, was laid down in great detail in the government regulations.

MEN OF THE SWORD

Ameers of one hundred received an outer robe of red satin, underneath which was an inner robe of yellow of the same material. The outer robe was embroidered with gold thread and trimmed with miniver. The inside garment was fringed and the cloak was of beaver. A skull-cap of gold brocade was worn on the head, the turban, a long strip of muslin, being wound round it. The end of the turban was ornamented with bands of white silk, on which were inscribed the titles of the sultan, and decorated with stripes of silk in different colours.

Ameers wore gold belts round their waists, the details of which varied with the rank of the wearer. The most senior officers wore gold buckles on their belts, decorated with rubies, emeralds and pearls. Officers of lower rank had buckles of plainer design, but still decorated with precious stones. Junior ameers had gold buckles without jewels. All senior officers also received swords of which the hilt and scabbard were decorated with varying amounts of gold. An important ameer received with his robe of honour, also, a horse covered with a sheet of cloth of gold. The horse was from the royal stables and was presented complete with his harness and saddlery. It was the duty of a special court officer to prepare the ceremonial harness and saddlery.

The Prince of Hama, the last royal Ayoubid prince, received even more elaborate robes. His turban was of white silk instead of muslin, and was embroidered with gold thread. He received two horses, one with gold housings as above, the other covered by a scarlet horse rug. Similar equipment was given to the Viceroy of Damascus, who also had a gold fringe round the edges of his outer robe.

Officers of lower rank received robes, consisting of bands of material of different colours, embroidered with gold thread and bordered with a gold fringe. In the case of somewhat more senior officers, the material was bordered with gold lace and edged with miniver or beaver.

MEN OF THE PEN

Wazeers and civil officials received white silk robes, bordered with miniver or beaver. Sometimes the sleeves were also lined with beaver. Officials of lower rank received robes without lined sleeves. For still more junior officials, the robe might be coloured, not white. Officials who received white silk robes were presented also with an inner robe of green.

MEN OF RELIGION

The robes of qadhis and men of religion were of wool, without borders or fringes. For the most senior, the outer robe was white, the inner green. Clerks wore black robes, the colour which formerly distinguished the Abbasids. Their turbans were of black muslin, over which was thrown a black scarf.

*   *   *

On normal occasions, the military class wore fur caps, whereas the clerical class wore an imama, or turban. Their body clothing consisted of robes or short coats, usually of bright colours but sometimes white in summer. On their feet, the Mamlukes wore boots of soft leather, black, red or white, to which spurs were attached. Armour consisted largely of chain-mail, occasionally stiffened by strips of steel. Helmets of various shapes were worn in battle.

NOTABLE DATES

Elevation of Malik-al-Aadil Salamish	August, 1279
Deposition of Malik-al-Aadil Salamish	27th November, 1279
Elevation of Malik-al-Mansoor Qalaoon	4th December, 1279
Death of Malik-al-Saeed Baraka in Kerak	24th March, 1280
Revolt of Sonkor al Ashqar in Damascus	3rd May, 1280
Sonkor defeated south of Damascus	21st June, 1280
Recognition of Ali, son of Qalaoon, as heir-apparent	25th October, 1280
Tatars destroy Aleppo	20th–25th October, 1280
Qalaoon leaves Cairo for Syria	April, 1281
Qalaoon signs ten-year truces with the Franks	April, 1281
Qalaoon enters Damascus	11th May, 1281
Qalaoon camps outside Hims	27th October, 1281
Battle of Hims	31st October, 1281
Qalaoon returns to Cairo	13th December, 1282
Arrival of an embassy from Il-Khan Tequdar	December, 1282

PERSONALITIES

Mamlukes
Malik-al-Saeed Baraka, son of Baybars
Malik-al-Aadil Salamish, son of Baybars
Malik-al-Mansoor Qalaoon
Ameer Sonkor al Ashqar rebel Viceroy of Damascus

Arabs
Malik-al-Mansoor Muhammad, Ayoubid Prince of Hama
Isa ibn Mahanna, chief of the bedouins of the Syrian desert

Mongols
Il-Khan Abagha, son of Hulagu
Mangu Timur Khan, brother of Abagha
Il-Khan Tequdar (alias Sultan Ahmed)

VI

Wealth and Power

The ruling class, the Mamlukes, lived on the usually generous grant of fiefs which could not develop into family properties since the transmission of estates was unlawful ... Commerce flourished extraordinarily during the Mamluke period, since at that time, Egypt and Syria were still the transit country for the rich Indian trade of the Italian merchant republics. In this way, great revenues flowed in to the Mamluke sultans.

CARL BROCKELMANN, *History of the Islamic Nations*

Qalawun vigorously prosecuted the war which his great predecessor had left unfinished ... The lords of the southern Latin cities hastened to make treaties with the sultan but it was too late—Qalawun could not afford the risk of having the Christians again attempt to assist the Mongols. The chief conquest of his reign was Tripoli, which was indulging in a petty civil war ... Qalawun came, but there was nothing left in Tripoli when he departed.

JOHN L. LAMONTE, *Crusade and Jihad*

The journey ended for me in Tripoli, a fitting terminus to this re-tracing the footsteps of the Crusades. For it was from the turrets of her castle of Tripoli that the Lady Melisende—the *Princess Lointaine*, the Queen of Outremer—inspired in the knights and poets of Christendom that intangible, ethereal love which could never be consummated, the essence of what poetry underlay the spirit of the Crusades.

SIR HARRY LUKE, *Cities and Men*

IN April 1283, Malik-al-Mansoor Muhammad, the Ayoubid Prince of Hama, paid a visit to Cairo. Qalaoon rode out to meet him, treated him with honour and allowed him to appear in public with the insignia of royalty. Abulfeda, one of his descendants, quotes a nice example of courtesy on this occasion. When Qalaoon enquired the reason for the prince's visit, the latter replied, "I wish to be freed from bearing the throne-name which was given to me, for I cannot decently continue to call myself Al-Malik-al-Mansoor, since that has become the name of our Lord the Sultan."

"I only assumed that name," replied Qalaoon, "because of the affection I feel for you. If you had been called by any other name, I would have chosen that one. What I did out of my affection for you cannot now be changed." Although we may consider the Mamlukes barbarians, they were not unversed in the flattering language of diplomacy.

On 6th April, 1283, the sultan, accompanied by the Prince of Hama, rode to the Province of Buhaira to supervise the digging of a new canal. Troops were called out and completed the work in ten days. The new canal irrigated a large area previously waterless. We see here a Mamluke sultan in person with his soldiers, digging a canal to increase the prosperity of Egypt.

On 14th April, 1283, an embassy arrived from the King of Ceylon seeking a treaty. The king described the wealth of his country which included many precious stones (especially rubies), elephants, and other objects of value. The late Dr. Muhammad Mustafa Ziyada, in a footnote to his edition of Maqrizi, explains that Qalaoon had made special efforts to encourage trade between Egypt and the East.

In August 1283, Arghoon, the son of Abagha, rebelled against his uncle Tequdar but was defeated and imprisoned. But Arghoon talked to his prison guards, pointing out that his uncle was a Muslim, and that in future only Muslims would be promoted. "Why," he asked, "should Mongols give up the laws of Jenghis Khan and follow the Arab religion?" This propaganda was quickly successful. The troops released Arghoon, proclaimed him Il-Khan and murdered Tequdar. Arghoon chose as his wazeer a Jew named Saad-al-Dowla.

From August 1283 to January 1284, the sultan was in Syria. A number of provincial governors were dismissed or transferred. In view of the ever-present possibility of plots against the sultan, it was thought inadvisable to allow a governor to remain long in one place and thereby to gain local influence.

An incursion was made into the Christian Armenian Kingdom of Cilicia. Great numbers of people were killed, and the country laid waste with fire and sword. The town of Ayas, or Lajazzo, was again taken and looted. This port enjoyed great prosperity. It imported oriental goods through the Il-Khan's dominions and shipped them to the West. The Mamlukes, as already indicated, wished to destroy this trade route and to monopolise the eastern trade through Egyptian territory.

Early in 1284, an embassy came to Cairo from Tuda Mangu, chief of the Golden Horde, a great-nephew of Baraka.[1] Maqrizi calls Tuda Mangu ruler of the Qipchaqs. As we have seen, the Qipchaqs were Turks, and both Baybars and Qalaoon were Qipchaqs. Their country, however, had been conquered by the Golden Horde.

Tuda Mangu claimed to have been converted to Islam, and requested the despatch of a flag blessed by the khalif. It will be seen that the Mamluke sultan gained considerable prestige as the world's greatest Muslim ruler, with whom the khalif resided.

This year grain rose to famine prices in Egypt owing to a bad Nile. The sultan ordered all Mamluke ameers to sell their grain, which they had been holding back for higher prices. The price of grain immediately fell to one-half, showing how large a percentage of the grain crop of Egypt belonged to ameers.

Isa ibn Mahanna died this year. He was of the Fadhl tribe, and ameer of all the nomad tribes of the Syrian desert. Isa had been treated with honour by both Baybars and Qalaoon. A deeply religious man, he was kind, generous, noble and benevolent. In his lifetime, the usually turbulent bedouins remained quiet. He was succeeded by his son, Mahanna ibn Isa ibn Mahanna.

One day, the sultan's two sons, Ali and Khalil, went out shooting birds with crossbows, and Ali killed a pelican. When a young boy killed his first game, it was the custom for him to offer it to a distinguished sportsman, who thereby became his sporting patron. Ali consulted his father regarding his choice of a patron and Qalaoon indicated Malik-al-Mansoor Muhammad, the Ayoubid Prince of Hama. Unfortunately Malik-al-Mansoor died the same year. He was succeeded by his son, Malik-al-Mudhaffar[2] Mahmood.

On 27th March, 1285, Muhammad, Qalaoon's third son, was born in the Citadel of Cairo. The sultan received the news as he was

---

[1] See page 77 and Genealogical Tree 5, page 78; also Genealogical Tree 4, page 58.
[2] The Conquering King.

entering Damascus on 31st March. We shall hear a great deal more of this boy. The sultan left Damascus almost immediately to attack the fortress of Marqab, which was held by the Hospitallers. It will be remembered that Qalaoon had concluded a ten-year truce with the Hospitallers, as a result of which this attack was a breach of faith. These truces had been concluded before the Battle of Hims, to prevent the Crusaders joining the Mongols. Now that he no longer feared the Tatars, Qalaoon broke faith with the Franks.

The knights, relying on the truce, were taken by surprise. On 17th April, 1285, the Mamlukes opened a mass bombardment on the castle. The situation of the Hospitallers was hopeless with no possibility of relief, for the Crusaders could no longer put an army in the field. The Muslims drove mine galleries beneath the walls and, on 23rd May, 1285, one of the main towers collapsed. The Mamlukes mounted the breach but were repulsed. Next morning, however, the knights asked for terms. Twenty-five senior officers of the Hospital were allowed to leave, armed and mounted, with the honours of war. The remainder left on foot on 27th May, all reaching Tripoli safely. A messenger was at the same time sent to Sonkor al Ashqar in his castle at Sahyoun, informing him that Qalaoon was aware of his former correspondence with the Tatars. Sonkor returned a soft answer.

On his return to Cairo, the sultan found waiting for him embassies from the German Emperor, from the Republic of Genoa and from the Greek Emperor of Constantinople. The German Emperor sent lavish gifts including rare furs, miniver and sable, and robes of scarlet, of yellow silk and of Venetian cloth. The Genoese had sent silk, hunting falcons and a dog "as big as a lion". (Could it have been a St. Bernard?) The Byzantine Emperor sent large amounts of silk and carpets. A few days later, an embassy from the Yemen brought a royal gift of thirteen eunuchs, ten horses, an elephant, a rhinoceros, eight parrots, three large pieces of amber, seventy camels laden with spices and many chests of textiles.

The constant arrival of embassies from emperors and kings bearing such valuable gifts proves that the Mamluke Empire was considered one of the world's greatest states, the friendship of which was sought by the most powerful monarchs.

An interesting point mentioned by Maqrizi regarding the encouragement of trade is that, in 1288, travel permit forms were sent from Cairo to notable merchants in the Yemen, Sind, India and China. The forms were to be filled in before departure from their countries of origin, and produced by the merchants when they entered Egyptian territory with their goods.

In February 1268, a force went to Kerak and brought the sons of
Baybars, Khidhr and Salamish, to live in Cairo. They were well
treated, lived in the Citadel and rode out with the sultan or his sons
to enjoy sport or play polo. Qalaoon probably thought they were
safer as members of his own household rather than in a distant
fortress where they could not be observed. Qalaoon then visited
Kerak in person, stored it with provisions sufficient to last a siege,
and placed in it a garrison of Bahri Mamlukes.

An army was sent to besiege Sonkor al Ashqar in Sahyoun, on the
grounds that he had not assisted the sultan or even visited him, when
he was attacking the Hospitallers in Marqab. After a short siege,
Sonkor surrendered and was escorted to Cairo. The sultan went out
to meet him in person, accompanied by "his sons and a large ceremonial guard". They returned to the Citadel, where the sultan
invested him with a robe of honour, with gifts of golden belts,
valuables and horses. Sonkor assumed his duties as an ameer at
court.

We cannot but admire the patient diplomacy of Qalaoon in
dealing with a rebel who had invited the Mongols to Syria. But
Qalaoon bided his time until he finally, and without bloodshed,
transformed the rebel into a court official.

On 15th January, 1288, an army was sent to invade Nubia and a
sharply contested battle was fought outside the capital, Dongola.[3]
Many of the tribes north of Dongola were partly Arab, mixed with
Berber and African blood, though still boasting such Arab names as
Beni Umar, Beni Shaiban or Beni Hilal. The King of Nubia, with
the greater part of the population, retired to the south. After much
killing and looting, the Mamlukes placed the king's nephew on the
throne, left with him a Mamluke garrison, and withdrew to Cairo
with the loot.

Once the main army had left Dongola, however, Semamoun, the
King of Nubia, returned, drove out the Mamluke garrison and remounted the throne. The puppet king they had appointed fled with
the Mamlukes to Cairo. The sultan was angered by this reverse, but
was obliged to leave for Syria as will be told below.

On his return, however, he immediately organised an army to
reconquer Nubia. According to Maqrizi, whose numbers are often
inaccurate, it consisted of forty thousand men, and left Cairo on 8th
October, 1289, escorting with it the puppet king. The column was
accompanied by five hundred boats on the Nile, carrying supplies
and warlike stores. Semamoun repeated his former strategy, retiring
to the south with the civil population, and the Mamlukes occupied

[3] Map 18, opposite.

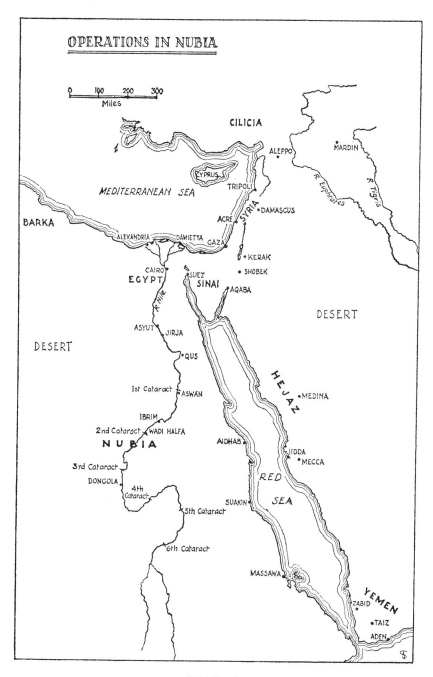

OPERATIONS IN NUBIA

0   100   200   300
Miles

CILICIA

MARDIN

ALEPPO

CYPRUS

MEDITERRANEAN SEA

TRIPOLI

R. Euphrates

R. Tigris

BARKA

ACRE   SYRIA   •DAMASCUS

ALEXANDRIA   DAMIETTA
GAZA

• KERAK

CAIRO   SUEZ   • SHOBEK

EGYPT   SINAI   •AQABA

DESERT

ASYUT   •JIRJA

•QUS

DESERT

R. Nile

HEJAZ

1st Cataract   •ASWAN   •MEDINA

IBRIM

2nd Cataract   WADI HALFA

NUBIA   AIDHAB

•JIDDA
•MECCA

3rd Cataract

DONGOLA   4th
Cataract

RED

SUAKIN   SEA

5th Cataract

6th Cataract

MASSAWA   YEMEN
•ZABID

•TAIZ

ADEN

MAP 18

Dongola without opposition. All along their line of march they had killed everyone they caught, smashed the irrigation water-wheels, ruined the crops and turned the country into a desert.

As the boats could go no further owing to the cataracts of the Nile, a light column continued the pursuit and found the king and the refugees fifteen days' march to the south. King Semamoun escaped and continued his flight, but a large number of civilians were rounded up and taken back to Dongola. The puppet king was re-installed, the Nubian tribute to Egypt was fixed, and a Mamluke garrison was left behind. The main column returned to Cairo, where it arrived in May 1290 with an immense amount of plunder.

Once again, no sooner had the army left Dongola than Semamoun returned. The Mamluke garrison withdrew and the puppet king was done to death. Semamoun, however, wrote to Cairo, promising to pay the tribute fixed in his absence. Qalaoon, a reasonable man, was pleased to accept this face-saver and informed the Nubian king of his agreement.

*   *   *

We have departed from strict chronology to describe the conclusion of the Nubian war. Between the two expeditions to Dongola, in 1288 and in 1289, a number of other important events occurred, to which we must now return.

In February 1288, the chief collector of taxes and the chief qadhi of Damascus—both, of course, Syrians—came to Cairo to complain against the Mamluke viceroy of Damascus, Sanjar al Shujai. It is noticeable that Maqrizi says that "they dared to lodge a charge". Qalaoon summoned the viceroy to Cairo and heard the case himself. The accused was convicted of selling lances, armour and warlike stores to the Crusaders. The sultan was furious, ordered the viceroy to be tortured, and to pay a large sum of money in gold. It also appeared that the viceroy had imprisoned a number of innocent citizens, refusing to release them until they gave him a bribe.

The affair sheds further light on the Mamluke régime. Many of the ameers were ruthless tyrants when occasion offered, though fearless fighters in battle. The system of government allowed extensive powers to provincial viceroys, who rarely referred to Cairo. The significance of the incident lies in the statement that two Syrian officials *dared* to complain to the sultan against the viceroy. On the other hand, the affair was not a case of the community oppression of Syrians by Mamlukes, for the sultan was enraged and treated the viceroy as a criminal. In point of fact, Syrians and Egyptians themselves often oppressed their own compatriots, as we shall see.

When we criticise the disloyalty of Sonkor al Ashqar or the tyranny of Sanjar al Shujai, we must remember the constant rebellions and "barons' wars", which occurred in England, almost down to Hanoverian times. How many dukes, earls and barons were imprisoned in the Tower of London without trial, or lost their heads under the executioner's axe?

After reporting this affair, Maqrizi adds that when Qalaoon next appointed a Mamluke governor of Egypt, he ordered him to meet the Egyptian qadhi every Wednesday, and to seek his advice on administrative problems.

In August 1288, Qalaoon's eldest son, Malik-al-Salih Ali, was taken ill with internal pains, vomiting and diarrhoea. Qalaoon was much distressed and appealed to all men of religion to pray for his son. Nevertheless, he died on 4th September, 1288. A week after the death of Ali, the sultan's second son, Khalil, was made heir apparent, and rode through Cairo with the insignia of royalty.

The principal problem of state in 1288–1289, however, was the question of Tripoli. The last Count, Bohemond VII, had died childless on 19th October, 1287. The two possible heirs were his mother and his sister, Lucie, who was married to the grand admiral of Sicily. A number of the notables of Tripoli declared a commune and abolished the hereditary title. They then wrote to the Republic of Genoa, placing Tripoli under her protection. The city was torn by rival intrigues.

Unfortunately, Genoa and Venice were at daggers drawn. The Venetians had a fleet in Acre and were determined not to allow a Genoese fleet to be based on Tripoli. As a result, two Italians, possibly a Venetian and a Pisan, went up from Alexandria to Cairo, and obtained an audience of Qalaoon. They told the sultan that, if the Genoese secured a naval base in Tripoli, they would dominate the eastern Mediterranean and prevent any Muslim ships putting to sea. As Rene Grousset rightly says in his *Histoire des Croisades*, "the histories of the baronies and republics of the Franks in Syria in the thirteenth century is the history of a suicide". The Mamlukes already disliked Tripoli because, in 1260, Bohemond VI had ridden into Damascus with the Mongols.

The sultan left Cairo with the army on 9th February, 1289, and entered Damascus on 9th March. A week later, he left Damascus for Tripoli. Not until he was almost in sight of the walls did the Franks cease their internal feuds. The Mamlukes immediately opened a massive bombardment with nineteen mangonels, while one thousand five hundred sappers drove galleries beneath the walls, or sprayed them with Greek fire. Soon two towers in the wall collapsed.

A number of Venetians who were in the town fled to the harbour. Others, seeing them, panicked and followed them. Qalaoon noticed the movement and, on 25th April, 1289, ordered a general assault. The city was carried, every man in it was killed and the women and children were driven off as slaves. The city and the walls were then methodically razed to the ground, stone by stone. Another rival of. Alexandria in the oriental trade had been obliterated.

Tripoli had been extremely rich, particularly through the textile industry. There are said to have been four thousand looms in the city, manufacturing luxury textiles, silk, camlet and cloth of gold, which fetched very high prices in the West.

The Lord of Jubail, head of the Gibelet family, rode boldly into Qalaoon's camp and did homage for the town of Jubail, which the sultan accepted in return for tribute. All the rest of the County of Tripoli surrendered to the Mamlukes without resistance. The only towns now left to the Franks were Acre, the capital, Beirut, Sidon, Tyre and Athlit. Tripoli had, it is true, a ten-year treaty with the sultan, of which this attack was a breach, but the sultan's pretext was that the agreement had been signed with Bohemond, not with the commune.

The fall of Tripoli produced no reaction in Europe, which was absorbed by its own power politics. The Armenian Christian King-dom of Cilicia, however, saw the writing on the wall. When Qalaoon returned to Damascus, he received a deputation from Cilicia implor-ing peace. The request was granted, in return for the surrender of more frontier fortresses.

The sultan arrived back in Cairo in the middle of September and began immediately to organise the second expedition to Nubia, which has already been described.

In July 1290, the sultan gave orders for the dismissal of all Jews and Christians from appointments in the civil government. Orders to the same effect were regularly repeated throughout the whole Mamluke period. In every case, however, they were all back at their appointments within a short time. The Christians at administration and the Jews at finance were extremely efficient office-workers, and government departments found themselves obliged to re-appoint them, as soon as the sultan's decree had blown over.

Henry II de Lusignan was at this time both King of Cyprus and also titular King of Jerusalem. Abandoned by Europe, the king sent an embassy to Qalaoon to sue for a renewal of the truce, which the sultan agreed to prolong for another ten years. We have seen that Venice had played an unsavoury part in urging Qalaoon to attack

Tripoli, the protégé of her commercial rival, Genoa. Now, with Tripoli destroyed, Acre, the Venetian naval base, would enjoy virtual monopoly.

In the summer of 1290, the Venetian Council sent a fleet of twenty galleys to Acre, with a volunteer force of Italian men-at-arms on board. The Venetians, however, had provided no pay for their troops, hoping that the Pope would put his hand in his pocket, which he failed to do. The volunteers were poor Italian peasants, without money, training or discipline.

As a result of the new truce, commercial relations had been resumed between Acre and the Muslim hinterland. Caravans arrived from Damascus and the local villagers brought in their farm produce to market. Suddenly, one day in August, the Venetian volunteers burst out of Acre and began to kill and rob the peasants and merchants, who were bringing their wares to the town for sale.

Then, with their blood now heated, they returned to Acre and commenced to massacre the Arabs in the streets, killing Christian and Muslim Arabs alike. The orders of knights and the old Frankish inhabitants rushed to rescue the victims of the Italian rioters, and succeeded in saving the lives of a few Arab merchants. The relatives of the dead hastened to Cairo where, amid much weeping and wailing, they spread the blood-soaked garments of the victims before the sultan. Qalaoon was speechless with fury, for the ink was scarcely dry on the new ten-year treaty.

He instantly wrote to all the provinces of Syria, ordering the preparation of mangonels, catapults, battering rams and ladders for the siege of Acre. Anxious, however, to show the correctness of his attitude, he wrote to Acre demanding that the offenders be handed over to him.

The council of the city—the titular king lived in Cyprus—was in a dilemma, for the offenders were Venetian soldiers. The knights pointed out that there were criminals in the prison already sentenced to death, who could be handed over as the offenders. But the volunteers were out of hand and mobs rioted in the streets, protesting against the surrender of any Christians to the Muslims. Guillaume de Beaujeu, the Grand Master of the Templars, warned that Qalaoon would destroy Acre, but was shouted down. The council sent a feeble reply, expressing regret at the incidents, but excusing themselves on the grounds that the offenders were Venetians. The answer perfectly suited Qalaoon, who wished to destroy Acre, and was able to claim that he had waited patiently for the reply to his diplomatic protest, but that the Franks had refused him all satisfaction for the outrage.

On 5th November, 1290, the sultan formed a camp outside Cairo in which the army began to mobilise. The same night, however, he was attacked by fever and died five days later, on 10th November, 1290, at the age of seventy years. His reign of eleven years had been a prosperous one. The climax of his career had been the defeat of the Mongols at Hims in 1281. He had eliminated the Frankish County of Tripoli, but failed to conquer Nubia.

In politics, he was shrewd, patient and careful. He extracted a good deal of money, especially from rich Syrians, but these haphazard methods of raising cash were everywhere practised in those days. Ibn Taghri Birdi, writing some forty years later, says that the cultivated area of Egypt was doubled in Qalaoon's reign. This is doubtless an exaggeration but indicates that he made great efforts to improve agriculture and irrigation.

Although himself a Bahri Mamluke, he regarded them with suspicion when he became sultan, owing to their past attempts to intervene in politics. As a counterweight to the River Mamlukes, who were (like himself) mostly Qipchaq Turks, he raised another Mamluke force, which he recruited principally from the Crimea, and from the Circassians of the Caucasus. The Circassians were a mountain people, entirely distinct from the nomadic Turkish tribes of the steppes. The new force was stationed in the Citadel and was called the Burji or Tower Mamlukes. In Qalaoon's time, they reached a strength of three thousand seven hundred men.

Qalaoon had been a handsome man with a presence which inspired respect. He was broad-shouldered with a short neck. He spoke Turkish and the Qipchaq dialect, but knew scarcely any Arabic. He left one wife, three sons and two daughters.

*   *   *

It would be extremely interesting to know the numbers and organisation of the Mamluke army under Qalaoon, but unfortunately all our historians are civilians, who write at length of military interventions in politics, but give no professional details of the organisation or strength of the army. The Royal Mamlukes were the backbone of the Mamluke army. Under Baybars and Qalaoon, they may have numbered some twelve thousand. Malik-al-Salih Ayoub, the Ayoubid, is said in one place to have had ten thousand mamlukes, so it would be reasonable to assume that this figure was inherited from Ayoubid days.

In addition, as we have seen, there were twenty-four ameers of one hundred, giving two thousand four hundred mamlukes. The total of the personal mamlukes of ameers of drums and ameers of ten might rise to another two thousand six hundred, giving a total of five thousand ameers' mamlukes.

The next category we encounter, also a relic of Ayoubid times, was the *halaqa*. The word in Arabic means a ring, and it seems possible that they originally constituted the personal bodyguard of the sultan, and surrounded him to protect him. At the Battle of Tel al Jazar on 25th November, 1177, for example, Saladin's life was saved by his bodyguard of one thousand mamlukes, all dressed in yellow tunics. The actual word *halaqa* is first used in 1174. Poliak, on the other hand, suggests that the word refers to the tactics of mounted Turks in galloping round an enemy army, shooting arrows into it, without closing. Such a word might be used to describe a force of mounted Mamlukes, who employed this system. At the siege of Acre, described in the next chapter, however, reference is made to the *halaqa al sultaniya*, which sounds like the sovereign's escort.

Early in the Mamluke period, the *halaqa* is sometimes mentioned as a unit like the Bahris. At this time, the soldiers of the *halaqa* were allotted fiefs to live on, just as Royal Mamlukes did. Maqrizi says that, in early Mamluke times, a soldier of the *halaqa* would own a string of chargers, suggesting that they were a wealthy, fashionable unit. Later on, as we shall see, the *halaqa* became a reserve unit, but under Baybars and Qalaoon it seems to have been an active corps of cavalry. In 1279, a certain man is mentioned as being the first ameers' mamluke to get a fief in the *halaqa*.

It will be remembered that ameers of a hundred were sometimes described alternatively as commanders of a thousand. It appears that, while the hundred were the ameer's personal mamlukes, the thousand were *halaqa*, whom he commanded only in war. *Halaqa* sub-units of a hundred were commanded by a *bash* (head) and a *naqeeb* (sergeant). An ordinary *muqaddam*, or officer of the *halaqa*, commanded forty troopers. These sub-divisions almost correspond to the regiment, squadron or troop of British cavalry. At the end of the campaign, the *muqaddam* gave up his command, which again suggests a reserve force. At the Battle of Hims, however, we hear of four thousand soldiers of the *halaqa* fighting in the very centre of the battle line.

To form any estimate of the strength of the *halaqa* is extremely difficult. At the beginning of the Mamluke period, there is a mention of their strength as being twenty-four thousand. On the other hand, another account states: "The soldiers of the *halaqa* had no routine duties, only special services for the sultan. Their numbers were twelve thousand but later were reduced."

Approximately, therefore, we may guess the numbers of the army under Qalaoon to have been:

Royal Mamlukes	12,000
Ameers' Mamlukes	5,000
Halaqa	12,000
	29,000

Twenty-nine thousand was, therefore, approximately the strength of the "Mamluke-type" troops from Egypt. Before discussing the provincial contingents, we will give a few more details on these Royal Mamlukes.

ROYAL MAMLUKES

These may be divided into four categories:

(a) Young mamlukes purchased from merchants who brought them from the Steppes, the Caucasus or Asia Minor. These were called *julban* or imported.

(b) Adult or veteran mamlukes of former sultans, engaged to serve under the reigning sultan. These were sometimes called *qaranis*.

(c) *Khassikiya*, or "specials", were selected from the *julban* for intimate service in the royal household, as pages, cupbearers or positions near the sultan. Growing up in the family, they often enjoyed the sultan's confidence. Hereafter I have called them "intimate mamlukes". Intimate mamlukes were not a military unit, but merely a number of young mamlukes chosen by the sultan for duties as pages or orderlies in the palace. As they thus became personally known to the sultan, they often achieved rapid promotion. Under the Bahri Sultans, there were sometimes about forty. Barsbai, who was sultan from 1422–1438, had a thousand intimate mamlukes.

(d) Former mamlukes of ameers, who had passed into the service of the sultan. These were often called *saifiya*.

Royal Mamlukes do not appear to have been permanently subdivided into tactical units, such as regiments. When a campaign was imminent, they seem to have been divided into units by the sultan, who appointed the commander for each. This statement, however, is made by Ibn Iyás, who wrote in the late period, when the efficiency of the army was low. It may not have been so under the Bahri Sultans.

Royal Mamlukes received fiefs of land, and also sometimes pay in cash, clothing allowance, rations of meat and forage, money grants before a campaign and donatives on the accession of a new sultan.

AMEERS' MAMLUKES

After the Royal Mamlukes, the next category in the army consisted of Ameers' Mamlukes. These were men who, on arrival in Syria or Egypt, had been bought by ameers to be their private mamlukes and had been trained, freed and equipped by their respective masters.

AULAD AL NAS AND THE HALAQA

The expression *aulad al nas* means literally "sons of people", the idea of *nice* people being implied. Normally *aulad al nas* were the sons born in Egypt of ameers or mamlukes. As we have seen, real mamlukes were all born on the Steppes. If such ameers or mamlukes married and had children in Egypt, their sons could become *aulad al nas*. The *halaqa*, already referred to, consisted largely but not exclusively of *aulad al nas*.

THE PROVINCIAL CONTINGENTS

But whereas, at the Battle of Hims, Qalaoon is said to have had sixty thousand men, our attempted reconstruction of the Mamluke army in Egypt has given us a figure of only twenty-nine thousand men. The remainder, amounting to about half the army, must have consisted of provincial contingents, concerning whom little accurate information is available.

There were, at first, five governorates or viceroyalties in Syria, later increased to seven. The original five were Damascus, Aleppo, Hims, Hama and Gaza. Safad and Tarablus were added when captured from the Franks. Each viceroyalty was a miniature sultan's court and maintained its own forces. Poliak, quoting Al Zahiri, gives the following establishments for Syria:

Damascus
>Twelve ameers of one hundred.
>Twenty ameers of drums (or forty).
>Sixty ameers of ten.
>Twelve thousand *halaqa*.

Aleppo

Six to nine ameers of one hundred.
Ten ameers of drums.
Twenty ameers of ten.
Three thousand *halaqa*.

Smaller viceroyalties were in proportion, such as:

Gaza

Two ameers of drums.
One thousand *halaqa*.

On the other hand, Godefroye-Demombynes, gives for Damascus:

Eight ameers of one hundred.
Twenty-one ameers of drums.
Twenty-two ameers of twenty.
Fifty-one ameers of ten.

The basic ranks of ameers were of one hundred, forty (drums) or ten, but occasionally we find other numbers, such as ameers of twenty cited above. At other times, we hear of an ameer of five, but these seem often to have been merely an excuse to give a small fief to the son of an important man. In the later decadent period, the misuse of military fiefs to support penurious relatives became frequent.

That we should find variations in the numbers of the army is not surprising, seeing that we are covering a period of two hundred and sixty-seven years. It would be impossible to write a description of the British army covering the period from 1705 to 1972. Indeed the remarkable thing about the Mamluke army is that it changed so little. The total strength of these viceroyalty contingents seems to have amounted, in the time of Qalaoon, to some twenty or twenty-one thousand men.

All ameers were made by the sultan, whether serving in Egypt or Syria. Those serving in Syria received fiefs in the provinces where they were stationed. If transferred, they normally surrendered their fiefs and received other feudal holdings in their new province. The rank and file of the *halaqa* in the provinces also received fiefs in the areas where they served. It is not certain that the *halaqa* in the provinces were all the descendants of Mamlukes. The provinces had not the same training facilities as were available for purchased mamlukes in Egypt. Moreover mamlukes were costly, owing to the long period of training which they received as boys. It is, therefore, probable that some of the provincial *halaqa* were local men, voluntarily enlisted as adults.

IRREGULAR FORCES

We have estimated the strength of the Mamluke army up till now as follows:

Royal Mamlukes (all in Egypt)	12,000
Ameers' Mamlukes (Egypt)	5,000
Halaqa (Egypt)	12,000
Provincial Contingents	21,000
	50,000

The remaining ten thousand required, to make up sixty thousand at the Battle of Hims, probably came from the tribes, of which the principal were:

(1) The bedouin tribes of the Syrian desert.
(2) The Turkman tribes, living around and north of Aleppo.

Each of these classes could reasonably produce five thousand horsemen. The bedouin tribal chiefs were given fiefs and the honorary rank of ameers, though they were not, of course, interchangeable with Mamluke ameers, and could not command regular troops. In addition to their war-time duties they were made responsible for public security in their tribal areas.

The cultivating tribes in Jebel Nablus (Samaria) and in the Lebanese mountains were hardy, warlike and good archers. But most of them were on foot, whereas the Mamluke army consisted solely of cavalry. The Nabulsis and the Lebanese were, however, sometimes called upon, where static operations were involved, such as the siege of Acre, described in the next chapter. The mountain tribes were called *ashair*, whereas the bedouins were designated as *Arab*.

ADDITIONAL TERRITORIES

During the second half of its lifetime, the Mamluke Empire acquired a number of additional territories, such as Barqa (Cyrenaica, now in Libya), Nubia (now part of the Sudan), the Hijaz, Cyprus, Diyarbekr, and Cilicia. These were more or less autonomous states, paying a varying degree of tribute. They were not divided into fiefs, nor incorporated in the Mamluke military system.

SERFDOM

Large areas of land, especially in Egypt, were, as we have seen, used as fiefs to pay the ameers, mamlukes and *halaqa* of the army. The farm labourers were serfs, bound to their land. If they escaped, the authorities helped the fief-holder to arrest them and bring them back. The Mamluke "owner" of the fief normally kept an agent on the land to collect his dues, whether in grain, or money. On land watered by rain, the fief-holder took one third to one quarter of the produce; on irrigated land, his share was one half of the crop. The farm worker also had to pay a number of minor dues.

The system was extremely hard on the farm labourer or fellah, but it was not introduced by the Mamlukes. It was an extremely ancient institution, possibly dating from the Pharaohs. After the collapse of the Mamlukes, it continued under the Ottomans. Similar systems were in force in various parts of Europe in the fourteenth century.

MILITARY TRAINING AND EFFICIENCY

The efficiency of the Mamluke army under the Bahri Sultans may be said to have been based on the following factors:

(a) The long period of training as boys, under the strictest discipline. The training took place in special barracks. The boys were commanded by eunuchs.

(b) Blind dedication of the mamluke to his master; in the case of Royal Mamlukes, their master was the sultan.

(c) Unswerving loyalty of every mamluke to his barrack-comrades. Old soldiers will remember that loyal comradeship constituted the real happiness of the military life.

(d) Ability was the only criterion of promotion, there being no "family" or private influence.

(e) Promotion was very slow. Clever boys were not allowed to shoot ahead, until their characters and experience made them mature soldiers.

(f) Veterans and senior mamlukes, even if they were never "commissioned" as ameers, were treated with great respect by young mamlukes.

These rigid military rules were relaxed when the Mamluke system fell into decline, but under the great Bahri Sultans, these disciplinary regulations produced the world's finest soldiers for a hundred and twenty-five years.[4]

NOTABLE DATES

Rebellion of Arghoon, son of Abagha } Il-Khan Tequdar killed }	August, 1283
Failure of Nile in Egypt	1284
Birth of Muhammad ibn Qalaoon	27th March, 1285
Capture of Marqab from the Hospitallers	27th May, 1285
Abortive campaigns in Nubia	1288–1290
Death of Ali ibn Qalaoon	4th September, 1288
Death of Bohemond VII of Tripoli	19th October, 1287
Capture of Tripoli by Qalaoon	25th April, 1289
Massacre of Arabs by Venetian levies of Acre	August, 1290
Qalaoon orders mobilisation	5th November, 1290
Death of Qalaoon	10th November, 1290

PERSONALITIES

Mamlukes
Al-Malik-al-Mansoor Qalaoon al-Salihi
Ali, his eldest son
Khalil, his second son
Muhammad, his third son

Arabs
Al-Malik-al-Mansoor Muhammad, Ayoubid Prince of
    Hama
His son, Al-Malik-al-Mudhaffar Mahmood
Isa ibn Mahanna, chief of the Syrian bedouins
Mahanna ibn Isa ibn Mahanna, his son

Mongol Il-Khans
Tequdar, son of Hulagu
Arghoon, son of Abagha

[4] The best modern sources for the army are David Ayalon, *Studies in the Structure of the Mamluke Army*, and Poliak, *Feudalism in Egypt*. But hints and casual remarks can be found scattered through all the Arab historians.

Khan of the Golden Horde
Tuda Mangu

Franks
Bohemond VII, last Count of Tripoli
Henry II de Lusignan, King of Cyprus and Jerusalem

Nubians
Semamoun, King of Nubia

VII

The Problem of Succession

On Friday 15th May at dawn, Al-Ashraf launched the final assault . . . The Mamlukes, advancing on foot in deep columns, overran everything . . . The marshal of the Hospitallers, Matthew de Clermont, for a short time forced back the enemy . . . But against the ever-increasing masses of Muslims, all efforts were in vain. Blinded by the smoke of Greek fire and jets of flame, beneath a rain of arrows, they fought on still . . . The battalions of Mamlukes forced their way into the heart of the town . . . The mass of the population were abandoned to the fury of the Mamlukes . . . Women and girls fled through the streets, their children in their arms, terror-stricken and weeping.

RENÉ GROUSSET, *History of the Crusades*

The great officers of the court and of the army were of course the most powerful men next to the sultan, and each deemed himself a fit successor to the throne . . . A coalition would be formed among a certain number of disaffected nobles, while a trusted cupbearer or other officer . . . would strike the fatal blow . . . and the conspirators would forthwith elect one of their number to succeed to the vacant throne. This was not effected without a struggle . . . then there would be a street fight; the terrified people would close their shops, and the rival factions of Mamlukes would ride through the streets.

STANLEY LANE-POOLE, *The Story of Cairo*

AL-MALIK-AL-ASHRAF[1] KHALIL

ON 12th November, 1290, Khalil[2] mounted the throne of his father, Qalaoon. When the decree appointing him heir was called for, it was found that Qalaoon had never signed it. "I will not give the Muslims a king like Khalil", the old man was alleged to have said. Rumour had accused the new sultan of having poisoned his elder brother, Ali.

On 18th November, Khalil set out to ride in state through the city, but when halfway along the route, he turned and rode hastily back to the Citadel. He had been told that the Viceroy of Egypt, the Ameer Torontai, was lying in wait to kill him. Summoned to the Citadel, Torontai went fearlessly to see the sultan but was immediately seized and put to death. His house was searched and found to contain one million six hundred thousand dinars in gold, together with silver, jewellery, textiles, horses, carpets and other forms of property, showing the amazing wealth which senior ameers were able to amass.

A few days later, Torontai's son, who was completely blind, obtained an audience. Holding out his hands like a beggar, he said, "Please let us have something to eat, for God's sake." Those who had seized Torontai's wealth had left the family utterly destitute. Khalil was touched and ordered the return of enough for them to live on. The Ameer Baidara was made Viceroy of Egypt.

The new sultan had a young friend called Muhammad ibn al Salous, whom he appointed wazeer. No wazeer had ever been so powerful as this sultan's favourite. When he rode from his house to the Citadel, his escort included the Mamluke Governor of Cairo, and all the senior officers, judges and notables. Drunk with pride, he treated everyone with contempt, even the Viceroy of Egypt, Ameer Baidara. This was all the more surprising in that he, Ibn al Salous, was a Syrian, not a Mamluke.

A deputation came from the Franks of Acre to implore the sultan's mercy, but Khalil refused to receive it. Sonkor al Ashqar, released by Qalaoon, was arrested and imprisoned. A certain Ameer

---

[1] The Most Noble King.   [2] Pronounced Khaleel.

Kitbugha, who had been accused with Torontai, was, however, released. We shall hear more of him.

Khalil urged on the preparations for the siege of Acre with great zeal. On 25th March, 1291, the Viceroy of Damascus, the Ameer Lajeen, left the city with the forces of Syria. On 28th March, Malik-al-Mudhaffar Mahmood, the Ayoubid Prince of Hama, reached Damascus with his troops, his siege train and field workshops. All the Syrian governors marched with their contingents to Acre.

The sultan set out with the army from Cairo, and camped on 5th April, 1291, beneath the walls of Acre. Next day, ninety-two mangonels arrived and within four days were established in their shooting positions. Screens were erected to prevent the enemy seeing or aiming at the troops. When the bombardment was opened, sappers also drove forward a great number of mine galleries towards the walls.[3]

René Grousset estimates the Muslim army at sixty thousand cavalry and a hundred and sixty thousand infantry. These numbers seem absurdly exaggerated. The Mamluke armies used against the Mongols numbered about sixty thousand, nearly all cavalry. They had no large infantry formations. Frankish historians give the strength of the defenders at eight hundred knights and fourteen thousand foot, including the lately arrived Venetian levies, who had provoked the trouble.

On 15th April, Guillaume de Beaujeu, Grand Master of the Templars, and Otto de Grandson, with a party of English, altogether a total of three hundred knights, made a moonlight sortie from the Porte Saint Lazare. They attacked their immediate opponents, the Hama contingent, drove in the outposts and reached the tents, but failed to destroy the siege engines. De Grandson was a Swiss officer employed by Edward I.

Later in the month, another sortie was attempted from the Porte Saint Antoine. But this time the Mamlukes were completely prepared, thousands of torches were lit and the Franks were glad to get back to their walls.

The Mamlukes relied largely on their sappers. The Franks do not seem to have attempted to drive counter-mines, the only way to repulse this form of attack. On 15th May, 1291, a long stretch of wall near the Porte Saint Antoine collapsed. On 16th May, the Mamlukes put in a local attack and occupied the New Tower.

[3] Mining was extensively used in war in the Arab countries, but far less in thirteenth-century Europe. The galleries were held up on wooden props. Then a fire was lighted, the pitprops burned, and the gallery fell in under the foundations of the walls.

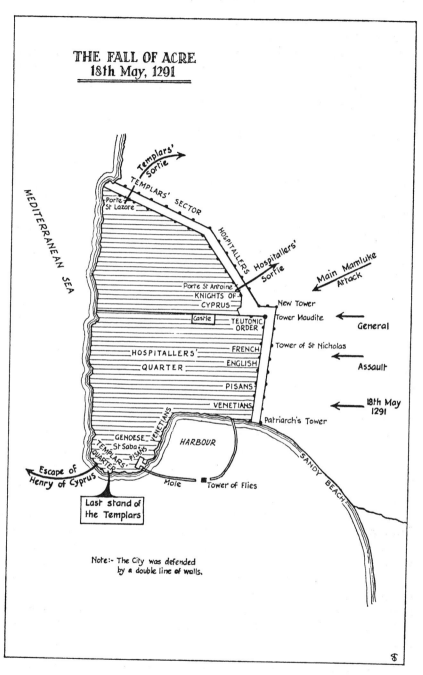

THE FALL OF ACRE
18th May, 1291

MEDITERRANEAN SEA

Templars' Sortie

TEMPLARS' SECTOR

Porte St Lazore

HOSPITALLERS

Hospitallers' Sortie

Main Mamluke Attack

Porte St Antoine
KNIGHTS OF CYPRUS

Castle

New Tower

Tower Maudite

General

TEUTONIC ORDER

Tower of St Nicholas

FRENCH

Assault

HOSPITALLERS' QUARTER

ENGLISH

PISANS

18th May 1291

VENETIANS

Patriarch's Tower

GENOESE
St Saba
TEMPLARS' QUARTER
VENETIANS
PISANS

HARBOUR

Escape of Henry of Cyprus

SANDY BEACH

Mole

Tower of Flies

Last stand of the Templars

Note:- The City was defended by a double line of walls.

MAP 19

On 18th May, when it was still dark, the sultan massed the drums of the whole army on the backs of three hundred camels, and ordered all to beat together. The noise of the drums was deafening and is spoken of with horror by all the Frankish survivors. At the earliest light of dawn, the Muslims advanced in deep columns which overran all opposition by sheer weight of numbers. Before the sun rose above the horizon, the Mamluke banners were fluttering on the walls by the Porte Saint Antoine. The Mamlukes were already pouring into the town, though the Templars and the Hospitallers held on to the walls on either side of the breach until three o'clock in the afternoon, when Guillaume de Beaujeu was killed.

The Templars resisted in their castle for a further ten days, but on 28th May, when the Mamlukes advanced to the assault, the massive castle collapsed, burying friend and foe beneath the rubble. Acre was then laboriously demolished, and the lighter buildings burnt. The remaining towns held by the Crusaders were evacuated almost without resistance. After one hundred and ninety-two years of fighting, the only relic of the Crusaders was the Lusignan Kingdom of Cyprus.

Before the fall of Acre, the Viceroy of Damascus, Husam-al-Deen Lajeen, was arrested by the sultan and sent to prison in Cairo, on the strength of a report from another ameer. In the atmosphere of intrigue at court, senior ameers must have lived in constant anxiety. The young sultan Khalil was already behaving like Baraka, the son of Baybars, promoting his own young friends, and ordering the arrest of senior ameers.

On 3rd June, 1291, Sultan Khalil made a triumphal entry into Damascus to celebrate the end of the Frankish States. Thence he returned to Cairo where he held another triumph on 8th August, 1291.

We have already noted that Ibn al Salous, a young Syrian friend of his, had been made wazeer in Cairo. He had red hair, a portly figure and spoke well. Commencing his career in business, he came to Egypt, where he incurred the anger of Qalaoon, though protected by Khalil. He went on pilgrimage to Mecca, perhaps to keep out of Qalaoon's way, and was still in the holy city when the old sultan died. Khalil had immediately recalled him in a scribbled note by his own hand, "Little redhead, it will be good to see you. Come back quickly." As already mentioned, he was made wazeer, the head of the administration for the whole empire.

Ibn al Salous was educated and well-spoken. The unlimited support of the sultan made him a man of power and importance, but his head was turned by his sudden promotion and he behaved with the utmost arrogance. The chief qadhi of Cairo, Ibn bint al Aaz, was an old man widely respected. Ibn al Salous decided to be rid of him, and arranged for some of his friends to complain to the sultan against the qadhi. The sultan, a foolish youth, ordered that the chief qadhi be paraded through the streets in an ignominious manner to prison. Ibn al Salous ordered that the chief qadhi—we might say the chief justice—be taken to the Citadel on foot by a police guard through the crowded streets.

Three passing Mamluke ameers, to their horror, saw the qadhi being hustled through the streets on foot. They spoke strongly to the sultan, condemning the arrogance of Ibn al Salous, and secured the release of the judge. The latter had spent a long life in the public service and had held many important appointments. Now, a broken man, he was glad to accept a small post as a schoolteacher, which the Viceroy of Egypt, the Ameer Baidara, had obtained for him. In this incident, the oppressor was a Syrian, the victim an Egyptian, and three Mamluke ameers rescued the oppressed.

In this year, 1291, the rebuilding of Aleppo was completed. Thirty-three years had elapsed since it had been razed to the ground by Hulagu.

*   *   *

On 17th March, 1291, Arghoon, the grandson of Hulagu, died in Persia and was succeeded as Il-Khan by his brother, Kaikhatu, a drunkard addicted to sexual orgies. The Mongols selected him as being a degenerate, and unlikely to try to introduce reforms as Arghoon had done.

On 1st April, 1292, Khalil and the army left for Aleppo and, on 29th May, laid siege to the Mongol fortress of Qilaat al Roum, or Roman Castle. Twenty mangonels soon battered breaches in the walls, scaling ladders were brought and the fortress was taken by assault on 1st July, 1292, after a siege of thirty-three days.

All the men were massacred, the women and children being taken as slaves. The sultan renamed the place Qilaat al Muslimin, or Muslim Castle. A permanent garrison was established there, with an armoury and a field workshop, and the walls were repaired. On 6th October, 1292, Khalil held the usual victory march on his return to Cairo. His head had been turned by the capture of Acre and of Qilaat al Roum. At the age of twenty-eight, he was an arrogant young tyrant, arresting and executing any ameers he did not like, especially those veterans whom his father had trusted.

On the evening of 2nd December, 1292, he ordered the strangulation in his presence of six ameers, one of them being Sonkor al Ashqar, who had been so patiently handled by Qalaoon. Five having died, there remained only Husam-al-Deen[4] Lajeen, former Viceroy of Damascus, whom Khalil had caused to be arrested during the siege of Acre. When he was almost dead, the bowstring broke and Lajeen fell at the sultan's feet. The Ameer Baidara, Viceroy of Egypt, and others present, joined in begging for a pardon. Khalil, perhaps thinking that Lajeen could not recover, granted their request. Lajeen was carried out, seemingly dead, but revived and ultimately recovered and lived to take his revenge.

The wazeer, Ibn al Salous, disliked or feared the Ameer Baidara and poisoned the sultan's mind against him, saying that his income was greater than that of Khalil himself. The latter, however, merely took back some of his fiefs.

One of the most remarkable features of the Mamluke régime was that ameers were paid for their military service by grants of land but that, unlike the feudal systems of Europe, the fiefs were never allowed to become hereditary and consequently never produced an aristocracy. The sultan always retained the power to take back the fiefs, which automatically reverted to the treasury when the holder died.

In January 1293, the sultan left Cairo with the declared intention of annexing the Christian Armenian Kingdom of Cilicia. In Damascus, however, he found an embassy from Sis, the capital of Cilicia, begging for peace. Khalil agreed, on condition that the Armenians surrender their frontier fortresses of Behesna, Marash and Tel Hamdoon.[5] From Damascus, the sultan suddenly marched to Salamiya and arrested Mahanna ibn Isa ibn Mahanna, chief of the Syrian bedouins. Mahanna, unaware that he had done anything wrong, was taken by surprise.

While Khalil was still in Damascus, an ambassador arrived from the Il-Khan. He brought a letter from Kaikhatu, stating that in future he proposed to reside in Aleppo, which had been annexed by his father, Abagha. Should his intention be obstructed, he might be obliged to conquer all Syria. Khalil, a facetious young man, replied that he had been interested in the Il-Khan's letter. Curiously enough, he had himself conceived a rather similar idea. He proposed to move his residence to Baghdad.

On 5th July, the sultan was back in Cairo.

*   *   *

[4] Sword of the Religion.   [5] Map 17, page 109.

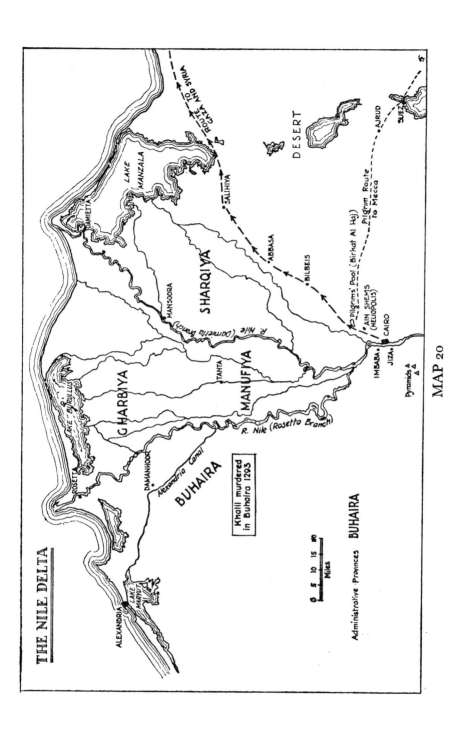

THE NILE DELTA

LAKE MARYUT

ALEXANDRIA

ROSETTA

LAKE BURULLUS

DAMANHOOR

Alexandria Canal

BUHAIRA

R. Nile (Rosetta Branch)

GHARBIYA

TANTA

MANUFIYA

DAMIETTA

LAKE MANZALA

MANSOORA

R. Nile (Damietta Branch)

SHARQIYA

ROUTE TO GAZA AND SYRIA

SALIHIYA

ABBASA

BILBEIS

Pilgrims' Pool (Birkat Al Haj)

AIN SHEMS (HELIOPOLIS)

CAIRO

IMBABA

JIZA

Pyramids

Pilgrim Route to Mecca

AJRUD

SUEZ

DESERT

Khalil murdered in Buhaira 1293

0 5 10 15 20
    Miles

Administrative Provinces BUHAIRA

MAP 20

On 5th December, 1293, the sultan crossed the Nile to shoot birds. He was accompanied by the Ameer Baidara and by the wazeer, Ibn al Salous. The latter went on to Alexandria, whence he wrote the sultan yet another letter of denunciation against Baidara. Infuriated by the letter, Khalil summoned Baidara to his presence. Before a large gathering, he loaded the ameer with abuse, shouted that he would tell Ibn al Salous to have him flogged and used other expressions which the genteel Maqrizi says it would not be nice to repeat. Baidara was deeply alarmed, but returned a mild answer and shortly after left the gathering.

Khalil was a foolish young man, who always believed what he was told and took immediate and violent action. Baidara, back in his tent, contacted a number of other ameers including Lajeen, who had narrowly escaped strangling the year before. A few days later, the shooting party struck camp to return to Cairo. The sultan's escort left with his baggage.

Baidara and his friends went to the sultan's tent before it was struck, hoping to kill him as he came out to mount. But it so happened that Khalil that morning had heard that there was a large number of birds on a near-by lake and had ridden out with his cross-bow, taking with him only one companion. The tent was struck and the convoy left for Cairo without the sultan.

Khalil spent the morning shooting with his companion, the chief huntsman.[6] Baidara had sent scouts to locate the sultan. These now returned and reported that he and one companion were shooting by the lake. At noon, Khalil was hungry and the huntsman produced a loaf of bread and a chicken. While he ate his lunch, Khalil saw a cloud of dust approaching and sent the ameer shikar to see what it was. But Baidara galloped straight past him. His drawn sword in his hand, he rode straight at Khalil and struck him a blow, which broke his arm. Another ameer followed and, aiming at his head, smashed his shoulder.

Lajeen came third, the man whose life had been saved the year before by the breaking of a bowstring. Calling out to Baidara, "He who would rule Egypt and Syria, let him strike a blow like this," he struck the sultan with his sword, laying him prostrate on the ground. The others jumped down from their horses and, one after another, ran him through with their swords. The body lay alone on the ground for two days until a local official loaded it on a camel and removed it for burial.

Meanwhile, Baidara and his accomplices galloped back to the sultan's tent, which seems to have been pitched again. Baidara sat

[6] Ameer Shikar.

on the throne and his supporters swore allegiance to him. They then remounted and rode for Cairo.

The Ameer Kitbugha and some brother-officers had spent the morning shooting birds in another direction. On the way back, they met some of the sultan's mamlukes, who had seen Baidara sit on the throne. The whole party galloped off in pursuit of Baidara.

The latter, meanwhile, had met other officers and told them he had killed Khalil, accusing him of persecuting the men who had faithfully served his father, of frivolity in handling affairs of state, his appointment of Ibn al Salous, his murder of Sonkor al Ashqar and many other charges. Moreover, he added, he has no religion, drinks wine in Ramadhan and holds orgies with beardless boys.

In the interval, Kitbugha had collected some two thousand horsemen, with whom he overtook Baidara and his party. First discharging a cloud of arrows, they then drew their swords and closed in, killing the whole of Baidara's party. Baidara's head was paraded through Cairo on the end of a lance. Lajeen, of bowstring fame, however, made good his escape, and hid himself in the city of Cairo.

The Ameer Sanjar al Shujai who was in command of the Citadel, hearing of these events, collected all the boats on the Nile on the east bank. When Kitbugha reached the west bank he was unable to cross, and was obliged to camp where he was, and open negotiations with Sanjar al Shujai. Agreement was eventually reached to place upon the throne the late sultan's younger brother, Muhammad, the son of Qalaoon. The agreement was not based so much on loyalty to the house of Qalaoon as on the need to gain time and avoid a blood-soaked civil war. The whole incident, indeed, illustrates the reason for the nomination of an heir-apparent before any sultan died. Otherwise, a free-for-all battle between rival ameers might break out at a moment's notice.

*   *   *

Khalil was twenty-nine when he died and had reigned for three years and one month. He left only two daughters. His misfortune was to have become sultan when so young, amid the rough, proud and violent ameers of the Mamluke régime. He himself had been born in Egypt. During the eleven years of his father's reign—that is during the time when he was sixteen to twenty-seven years old—he had lived as a prince. His youth, his conceit and the lack of respect which he had shown to those senior ameers who had served his father, earned him the resentment of many.

On the other hand, he was gifted by nature. He was generous, and extremely active and energetic. He was educated, unlike Baybars or Qalaoon, and Maqrizi states that he never signed an official document without first reading it, and sometimes ordering corrections to be made. He could be pleasant in conversation when he wished, and was remarkably intelligent. He might have made a distinguished ruler if he had mounted the throne at a more mature age.

As it was, he was frivolous, credulous of what he was told, and extremely hasty and indiscreet in his speech. He became arrogant after his campaigns against Acre and Qilaat al Roum, but both these victories were gained over extremely weak enemies. These minor successes could not be compared with Ain Jaloot or the Battle of Hims, when the whole Mongol army had been defeated in the field.

*   *   *

The reader will by now have realised that, at this stage, the principal problem facing the Mamluke régime was that of the succession. In other respects, their system, which had come into existence by accident, had been amazingly successful. It had produced four capable rulers, of whom Baybars and Qalaoon would have been outstanding sovereigns in any country.

Every boy brought from the steppes had a sultan's sceptre in his knapsack. None possessed wealth or influence to assist him. Every man relied on himself alone. Every Mamluke who rose to be a sultan or an ameer was inevitably capable, brave, determined and a born leader. But the problem was how to find successors to men like Baybars and Qalaoon.

The Ayoubids had been cultured and highly civilised, and Arabic was their mother tongue. The Mamlukes in most cases did not know Arabic and were devoid of culture, but they saved Syria and Egypt from the Mongols, which it is unlikely that the Ayoubids could have done. The prestige which they acquired thereby, all over the world, made their empire not only respected but wealthy.

But they never solved the problem of the succession. A régime under which the rulers fought their way up would obviously produce capable leaders. But the process of allowing potential sultans to fight it out gave rise to frequent rebellions and civil wars. As a result, when a sultan died, there was a readiness to accept his son, in the hope of maintaining peace. More often than not, the sultan's son was a failure, for he had not been exposed to the biting blizzards of the steppes as a child, nor had he fought his way to the top in Egypt. After a short time, he was deposed or murdered.

If an outstanding leader emerged quickly, the son of the former sultan was hustled out of the way, as had happened to the sons of Baybars when Qalaoon mounted the throne. But if no dominating personality appeared, a prolonged period of struggle might ensue, as was to occur after the murder of Khalil.

*　　*　　*

We have no reason to feel supercilious when we consider the difficulties experienced by the Mamlukes. To this day, the problem of choosing a successor to the ruler of a state remains unsolved. Hereditary monarchy was invented to provide an heir without a civil war, but it was, of course, impossible to ensure that the king's son would be a capable ruler.

The Arabs had adopted a compromise. Under their system, the most capable member of the royal family could succeed, not necessarily the king's son. This method allowed a wider field of choice, but did not preclude rivalry between different princes.

The Byzantine Emperors were despotic, but if they failed to make good, they were often assassinated or removed. The dictators of many modern states have fallen in the same manner. But if a dictator rules for a long time with complete success, the problem arises in a more acute form when he dies.

The Western nations today may claim that they can ensure the peaceful succession to leadership by means of elections. Yet many people in these countries profess contempt for the politicians whom they themselves elect. The West today has avoided civil wars by resigning itself to be ruled by persons whom it neither trusts nor respects. The emergence of Stalin, on the other hand, is not unlike the method used by the Mamlukes.

*　　*　　*

AL-MALIK-AL-NASIR[7] MUHAMMAD IBN QALAOON
(First Reign)

Muhammad was the third son of Sultan Qalaoon. The first, Ali,

[7] The Victorious King.

had died, the second, Khalil, had been murdered. Muhammad had been born in March 1285, in the Citadel of Cairo, and was eight years old when he became sultan in 1293.

The Ameer Kitbugha, when he obtained boats to cross the Nile, conferred with Sanjar al Shujai, the commandant of the Citadel. Then the other senior ameers were called in, most of them being Salihis, old men who had served under Malik-al-Salih Ayoub, or Mansooris, former mamlukes of Qalaoon. All agreed to the elevation of Malik-al-Nasir Muhammad. On 18th December, 1293, the child-sultan sat on the throne in the Hall of Audience. A gratuity was paid to the troops, who thereupon swore allegiance.

The Ameer Kitbugha was made Viceroy of Egypt, while Sanjar al Shujai became wazeer, a post normally held by an Egyptian or a Syrian. The precarious balance of power between Kitbugha and Sanjar made it necessary for the latter to have a rank equal to the former.

Kitbugha was made regent and assumed control of the government, leaving the child-sultan in his nursery. The regent forged a decree, in the name of Khalil, appointing Muhammad as his heir, a copy of which was sent to Damascus, where the ameers swore loyalty to Muhammad as heir before they learned of the death of Khalil. Two ameers in Damascus were executed and seven others arrested and sent to Cairo, on the grounds that they had been associated with Baidara. On 20th December, 1293, the alleged accomplices of Baidara suffered the amputation of their hands. They were then nailed to planks tied to the backs of camels and were paraded through Cairo, preceded by the head of Baidara on a lance.

The authorities caused the procession to pass in front of the houses of the victims. When it reached the house of the Ameer Altunbugha, his young girl slaves burst out bareheaded into the streets with their children, weeping and beating themselves on the breast and face. His pages tore their clothes, giving vent to lamentable cries. His wife had gone up on to the roof in order to jump down and die with her husband, but her girl slaves held her back, while she screamed passionately, "Would to God that I could sacrifice myself for you." The crowds of onlookers burst into tears.

Meanwhile, the young slaves of Khalil and other palace servants blacked themselves and ran through the streets accompanied by professional weeping women. "Never," comments the civilised Maqrizi, "had Egypt seen such days of horror." There was still no news of Lajeen, the actual murderer of Khalil.

The former wazeer, Ibn al Salous, returned to Cairo when he heard of the death of Khalil, and lived openly in his house. Having been a boon companion of Khalil, he was presumably about thirty years old. He still retained the arrogant manner which he had affected in the lifetime of his patron.

Five days later, he was arrested and subjected to repeated floggings and torture. In between the floggings, he was led through the streets on a donkey, exposed to the ridicule of those whom he had treated with contempt in the days of his glory. "It is impossible," says Maqrizi, "to tell all that this unhappy man had to suffer in the way of insults and cruelty." Eventually death ended his misery.

When expressing our horror at the brutality of the Mamlukes, we must remember that, three hundred years after this date, people were still being tortured and burned alive in Western Europe.

*   *   *

Meanwhile, the two Ameers Kitbugha and Sanjar were together at the head of the state. But equality between two ameers was impossible. Sanjar decided to have Kitbugha assassinated.

On 23rd January, 1294, as Kitbugha entered the Citadel, an officer warned him that Sanjar had arranged to have him murdered in the banqueting hall. A few minutes later, a supporter of Sanjar drew his sword to kill Kitbugha, but was immediately cut down by his mamlukes, who had been warned to be on the alert. As Sanjar was the commander of the Citadel, Kitbugha hastily escaped. Then, calling up his men, he blockaded the fortress from the outside. The young sultan, in the palace inside the Citadel,[8] was a helpless spectator of the civil war.

When the blockade had lasted for seven days, the queen mother called from the ramparts asking the besiegers what they wanted. They replied, expressing loyalty to the sultan but denouncing Sanjar. The queen mother succeeded in having Sanjar locked in his apartment, the gates were immediately opened and the besiegers rushed in and killed Sanjar. The shops in the city, closed for fear of fighting and looting, were opened, and the streets resumed their normal activity.

On 14th February, 1294, Muhammad ibn Qalaoon made a state progress through Cairo with the insignia of royalty. Kitbugha and the ameers walked on foot beside the sultan's horse.

The facts of history can be obtained from the records, but the most difficult task of the historian is to recover the spirit which animated the historical personages whose adventures he describes. With our modern ideas of nationality, it is surprising to us to learn that

[8] Map 21, page 158.

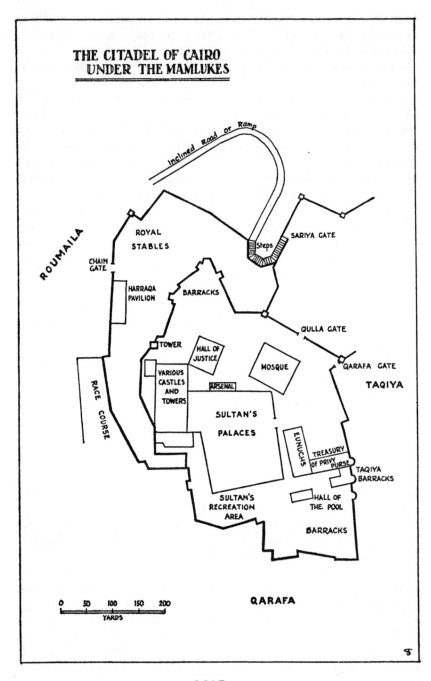

THE CITADEL OF CAIRO
UNDER THE MAMLUKES

Inclined Road or Ramp

ROUMAILA

ROYAL
STABLES

CHAIN
GATE

Steps

SARIYA GATE

HARRAQA
PAVILION

BARRACKS

QULLA GATE

TOWER

HALL OF
JUSTICE

VARIOUS
CASTLES
AND
TOWERS

MOSQUE

QARAFA GATE

TAQIYA

ARSENAL

RACE
COURSE

SULTAN'S

PALACES

EUNUCHS

TREASURY
OF PRIVY
PURSE

TAQIYA
BARRACKS

SULTAN'S
RECREATION
AREA

HALL OF
THE POOL

BARRACKS

0   50   100   150   200

YARDS

QARAFA

MAP 21

Kitbugha, who was now virtually dictator, was a Mongol, who had deserted to the Mamlukes when Qalaoon was sultan.

Six months after these events, the Ameer Lajeen, who had lain concealed since the murder of Khalil, emerged from hiding and was pardoned.

On 1st December, 1294, more than three hundred of Khalil's former mamlukes seized horses from the sultan's stables and ran amok through the streets of Cairo. Hearing of the riot, a number of ameers armed and mounted and quickly dispersed the mamlukes. Some were beheaded, others had their hands cut off or were drowned in the Nile. The whole affair was senseless, an outbreak of emotional frustration which ended in butchery.

Kitbugha had now ruled the empire as regent for a year, during which he had never even troubled to inform the little sultan of current events. The morning after the riot he assembled the leading ameers and addressed them as follows: "The majesty of the throne has been insulted. The conditions necessary for its proper maintenance cannot exist as long as the sovereign is a child like Malik-al-Nasir." The ameers agreed forthwith to depose the young sultan and to proclaim Kitbugha sultan in his place. All immediately took the oath of allegiance.

A horse was quickly brought and decked with the yellow hood of royalty.[9] Kitbugha mounted and rode up to the Citadel from his house, the ameers walking before him on foot. Seating himself on the throne, he announced that he had chosen the throne-name of Malik-al-Aadil, the Just King.

- -

AL-MALIK-AL-AADIL KITBUGHA

- -

Malik-al-Nasir Muhammad and his mother were removed from the palace and given an apartment in the Citadel. Lajeen (of the bowstring), the murderer of Khalil, was made Viceroy of Egypt. On 20th January, 1295, Malik-al-Aadil Kitbugha rode in state through Cairo with the insignia of royalty.

But soon after the accession of Kitbugha everything seemed to go wrong. Human life in Egypt depended on the Nile.[10] For two years, the Nile failed to rise and Egypt lay parched and dusty. In Barka (Cyrenaica) the crops were eaten by locusts. Famine prevailed

[9] In addition to the golden saddlecloth and yellow parasol, the sultan's horse on state occasions wore a hood extending from the ears to the saddle and made of heavy yellow silk embroidered with gold thread.

[10] "The blessèd Nile" Maqrizi calls the river.

in Syria, Egypt and North Africa. Starving wretches chased and ate dogs and cats, and even cases of cannibalism were reported. The superstitious public attributed these disasters to divine displeasure at the deposition of the young Malik-al-Nasir Muhammad.

*   *   *

While these events were taking place in Egypt, the Il-Khan Kaikhatu was assassinated on 25th April, 1295. He had reigned three years and nine months, spending most of his time in debauchery. His cousin Ghazán seized the throne.[11] As soon as he was well established, he announced his conversion to Islam.

*   *   *

The position in the Holy City of Mecca was somewhat precarious. In 1173, more than a century before, Saladin had sent one of his brothers to seize power in the Yemen, accompanied by a trusted retainer, Umar ibn Rasool. Five Ayoubids in succession had ruled the Yemen but, after the fifth, the Rasool family had seized the throne.

In 1295, both the Mamlukes and the Rasools claimed suzerainty over Mecca, while the Sharifs, the descendants of Muhammad, strove to retain their independence. Each year, the Mamlukes sent an escort with the pilgrimage, but they did not attempt to maintain a permanent garrison. Between pilgrimages, the King of the Yemen sent troops. At other times, rival Sharifian princes disputed the coveted position of Ameer of Mecca.

*   *   *

In January 1296, reports reached Cairo that the Uwairat, a Tatar tribe, had crossed into Syria, escaping from the new Il-Khan, Ghazan. Maqrizi gives their numbers as eighteen thousand, probably an exaggeration. Their chief, with a thousand horsemen, came to Cairo. Kitbugha received them with high honours, being himself, it will be recalled, a Mongol.

The Uwairat refused to accept Islam, lived largely on horse flesh and refused to observe Muslim customs. Kitbugha was severely criticised for admitting these heathen. They were dispersed in various areas, and the younger generations were gradually assimilated.

[11] Genealogical Tree 5, page 78.

Their daughters, it is alleged, were in demand as wives, being reputedly remarkably beautiful.

*   *   *

In Egypt the famine continued, until about a thousand persons a day were said to be dying in Cairo. Wide pits were dug and every morning the corpses were collected and thrown pell-mell into the pits. In Syria conditions were little better until, on 19th December, 1296, a religious teacher called Ahmad al Fazari read through the whole of Bukhari's Traditions of the Prophet in one session, in the Great Umaiyid Mosque in Damascus. The very same night, it began to rain and continued to do so for forty days.

*   *   *

On 20th August, 1296, Kitbugha left for Syria with the army. He remained some time in Damascus and then went into camp near Hims. On 21st November, 1296, he set out to return to Egypt.

Accounts of royal visits to Syria always include brief notices of the dismissal and possible arrest of ameers or officials. Many of the charges were for peculation, but our historians never mention a public enquiry or a trial. The sultan merely pronounced an order of dismissal. Sometimes, a few months later, the same officer received a robe of honour and a new appointment, usually without any explanation. To the historians, the procedure was probably obvious, but not to us.

The sultan, doubtless, had many spies and other sources of information, the public being often afraid to complain. In such circumstances, in the hands of a conscientious and energetic sultan, an intelligence system and arbitrary dismissals may have been the best way to suppress corruption. It avoided the endless prevarications of the legal trials, and the bribery or intimidation of witnesses.

On the return march to Egypt, the army camped one night at Al Auja in southern Palestine. Maqrizi states that the ameers were already incensed against the sultan, without specifying the reason. Kitbugha sent for an ameer called Baisari and spoke to him harshly in the presence of other ameers. The latter assembled in the tent of Lajeen, the murderer of Khalil. Lajeen told the others that some of the sultan's mamlukes had forged letters, ostensibly written by Baisari to the Mongols, and had convinced Kitbugha that they were genuine. When they reached Cairo, Lajeen asserted, Baisari would be imprisoned. The ameers resolved to anticipate any further action by the sultan.

At midday, on 26th November, 1296, the ameers armed and mounted and, each preceded by drums and surrounded by his personal mamlukes, marched across the camp to the sultan's tent. Several of Kitbugha's mamlukes were killed defending his tent. Although he was completely surprised, the sultan profited from the time gained by the resistance of his mamlukes. Slipping out of the back of the tent, he mounted the "duty horse", which was always kept saddled and bridled outside the sultan's quarters, and rode for his life for Damascus, accompanied by only four of his mamlukes.

A few seconds later, Lajeen, sword in hand, burst into the tent, ready to add a second sultan to his score, but Kitbugha was nowhere to be seen. When Lajeen rode back to his tent, the ameers walked on foot beside his horse, a tacit acknowledgment of their new ruler. Kitbugha had reigned two years all but six days.

*   *   *

It is noticeable throughout the lifetime of the Mamluke Empire that Damascus was the starting point of many rebellions and thus was a constant source of anxiety to Cairo. Both nature and history had made the two cities rivals. Egypt and Syria were two entirely distinct countries, separated by the one hundred and fifty miles of the desert of Sinai, a barrier as formidable as the sea. The people of Syria were of mixed descent, partly immigrants from Arabia but also to a large extent mixed with Greeks, Italians and races from Asia Minor, Persia or the Steppes. The people of Egypt, on the contrary, also included immigrants from Arabia, but mixed with others from Central Africa and with Berbers from the North African countries. Egypt and Syria were thus two distinct countries inhabited by different races, each with its natural capital, Cairo or Damascus, at its centre.

Cairo, as the capital of the Mamluke Empire, naturally feared Damascus as a potential rival. For this reason, the Mamlukes had divided Syria into six provinces, the viceroy of each of which dealt direct with Cairo. Damascus was not allowed to be the political capital of Syria.

Damascus, which is mentioned in the book of Genesis, is one of the oldest cities in the world, and still is one of the most beautiful. It lies at the foot of a range of mountains, which dominate it on the west, crowned by the snowy crest of Mount Hermon. The springs and melting snows from the mountains pour down to the plain, filling it with the babble of flowing streams, which water an extensive area covered with gardens and orchards. Here grew a profusion of fruit trees, apples, plums, mulberries, pomegranates, figs, apricots and fresh vegetables such as lettuce and asparagus. Flowers also were cultivated, especially lilies and violets, which were valued for their perfume.

The later Seljuq period and the wars of the Crusaders had resulted in disturbances, but the thirteenth century brought more stability, especially after the defeat of the Mongols at Ain Jaloot. As a result, the economic situation improved, Damascus became prosperous and the population increased. People no longer crowded together inside the walls. Suburbs and country houses sprang up in the garden areas and along the banks of the streams. Thus although Damascus was humiliated by being made politically subordinate to Cairo, she profited immensely by the order and security established under the Bahri Mamlukes.

According to Nicola Ziadeh,[12] the population of Damascus under the Mamlukes was about a hundred thousand persons, "bigger than Paris or Florence" as Western merchants admitted. According to the Jewish traveller, Benjamin of Tudela, there were some three thousand Jews. The European commercial community, in Mamluke times, consisted chiefly of Venetians, Genoese, Florentines, Catalans and French. Both the Christian and the Jewish communities enjoyed a large measure of autonomy. The Christian Patriarch and the Jewish Rais, or Head, were elected by their own communities, for whom they were responsible to the government.

Throughout the Mamluke period, while Cairo enjoyed political leadership, Damascus was a centre for Muslim theology, religion and mysticism, partly, perhaps, because the intellectual atmosphere was freer than in Cairo. Damascus also harboured many Muslim learned men, who had escaped from Baghdad or the cities of the north at the time of the Mongol invasions.

One of the most famous Muslim divines was Ahmad Ibn Taimiya, who died in Damascus in 1328. An active and dynamic reformer, he was a puritan, who preached strict and simple adherence to the Qoran and the early traditions. In modern times, the Wahhabi movement in Arabia and the Senussi in North Africa derived much from his writings.

A religious teacher contrasting with Ibn Taimiya was Ibn al Arabi, who died in Damascus in 1240. He was a mystic, who believed that man by contemplation could establish direct contact with God.

During the Mamluke period, great numbers of persons, from sultans downwards, established charitable or religious endowments. Schools were thereby enabled to maintain their independence,

[12] Nicola A. Ziadeh, *Damascus under the Mamlukes.*

without bowing to government interference or asking fees from their pupils. Under the Mamlukes, school buildings were often spacious and their architecture beautiful. In Mamluke times, there were seventy-eight monasteries for men and two for women in Damascus. All these institutions were endowed and were devoted to religious learning and Sufi mystic contemplation. The Sufis belonged to different orders in the same way as Christian monks.

There were also six hospitals in Damascus in Mamluke times from 1150 to 1516. All medical treatment was free. Some of the hospitals had medical teaching schools.

The famous traveller Ibn Batuta tells of the great variety of remarkable charitable endowments in Damascus, such as for paying the wedding expenses of poor girls, for ransoming prisoners, for assistance to travellers or for paving the streets.

Altogether Damascus, in the Mamluke period, was a great, beautiful and cultured city. The fact that Cairo held the political power caused Damascus to specialise in religion, literature and intellectual activities. When they stayed in Damascus, the sultans used the same pomp as in Cairo, riding through the city with the insignia of royalty and the yellow parasol, and preceded by a band. By this means, they attempted to placate the jealousy of their second capital, of which they were always a little apprehensive.

NOTABLE DATES

Accession of Malik-al-Ashraf Khalil	12th November, 1290
Commencement of the Siege of Acre	5th April, 1291
Fall of Acre	18th May, 1291
Capture of Qilaat al Roum	1st July, 1292
Assassination of Sultan Khalil	December, 1293
Elevation of Malik-al-Nasir Muhammad	18th December, 1293
Deposition of Malik-al-Nasir Muhammad } Elevation of Kitbugha	2nd December, 1294
Years of famine in the Mamluke Empire	1295 and 1296
Assassination of the Il-Khan Kaikhatu } Elevation of Il-Khan Ghazan	25th April, 1295
Immigration of the Uwairat	January, 1296
Deposition of Kitbugha by the ameers	26th November, 1296

PERSONALITIES

Mamlukes
Sultan Malik-al-Ashraf Khalil ibn Qalaoon   1290–1293
Sultan Malik-al-Nasir Muhammad ibn Qalaoon 1293–1294
Sultan Malik-al-Aadil Kitbugha   1294–1296
The Ameer Husam-al-Deen Lajeen, murderer of Khalil
Syrian wazeer of Khalil, Muhammad ibn al Salous

Mongols
Il-Khan Kaikhatu   1291–1295
Il-Khan Ghazan   1295–1304

VIII

The Sultan's Favourite

The wordly hope men set their hearts upon
Turns ashes—or it prospers; and anon,
Like snow upon the desert's dusty face
Lighting a little hour or two—is gone.
Think in this battered caravanserai
Whose doorways are alternate night and day,
How sultan after sultan with his pomp
Abode his hour or two, and went his way.

EDWARD FITZGERALD, *The Rubaiyat of Omar Khayyam*

What though the field be lost?
All is not lost; the unconquerable will
And study of revenge, immortal hate,
And courage never to submit or yield.

JOHN MILTON, *Paradise Lost*

The sultan led his armies to meet the Mongols. People in the city prayed and recited liturgies for victory. But at Wadi al Khaznadar, near Hama, the Mongols defeated the Muslim army . . . The Damascenes were frightened; Ghazan was approaching their city.

ISMAIL IBN KATHIR, *Al bidaya wa al nihaya* (Eng. trans. Nicola Ziadeh)

THE series of incidents from the murder of Khalil to the fall of Kitbugha illustrates the extraordinary violence and jealousy of the Mamluke ameers. Kitbugha killed Baidara, professedly out of loyalty to the family of Qalaoon, but as soon as he himself was firmly established, he deposed Muhammad, the son of Qalaoon, and made himself sultan.

When two ameers, Sanjar al Shujai and Kitbugha, were left in a dominating position, the latter killed the former. When, six months later, Lajeen emerged from hiding, it was Kitbugha who pardoned him and made him Viceroy of Egypt. But now Lajeen had tried to kill Kitbugha and to make himself sultan.

We may also contrast the wisdom of Qalaoon with the foolishness of Kitbugha. For when Qalaoon obtained the original letters of Sonkor al Ashqar to the Mongols, he burned them and said nothing. But later on, when the situation was more stable, he arrested Sonkor. Kitbugha, apparently on the basis of forged letters attributed to Baisari, had immediately sent for the latter and abused him harshly in the presence of other ameers.

- -

AL-MALIK-AL-MANSOOR LAJEEN AL MANSOORI

- -

When Lajeen came to Egypt, he had been a mamluke of Malik-al-Mansoor Ali, the son of Aibek. When the boy sultan was deposed by Qutuz, Lajeen was bought by Qalaoon, then an ameer. He was nicknamed "red-head", suggesting that his racial origin was mixed, for the Central Asian Turks were dark. He became a page to Qalaoon, and was called little or young Lajeen, presumably to distinguish him from some old Lajeen, for the name was not uncommon.

As an ameer and later as Viceroy of Damascus under Qalaoon, Lajeen had proved to be an ideal governor, for he earned the affection of the public and abstained from greed and extortion. Perhaps Khalil had ordered that he be strangled simply because he disliked the men whom his father had trusted. When the bowstring broke, Lajeen was pardoned, but he continued to feel insecure.

*   *   *

Lajeen now sat in the sultan's chair in the camp at Al Auja. The following evening, the ameers went to Lajeen in a body and offered to swear loyalty to him as sultan, but on certain conditions. Firstly, they asked that, as sultan, he would continue to consult them as equals—presumably Kitbugha had not done so. Secondly, they insisted that he would not delegate power to his personal mamlukes. They were particularly afraid of one of these called Mangu Timur, who enjoyed great influence over his master. Lajeen swore to these terms, whereupon the ameers gave their oaths of loyalty to him.

The sultan issued a decree, remitting all arrears of taxation and, on 8th December, 1296, rode in state through Cairo and took up his residence in the Citadel. The day of the arrival of the new sultan in Cairo, the price of food dropped to one-half, and prosperity and security were believed to be returning. The Ameer Kara Sonkor Al Mansoori was made Viceroy of Egypt and Kanjak al Mansoori Viceroy of Damascus.[1] Officials were strictly ordered not to extort money by illegal means. The public implored the blessing of God on their new and popular sultan.

Meanwhile, Kitbugha had arrived in Damascus and mounted to the Citadel, where the ameers and notables visited him and re-newed their oaths of allegiance. A few days later, the accession of Lajeen in Cairo became known in Damascus. Soon afterwards, messengers from Egypt contacted most of the ameers in Syria and secured their adherence to the new régime. Kitbugha found himself deserted. Then orders came, appointing him governor of Salkhad.[2] Kitbugha declared himself satisfied, swore loyalty to Lajeen and proceeded to his new post. His family joined him at Salkhad.

Lajeen released a number of ameers from prison and gave them robes of honour, including Baybars the Jashnekeer, of whom we shall hear more. He also promoted several of his private mamlukes to be ameers, including that Mangu Timur against whom the other ameers had warned him.

Every ameer, as we have seen, had between ten and a hundred private mamlukes of his own. Once freed, at the age of perhaps seventeen or eighteen, they considered themselves socially his equals. The senior men among them shared his meals and his councils. No mamluke would do menial work, such as clean out the stables or groom the horses, tasks which were performed by servants.

When an ameer became sultan, the position of his private mam-lukes became delicate. They had been the new sultan's companions

---

[1] These ameers had been mamlukes of Malik-al-Mansoor Qalaoon and barrack-comrades of Lajeen.
[2] Map 17, page 109.

and confidants, but they were not ameers. The existing senior ameers had many years of service, had commanded armies or governed provinces. They were afraid that the sultan might promote his own private mamlukes over their heads.

Kitbugha's fall had pointed the lesson, for his private mamlukes, whom he trusted, had forged a letter incriminating a senior ameer. It was with this affair in mind that the ameers heard with misgiving that Lajeen had promoted his mamluke, Mangu Timur, to be an ameer.

Meanwhile, however, Lajeen was behaving with generosity and tolerance and was gaining a reputation for piety. It will be remembered that, after the murder of Khalil, he had disappeared for six months. It now transpired that he had hidden in the ruined minaret of the mosque of Ibn Tulun, which is still to be seen in Cairo. Lajeen now gave twenty thousand gold dinars[3] to repair the mosque and to establish pious foundations to maintain religious schools.

The Khalif Hakim, who had been appointed by Baybars, had been under virtual house arrest in the Citadel for many years. He was now allowed to move to a house in the city and given a handsome allowance for expenses.

But the sultan's honeymoon with his subjects soon came to an end. The Ameer Kara Sonkor, Viceroy of Egypt, was imprisoned. His Egyptian secretary, Sharf-al-Deen Yaqoub, was flogged to death. It was rumoured that Lajeen proposed to make his mamluke, Mangu Timur, Viceroy of Egypt, over the heads of all the ameers. This was just what they had feared. They now waited on the sultan to remind him of his oath.

Lajeen was annoyed and began posting those who had protested to distant outposts. Then the announcement of Mangu Timur's promotion as viceroy was published. All the time, Lajeen continued to increase his reputation for sanctity. He forbade the wearing of expensive clothes or gold embroidery, and the court adopted simple and cheap forms of dress.

The sultan sat twice a week in the Hall of Justice to redress grievances, as the Arab Khalifs had been wont to do in their great days. He disapproved of gambling. Whereas Islam prescribed one month a year for fasting, Lajeen fasted for two, Shaaban and Ramadhan.

One day the sultan broke a bone and several ribs and dislocated an ankle in a polo accident, and was obliged to remain in his room for two months. On 9th December, 1297, he rode through the city

---

[3] A dinar may be very roughly assumed to have been worth £1 or $2.50 (1972).

once more, the drums were beaten, Cairo and Fustat were splendidly decorated and great public rejoicing took place. Large sums were paid for seats in houses on the route of the procession, and shopkeepers charged money to allow spectators to sit in their shops and watch their beloved sultan ride by. "There was great public rejoicing," explains Maqrizi, "for he was much loved by the people."

The spontaneous love of the Egyptians for Lajeen is to be noted. With our modern ways of thought, we must not assume that the people of Egypt hated the Turks, as they called them, as foreigners. Mamluke rule was well integrated into the Egyptian scene. Some sultans were loved and some hated—not for their nationality—but for their personal qualities.

Also in December 1297, Lajeen held an interview with Malik-al-Nasir Muhammad, the son of Qalaoon. The boy-sultan deposed by Kitbugha had been living for some three years with his mother in an apartment in the Citadel and was now thirteen years old. Lajeen told the boy that he had been the mamluke of his father, Qalaoon, and that he was only occupying the throne until Muhammad was old enough to reign. Meanwhile, however, he said, it would be better for Muhammad to move to Kerak, where he could lead a free and healthy life. The two swore mutual loyalty and the boy-sultan rode away to Kerak.

A few days later, the Ameer Baisari was arrested. He had been the first to recognise Lajeen as sultan and the two had remained close friends. When the sultan was ill after his polo accident, Mangu Timur was afraid that he might die. He consequently sent some of his friends to Lajeen to suggest that he should nominate Mangu Timur as heir to the throne.

Soon afterwards, the Ameer Baisari came to visit the sick sultan, who consulted him on the advisability of making Mangu Timur heir to the sultanate. But Baisari replied, "Mangu Timur is not fit to be a private soldier but you have made him Viceroy of Egypt. Have you forgotten that you swore not to promote your personal mamlukes above the senior ameers?" No sooner had Baisari left, than the sultan told Mangu Timur all that he had said. The latter accordingly bribed certain persons to tell Lajeen that Baisari was plotting to kill him. He also won over a favourite mamluke of Baisari, called Arslan, promising to make him an ameer of drums.

One day Baisari invited the sultan to a banquet on the Nile. Mangu Timur told Arslan to warn Lajeen that Baisari intended treachery at the banquet. Soon afterwards Baisari dined with the sultan one evening. As he left the palace, he was arrested and imprisoned. He was given a comfortable apartment, where his wife joined him, but he remained in prison till his death. The remarkable part about this affair was that Lajeen and Baisari had been lifelong friends and that both of them were betrayed by their favourite mamlukes.

Shortly afterwards, the sultan consulted an Egyptian qadhi regarding the grant of further powers to Mangu Timur. The judge replied, "Mangu Timur is a proud young man, who will not listen to advice. His further advancement would cause trouble." Lajeen reported the qadhi's remarks to Mangu Timur, who soon found a pretext to imprison him and to confiscate his property.

In February 1298, an army was sent to Syria to invade Armenian Cilicia once again. The southern part of the kingdom was laid waste, though the king begged for peace.

*　　*　　*

The lands of Egypt had hitherto been divided under the Mamlukes into twenty-four portions. Of these, four had been the property of the sultan, ten were used as fiefs for ameers and ten as fiefs for the *halaqa*.[4] It does appear that any land was owned by Egyptian cultivators. Many Egyptians were extremely rich, but these were city merchants or government officials.

Lajeen decided to reduce the twenty shares allotted to the ameers and the *halaqa* to eleven. A survey was carried out in order to effect this large-scale redistribution of land. The ostensible reason for the changes in land allotment was to save nine portions out of the twenty-four and use them to raise more troops. When, however, the new land registry lists were published, many areas were found to have been registered under the personal name of Mangu Timur. This may, indeed, have been the object of the operation.

On 23rd April, 1298, new title deeds were distributed to the ameers by the sultan, who noticed the discontent they showed at the drastic reduction of their fiefs. Mangu Timur handed out the new deeds to the *halaqa*, who, as we have seen, were a kind of army reserve. Many refused to accept their deeds and announced their intention of resigning from the service. Mangu Timur angrily ordered that those who complained be flogged or imprisoned.

A wealthy merchant having died, leaving his property by will, Mangu Timur sent for the judge before whom the will would be proven and told him to disallow it. The Egyptian judge refused to take orders and a struggle ensued, the case ultimately reaching the sultan, who summoned the qadhi to the palace and thanked him for

[4] Page 135.

his constancy. The quiet courage of the judge in refusing to give an illegal decision earned the admiration of many ameers. The qadhi left his cloak in the palace, where the ameers tore it into strips, which they took home as holy relics. This incident gives yet another insight into the Mamluke mentality.

In October 1298, Mangu Timur sent agents to Syria to arrest a number of leading ameers, wishing to appoint more of Lajeen's personal mamlukes in their places. The ameers, however, heard of the plot and deserted to the Mongol ruler, the Il-Khan Ghazan. The explanation of this grossly corrupt government under so pious and popular a sultan seems to have been that Lajeen was now virtually a religious recluse, while Mangu Timur acted as if he were sultan.

One day in December 1298, Lajeen had fasted all day. It was not a set fast-day, but he now frequently performed extra fasts. At sunset, he broke his fast, and sat down to play chess with the chief qadhi. A number of ameers had meanwhile agreed to kill the sultan and Mangu Timur, not that they disliked Lajeen but because he left everything to the former.

The Ameer Kurji entered the sultan's room as he often did, having posted his accomplices in the corridors. Soon the duty officer for that night, the Ameer Nougai Karmouni, entered the room. "Is our lord the sultan going to say the evening prayer?" asked Kurji.[5] The sultan said he would do so and rose from the chess table, having previously taken off his sword. Nougai quietly moved the sword away out of reach. Thereupon Kurji drew his sword and struck Lajeen on the shoulder. The sultan put out his hand for his sword but, not finding it, threw himself on Kurji and brought him to the ground. Nougai, however, struck Lajeen with his sword, causing him to collapse. The other conspirators then burst into the room and Lajeen was hacked to pieces.

News of the murder reached the city, where men with lighted torches crowded into the streets. Mangu Timur allowed himself to be persuaded to go up to the Citadel where he was quickly seized and killed.

Maqrizi describes Mangu Timur as zealous for the empire and hard-working. He inspired respect and never used abusive or coarse language. But he was somewhat irresponsible and extremely arrogant. The ameers liked Lajeen but loathed Mangu Timur.

Lajeen had reigned for two years and was fifty years old. He had reddish hair and blue eyes, and was a tall, imposing figure. Brave, pious, intelligent and just, he was much given to good works. He also considerably reduced taxation. He liked the people, talked amicably

---

[5] Muslims, of course, pray five times a day.

with them, and was much loved. His only real defect was his sub-
missiveness to Mangu Timur.

The night of the murder, the ameers assembled to choose a successor. Some advocated the recall of the boy, Malik-al-Nasir
Muhammad, and the appointment of the Ameer Taghji, who had
planned the assassination, as regent. The Ameer Kurji, who had
actually killed Lajeen, demanded Taghji as sultan and himself as
viceroy. The meeting broke up without a decision.

Shortly afterwards, the army returning from Cilicia reached
Bilbeis. It was led by the Ameer Bektash al Fakhri, the commander-
in-chief, an old man with many years of honourable service, who had
never taken part in power-struggles or intrigues. A simple soldier, he
was devoted to duty, not to private ambition.

The ameers adjourned their discussions and rode out to meet
Bektash. The Ameer Taghji, aspiring to be sultan, rode in front.
When Bektash heard that Taghji had arranged the sultan's murder,
he gave a roar of anger. A staff officer rode at Taghji and split his
head open with his sword. Kurji, the actual killer, was also struck
down.

On reaching Cairo, Bektash rode to his house, refusing to join in
the frenzied intrigues of the ameers for the choice of a sultan. Two
other candidates now came forward. The Ameer Salár, who was
supported by the Salihis and Mansooris (old mamlukes of Al-Salih
Ayoub and Al-Mansoor Qalaoon), and Baybars the Jashnekeer,
favoured by the Burji Mamlukes.

Finally, to avoid civil strife, it was agreed to recall the young
Malik-al-Nasir Muhammad from Kerak. Meanwhile, the senior
ameers in council governed the empire.

MALIK-AL-NASIR MUHAMMAD
(Second Reign)

Messengers from the ameers had meanwhile reached Kerak and the
young Malik-al-Nasir Muhammad had set out for Cairo. So intense
was the public joy that the whole population of the city turned out to
welcome him. Although the Mamlukes were "foreigners", the
Egyptian public took a passionate interest in their rulers. The
thirteen-year-old sultan entered Cairo amid wild enthusiasm. The
city was splendidly decorated and the bands played.

Seated in the Hall of Audience, the boy-sultan received the oaths
of loyalty of the ameers and notables. The Ameer Salar, a Mongol,
was made regent, the Ameer Aqoosh al Afram became Viceroy of

Damascus, and Baybars the Jashnekeer occupied an important position at court. Salar and Baybars issued orders as if both were sultans, for Malik-al-Nasir, being a minor, had no executive power.

* * *

It will be remembered that a group of senior ameers in Syria had heard that Mangu Timur was about to have them all arrested, in order to promote his own friends. As a result, the Ameer Qipchaq, the Viceroy of Damascus, and several others had deserted to the Mongols. As soon as Lajeen and Mangu Timur were murdered, messages were sent post-haste to tell the deserters. When the letters reached them, however, they were already guests of the Mongol governor of Mardin (pronounced Mardeen) and were unable to return.[6]

The Mamluke ameers were obliged to proceed to the camp of Il-Khan Ghazan near Tabriz, where they were received with well-nigh royal honours and loaded with many gifts. A month later, in March 1299, reports reached Cairo that Ghazan was about to invade Syria. The Ameer Aqoosh, nicknamed the Lion-Killer, was sent with a column of troops from Cairo to Damascus.

On the Mongol side, however, the Il-Khan's governor of Asia Minor, Salamish Afal, had allied himself with the Qaraman ameers to rebel.[7] Defeated by the Il-Khan's army, he arrived a fugitive in Cairo. The Mamlukes assisted him to return to Asia Minor, while another column took Mardin, which belonged to Ghazan. The Mamlukes and the Mongols were drifting into war.

Soon detailed reports were to hand regarding Ghazan's plans to invade Syria. Orders were given in Cairo for mobilisation, with the result that the prices of horses, camels, weapons and supplies rose rapidly. The Mamlukes were obliged to supply their own horses and equipment, with the result that prices soared before a campaign. The troops asked for a money grant to buy their necessaries, but Baybars and Salar refused.

Morale was lowered by the constant jealousy of the two ameers, though both were agreed to deny all power to Malik-al-Nasir, who was now fifteen and wished to discuss public affairs. They allowed the young sultan very little money, to prevent his acquiring any influence.

On 22nd September, 1299, the army left Cairo for Damascus, with the two ameers and the sultan. At Gaza, the column halted to rest. It will be remembered that the Uwairat Mongols had come over to

[6] Maps 13 and 22, page 66 and opposite.   [7] Map 17, page 109.

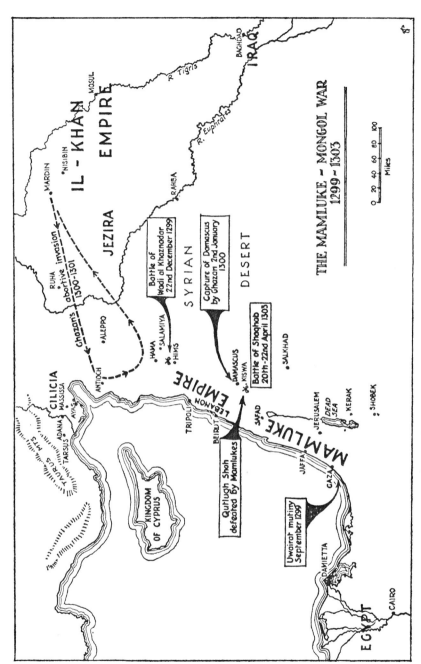

THE MAMLUKE – MONGOL WAR
1299 – 1303

Miles
0 20 40 60 80 100

IL – KHAN EMPIRE

MOSUL

R. Tigris

BAGHDAD

IRAQ

MARDIN

•NISIBIN

Ghazan's abortive invasion 1300-1301

JEZIRA

RUHA•

R. Euphrates

RAHBA•

SYRIAN DESERT

ALEPPO•

ANTIOCH•

CILICIA

MASSISA•

ADANA•
TARSUS•
AYAS•

TAURUS MTS.

KINGDOM
OF CYPRUS

HAMA•
•SALAMIYA
•HIMS

Battle of
Wadi al Khaznadar
22nd December 1299

Capture of Damascus
by Ghazan 2nd January
1300

DAMASCUS•
•KISWA

Battle of Shaqhab
20th–22nd April 1303

•SALKHAD

•KERAK

•SHOBEK

TRIPOLI•

BEIRUT•

Quhlugh Shah
defeated by Mamlukes

LEBANON

EMPIRE

MAMLUKE

SAFAD•

JERUSALEM•

DEAD
SEA

JAFFA•

GAZA•

Uwairat mutiny
September 1299

DAMIETTA•

EGYPT

CAIRO•

MAP 22

the Mamlukes in the reign of Kitbugha, himself a Mongol. They had resented the deposition of Kitbugha, with the result that Lajeen had imprisoned their leaders. They now decided to kill Salar and Baybars, and to replace Kitbugha on the throne, for he was still governor of Salkhad.

In camp near Gaza, one of the Uwairat attacked Baybars, killed his horse and wounded him, but was forthwith killed himself. Immediately all was in confusion. The Uwairat attacked the sultan's tents, but his mamlukes mounted and unfurled his war-banner. Everyone armed and mounted, but no one knew what had happened. Some ameers thought that the sultan might have planned to kill Salar and Baybars, and himself to assume power. They sent to ask his orders but the boy sultan burst into tears and said he did not know what was happening.

Some ameers sent to ask orders from the old Ameer Bektash, the commander-in-chief, who was some miles ahead with the advanced guard. The Burji Mamlukes, who supported Baybars, tried to blame Salar. Finally the Uwairat were put to the torture and confessed their intention to restore Kitbugha. Fifty Uwairat were strangled on the spot. After four days of chaos, the army marched on, but spirits were low.

A few days later, a cloudburst deluged the bivouac at night. Horses, camels, baggage and rations were swept away in the floods. Many soldiers lost all their equipment. Shortly afterwards, clouds of locusts filled the air. The morale of the army fell to zero, everybody foretelling a disastrous campaign.

The sultan entered Damascus on 28th November, 1299. On 5th December, crowds of terrified fugitives arrived from Aleppo. Ghazan had reached the Euphrates. Everyone in Damascus spoke of the impending defeat of the Mamluke army. A gratuity of thirty to forty dinars was paid to every soldier to raise morale.

On 15th December, 1299, the sultan at the head of the army left for Hims. Arab scouts located the Tatar army near Salamiya.[8] The Mamluke army rested three days near Hims, but all ranks were plunged in gloom. On 22nd or 23rd December, 1299, the boy sultan led the army forward on horseback until, at ten o'clock in the morning, the Mongol outposts were sighted. For some reason unexplained, the Mamlukes were ordered to drop their lances, and to use only swords or maces. Advancing for a further quarter of an hour, they formed line of battle at a place called Majma al Murooj, the meeting of pastures. Later on, the same place became known as Wadi al Khaznadar, the Treasurer's Valley.

[8] Map 22, page 177.

Maqrizi claims that the Mamlukes had only twenty thousand men, while the Mongols were a hundred thousand strong. Such figures are completely unreliable. On the Mamluke right flank were the bedouins and the contingents of Aleppo and Hama. On the left was the old campaigner, the Ameer Bektash, recently commander in Cilicia, and with him Aqoosh, the "Lion-Killer". The Ameer Salar, the Regent, was in the centre, and commanded the whole army. The young sultan was sent to a place of safety in the rear. Baybars the Jashnekeer was taken ill before the battle and was carried from the field in a litter.

The Ameer Salar, with a number of religious leaders, rode down the ranks encouraging the troops, some of whom were moved to tears by the religious appeals of the shaikhs. Five hundred Mamlukes who had been specially trained as artificers took post in front of the army. Ghazan had ordered his men to stand fast on the defensive until he himself led the decisive counter-attack.

The artificers, armed with naphtha, now lit their weapons and charged the enemy on horseback. Naphtha was the original "Greek fire" first used by the Byzantines, and then copied by the Arabs and now by the Mamlukes. Our historians do not explain how it was used on horseback. On the present occasion, the liquid fire attack was a fiasco, the flames going harmlessly out.

Ghazan is then alleged to have brought forward ten thousand archers on foot, who poured a stream of arrows into the Mamlukes, killing especially great numbers of horses. (English readers may be interested to note that, in 1346, some fifty years later the French were defeated at Crécy in a similar manner by the steady and continuous shooting of the English long-bows.)

The tactics employed in this battle seem to be peculiar, for both Mongols and Mamlukes were essentially horsemen. Both sides seem to have tried new weapons, the Mamlukes liquid fire, the Mongols foot-archers. The brunt of the arrows discharged by the foot-archers seems to have fallen upon the bedouins, and the contingents of Aleppo and Hama, on the Mamluke right. These lost so many horses that they fell back in confusion. Meanwhile, however, the Mamluke left, commanded by old Bektásh, had broken the Mongol right and pursued them off the field. It is alleged that Ghazan was about to order a retreat when the Ameer Qipchaq, the Mamluke deserter, encouraged him to fight on.

Deciding on a final effort, Ghazan himself led an impetuous charge against the Mamluke centre. Salar and the Tower Mamlukes took to flight with the Mongols close on their heels. The young sultan, seeing the débâcle, burst into tears, crying out, "O Lord! let me not be a means of bringing disaster on the Muslims." The fugitives swept past him, leaving him with only twelve mamlukes as his escort. By sunset the fleeing rabble were streaming past Hims.

Ghazan, fearing to lose control of his army in the dark, halted the pursuit. His action, opines Maqrizi, was an Act of God, for if the pursuit had continued not a Muslim soldier would have been left alive. The Mamlukes were always famous for their fiery attacks, but in retreat their discipline was not strong enough to make it possible to rally them.

On 26th December, 1299, the fugitives reached Damascus, but scarcely had they entered the city than the cry was raised that the Mongols were coming. The soldiers, throwing away their arms, equipment and baggage, continued their flight down the coastal plain of Palestine. The people of Damascus, catching the infection of panic, scattered wildly over the open country or headed for the mountains west of the city. The tribes and the country people robbed the terrified soldiers and city dwellers as they fled.

The Mamlukes and the Mongols both consisted of tribes born on the steppes, living on horseback, exposed to extremes of heat and cold. Yet in some ways, they were utterly different. The family of Jenghis Khan—the Golden Family—ruled with absolute authority the wild horsemen of the steppes. Among the Mamlukes, there were no leading families. They were no respecters of persons and spent much of their lives fighting one another. It was these internal hatreds which had undermined Mamluke morale at the battle. Where resistance to authority is preached in peace time, under the guise of freedom, military discipline in times of crisis is difficult to maintain.

*   *   *

Ghazan seized all the Mamluke base stores and treasure, which had been deposited in Hims. He had shown himself a capable commander, who had held his troops well in hand until he gave the order for the counter-attack. The use of foot-archers seems to have been original for Mongols. Mamlukes and Mongols normally used short bows from horseback. Salar, by contrast, showed very poorly in the battle, being perhaps rather a politician than a soldier. But the morale of the Mamlukes had already been lowered by the mutual intrigues of Salar and Baybars the Jashnekeer.

On the morning of 27th December, 1299, a terrible panic swept Damascus, men and women abandoning their homes and their shops and fighting like wild cats to get out of the city gates. The prison wardens having fled, the convicts broke out and began to loot.

On the morning of 29th December, such men as were left chose two religious leaders to go out to meet the Il-Khan Ghazan. They were the Chief Qadhi, Muhammad ibn Jumaa, and the Shaikh al Islam, Ahmad ibn Taimiya, who met Ghazan at Nebk, forty-five miles north of Damascus. The Il-Khan reined in his mare and the Syrians hastily dismounted and kissed the gound, begging for an amnesty for the city. "I have already sent such an order as you wish," replied Ghazan, and rode on.

In fact, a missive had already been sent by the hand of a Tatar officer, escorted by a troop of cavalry. After many claims to be the servant of the Most High God, Ghazan had announced that he came only to drive out the Mamlukes, whose crimes had desecrated the country. No soldier of his, he said, would commit any crime against man or woman. All religions would be respected.

When Ghazan reached Damascus, he camped outside the walls, together with the Ameer Qipchaq, the former Mamluke viceroy of the city. The Mongol troops, however, continued southwards to Jerusalem and Kerak, killing and looting as they went. The Mamluke commander of the Citadel, Sanjar al Mansoori, commonly called Arjuwash, closed the gates and refused to surrender. Even Qipchaq could not persuade him. A decree appointing the Ameer Qipchaq governor of all Syria under Ghazan was read out from the roof of the great mosque, after which handfuls of gold and silver were scattered over the crowd.

On 11th January, 1300, however, the Tatars began to plunder Salihiya, the northern suburb of the city, later extending their depredations to Mezza, south of the city. They stripped the mosques and colleges of lamps and carpets and then set fire to the buildings. The Mamlukes had often carried fire and sword through the Armenian Christian Kingdom of Cilicia and some at least of the plundering of Damascus was due to the Armenians. It was alleged that nine thousand nine hundred persons in Damascus were killed or driven off as slaves.

Ibn Taimiya went to Ghazan's camp to protest, but could not see the Khan, who was drunk. The wazeer, however, suggested a large cash payment to the Mongol treasury as a simple way to settle the difficulty. The great Umaiyid mosque had been turned into a place of ill repute, where women were brought in for the amusement of the drunken Tatars.

Siege engines were erected to bombard the citadel, but the indomitable Arjuwash sent raiders out from the citadel, who destroyed the mangonels and killed the engineers who had erected them.

[9] The text is in Nuwairi, *Nihaya al Arab.*

Ghazan's amnesty was wearing thinner and thinner. The Mongols were demanding more and more money, and passing soldiers seized men in the streets and flogged and tortured them. In the suburbs and the rural areas, looting and massacre ran wild. Maqrizi alleges that about one hundred thousand persons were killed in the country altogether. Eventually three million six hundred thousand dirhems were paid by the city, the equivalent of some hundred and eighty thousand gold dinars. More than twenty thousand pack animals, horses and camels, were also commandeered.

After a stay of just over a month, Ghazan marched away with his army on 5th February, 1300, and re-crossed the Euphrates. His Mongol cousins and rivals, the descendants of Jagatai, had invaded his empire from the east and had occupied Khurasan.[10] Once again the internal jealousies of the descendants of Jenghis Khan had saved Syria from the utter destruction which was everywhere the result of Mongol rule.

Ghazan had left Qipchaq, the Mamluke deserter, as Governor of Syria. Bektimur, who had deserted with Qipchaq, was made Governor of Aleppo. These two renegade Mamlukes had some twenty-four thousand Mongol troops under their command. Some Tatar units had already reached Gaza when they were recalled. They now withdrew slowly northwards until Qipchaq had concentrated the great majority of them in the Aleppo area.

The situation slowly settled down in Damascus, and a few shops began to open. Indignation, however, was aroused when Qipchaq farmed out to an Armenian woman for four million dirhems the right publicly to sell wine in the city. The amount of the contract, equivalent to two hundred thousand gold dinars, seems to indicate that there were many wine drinkers in Damascus.

NOTABLE DATES

Assassination of Khalil	December, 1293
Deposition of Malik-al-Nasir ⎫ Elevation of Kitbugha ⎭	2nd December, 1294
Deposition of Kitbugha	26th November, 1296
Elevation of Lajeen in Cairo	8th December, 1296
Lajeen's revised distribution of fiefs	23rd April, 1298
Desertion of Qipchaq and other ameers to the Mongols	October, 1298

[10] Map 9, page 52.

Assassination of Lajeen ⎫
Elevation of Malik-al-Nasir ⎬ December, 1298
  (Second Reign) ⎭
Battle of Wadi al Khaznadar   22nd December, 1299
Occupation of Damascus by
  Il-Khan Ghazan   2nd January, 1300
Retirement of Ghazan from Syria ⎫
Qipchaq left as Governor   ⎬ 5th February, 1300

PERSONALITIES

Mamlukes
Sultan Khalil ibn Qalaoon
Sultan Malik-al-Nasir Muhammad ibn Qalaoon
Sultan Malik-al-Aadil Kitbugha
Sultan Malik-al-Mansoor Lajeen
Regent Salar
Ameer Baybars al Jashnekeer
Ameer Qipchaq, Viceroy of Damascus, deserter to the Mongols

Mongols
Il-Khan Kaikhatu   1291–1295
Il-Khan Ghazan   1295–1304

IX

Defeat into Victory

The Moghuls (Mongols) spread beyond the Tigris and Euphrates, pillaged Aleppo and Damascus . . . But the Mamlukes had breathed in their infancy the keenness of a Scythian air; equal in valour . . . they met the Moghuls in many a well-fought field; and drove back the stream of hostility to the eastwards of the Euphrates.

EDWARD GIBBON, *Decline and Fall of the Roman Empire*

The saddest of all kings
Crown'd and again disowned.

L. P. JOHNSON

S O hysterical had been the panic which swept the army after the Battle of Wadi al Khaznadar that the young sultan found himself virtually alone, and made his way back to Egypt with only a handful of companions. He re-entered the Citadel of Cairo on 7th January, 1300. Day by day, the exhausted soldiers straggled in, by ones and twos, in a lamentable condition, among them the former sultan, Kitbugha.

The ameers set themselves immediately to repair the catastrophe. All over Egypt, armourers were commissioned to make swords and lances. The price of horses trebled, and even the poor horses which turned the Nile water-wheels were impressed as chargers. Many ameers raised military units at their own expense. A capital levy was imposed on the merchants and notables and new taxes were demanded.

When news reached Cairo that Ghazan had left Syria, the young sultan, Al-Nasir Muhammad, wrote to Qipchaq, Bektimur and the other ameer deserters, calling upon them to submit. They readily complied and, abandoning their posts under the Mongols, set out for Egypt. Seeing that the tide was turning against them, the remaining Mongols in Damascus joined the main body in Aleppo. The gallant Arjuwash, who had held the Citadel of Damascus against the Mongol army for a hundred days, assumed control of the city. The wineshops were closed, the great mosque was cleaned out and hope revived.

On 31st March, 1300, the sultan left Cairo, preceded by the Ameers Salar and Baybars the Jashnekeer and with the army. North of Gaza, they met Qipchaq, Bektimur and the other ameers who had been with the Mongols. Both sides dismounted and embraced one another weeping. This tearful scene would have been more affecting if Qipchaq had not been the man who had persuaded Ghazan to invade Syria. On 2nd May, 1300, the leading troops from Egypt entered Damascus. Prominent among the commanders was old Bektash, who had routed the Mongol right wing at Wadi al Khaznadar.

A column sent on ahead surprised the Mongol garrison of Aleppo. As many of the enemy as were caught were killed in cold blood, while the remainder re-crossed the Euphrates. When Salar re-entered Damascus, persons who had collaborated with the Mongols suffered a savage retribution, some being strangled and others tortured. Local tribes which had plundered the fugitives were made to return the loot. A month later, all being quiet, Salar and Baybars returned to Cairo. Qipchaq was made governor of Shobek, a small town south of Kerak.[1]

The Druzes of Lebanon had been active in plundering the fugitives after the Battle of Wadi al Khaznadar, and a punitive column was now sent against them. But they are alleged to have had twelve thousand archers, who, for six days, repulsed the mounted Mamlukes in the precipitous mountains. The Druzes were a sect which practised a secret religion in the Lebanese mountains, and who are still numerous in Syria and Lebanon. Eventually peace was concluded and the Druzes returned a part of the loot.

*   *   *

In September 1300, reports were received that Ghazan was returning to Syria. Preparations were made for another campaign, and more money was extorted from the public, many of whom began to show signs of resentment. People taunted the soldiers saying, "Yesterday you ran away from the enemy, now you want to rob us. You are brave enough against civilians, but your courage fails against the Mongols."

In Syria, the same procedures were followed. Householders were charged additional taxes and farmers found their crops seized. These drastic measures ruined the country, coming on top of the looting and massacres committed by the Mongols.

In Cairo, artisans were enrolled to make lances, swords and armour. The *halaqa* was called to arms.[2] On 29th October, 1300, the young sultan and the army left for Syria, suffering great hardships in their march up the coastal plain, owing to torrential rains which fell without respite for forty-one days. The troops were constantly soaked to the skin, the country was flooded, transport was bogged down and ration convoys were stuck, leaving the troops without food.

Ghazan had crossed the Euphrates and marched to Antioch, the whole population fleeing before him. His transport animals died like flies and no forage was obtainable. The Il-Khan turned south-east from Antioch towards Hama,[3] driving before him great numbers of people and immense herds of looted animals. He was believed to be marching on Damascus.

But God, says the good Maqrizi, sent His rain and snow in

[1] Map 22, page 177.   [2] Page 135.   [3] Map 22, page 177.

quantities never before seen. Ghazan was said to have lost ten thousand horses, and a great part of his cavalry was on foot. Some were riding pillion behind their companions. Eventually he abandoned the campaign and recrossed the Euphrates on 23rd January, 1301. Two thousand Mamluke cavalry were sent to the north to raise the public confidence and persuade people to return to their homes. Syria was almost depopulated while Egypt swarmed with destitute refugees.

*   *   *

In the year 1301, "the wazeer of the King of the Maghrib" visited Cairo on his way to the pilgrimage of Mecca. The King of the Maghrib was presumably the Beni Merin ruler of Morocco. Ever since the rise of Islam in the seventh century, large communities of Christians had remained, living peaceably among the Muslims, in Egypt, Palestine and Syria. In Morocco, however, Christianity had almost disappeared.

The Moroccan wazeer was horrified at the wealth of the Christians in Cairo. "How do you expect to defeat the Mongols," he indignantly asked Salar and Baybars, "while among you Christians live in luxury and even employ Muslim servants?" The wazeer wept copiously at seeing this lamentable situation. Persecution of Jews and Christians had never been the policy of Egypt or Syria. The Mamlukes prided themselves on being soldiers and left commerce and much of the civil service to Christians, who often became rich.

Salar and Baybars,[4] were put to shame by the Moroccan. They summoned a meeting of qadhis and decreed that Jews must wear yellow turbans and Christians blue. Members of both religions were to ride donkeys, not horses. Christians, many of whom held high administrative posts, were not to be employed in the sultan's offices or on the staffs of ameers, but apparently retained junior government posts. A few Christians in the highest positions adopted Islam rather than lose their appointments and social status, but the remainder bowed to the new rules.

Encouraged by the new attitude of the authorities, the mob wrecked a number of churches and synagogues. The ameers called a meeting of qadhis and religious teachers to consult them on the legal aspects of these incidents. The majority ruled that newly erected churches and synagogues could be demolished, but that long established religious buildings should not be damaged. Orders were sent to Syria for the changes in the colours of turbans, but there is no

---

[4] Salar was by origin a Mongol, Baybars a Circassian.

mention of destruction of churches. In Egypt, all churches were closed for a year, but then were gradually allowed to re-open. The Byzantine Emperor and other Christians monarchs also made representations.

In Europe, such acts of intolerance had been practised periodically by Jews and Christians against one another. The narrow intolerance of man for man is almost incredible, as much today as seven centuries ago.

*   *   *

The preoccupation of the government with the Mongol war had resulted in the neglect of the administration of the southern provinces, where taxes were in arrears and breaches of the peace had occurred. A column was sent to "restore order", which it did by killing a great number of people and driving off immense flocks of horses, sheep and camels. "By this means," according to Maqrizi, "the evil in these provinces was quieted." The means of livelihood of the inhabitants had also, incidentally, been destroyed.

The brutality used by the Mamlukes towards their rural and tribal subjects was to be one of the causes of their ultimate collapse, although they behaved well on the whole to the city populations. Their ruthless repression of the country people was, unfortunately, imitated by the Ottomans and, in some places, survives to the present day.

In the summer of 1301, a deputation arrived from the Il-Khan Ghazan, boasting of his victories, expressing contempt for the sultan and his army, but also suggesting peace. The Mongol ambassadors were received by the sultan in the palace on 24th August, 1301. The event took place at night in the light of a thousand torches. The ameers and mamlukes were dressed in their most splendid uniforms, glittering with cloth of gold. A reply was returned to Ghazan in the same style as his own missive, half threats and half hopes of peace.

In 1302, the Khalif Hákim died. He had held the position for forty years, deprived of all power but occasionally produced to pronounce a blessing on state occasions. He was succeeded by his son.

In 1302, the tribes of southern Egypt rebelled in spite of—or perhaps because of—the severe treatment they had received the year before. The whole army marched to the south, led by both Salar and Baybars. All ranks received orders to kill every man and child without pity. The women were carried off. Some sixteen thousand men are said to have been disembowelled. Everyone was killed as far south as the borders of Nubia, and the whole country stank of corpses.

The booty included eighty thousand sheep, thirty-two thousand camels, eight thousand head of cattle and four thousand horses, not to mention immense sums in cash.

The army began its withdrawal on 18th March, 1302, leaving behind it an empty land. The Mamlukes had made a desert and they called it peace.

* * *

But once again a despatch from Aleppo announced that the Mongols were preparing to invade Syria. Mobilisation was ordered yet again, and columns of troops set out for the north. The people of Aleppo and Hama once more wearily abandoned their homes and plodded southwards towards Damascus. Ghazan accompanied his troops to the Euphrates, but turned back from there, sending the army on under command of Qutlugh Shah. He advanced by forced marches, hoping to occupy all Syria before the main Mamluke army could arrive from Egypt.

The Mongol army reached Hama on 3rd April, 1303. Meanwhile, the sultan and the main Mamluke army had left Cairo on 24th March. The people of Damascus began to leave the city, fleeing to the mountains to the west or scattering over the country. Mongol scouts appeared from every direction outside the city. The Damascenes spent the whole night in the mosques, imploring God to save them. Next morning the Tatars had vanished.

Qutlugh Shah, hearing that the sultan and the Mamluke army were approaching, left Damascus and moved southwards to meet him. It was 19th April, 1303. The Mamlukes took up a position at Shaqhab, below the rocky ridge of Ghabaghib past which ran the main road leading south from Damascus. Here the road crossed a number of stony ridges, running east and west, constituting natural defensive positions, where battles to protect Damascus have been fought again and again throughout history. Ghabaghib is some twenty-five miles south of Damascus.[5]

Qutlugh Shah had taken up his position on high ground, while the Mamlukes had formed a line below him, along a small stream. In the centre was the young sultan with the new khalif, who was about his own age. With them were Salar and Baybars the Jashne-keer. In the left centre was Qipchaq, the former deserter, while on the extreme left was old Ameer Bektash.

On the morning of 20th April the two young men, the sultan and

[5] In my book, *The Lost Centuries*, I called this battle Marj al Suffer, which is close by. Maqrizi calls it Shaqhab (pronounced Shuck-hub).

the khalif, stepped out on foot in front of the army. With them were Qoran readers, reciting portions of the Qoran and promising the joys of paradise to those who fell as martyrs at the hands of the infidels. The sultan stood still, while the young khalif beside him cried in a loud voice, "Defenders of the faith! See your sultan is with you. Fight for your women and for the defence of the religion of your Prophet (on whom be the blessing and salvation of God)." Tears flowed down the cheeks of many men standing in the ranks.

The troops were still not all in their battle positions when, about midday, the squadrons of Tatars began to advance in a dark, solid mass. Qutlugh Shah, who had some fifty thousand men, now led a dashing charge of ten thousand horsemen against the Mamluke right wing. The troops, however, stood firm, and after a desperate struggle the attackers drew off. A thousand mamlukes and six senior ameers had been killed.

A fresh Mongol attack was launched against the centre, where Salar, Baybars and the Burji or Tower Mamlukes resisted valiantly and once more the enemy fell back. But new attacks were delivered on the right wing and the centre, and some units commenced to give way. Stragglers, escaping to the rear, began to loot the baggage, which had been parked behind the army. Groups of women who had followed the army when it evacuated Damascus, and had crowded round the baggage, screamed, tore their hair and cried to God for help.

As darkness drew in, fighting ceased. Qutlugh Shah withdrew to the high ground a short distance north of the battlefield. Having seen a number of Mamluke units retreat, he seems to have thought that the battle was won, but when he reached the ridge behind his position and could overlook the battlefield, he saw that most of the Mamluke army was still intact. He also learned for the first time, from a prisoner, that the sultan was with the army facing him. Instead of plying sword and lance in the mêlée, he would have done better to remain himself on the high ground, observing the Mamluke army.

The Mamlukes remained under arms all night, many of them on horseback. The drums continued to beat until dawn as a signal for stragglers to rejoin their units. All night long, Baybars, Salar, Qipchaq and the senior ameers continued to circulate among the troops, encouraging them, advising them and urging them to stand fast.

At dawn on the second day, the sultan's army stood in perfect battle order, each ameer at the head of his command. Soon after sunrise the Mongol army, which had reformed on the high ground, advanced down the slope in one long line. The sultan's Mamlukes advanced with great gallantry to meet the Mongol centre. On both flanks, the ameers held their ground but the honours of the day went to the Royal Mamlukes, many of whom had three horses shot under them.

When Qutlugh Shah had withdrawn to the high ground the previous evening, he took up a position militarily impregnable but without water. The Mamlukes were drawn up along the stream in the valley below. At noon on the second day, the Mongols withdrew. Horses and men were too thirsty to fight on.

Qutlugh Shah and his officers decided to advance again at four o'clock in the morning on the third day. Their vital objective was to reach the water. A report on their condition was brought to the sultan by a mamluke who had been taken prisoner, but had escaped. The ameers decided to let the Mongols reach the stream.

At four in the morning, the Tatars mounted and rode down to the stream. They rushed pell-mell into the water, men and horses intent only on slaking their thirst. As they pushed and crowded into the stream, the Mamlukes fell upon them, "harvesting their heads as men harvest barley with a sickle". The whole Mongol army fled in disorder, hotly pursued by the triumphant Mamlukes.

*   *   *

Pigeons were immediately flown to Gaza with news of the victory, and also to the towns and fortresses of Syria. The battle had been fought on 20th, 21st and 22nd of April. On 23rd April, the sultan moved forward as far as Kiswa.[6] The next morning, the whole population of Damascus flooded out of the city to meet the sultan. The notables rode on horseback and a seething mass of persons crowded round on foot, townspeople, men, women and children. "None could reckon their numbers save He who created them," says the pious Maqrizi. All were calling out prayers and praises to God and congratulations to the sultan. Tears flowed abundantly and the drums rolled continuously as the troops marched by. Never before had such a day of joy been seen. The whole city was soon gaily decorated.

Meanwhile a number of units pursued the enemy, whose troops were so demoralised that they threw away their arms, passively allowing themselves to be killed, even by civilians.

Ramadhan, the month of fasting, had begun on the first day of the battle, 20th April. The sultan fasted the rest of the month in Damascus, every evening being devoted to joyful festivities.[7] The

[6] Map 22, page 177.
[7] During Ramadhan, Muslims fast from dawn to sunset, but can eat and drink at night.

sultan celebrated the feast of the end of the fast in Damascus. On
23rd May, 1303, he left the happy city behind him to return to
Cairo.

*   *   *

The great majority of the Tatars were killed by the people of
Syria, only one-tenth it was estimated, reaching home. Ghazan was
dumbfounded at the magnitude of the catastrophe. When Qutlugh
Shah returned, Ghazan summoned him to court. Seated on his royal
couch, the Il-Khan loaded his army commander with abuse and
then ordered his execution. At the entreaties of the courtiers, he
agreed to spare his life, but ordered him to stand at the further end
of the Hall of Audience. Then everyone in the crowded hall was told
to file past and spit in his face.

Ghazan never recovered from the disaster. He fell ill and died on
17th May, 1304. Although unsuccessful in his invasions of Syria,
Ghazan was the only Il-Khan who attempted to govern justly. He
had a real sympathy and affection for his subjects, and his death was
deeply lamented.

*   *   *

When news of the victory reached Cairo, the people abandoned
themselves to wild rejoicing. The city was quickly decorated with
wooden towers covered with carpets and draperies. All through
Ramadhan the people worked joyfully to prepare for the sultan's
return, decorating the fronts of their houses with hangings of silk,
and even with pearls and jewels. The governor erected a tower
beneath which he placed troughs full of sweets, sugar and lemons.

The sultan reached Cairo on 12th June, 1304. The whole population of the city and the countryside turned out to greet him. High
prices were paid for seats in houses along the route. At the head of
the procession came one thousand six hundred Mongol prisoners,
each with the severed head of one of his comrades hung round his
neck. A thousand other Tatar heads went by on the points of lances.
Then the Mongol drums torn and broken and their captured banners
were dragged along in the dust.

On entering the city, the ameers dismounted, leaving the sultan
alone on horseback. The first to dismount was the old Ameer
Bektash, who held the ceremonial post of the sultan's armour-
bearer. In view of his great age and long service, the sultan ordered
him to remount and to have the armour carried by a mamluke. But
old Bektash refused and carried the sultan's armour on foot, all

through the procession. There followed three ameers, the first carrying the royal parasol, the second the sceptre and the third the mace. The streets had been spread with carpets over which the sultan rode. When the procession ultimately reached the palace, visitors, come to offer their felicitations, were presented to the sultan. "This was indeed the greatest of days," cries the good Maqrizi ecstatic ally.

* * *

When Ghazan died in May 1304, he was succeeded by his brother Oljaitu (1304–1316), who also professed Islam. He wrote to the sultan to inform him of his accession, and asking that the two empires remain at peace. The Mamlukes had no wish for further Mongol wars and returned a cordial reply.

Soon afterwards, ambassadors arrived from Toktai (1290–1312), the Khan of the Golden Horde, who ruled the country from the lower Volga to the Black Sea, the former land of the Qipchaqs.[8] These were the descendants of Juji, the eldest son of Jenghis Khan.[9] Toktai informed the sultan that he proposed to make war on Ghazan, and he asked for Mamluke co-operation. These advances would have been warmly welcomed if Ghazan had still been alive. But Ghazan had died since the embassy left home. An answer was returned that the sultan had made peace with Oljaitu, and a royal gift was sent to Toktai.

* * *

The sultan was growing up. Salar and Baybars became increasingly unwilling to allow him any money lest he gain friends and influence, although they themselves lived in the height of luxury.

In the year 1305, Salar went on the Meccan pilgrimage, where he gave away vast sums of money to charity and pious bequests, though the sultan in Cairo had barely enough to eat. In his absence, a party of two hundred Mongol deserters arrived with their families. Two of them proved to be brothers of Salar, who had originally himself been a deserter, though, to our surprise, he was now head of the Mamluke empire. The party was received with honour in Cairo and Salar's brothers were made ameers.

It is of interest to note, in view of our total preoccupation with "race", that in the fourteenth century, the idea counted for nothing at all. No one had commented on the fact that, at the Battle of Shaqhab, the Mamluke army had been commanded by a Mongol

[8] Map 9, page 52.   [9] Genealogical Tree 4, page 58.

deserter. In spite of this attitude, however, we may well suspect that some Mamluke ameers, who had served thirty years for their promotion, were not pleased when Salar's relatives were given the immediate rank of ameers.

Salar and Baybars received intelligence that the wazeer, Muhammad ibn al Shaikhi, had met the sultan and had lent him two thousand gold dinars. They accordingly instructed a Christian treasury clerk to produce forged accounts, to prove that the wazeer had embezzled a large sum of money. Salar ordered the wazeer to be first flogged and then tortured to death. Ibn al Shaikhi was a native of Damascus, who had worked his way up to the head of the civil service by sheer clerical ability. But then he became involved in the power struggle between Salar, Baybars and the sultan, and was crushed like a fly.

It is of interest to note that, fifty years after the commencement of the Mamluke régime, it was still rare to find an ameer who spoke Arabic or an Egyptian or Syrian who spoke Turkish. Any Egyptian who did know Turkish, Maqrizi reports, obtained an advantage over his colleagues. The position must have been similar to that of American or European experts or advisers today, serving in Asian or African countries.

Another sidelight of Mamluke mentality is provided by the case of a senior Mamluke ameer, close to the sultan, who struck a qadhi. The latter was, of course, an Egyptian, but the ameer was instantly dismissed. In 1306, died the old Ameer Bektash at the age of eighty. He was the last surviving mamluke of the Ayoubid Sultan Malik-al-Salih Ayoub. He had refused to be sultan, and was famous for his sterling virtues, his impartial mind and his acts of benevolence. It is strange that, in every age, loyalty and honesty are called "old-fashioned virtues".

Bektash had fought in all the campaigns he could, for he cherished the hope of dying a martyr, in battle with the infidels. But God, he sadly admitted, had not wished it so and he died in his bed. When we consider the careers of political ameers who ruthlessly intrigued and fought their way to the top, it is well to remember old Bektash al Fakhri, the simple soldier who spent all his life at the wars, refused to be a sultan and never pursued a selfish aim.

Several of the Muslim historians give obituaries of persons who died each year. Among such, there is often mention of ameers who were honest, loyal, religious and generous, though the day-to-day narratives of war and politics give such persons no publicity.

*   *   *

Tension continued to increase between Salar and Baybars. Salar was a subtle intriguer, Baybars a violent, loud-voiced man. Soon they were no longer on speaking terms.

During the winter of 1307 to 1308, the young sultan grew increasingly resentful of the authority exercised over him by Salar and Baybars. He was now twenty-two, but was almost under house-arrest. No officer or officials were allowed to see him, the two regents never spoke to him of public business and he lived in penury.

He planned a coup, in which his personal mamlukes, led by the Ameer Bektimur, were to arrest Salar and Baybars. An announcement would then be made that the sultan had assumed power. But the regents had spies in the palace. On the evening on which the coup was to take place, Bektimur was arrested. Rumours spread in the city that the regents had murdered the sultan.

An immense crowd emerged from the streets, shouting furiously, for the public was devoted to Malik-al-Nasir Muhammad. The ameers sent a troop of cavalry, which charged the crowd with batons. The demonstrators, however, continued to roar, "O Nasir! O Victorious! God curse those who betray the son of Qalaoon," until in the evening they gradually dispersed. A few days later, a letter arrived from the Viceroy of Damascus, threatening to march on Cairo if the two ameers maltreated the sultan.

In government circles, most of the ameers supported Salar, a skilful and prudent politician. The Burji Mamlukes, however, now the strongest military force in the capital, were all for Baybars. To escape from the intolerable atmosphere of the palace, the young sultan expressed a desire to make the pilgrimage to Mecca. The two ameers agreed, feeling that it would be a relief to have him out of the way.

The sultan left for Mecca on 10th March, 1308. Vast crowds came out of the city, weeping and calling down blessings on his head, for the kindly Egyptians had taken the unhappy young man to their hearts. The convoy reached Kerak on 26th March, 1308, where the sultan sent for the ameers of his escort and told them that he had decided to abdicate and to live in peace in Kerak. He gave them a letter to Salar and Baybars with his abdication. When the letter reached Cairo, Salar and Baybars, completely taken aback, replied angrily telling him to return forthwith and not to behave like a child. Otherwise he would live to regret it.

Consternation reigned in Cairo. The existence of a child-sultan had enabled Salar and Baybars to maintain a precarious balance of power. But if the sultan disappeared, a showdown between the duumvirs would be inevitable.

The Tower Mamlukes began to prepare for battle. Salar, the politician, urged his friends to avoid violence. The next morning, surrounded by his supporters, he went to his office in the viceroy's palace. Soon Baybars appeared, and then the khalif and the qadhis were summoned and told of the sultan's abdication. Several senior ameers expressed the view that Salar should be sultan.

Salar rose to his feet and replied diplomatically, "O Ameers, I doubt if I am worthy of the office. My friend Baybars here is a more suitable candidate." It is impossible to know whether this was a suitable expression of modesty or whether Salar was perhaps afraid of violence, for Baybars had packed the hall with Burji Mamlukes. Scarcely were the words out of his mouth than the Burjis began to shout, "The ameer is right!"

Seizing Baybars, they placed him on a horse, threw over his shoulders a black cloak, such as was worn at the inauguration of sultans and led him into the streets, while criers announced his elevation to the throne. Riding up to the palace in the Citadel, Baybars sat on the throne and accepted the oaths of allegiance, Salar being pushed forward with the other ameers and obliged to swear. Couriers immediately left for the provinces, announcing the abdication of Malik-al-Nasir Muhammad and the elevation of Malik-al-Mudhaffar Baybars. A decree was sent to Kerak, appointing Malik-al-Nasir Muhammad governor of the fortress.

NOTABLE DATES

Battle of Wadi al Khaznadar	22nd December, 1299
Occupation of Damascus by Ghazan	2nd January, 1300
Return of Mamlukes to Damascus	2nd May, 1300
Ghazan's abortive invasion of Syria	October, 1300 to January, 1301
Punitive expeditions to southern Egypt	1301–1302
Battle of Shaqhab	20th–22nd April, 1303
Death of Il-Khan Ghazan	17th May, 1304
Oljaitu becomes Il-Khan	21st July, 1304
Al-Nasir Muhammad leaves, ostensibly for Mecca	10th March, 1308
Abdication of Al-Nasir Baybars the Jashnekeer becomes sultan	April, 1308

PERSONALITIES

Mamlukes
Sultan Malik-al-Nasir Muhammad, the son of Qalaoon
Sultan Malik-al-Mudhaffar Baybars, the Jashnekeer
Regent Salar
Ameer Bektash al Fakhri, commander-in-chief

Mongols
Il-Khan Ghazan
Il-Khan Oljaitu
Qutlugh Shah, commander of the Mongol army at Shaqhab

X

Third Time Lucky

Woe to the land that's governed by a child.

SHAKESPEARE, *King Richard III*

The idea of hereditary succession was wholly foreign to the Mamluk system; yet it presented the only correction to these scenes of violent supersessions, and after a time some sort of hereditary title seems to have been established. Kalaun (Qalaoon) had been succeeded by his son Khalil and then by a younger son Al-Nasir Muhammad. Thus, from 1279 to 1382 Egypt was ruled, except for six or seven years, by members of the house of Kalaun. Like most of the Mamluk sultans, he was a notable builder. It is extraordinary how these men of war, in the midst of alarums and intrigues, took a delight in architecture. The long reign of Al-Nasir was a golden age of Mamluk architecture . . . It was an age of brilliant artistic production, and the immense sums spent . . . on building and decorative works show that the wealth of the country was vast and was nobly expended.

STANLEY LANE-POOLE, *The Story of Cairo*

When our actions do not
Our fears do make us traitors.
SHAKESPEARE, *Macbeth*

2 Mamluke tombs on the plain east of Cairo, erroneously called "The Tombs of the Khalifs"

X

MALIK-AL-MUDHAFFAR BAYBARS AL JASHNEKEER

BAYBARS was not a clever politician. Suspecting that Malik-al-Nasir might attempt to return to the throne, he sent an order to Kerak to seize all his money, his horses and his mamlukes. The ex-sultan sent a submissive reply, but kept back some of his possessions. But Baybars sent once again, demanding the surrender of more possessions. It seems probable that when Al-Nasir came from Cairo, he really had intended to live in peace in retirement, but that Baybars' persecutions persuaded him that he would not be left alone. He accordingly wrote secretly to his friends in Egypt and Syria to complain.

Meanwhile, the blesséd Nile joined his allies and refused to rise, a disaster which the public interpreted as a sign of the divine displeasure at Baybars' seizure of the throne. The fact that Salar and Baybars were still at loggerheads added to the general insecurity. Public dissatisfaction soon asserted itself. Sixty mamlukes deserted from Cairo and joined Al-Nasir, followed by a hundred and twenty more.

From Syria, the Governors of Aleppo, Hama, Safad and Jerusalem declared their loyalty to Al-Nasir, but the Viceroy of Damascus temporised. Meanwhile Al-Nasir left Kerak and camped at Ziza on the road to Damascus. The whole of Syria and Egypt was seething with rumours, with reports of desertion, and with wild alarms. In Damascus, the viceroy collected the ameers, the judges and the notables and announced, "Good people of Damascus! You have no sultan but Malik-al-Mudhaffar Baybars", whereupon those present replied in one shout, "No! No! We have no sultan but Malik-al-Nasir!"

Every day more ameers and mamlukes deserted to Al-Nasir Muhammad, who was now approaching Damascus in a triumphal procession. Those in the city prepared the insignia of royalty and decorated the streets. At length, amid wild popular enthusiasm, Al-Nasir rode into the streets of Damascus, which had been spread with carpets beneath the feet of his horse. The Viceroy of Damascus, who had supported Baybars, gave himself up, carrying his own winding sheet under his arm, signifying his readiness to die, but Al-Nasir received him cordially and confirmed him in his post.

The triumphal progress then left Damascus for Cairo, officers and men alike deserting their posts to meet the returning sultan. Baybars, seeing that he was lost, rode out of Cairo with his mamlukes. Salar, however, remained in Cairo, loudly announcing his loyalty to Malik-al-Nasir, and preparing a banquet for the returning sultan. At last, surrounded by his staff and welcomed by seething crowds of citizens, Al-Nasir Muhammad, for the third time, mounted the throne and put an end to his travels.

AL-MALIK-AL-NASIR MUHAMMAD
(Third Reign)

Malik-al-Nasir, now twenty-four years old, could not quite resist the temptation to revenge himself for his previous humiliations. He had at first appeared lenient towards Baybars and inveigled him into giving himself up. But he reproached him bitterly, when Baybars was brought before him, reminding him of an occasion when he, Al-Nasir, had asked for roast goose for dinner. But Baybars had replied to the messenger, "What does he want with roast goose? Does he want to eat twenty meals a day?" Baybars the Jashnekeer was held under arrest, and the same night was quietly strangled.

Salar had been made governor of the little town of Shobek,[1] but the sultan was anxious lest he desert to the Tatars. As a result, he persuaded him with fair words to come to Cairo, where he was immediately imprisoned, and shortly afterwards put to death. Salar, as already mentioned, had been taken prisoner in Qalaoon's wars with the Mongols, but the sultan had taken a fancy to him and given him employment. The extraordinary manner in which a career was open to talent under the Mamlukes is shown by the fact that this "enemy alien" became virtually the head of the empire. After his death, Salar was found to possess many millions of gold dinars and incalculable wealth in jewels, textiles, horses, camels, slaves and artistic treasures.

The deaths of Salar and Baybars frightened the ameers, among whom was Kara Sonkor, the Viceroy of Aleppo, who had assisted Al-Nasir to regain the throne but later criticised him for killing Baybars. Alarmed at his own temerity, he deserted to the Mongols,

[1] Map 22, page 177.

with five ameers of drums, six ameers of ten and a number of mamlukes and Turkmans. They crossed the Euphrates, passed through
Mardin and reached Oljaitu's camp south of Tabriz, where they
received an enthusiastic welcome.

Before leaving Syria, all the ameers sent their wives and children
to Cairo with letters to the sultan, explaining that fear of him was
the cause of their flight and asking him to care for their families.
While fear of the sultan was the only way to keep the unruly ameers
in order, too great a fear at times drove them to desert to the
Mongols.

But if the young Al-Nasir was severe in his handling of the ameers,
he retained a real love for the people. He sat twice a week in open
court in the Palace of Justice to hear complaints from any who
thought themselves aggrieved. A number of cases of oppression were
hastily settled out of court, lest the sultan hear about them.

A false alarm regarding a Tatar invasion having blown over, the
sultan decided to go on pilgrimage, returning in April 1313 direct
to Damascus, where he remained a fortnight before riding back to
Cairo. On his return, the race course was constructed below the
Citadel, extending from the royal stables to the Qarafa Gate.[2] It was
enclosed by a wall, wells were sunk for irrigation and trees and date
palms were planted. The sultan himself inaugurated it by playing
polo on it with the ameers.

The principal shaikh of the bedouins of the Syrian desert, Mahanna
ibn Isa, had been a friend of Kara Sonkor, the Viceroy of Aleppo,
who had gone over to the Mongols. Finding himself out of favour,
Mahanna moved to the east and camped on the Euphrates, whence
he instructed his tribesmen to cut the roads in Mamluke territory
and to rob travellers. So much trouble resulted that the sultan, who
could not catch the desert nomads, was obliged to invite Mahanna to
return to favour. The principal tribes of the Syrian desert enumerated
by the historians were Beni Kilab, Al Murra, Al Fadhl and Al Ali.
Mahanna himself belonged to Al Fadhl.

The international situation being quiet, the sultan spent much
time on public works, buildings, and the construction of roads and
bridges, schools and mosques. Always active, he constantly rode out
himself to inspect the work. The ameers and the notables imitated
his interest in construction, and the suburbs of Cairo filled up with
new houses and gardens.

In the summer of 1313, work began on a new survey and redistribution of land. These surveys were called *rawks*,[3] and that undertaken by Malik-al-Nasir was called the *rawk al Nasiri*. That

[2] Map 21, page 158.   [3] Pronounced like coke, poke.

undertaken in 1297 in the reign of Lajeen had been called the *rawk al Husami*, his religious surname being Husam-al-Deen. As has already been explained, the Mamluke army was paid by the allotment of fiefs, or land-estates, to the ameers and the Royal Mamlukes. But all the land belonged to the government and it was, at this stage, never given in ownership to the members of the army. The system, therefore, never became a hereditary feudal system producing an aristocracy. When the holder of the fief died or was dismissed from the army, his feudal holding returned to the Army Office and was reallotted to someone else.

Periodical surveys and redistribution of fiefs were rendered necessary for several reasons.

(a) Changes in the productivity of the land—if a new irrigation canal were opened or an old one silted up, the value of the agricultural lands changed.
(b) Changes in policy, as will be explained below.
(c) Perhaps also, the object of reallocating all feudal holdings was to impress on all feudatories their dependence on the sultan, and precisely to prevent the crystallisation of fiefs into hereditary estates.

In Europe and in the Crusader states, feudal holdings had become hereditary and had produced aristocracies.

In the Seljuq Empire, Malik Shah had distributed fiefs to his Turkish commanders, probably not intending to allow them to become hereditary. But civil war broke out on his death and thereafter the sultans were never strong enough to take back the fiefs granted. From these Turkish lords sprang independent dynasties, such as that of the Zengids.

Saladin had overthrown the Zengids and taken over their empire, which he distributed among the junior members of the Ayoubid family. This policy was a failure, for each feudal Ayoubid prince regarded himself as independent, and refused to obey the Ayoubid sultan. The Ayoubid period was peculiar in that all the aristocracy were members of the ruling Ayoubid family.

* * *

Malik-al-Nasir Muhammad in 1313 began a reallocation of fiefs in Syria. We have no details of this operation, except that it effected a saving of land sufficient for fiefs for six ameers of drums and three ameers of ten. Then, in 1315, reallocation of fiefs was commenced in Egypt.

Under Baybars and Qalaoon, the total cultivable land of Egypt had been divided up into twenty-four "units", allotted as follows:

4 Units to the sultan and the Royal Mamlukes.
10 Units to the *halaqa*.
10 Units to the ameers.

Thus of the twenty-four units, only one-sixth belonged to the sultan and his own mamlukes. The result of Lajeen's reallocation was to give:

4 Units to the sultan in person.
9 Units to the Royal Mamlukes.
11 Units to the ameers and the *halaqa* together.

As a result of the survey of Al-Nasir in 1315 in Egypt, the following division was made:

10 Units to the sultan personally.
14 Units to all other fief-holders.

As ameers and mamlukes constituted the standing peace-time army, which *must* be retained, the economy was made at the expense of the army reserve—the *halaqa*. This change of policy had been made possible by the collapse of the Il-Khan Empire and the disappearance of the threat of Mongol invasions, which had hitherto necessitated a large army reserve.

According to Maqrizi, the fiefs allotted to the *halaqa* had, under Qalaoon, been worth annual incomes varying from ten thousand to thirty thousand dirhems, but these were reduced to incomes of from five thousand to twenty thousand dirhems, according to rank. Many members of the *halaqa* abandoned the service altogether and sought other means of livelihood.

The sultan's wealth and power, however, increased greatly, and also the sums expended by him on the Royal Mamlukes. The final result was to increase the regular army, all of whom were the personal mamlukes of the sultan, and to downgrade the reserve.

The actual process of survey in Egypt occupied seventy-five days, and was not topographical. Every village was visited by committees of judges, surveyors and officials, who drew up registers on the evidence of local residents. From these and previous records, new registers were compiled showing the crops, number of ploughs and the income paid to the military holders of the fiefs, whether in cash, grain, chickens, lucerne, beans, lentils or any other forms of produce. Several copies were made of all registers, the originals being handed into the army pay office, for the fiefs of ameers and mamlukes were derived from the land. The system was hard on the cultivators, who had to pay the military holder of the fief and many minor dues as well. Al-Nasir caused some of these petty charges to be reduced.

The fiefs were then reallotted. Every officer and man received his new title deeds from the sultan in person, who asked each in turn, "Who are you, where are you from, whose mamluke are you? In what battles have you fought?"

One young soldier came up to the table with a long scar across his face. "In what battle did you get that sword wound?" asked the sultan. "That is not a sword wound, O king," answered the boy. "I fell off a ladder and hurt myself." The paymaster quickly intervened, saying, "O king, he ought not to have so good a fief if he was not wounded in battle." The sultan smiled and handed the soldier his title deeds. "Let him be," he said. "He told me the truth. If he had named some battle, no one could have contradicted him."

The sultan also went through the list of pay and pensions, for some men received cash instead of fiefs. The care and perseverance with which Al-Nasir himself checked all the documents of every officer and man, and the time he spent seeing and speaking to every soldier are truly amazing. But all the time, he kept a close eye on economy. Many fiefs were reduced and the extensive lands acquired by Salar and Baybars were all made over to the treasury. The sultan's decisions however, brooked no argument. Anyone who protested at the smallness of his fief might well be deprived of it altogether, if indeed he were not arrested.

*　　　*　　　*

In March 1316, news was received in Cairo of the death of the Il-Khan Oljaitu (1304–1316) and the elevation of his son Abu Saeed (1316–1334) as his successor. The prestige and power of the Il-Khanate were rapidly declining.

The endless confusion with Nubia continued. A member of the royal family having been brought up in Egypt, the sultan had the idea of making him king and sent him to Dongola with an army. But the Egyptian candidate was killed and the plan failed.

Some of the eastern trade from Aden was landed at Aidhab and Suakin and transported[4] to Egypt by land, exposed to raids by the local nomads. As usual, however, the Mamlukes completely failed

[4] Map 18, page 129.

to win the co-operation of the Nubians or of the tribes, but sought only to cow them with military expeditions, which killed and plundered these unhappy people, leaving the survivors ever more filled with hatred.

The far-reaching prestige enjoyed by the Mamluke Empire is illustrated by the great number of embassies reaching Cairo—eight in one year at this time—including some from the Il-Khan Abu Saeed, the King of Georgia, the Byzantine Emperor, the Khan of the Golden Horde and the Kings of Nubia and of the Yemen.

In 1319, the sultan again went on the pilgrimage, with great pomp and splendour, in embroidered tents, with gold and silver plate and a large company, including the Ayoubid Prince of Hama, Malik-al-Muaiyad Ismail.[5] The sultan assumed a humble and contrite manner. "I behaved like someone of importance," he said to one of his intimates, "until I saw the Kaaba.[6] Then a great fear entered my heart, when I remembered how men kissed the ground before me, until I myself knelt down before Almighty God."

One of the qadhis having suggested that the sultan might perform the ritual circumambulations of the temple on horseback, the sultan replied, "Who am I that I should act differently from other people?" He would not even allow his escort to hold back the crowd when he went to perform his devotions.

With his own hands he rinsed down the walls of the Kaaba and washed the soiled clothing of his fellow pilgrims. On the return march, he stopped at Aqaba to supervise the improvement of the track where it climbed up the rocky defile from the Jordan valley to the plateau of Sinai. There is no reason to doubt the sincerity of the sultan's piety or the qualms of conscience which he suffered when he remembered the many rivals whom he had put to death. Yet what else could he have done, for the empire was strong and prosperous under a sultan who was feared, and was torn by civil wars under a weak ruler. Even Napoleon was alleged to have said, five hundred years later, that when a king was said to be kind, his reign was a failure.

Al-Nasir was the first Mamluke sultan who spoke Arabic fluently and sympathised not only with the peoples of Egypt and Syria, but with the tribes of the desert. These qualities, which made him so popular, he doubtless owed to his years of exile in Kerak, on the fringe of the deserts stretching down into Arabia. On his pilgrimage this year he met and talked to the shaikhs of Beni Mehedi of the Hejaz, of Beni Lam, Al Fadhl, and the sons of Mahanna. Never

---

[5] Malik-al-Muaiyad Ismail was the historian, generally known by the name of Abulfeda.
[6] The Holy of Holies in the Temple of Mecca.

before had bedouin chiefs gathered round a Mamluke sultan in this way, or talked to him with such freedom. Their equalitarian familiarity infuriated the Egyptian civil servants who, then as now, regarded the democratic manners of the nomads with dislike and contempt.

The sultan returned to Cairo on 24th February, 1320, in a magnificent procession, all the people of the city turning out to greet him. He was accompanied also by the Ayoubid Prince of Hama, Malik-al-Muaiyad Ismail, to whom he granted the favour of a special procession with the insignia of royalty.

The family of Jenghis Khan still enjoyed an extraordinary prestige, even a hundred years after the death of the conqueror. Mamluke sultans were perhaps more powerful, certainly more wealthy and more cultured, but they had no pedigree. Indeed their system was founded on equal opportunity for all, yet they could not resist the glamour of Mongol royalty.

Al-Nasir had written to Aibek, Khan of the Golden Horde,[7] to ask his daughter in marriage. The Mongols were at first indignant that a mere Mamluke should aspire to marry into the Golden Family, and Aibek eventually eluded the request by agreeing, but asking so large a dowry that the proposal was quietly dropped. Later, however, presumably to maintain diplomatic relations with Egypt, a great-great-great-granddaughter of Jenghis Khan was sent. She arrived by sea and was escorted up to the Citadel with great pomp.

Perhaps the lady had been selected for her ugliness, for she was accompanied by a somewhat take-it-or-leave-it letter, asking the sultan to take her if he liked her, and if he did not like her to be kind to her. Unfortunately, he did not like her. The morning after the wedding, Al-Nasir left on a shooting expedition.

This year, he also sent a group of assassins to murder Kara Sonkor, the former Viceroy of Aleppo, who had deserted to the Il-Khan. The Mongols had news of the plot and most of the gang were caught and killed, but some diplomatic tension ensued. The Mongols retaliated by sending assassins to kill Al-Nasir, which resulted in the adoption of safety precautions in Cairo, restricting the sultan from mixing in crowds, which formerly greeted him so warmly.

In April 1320, the sultan commenced the Nasiri race course and polo ground on the Nile.[8] He bought a number of nearby properties from which to borrow earth to level the area. On the boundary of the area was a Christian church, which the engineers wished to demolish in order to use the rubble. The sultan refused, but made a cryptic remark to the effect that it might collapse.

On 9th May, 1321, however, a crowd of roughs suddenly set to

[7] Genealogical Tree 4, page 58.   [8] Map 14, page 72.

work and demolished it. It was a Friday and the Muslims were at midday prayers. When they emerged from the mosques, they saw a party tearing down the church. Someone shouted, "The sultan has ordered the destruction of churches." Many churches were rich, containing gold vessels, vestments and crucifixes set with jewels. Soon the streets were full of people carrying off the plunder.

Al-Nasir was furious and called out troops to restore order, which was only done with great difficulty. Most of the churches, and a certain number of monasteries in Cairo were destroyed. Somehow the news spread over Egypt and churches were also demolished in Damanhoor, Damietta, and other cities. Almost sixty churches were destroyed altogether. It is not possible to decide whether the outbreak was planned or spontaneous.

Six days later, fires broke out in various parts of Cairo and continued for five days. All other work was abandoned and men of every race and class toiled to carry water and to demolish threatened buildings. The streets were crowded with women and children fleeing from their homes.

When the fires had raged for six days, two Christian monks were caught leaving a house with rags soaked in oil. Under torture, they confessed that the fires had been started by a party of Christians, in revenge for the destruction of their churches. The group consisted of fourteen monks, all from one monastery, six of whom were burned alive. The mob, however, refused to be pacified and continued to assault Christians.

Even the sultan lost something of his popularity. When out riding, he was greeted with cries of "May God give victory to Islam. Why do you protect Christians?" Al-Nasir was angry and ordered several ameers to lead their mamlukes against the crowd and strike them down. But before the troops moved off, he relented and told them to arrest rioters, not to kill them. In the end, the sultan, alarmed at the popular violence, left the Christians to their fate. New edicts were promulgated, forbidding the employment of Christians in government offices.

We should not dismiss these incidents as oriental fanaticism. Two hundred and fifty years later, in August 1572, in the Massacre of St. Bartholomew in France, fifty thousand Protestants were killed in cold blood. Moreover this was done at the order of the government, whereas in Cairo in 1321 the government did its best to restore order.

It is worthy of remark that both Muslims and Christians were acting contrary to their religions, under the influence of communal jealousies. The Prophet had forbidden the molestation of Christians, who were, he said, the people nearest to the Muslims. Christians likewise are ordered in the Gospels not to render evil for evil.

In 1332, the unhappy Armenian Kingdom of Cilicia was again invaded, the port of Ayas was destroyed and Oshin, the Armenian King, was killed. It has already been explained that the Mamlukes regarded Ayas as a rival to Alexandria.

It is typical of the sultan's energy that every morning a statement of the government's income and expenditure was placed before him and discussed with treasury officials. His physical energy was as great as that which he showed in clerical work. He constantly rode out to supervise the digging of irrigation canals or the erection of buildings.

*   *   *

In January 1325, there were in Cairo special embassies from the Byzantine Emperor, the King of the Yemen, the Il-Khan, the King of Nubia, the Armenian King of Cilicia, the Qaraman Ameer of Asia Minor and the ruler of Mardin. At the request of the King of the Yemen, a small force was sent to quell a revolt in that country, consisting of ten ameers of drums, ten ameers of ten, three hundred Royal Mamlukes and a thousand men of the *halaqa*. The total strength was some two thousand men, a small force to send one thousand five hundred miles, into wild tribal mountains.[9]

In June 1325, the Yemen column marched out of Mecca for the south. The rebels, thereupon, became reconciled to their king, Malik-al-Mujahid, who met the Mamluke column at Zabid. The king's soldiers were armed with primitive weapons, had no horses and aroused the contempt of the Mamlukes, clad in brilliant uniforms, with helmets and breastplates. Difficulties continued to increase. The Yemenis would supply neither food nor forage, possibly on the secret orders of the king who, being now reconciled with the rebels, wished to get rid of the Egyptian expedition.

Relations continued to deteriorate. The Yemenis cut off the water supply and stole the baggage camels at pasture. The king shut himself in the fortress of Taiz, the tribesmen took refuge in the mountains. Eventually the Mamluke column withdrew, reaching Mecca with some difficulty due to lack of supplies. It ultimately arrived back in Cairo after an absence of eight months, having narrowly escaped a military disaster.

*   *   *

[9] Map 23, opposite.

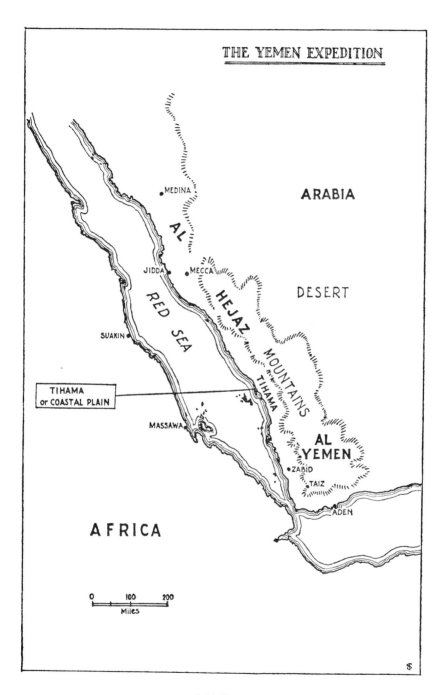

THE YEMEN EXPEDITION

ARABIA

• MEDINA

AL

JIDDA •   • MECCA

RED SEA

HEJAZ

DESERT

SUAKIN •

MOUNTAINS

TIHAMA
or COASTAL PLAIN

TIHAMA

MASSAWA •

AL
YEMEN

• ZABID

• TAIZ

AFRICA

• ADEN

0   100   200
Miles

$

MAP 23

In 1329, the sultan fell from his horse when out hunting and broke his arm. He was confined to his room for thirty-seven days. When his recovery was announced, Cairo was decorated as never before. All the bands played and the sultan's surgeon became a rich man. There is no doubt that the popular rejoicing was genuine.

A Christian of Kerak, converted to Islam, claimed that he could make gold. He put copper, silver and tin into a cauldron and heated them until they fused. When the product had cooled, a large block of metal was formed, seeming to be gold. The sultan was delighted and loaded the alchemist with money. Later, the deception was discovered and the alchemist met a painful death.

This year, the Il-Khan Abu Saeed sent an elephant with the Iraqi pilgrimage to Mecca, an action considered by the Mamluke authorities to be in rather bad taste.

In 1331, a number of young Royal Mamlukes went down into Cairo and made a disturbance. They were arrested, flogged and dismissed from the service, a notable punishment in view of what was to come.

Malik-al-Muaiyid Ismail, the Ayoubid Prince of Hama, died this year and was succeeded by his son, Malik-al-Afdhal Muhammad, who was twenty years old. He came to Cairo to pay his respects and rode in a state procession through the city with the insignia of royalty, after which he ascended to the Citadel and kissed the ground before the sultan.

It is extraordinary that this one little dynasty retained its hereditary throne for so long, in the heart of the Mamluke Empire, proving how strong can be the ties of a traditional friendship, apart from logical or material interests. It is surprising today how little trouble is taken by governments to foster such moral bonds, which formerly constituted the strongest cement uniting the British Commonwealth. Today financial interests or military alliances seem to take precedence of brotherly love.

In May 1332, the sultan's eldest son, Anook, was married to the daughter of the Ameer Bektimur al Saqi. The sultan sat in state on the wedding night and every ameer with his private mamlukes kissed the ground before him, all carrying candles. The sultan then moved to the private apartments, where the wives of the ameers also kissed the ground and offered wedding gifts. Every dancer and musician in Cairo had been brought up to the palace, and the rest of the night was passed in music and dancing, until the time came to escort the bride in a formal procession to the bridal chamber.

The next day the sultan held a reception, at which robes of honour were given to all ameers, civil officials and judges, and gifts were sent to their wives. More than twenty thousand animals are said to have been slaughtered for public feasting, including sheep, cattle, horses and chickens. The horses were eaten only by the Mamlukes, for horses were regularly slaughtered for banquets on the steppes. Nine hundred tons of sweets, and sweet drinks were served. Although every Mamluke had been born in poverty and hardship on the steppes, the most distinctive feature of their rule was magnificence.

*　　　*　　　*

As soon as the festivities were over, the sultan announced his intention of once more going on pilgrimage. Many ameers accompanied the royal convoy, those who stayed behind being ordered to live on their estates until the sultan's return.

As the great caravan approached Aila (the modern Aqaba) an informer told Al-Nasir that the Ameer Bektimur proposed to assassinate him on the pilgrimage. Bektimur's daughter had only just married the sultan's eldest son and his wealth and prestige were immense. To Al-Nasir, Bektimur seemed to have grown too great. The sultan was alarmed, changed his sleeping place several times each night and kept Bektimur under constant observation. On the way back from Mecca, he arranged for both Bektimur and his son to be poisoned.

In Mecca and Medina, the sultan showed his usual piety and gave many splendid gifts to religious and charitable causes. Rumours of troubles and intrigues had reached Cairo from the pilgrimage, and the public were in great anxiety. Immense numbers turned out to welcome the sultan's return. As he rode along the route, lined on both sides by seething crowds, he was wearing an Arab kerchief over his face in the bedouin style. Shouts rose from the spectators, "Take the kerchief off. Let us see your face!" When he did so, the crowd went mad with joy and roared, "Praise God for your safety." The dancing, the singing and the playing of bands lasted for three days. The sultan's triumphant return passed into a proverb. "As happy as the people, when Al-Nasir returned from pilgrimage" became a simile of human bliss.

*　　　*　　　*

An Egyptian Christian official called Neshu had begun his career as a finance clerk. His efficiency drew the attention of the sultan, to whom he complained of the alleged dishonesty of other officials, deeply impressing Al-Nasir, who was a simple soul, easily deceived.

The next step was that Neshu announced his conversion to Islam, and was placed in charge of revenue collection.

His method was to conduct secret enquiries into the wealth of every ameer, notable or merchant, often using old women as spies. When he located a rich man, he informed the sultan that he had obtained his money by dishonest means, and set himself to mulct his victim. Soon the public revenue increased by leaps and bounds, while Neshu told his master that, until he took over, these sums had been embezzled by dishonest officials.

When he began to enquire into the income and expenditure of all Mamluke ameers, one of the most senior, the Ameer Qusoon, complained to the sultan, who, however, took no notice. It was obvious that Neshu was more powerful than the greatest ameer. Soon his two brothers and his brother-in-law received important positions. Any official opposing him was accused of peculation, tried before a packed court and sentenced. The sultan seemed to be completely deceived.

Seeing that he enjoyed the sultan's full support, Neshu's outrages continued to increase. Almost daily, some rich man, usually an Egyptian, would be arrested and flogged until he handed over five thousand or ten thousand dinars, alleged to be owed by him to the treasury. Another story tells of a pregnant woman tortured in prison to reveal her husband's wealth, as a result of which she suffered a miscarriage. Neshu even grew so bold that he demanded money from ameers. Well aware of the sultan's almost puritan morals, he denounced to Al-Nasir as a secret alcoholic any Mamluke ameer who opposed his activities. The sultan would immediately write an angry order exiling the officer to a minor post on the frontier. When Tinkiz, the Viceroy of Damascus, tried to tell Al-Nasir of the outrages which were being committed in his name, the sultan only showed resentment. No sooner had the ameer withdrawn than Al-Nasir sent for Neshu and told him all that the viceroy had said.

In 1338, when the Coptic Patriarch died, Neshu seized all the gold, silver, ornaments, jewels and church furniture which he could find in the patriarchate. In 1340, the sultan's intimate mamlukes agreed together to speak to him. Yalbugha al Yahyawi, a mamluke whom he trusted, fell ill, and the sultan visited him in bed. The sick man said that he felt it his duty, on his deathbed, to warn his master that Neshu was destroying the loyalty of Al-Nasir's subjects. Yalbugha then burst into tears, and even the sultan began to sob. For the first time, he was deeply alarmed, and consulted the Ameers Tinkiz and Bushtak. Orders were given for Neshu's arrest, and a detachment of troops was sent to search his house.

Neshu had often complained to the sultan of poverty and had

borrowed a dinar or two ostensibly to buy food. Al-Nasir still believed him to be honest, though perhaps tactless. The ameers and the public, therefore, held their breath while the house was being searched. The first report stated that fifteen thousand dinars had been found in cash, two thousand five hundred loose pearls, sixty ropes of pearls, great quantities of jewels, gold and silver rings, a gold cross set with precious stones, silk tapestries embroidered in gold thread, valuable antiques, china dinner services, glass and articles of luxury. Large amounts of food were stored, such as two hundred jars of fish, quantities of cheese, large amounts of bacon,[10] four hundred jars of wine, four hundred suits of clothing not yet worn, women's dresses, textiles and other costly stuffs—the catalogue is a long one. The house of his brother-in-law also contained valuables worth some twenty-five thousand dinars.

The sultan, who had so often angrily defended Neshu, was ashamed before all the ameers. "May God damn all Copts," he cried angrily, "and everyone who trusts them or believes what they say." He gave orders for Neshu and his near relatives to be tortured to death. Neshu had held supreme power in the Mamluke empire for seven years and seven months.

Four days after Neshu's arrest, the streets of Cairo and Fustat were magnificently decorated by the people. All shops were shut and the public spent a week's holiday, in festivals, singing and dancing.

The Neshu affair is of great interest, for it has been often repeated throughout history. Al-Nasir, the son of a northern race, was completely unable to resist the machinations of the far more subtle city-dwellers of the Middle East. The same story was repeated again and again throughout the later occupations of Middle Eastern countries by north European powers. The colder climates of the north may produce courage, perseverance and frankness, but such races are often as gullible as children when confronted by the subtle minds of the peoples of the eastern Mediterranean seaboard.

[10] Neshu, it will be remembered, was by way of having become a Muslim.

NOTABLE EVENTS

Commencement of Al-Nasir's Third Reign	March, 1309
Death of Baybars the Jashnekeer } Death of Ameer Salar	1309
Desertion of Kara Sonkor to the Tatars	1310
Nasir's redistribution of fiefs	1315

Death of Il-Khan Oljaitu ⎫	1316
Elevation of Il-Khan Abu Saeed ⎭	
Destruction of churches in Cairo ⎫	May, 1321
Arson by a party of monks ⎭	
Invasion of Cilicia. Destruction of Ayas	1322
Abortive expedition to the Yemen	1325–26
Sultan's third pilgrimage ⎫	1332
Poisoning of Ameer Bektimur ⎭	

PERSONALITIES

Mamlukes
Sultan Malik-al-Mudhaffar Baybars
Sultan Malik-al-Nasir Muhammad
Ameer Salar, the "Regent"
Ameer Kara Sonkor, deserter to the Il-Khan
Ameer Bektimur al Saqi, poisoned by the sultan

Egyptians or Arabs
Neshu, the Collector of Revenue
Malik-al-Mujahid, King of the Yemen
Malik-al-Muaiyad Ismail, Prince of Hama
His son, Malik-al-Afdhal Muhammad

XI

Every Inch a King

Alas all this I bear, for what I seek I know
Peace, peace is what I seek and public calm:
Endless extinction of unhappy hates.
                    MATTHEW ARNOLD, *Merope*

Though God hath raised me high, yet this I count the glory of
my crown: That I have reigned with your loves.

                                        QUEEN ELIZABETH I

He was a man, take him for all in all,
I shall not look upon his like again.
                    SHAKESPEARE, *Hamlet*

The long reign of en-Nasir was a golden age of Mamluk architecture. This self-possessed, iron-willed man—absolutely despotic, ruling alone—physically insignificant, small of stature,
lame of a foot, and with a cataract in his eye—with his plain
dress and strict morals, his keen intellect and unwearied energy,
his enlightened tastes and interests, his shrewd diplomacy . . . his
superb court, his magnificent buildings, is one of the most remarkable characters of the Middle Ages. His reign was certainly
the climax of Egyptian culture and civilisation.
                    STANLEY LANE-POOLE, *The Story of Cairo*

An institution is the lengthened shadow of one man.
                                        EMERSON

IN 1335, the bléssed Nile failed to rise and the crops failed. The price of wheat soared and the poor faced starvation. The Mamluke ameers, who held most of the land in fief, refused to sell their grain, hoping for a further rise. Wheat was sixty dirhems the ardeb on the black market, the normal price being fifteen dirhems.

Al-Nasir was furious when he heard what had happened. He struck the great ameer Qusoon in the face, because his bailiff had refused to sell his master's wheat, and ordered the bailiff to be flogged in the palace. Officials were sent to open the ameers' barns every day and to sell their grain at thirty dirhems, a good price for the fief-holder, but only half the black market rate. Orders were sent to all the Syrian provinces for officials to ride out in person, collect all available wheat and send it by caravan to Egypt, where the owners were paid thirty dirhems. Inspectors were posted in all the bakeries in Cairo to superintend the sale of bread. Thus the famine was ended. The speed and efficiency of this rescue operation are a striking example of the sultan's determination, his powers of organisation, and his concern for the welfare of the people.

*   *   *

The sultan had been conducting a (to us) amusing game of bluff with Mahanna ibn Isa, the chief of the bedouin tribes of the Syrian desert. The sultan had a passion for thoroughbred horses, some of the best of which were bred by the bedouin. He accordingly wrote to Mahanna to send him some good mares, an order with which the shaikh complied with pleasure, for Al-Nasir paid very high prices. Then the sultan invited the old chief to visit Cairo, but he made excuses and sent his three sons. Living in the open desert, bedouins have a horror of prisons.

Al-Nasir was annoyed and wrote to the Viceroy of Aleppo to evict Mahanna from his estate in Syria. But nomads have a ready answer to high-handed rulers—they cross the border into a neighbouring state. Mahanna once again camped on the Euphrates and rode to the court of the Il-Khan, who gave him a royal reception. Eventually, however, wishing to remain on good terms with the Mamlukes, the Mongols invited the shaikh to return to Syria, much to Al-Nasir's delight.

Mahanna's sons persuaded him to go to Cairo, at which Al-Nasir was so overjoyed that "he nearly flew up into the air", to borrow Maqrizi's phrase, and sent a deputation of senior ameers to greet the nomad chief. The wily old man, when he met the sultan, told him that he had come because he had seen the Prophet in a dream and had been ordered by him to visit Al-Nasir—a subtle suggestion that the sultan enjoyed special protection from on high. Al-Nasir, a simple soul in spite of his energy and determination, was delighted and loaded Mahanna with honours, even though he refused to eat at a royal banquet, doubtless fearing poison. His humble excuse was that he was a poor bedouin, who lived on camels' milk.

The sultan ordered the Viceroy of Aleppo to give back Mahanna's estate and to increase it. A hundred robes of honour were heaped on him and his followers. In addition, he was given the village of Douma outside Damascus and a cash present of nine thousand gold dinars. So, in the end, the poor, simple-minded bedouin who lived on camels' milk was not unsuccessful in the game of bluff.

*   *   *

When Baybars the Jashnekeer had been made sultan in 1309, his elevation had been consecrated by the Khalif Mustakfi. Now, long afterwards, the khalif was brought into the Citadel where he was made to live under house-arrest. Then he and his family were exiled to Qus on the Nubian frontier, where they lived in poverty. It is difficult to analyse Al-Nasir's religious convictions. He went repeatedly on pilgrimage, mingling humbly in the crowd of pilgrims. He was severe to all persons who consumed alcohol, he closed all wineshops and brothels, obliging the inmates to marry and settle down. Yet he revenged himself on the khalif for recognising Baybars, which he doubtless did under pressure, and he made use of murder to dispose of his enemies. A number of ameers, arrested when Al-Nasir returned to the throne, were released in 1334, after some twenty to twenty-five years in detention.

*   *   *

In 1334 occurred the death of Abu Saeed, the Il-Khan, the great-great-grandson of Hulagu, "The enemy of God", who had destroyed Baghdad and killed the Khalif Mustasim. Abu Saeed, who was only thirty when he died, had been a sincere Muslim and a pleasant, civilised young man. He was generous and handsome, played the violin and composed music. He also forbade the consumption of alcohol, but with little effect. Unfortunately, it was the fierce Jenghis

Khan and Hulagu who had established the Mongol Empire. When the rulers became polite, pious and musical, the Il-Khanate disintegrated. Rival claimants soon tore the country apart.

The most powerful figure at court was Hasan Jalairi, head of the Jalair family, who had married a sister of the Il-Khan Ghazan. Another claimant to the throne was Musa ibn Ali ibn Baidu, also a great-great-grandson of Hulagu.[1] A certain Arpa was yet another competitor, but was quickly eliminated. Hasan, now nicknamed Buzurg or the Great, defeated Musa in a battle near Tabriz.

The whole area of the Il-Khanate[2] fell into anarchy, ceasing any longer to be a threat to the Mamluke Empire. Rival chiefs from Persia, Iraq and Asia Minor wrote to Al-Nasir Muhammad, offering to become his vassals and soliciting his protection. The sultan accepted these professions of devotion, but was wary enough not to promise military aid to any of the contestants. Hasan Buzurg attacked the Ameer of Sivas, but ultimately established his principal capital in Baghdad. A new Turkman family called Dulqadir seized power in Albistan.

The collapse of the Il-Khan Empire freed the Mamlukes from their only serious enemy, though it left them with the lesser problem of an eastern frontier in anarchy. It also made it easier for them to destroy the Armenian Christian Kingdom of Cilicia, which had in the past been a Mongol protectorate. As a result, in the winter of 1336–1337, yet another Mamluke expedition invaded Cilicia and again destroyed the port of Ayas. Nevertheless the Cilician kingdom still struggled on, though the Mamlukes occupied most of the frontier fortresses. The Armenian king was Leo V, who had married Eleanor of Aragon, the widow of Henry II, King of Cyprus. The force returned to Cairo on 12th August, 1337.

In 1339, the ruler of Nisibin[3] wrote to ask the sultan's protection, offering to mint coins in his name. Al-Nasir thanked him and gave the ambassador a robe of honour, but avoided undertaking any commitments. The object of such approaches to the sultan by these insecure minor rulers was partly to ensure for themselves a safe asylum, should they be obliged to flee from their countries.

*   *   *

The Ameer Tinkiz had been Viceroy of Damascus almost as long as Al-Nasir had been sultan. The two seemed to fulfil Aristotle's definition of friendship—one mind in two bodies. When Tinkiz visited Cairo, the sultan gave him a royal reception. Neither man,

[1] Genealogical Tree 5, page 78.   [2] Map 15, page 76.   [3] Map 22, page 177.

for more than twenty years, seemed to have any secrets from the other.

In 1340, a series of fires broke out unaccountably in Damascus. Investigation revealed that two Christian monks had come from Constantinople and had been guilty of these acts of arson, assisted by three Damascene Christians, who were arrested, tortured and paraded through Damascus nailed to planks on the backs of camels. The monks escaped to Constantinople. A curious detail is that the fires were started by "cakes" of some material containing naphtha, which did not ignite until three or four hours after they had been laid—an early type of time bomb.

The case file was sent to the sultan, who was angry at the severity of the torture inflicted on the three Christians. He wrote to Tinkiz, pointing out that Constantinople was full of Muslim merchants on whom the Byzantine Emperor might retaliate. Tinkiz, informed of the sultan's anger, began to transfer his wealth to Qilaat Jabir on the Euphrates in order, presumably, to be able to escape in an emergency and go to the Tatars. The sultan was informed of these precautions and decided to act before Tinkiz could desert.

Al-Nasir, accordingly, collected all the ameers in Cairo and made them renew their oaths of loyalty. He then told them that Tinkiz was in revolt. A large distribution in cash was made to ameers, officers of the *halaqa* and the Royal Mamlukes, and a military detachment was sent post-haste to Damascus. Tinkiz was taken by surprise and arrested.

On 4th July, 1340, Tinkiz arrived in Cairo. Transferred under escort to Alexandria, he was secretly put to death there a week later. He was not tortured or made a public spectacle. The sultan seems to have been unnecessarily hasty, but he himself had made Tinkiz so powerful that, in the end, he became afraid of him. We have seen that, under the Mamluke system, provincial governors in Syria were all directly under Cairo, and not under Damascus. Al-Nasir, in the days of their friendship, had changed this organisation and had ordered all provincial governors to take orders from Tinkiz, and not to write to Cairo.

Tinkiz had been Viceroy of Damascus for twenty-eight years, but his administration had deteriorated in the last three or four years. He had become difficult and irritable, possibly due to so long a period of autocratic power—indeed Al-Nasir himself had deteriorated in the same manner. The sultan, doubtless, noticed the deterioration in the administration of Syria, but Tinkiz had grown so powerful that his removal was a tricky operation. Two of the daughters of Tinkiz were married to the sultan's sons.

Tinkiz had become extremely rich during his long term as Viceroy of Damascus. His wardrobe included a thousand silk shirts and great quantities of embroidered robes in silk and satin. He possessed four thousand two hundred horses and riding camels, and many other forms of wealth.

Many of his qualities he shared with the sultan. He did away with oppression, enforced impartial justice, extended education and put an end to public immorality. He closed all brothels and drink shops in and around Damascus. He did not allow the ameers to wrong the public or the merchants, but sent both parties to the Law Courts. He never accepted gifts or bribes, and he everywhere prevented peculation. He repaired the great Umaiyid mosque in Damascus and improved the city water supply. He widened and improved the thoroughfares, and reformed the collection of taxes.

He was loved by the people and feared by the ameers, as was the sultan himself. He was devoted to hunting in the Mongol manner— which was to extend an immense arc of soldiers, who drove the game before them in a narrowing circle towards the hunters. The latter then enjoyed a wildly exciting few hours, using their bows to shoot down the galloping animals. The best game was gazelle, oryx or ostriches. So great was his prestige that if Tinkiz crossed the Euphrates on a hunting trip, says Maqrizi, the people of Baghdad and Tabriz prepared to flee from their homes. He was, in many ways, the ideal paternalistic administrator. Al-Nasir fully appreciated the outstanding qualities of Tinkiz, which so closely resembled his own.

Early in 1341, the sultan suffered a serious illness, possibly dysentery, and was confined for some time to his bed. He recovered, though his face had changed and he looked old. Nevertheless the public gave vent to their joy, decorated the streets, danced, sang and played.

In May 1341, however, the dysentery returned, to the general distress of the people, and the sultan once more took to his bed. The ameers eyed one another suspiciously, fearing civil war if the sultan died. The great Ameers Qussoon and Bushtak were particularly jealous of one another. People began to hoard supplies in their houses for fear of disturbances. A group of ameers waited on Al-Nasir to beg him to nominate one of his sons as heir. He appointed Abu Bekr, warning the ameers against his son Ahmad, who was in exile in Kerak. Thereafter he grew rapidly weaker, and died on 7th June, 1341, at the age of fifty-six.

Malik-al-Nasir Muhammad had been born on 25th March, 1285. He became sultan in 1293, at the age of eight. A year later he was deposed and Kitbugha seized the throne, followed by Lajeen. In

1298, he returned and remained as nominal sultan for ten years, though Salar and Baybars monopolised all the power. In 1308, under pretence of going on pilgrimage, Al-Nasir withdrew to Kerak and abdicated, while Baybars the Jashnekeer seized the throne. In 1309, Malik-al-Nasir returned and remained the sole autocrat of the empire for thirty-two years.

Malik-al-Nasir Muhammad was the greatest of all the Mamluke sultans and ruled longer than any other. Under him, the empire reached the highest pinnacle of its power, commencing to decline from the moment of his death. It may therefore, be worthwhile, briefly to summarise his qualities.

Firstly, his personality and his determination gave the empire thirty-two years of peace and prosperity. His authority was ruthlessly enforced. When he returned from Kerak for his third reign, he arrested thirty ameers in one day, some of whom were to spend twenty or more years in detention This determined action struck fear into the hearts of all potential rebels, and gave the empire thirty-two years of internal peace.

Secondly, he was genuinely devoted to the interests of the common people, and was sincerely loved by them.

Thirdly, his energy and industry were untiring, in checking the accounts and maintaining the files and records, in promoting public works, roads, irrigation and building, and in himself travelling round the empire. He knew all his mamlukes by name with their personal history; and he kept a stud-book, with a folio for each of the three thousand mares on his farm. He was always considerate to officials, even including his grooms and stable boys, the men who looked after his hawks, and the cooks and servants in the palace.

Fourthly, he was almost puritan in his morals. His conversation was always correct, and he never swore. His dress, amid his gorgeous court, was very restrained and he normally wore only plain cotton clothes of mediocre quality. He never wore gold, jewels or silk. He was resolutely opposed to alcohol, and any ameer suspected of drinking was exiled. He was strict in his sexual morals, closed all brothels and exiled persons guilty of immorality. Yet he liked the palace to be full of beautiful slave girls, who wore pearls, gold bangles and gold sandals, and had silk counterpanes on their beds.

Fifthly, one of the sultan's most unfortunate qualities was his credulity. Without this weakness, he could never have been deceived for seven years by a financial swindler like Neshu. Moreover, not only did he believe what he was told, but he acted rashly without further enquiries. We shall never know how many ameers were arrested and imprisoned on the mere report of an informer, or of a personal enemy of the victim.

Sixthly, he disliked wars and always sought a peaceful solution. He made use of assassination against his enemies rather than of military operations. Perhaps his distaste for war was due to his boyhood's experience at the battles of Wadi al Khaznadar and Shaqhab. The only military operations he sanctioned were against Nubia and the Armenian Kingdom of Cilicia, in both of which cases the Mamlukes behaved with great cruelty. He was fortunate, in comparison with Baybars the Bunduqdari and Qalaoon, that the Il-Khanate was in decline. On one occasion, when a qadhi protested to him over the priceless gifts he was sending to the Il-Khan Abu Saeed, the sultan replied, "You keep quiet, qadhi! You don't know what I know. By these means, I spare myself anxiety and my soldiers their lives."

Seventhly, although he was short, lame of one foot and physically insignificant, there was about him something which made all admit that he was every inch a king.

The magnificent reign of Malik-al-Nasir Muhammad, like that of Louis XIV of France, was followed by a deluge of troubles. Both were obsessed by glory, prestige and magnificence. Both dominated the age in which they lived, Louis largely by means of war, but Al-Nasir by wealth, by the arts of peace, by architecture, public works and the splendour of his court. Both could be described as Rois Soleils.

*   *   *

Al-Nasir left fourteen sons, eight of whom were in turn to be sultans, but none of whom were a success. He never succeeded in winning the affection of his own sons, though he himself was loved by the public. This failure may have been partly due to the fact that his days were so full. He abolished the post of wazeer, or prime minister, and himself acted as head of the administration, giving orders direct to the different departments. Working day and night, he had no time to give to his children.

*   *   *

But if Al-Nasir made the Mamluke Empire perhaps the greatest Power of his day, he bequeathed to it two factors which were ultimately to destroy it. The first of these was his treatment of his young mamlukes, the second was his survey of the land.

Previous sultans had bought large numbers of boys from the steppes, but when they arrived, they were sent to special training companies, commanded by eunuchs. Here the boys were taught the Muslim religion, dignity, deportment and good manners. But most of their time was spent in rigorous military training, horsemanship, shooting with bows and arrows, and the use of lance, sword and mace, under the strictest discipline. They wore plain cotton clothing and received a low rate of pay. When qualified, they were posted to a military unit. Even if, in later life, they rose to high rank, they appreciated that their success was the result of the long years of training and discipline which they had undergone.

Al-Nasir changed all this. He bought great numbers of boys (and girls) from the steppes, and paid very high prices. When a batch of primitive tribal boys arrived, he immediately gave them splendid horses to ride, and loaded them with fine clothes, weapons and handsome saddlery. "When a new mamluke sees such prosperity as satisfies all that he could desire," the sultan used to say, "his heart will forget his native country, and his only desire will be to serve his master." This policy of pampering the boys instead of disciplining them, was to lead to disastrous results after Al-Nasir's death. The powerful personality of the sultan enabled him to preserve discipline with ease, but when he was succeeded by weaker men, the indiscipline of the young mamlukes soon led to chaos.

The second tragic mistake which Al-Nasir bequeathed to his successors was his land survey, commonly called *Al Rawk al Nasiri.* Mention has already been made of the fact that the army, both ameers and mamlukes, were paid by the allotment of fiefs of land, which were cultivated by Egyptian farm workers, part of the value of their produce constituting the pay of the officer or soldier. The fiefs belonged to the Army Office, not to the soldier. When an ameer of drums was promoted to be an ameer of one hundred, for example, he surrendered his fief and received a larger one in proportion to the pay pertaining to his higher rank.

The Mamluke army (excluding local forces) consisted of three categories:

(1) The Royal Mamlukes
(2) The ameers and their personal mamlukes
(3) The *halaqa.*

The Royal Mamlukes obviously belonged to the sultan and received fiefs and several other perquisites, money, clothing, food and forage at certain intervals.

The fief allotted to an ameer was supposed to be sufficient for himself and his personal mamlukes, ten, forty or a hundred.

The *halaqa* was an army reserve. The men, often old mamlukes, lived off their fiefs, as did their officers, but could be mobilised in war time.

The principal object of Al-Nasir's reorganisation of fiefs was to increase the royal share, thereby enabling the sultan to maintain an increased number of regular, full-time Royal Mamlukes. This object was achieved by cutting down the fiefs allotted to the *halaqa*. In modern terms we should say that Al-Nasir increased the strength of the full-time regular army, by reducing the money allotted to reservists. This meant that the total strength of the army on mobilization was considerably reduced.

On the other hand, the despotic power of the sultan was greatly increased for a far higher proportion of the army was now composed of Royal Mamlukes, who were the sultan's personal property. The sultan, however, did not foresee that the Royal Mamlukes might realise, sooner or later, that they were the only serious military force in the empire, and might thus endeavour to impose their own military rule on the sultan and on the empire alike.

*   *   *

We naturally tend to condemn autocracy, but this is to judge the world by the mentality of the Western nations in the twentieth century. These ideas were not current in the fourteenth century either in England or France, in Egypt or Persia. Kings were expected to rule and especially to suppress lawless elements. It was the military class which threatened law and order, whether they were the feudal barons in Europe or the Mamluke ameers in Egypt and Syria. The confusion caused in Europe by lawless barons was cured by the establishment of the powerful Tudor or Bourbon kings. In the same manner, the restless Mamluke ameers could only be kept in order by strong sultans who, incidentally, were always popular with the general public.

The "perpetual round" from anarchic chiefs to strong monarchs, to democratic balances, to popular anarchy and then back again to authoritarian rule has repeated itself again and again in different countries. It is illogical to compare a nation in the stage of democracy to one in the stage of authoritarianism, as if these systems were permanent institutions in either. For political systems never stand still.

"A democracy cannot exist as a permanent form of government. It can only exist until the majority of voters discover that they can vote themselves largesse out of the public treasury. From that moment on, the majority always votes for the candidate who promises them the most benefits from the public treasury, with the result that democracy always collapses over a loose fiscal policy, always to be followed by a dictatorship and then a monarchy."

These words, so significant for us today, were not written by a modern fascist, but by an eighteenth-century historian of Scotland, Alexander Fraser Tytler. But the exciting feature of this "perpetual round" from autocracy to anarchy and back is that, under conditions apparently so completely dissimilar, it applied to Mamluke Egypt as much as to twentieth-century Britain. Suffice it to say that the Mamluke Empire rose to its pinnacle of greatness under the arbitrary rule of Baybars the Bunduqdari, Qalaoon al Elfi and Al-Nasir Muhammad. Moreover it was under these autocrats that the empire was rich and prosperous and *the common people were happy*.

Alexander Tytler ends his statement by saying that democracy is always followed by a dictatorship and then by a monarchy. Here he touches upon one of the problems which the Mamlukes never overcame. The best form of government may be a dictatorship and an angel from heaven. But the problem then arises how to find another dictator, when the angel dies. Monarchy can easily be denounced as illogical. No one family can produce an endless succession of capable rulers, but at least the death of one need not be followed by disturbances or civil wars until the next dictator emerges. Legitimate monarchy may produce mediocre rulers, but at least it insures a peaceful takeover.

The Mamluke system was completely equalitarian. Every Mamluke began his career as a nameless slave. The idea of heredity, or aristocracy was strange to them. But the penalty which they paid for equal opportunity was constant civil war. And so, throughout their history, we see the two objectives in conflict—strong orderly rule by capable leaders against the desire for a peaceful succession to the throne. The sons of dying sultans were accepted as their heirs in order to avoid civil wars, but, when they proved incapable, rebellions and civil wars marked the course of the search for a really capable successor. The tragic forty years following the death of Malik-al-Nasir Muhammad emphasise this endless Mamluke dilemma.

NOTABLE EVENTS

Death of the Il-Khan Abu Saeed Disintegration of the Il-Khan Empire	1334

Year of famine in Egypt	1335
Mamluke invasion of Cilicia	1336–1337
Arrest and execution of Tinkiz, Viceroy of Damascus	1340
Death of Malik-al-Nasir Muhammad	7th June, 1341

PERSONALITIES

Mamlukes
Sultan Malik-al-Nasir Muhammad
Ameer Tinkiz, Viceroy of Damascus
Abu Bekr, son of Al-Nasir

Mongols
Il-Khan Abu Saeed
Hasan Buzurg Jalairli
Musa ⎱ Pretenders to the Il-Khanate
Arpa ⎰

SUMMARY OF MAMLUKE SULTANS
1250–1341

1.	Spray-of-Pearls, Queen of Egypt, widow of the Ayoubid Sultan Malik-al-Salih Ayoub	1250
2.	Malik-al-Muizz Aibek and Spray-of-Pearls	1250–1257
3.	Malik-al-Mansoor Ali, son of Aibek (Guardian, Qutuz)	1257–1259
4.	Malik-al-Mudhaffar Qutuz	1259–1260
5.	Malik-al-Dhahir Baybars al Bunduqdari	1260–1277
6.	Malik-al-Saeed Baraka, son of Baybars	1277–1279
7.	Malik-al-Aadil Salamish, son of Baybars	1279
8.	Malik-al-Mansoor Qalaoon	1279–1290
9.	Malik-al-Ashraf Khalil, son of Qalaoon	1290–1293
10.	Malik-al-Nasir Muhammad, son of Qalaoon (First Reign)	1293–1294
11.	Malik-al-Aadil Kitbugha	1294–1296
12.	Malik-al-Mansoor Lajeen	1296–1298
13.	Malik-al-Nasir Muhammad (Second Reign)	1298–1308
14.	Malik-al-Mudhaffar Baybars, the Jashnekeer	1308–1309
15.	Malik-al-Nasir Muhammad (Third Reign)	1309–1341

When we see a list of fifteen sultans in ninety-one years, we seem at first to be faced with a hopelessly confused story, which we can never hope to remember. It is worth noticing, however, that, out of these ninety-one years, sixty years were occupied by three reigns alone, namely:

Baybars the Bunduqdari	17 years
Qalaoon	11 years
Malik-al-Nasir Muhammad (Third Reign)	32 years

The remaining thirty-one years were occupied by ten stop-gap sultans, some of them children, some of them soldiers of fortune, whose talents were unequal to the task. Thus, during this period, the free-for-all Mamluke system of selecting sultans resulted in sixty years of outstandingly capable government, and thirty-one years of insecurity.

XII

A Sequence of Sultans

The twelve descendants of Al-Nasir who followed him in rapid succession during forty-two years (1340–82) were mere figureheads; their ameers ruled, deposing or murdering the sultan at pleasure. None of these sultans distinguished himself in any field of endeavour and the only notable monument is the Mosque of Sultan Hasan, son of Al-Nasir, completed in 1362 and considered the most beautiful of those built on a cruciform plan.
PHILIP HITTI, History of the Arabs

> Boys must not have th'ambitious care of men,
> Nor men the weak anxieties of age.
> HORACE

THE DESCENDANTS OF QALAOON

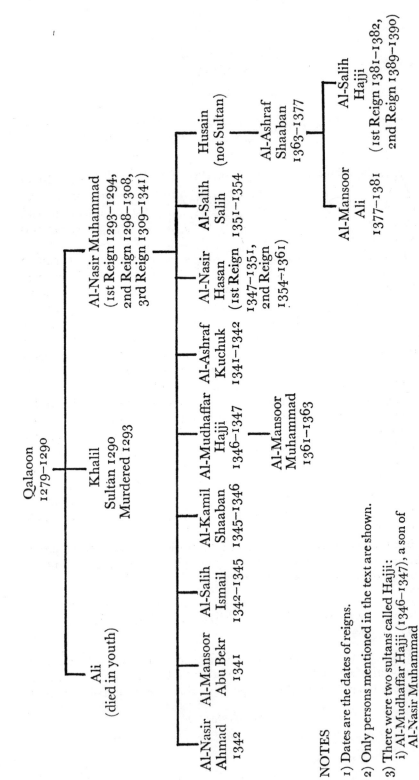

Qalaoon
1279–1290

Ali
(died in youth)

Khalil
Sultan 1290
Murdered 1293

Al-Nasir Muhammad
(1st Reign 1293–1294,
2nd Reign 1298–1308,
3rd Reign 1309–1341)

Al-Nasir Ahmad
1342

Al-Mansoor Abu Bekr
1341

Al-Salih Ismail
1342–1345

Al-Kamil Shaaban
1345–1346

Al-Mudhaffar Hajji
1346–1347

Al-Ashraf Kuchuk
1341–1342

Al-Nasir Hasan
(1st Reign 1347–1351,
2nd Reign 1354–1361)

Al-Salih Salih
1351–1354

Husain
(not Sultan)

Al-Mansoor Muhammad
1361–1363

Al-Ashraf Shaaban
1363–1377

Al-Mansoor Ali
1377–1381

Al-Salih Hajji
(1st Reign 1381–1382,
2nd Reign 1389–1390)

NOTES

1) Dates are the dates of reigns.
2) Only persons mentioned in the text are shown.
3) There were two sultans called Hajji:
   i) Al-Mudhaffar Hajji (1346–1347), a son of
      Al-Nasir Muhammad
   ii) Al-Salih Hajji, son of Al-Ashraf Shaaban.

Genealogical Tree 6

AL-MALIK-AL-MANSOOR ABU BEKR

ABU Bekr was not the eldest of Al-Nasir's sons, but his father on his deathbed had nominated him as his successor. He was installed on 30th May, 1341, took his seat on the throne and the ameers and the notables kissed the ground. The new sultan was twenty years of age.

The Ameer Taqazdemur was chosen as regent and the Ameer Qusoon was made commander-in-chief. The Ameer Tajar, the Duwadar or chief secretary, was a bitter enemy of Qusoon, and soon the army was divided into two cliques each supporting one of the rivals. The sultan, who was young, hasty and indiscreet, consulted one of his intimate mamlukes on the idea of arresting Qusoon, a proposal which had been made to him by Tajar. The intimate mamluke told Qusoon, who consulted a group of ameers of his party. They decided to dethrone the sultan.

A few days later, the Ameer Qusoon went up unexpectedly to the Citadel, arrested the young sultan, and sent him into exile at Qus, on the frontier of Nubia.[1] His reign had lasted three months. Qusoon then immediately arrested Tajar and his supporters and sent them to prison in Alexandria. He then despatched an order to the governor of Qus to kill the sultan, which was promptly done. This coup d'état was extremely well organised, and was over before anyone knew what was happening. There was no fighting, only the sultan himself being killed.

But the very ease with which the coup was executed was to prove disastrous. By demonstrating how simple it was to change a sultan, it ushered in long years of instability.

AL-MALIK-AL-ASHRAF KUCHUK

The Ameer Qusoon was now the dictator of Egypt, but hesitated to proclaim himself sultan—at least until he was more secure. A sultan of twenty years old, however, might have been awkward and

[1] Map 18, page 129.

had his own ideas. He accordingly selected an infant son of Al-Nasir Muhammad, aged only seven years. Al-Malik-al-Ashraf Kuchuk[2] was installed as sultan on 27th August, 1341. Qusoon moved his residence to the Citadel and took over the control of the government. The practice of choosing small children to be sultans was to become increasingly popular in future years with power-greedy ameers.

The seizure of power by Qusoon, however, caused widespread public bewilderment. After thirty-two years of stable rule under Al-Nasir, the descendants of Qalaoon had almost become a dynasty. The viceroys in the provinces were in doubt what to do, and the insecurity brought business to a standstill.

Qusoon arrested the Royal Mamlukes who had favoured his rival, Tajar, and sent orders to the Viceroy of Damascus to arrest the Viceroy of Aleppo, the Ameer Tushtimur. The latter, however, received warning, rode quickly to Kerak and took the Ameer Ahmad, another son of Al-Nasir, who was living there. The Viceroys of Tarablus, Safad and Hama, hearing of this development, declared for Ahmad. The Viceroy of Damascus also joined them.

A number of ameers in Cairo, including Yalbugha al Yahyawi, Al-Nasir's favourite, agreed to rise against Qusoon and assembled in the Roumaila, the open space outside the royal stables.[3]

The leader of this revolt was the Ameer Aidghamish, who broke into the Citadel, arrested Qusoon and sent him to prison in Alexandria. Kuchuk abandoned his throne and retired to his mother's apartments. He had "reigned" for five months. He was to remain, a child, with his mother, until he died a few years later.

*　　*　　*

AL-MALIK-AL-NASIR AHMAD

Ahmad was the third of Al-Nasir's sons to reign. His father had, on his deathbed, warned the ameers against making him sultan. He was installed on 21st April, 1342. He was the eldest of his father's surviving sons, and appeared to be a strong and handsome young man. He began his reign by ordering the execution of five ameers who were in detention in Alexandria. He then appointed as Viceroy of Egypt the Ameer Tushtimur, nicknamed "Green Peas", former Viceroy of Aleppo, who had initiated the movement to make him

---

[2] Malik-al-Ashraf means Most Noble King. Kuchuk in Turkish means small.
[3] Map 21, page 158.

sultan. A month later, he ordered the arrest of Tushtimur "Green Peas". He appointed Qutlubugha al Fakhri as Viceroy of Damascus, then immediately ordered his arrest. Tushtimur and Qutlubugha were the two principal ameers who had placed him on the throne.

Forty days after his accession, the sultan set out on a journey, without revealing where he was going, and taking Tushtimur and Qutlubugha with him in chains. He went straight to Kerak, where he had previously been living. The ameers in Cairo wrote to the sultan, asking him to return, but he replied that he preferred to live in Kerak. He then ordered the execution of Tushtimur and Qutlubugha in the Castle of Kerak. When the ameers heard of the executions, they decided to dethrone Ahmad and to elevate another son of Al-Nasir called Ismail.

Ahmad had been sultan for two months and twelve days. He was obviously insane, the reason, no doubt, why his father had refused to name him as his heir, and had warned the ameers against him.

AL-MALIK-AL-SALIH ISMAIL

Ismail, the fourth son of Al-Nasir, was installed on 18th July, 1342. The Ameer Aqsonqor al Salari was made viceroy and head of the government. The new Sultan Ismail behaved with great kindness and generosity, and distributed sums of money to his father's intimate mamlukes.

A force was sent to arrest the former Sultan Ahmad in Kerak, but the latter fortified himself in the castle, which the column was unable to take by assault. Ahmad resisted for two years, but then the garrison was left without food, and the former sultan was forced to surrender and was executed in July 1344. He had resisted with extraordinary courage, but was quite insane.

Unfortunately, a year later, Ismail fell ill and died on 17th July, 1345, after a reign of three years. He was the best of all Al-Nasir's sons and was generous, well-meaning and anxious to see equal justice for all his subjects. He was deeply mourned by all classes. It was indeed a tragedy that he, a man who might have made a great ruler, should die so young.

AL-MALIK-AL-KAMIL[4] SHAABAN

Nominated as his heir by his brother Ismail, Shaaban, raised to the

[4] The Perfect King.

throne on 23rd July, 1345, was the fifth of Al-Nasir's sons to become
sultan. The Ameer Argtai was made regent. Al-Nasir's favourite,
Yalbugha al Yahyawi, became Viceroy of Damascus. This year,
little Kuchuk, former sultan, died a natural death in the private
apartments of the palace.

Shaaban behaved with youthful foolishness, ordering arrests and
sequestrations. Scarcely had the Ameer Yalbugha al Yahyawi
assumed the post of Viceroy of Damascus than he declared himself
in rebellion. A force was mobilised to go to Syria.

Shaaban then sent for two of his brothers, Hajji and Husain, and
accused them of conspiracy. Both they and their two mothers denied
the charge with tears, but Shaaban gave orders for their confinement
in a room in the Duhaisha Palace. These were scarcely more than
nursery squabbles, partly due to the fact that the various sons had
different mothers.

On 12th September, the Ameer Maliktimur the Hejazi, with his
mamlukes in battle order, advanced across the Roumaila to the
Chain Gate.[5] The sultan mounted and ordered the drums to be
beaten to call the troops to arms, but no ameers or soldiers answered
the call. The sultan took refuge in his mother's apartments and the
insurgents entered the Citadel. They broke into the Duhaisha Palace
and brought out the Ameer Hajji, kissing the ground before him and
hailing him as sultan. They then sent for Shaaban and locked him
up in the same room from which Hajji had been released.

This bloodless coup d'état occupied only an hour immediately
after sunrise, so easy had it become to change a sultan. Breakfast
laid for Sultan Shaaban was eaten by Sultan Hajji. Three days later,
Shaaban was strangled in the Duhaisha. He had been a sultan for a
year and two months. He was fair-haired and blue-eyed, with a large
nose and his face was pockmarked. He was of a violent temperament
and was probably incapable of conducting public affairs. His
mother was said to have been a Greek, which might have merely
meant that she came from Asia Minor.

*   *   *

It is difficult to follow the anarchy of these years but the following
considerations may be relevant.

(1) None of the sons of Al-Nasir were of mature age. Ismail might
have made a good sultan but died of illness. The antics of the others

[5] Map 21, page 158.

were mostly the emotional outbursts of children, fomented by the rivalries of their mothers.

(2) In these circumstances, the only solution would have been a wise and firm regent, but any ameer who undertook this task immediately became the target of conspiracies by the other ameers. The brief careers of the regents were as tragic as those of the boy-sultans themselves.

(3) There was no agreed procedure for regents. Child-sultans seemed to issue orders which were obeyed, in spite of the presence of a regent.

(4) Al-Nasir had given little time to the training of his children, because he was always so busy. But even if he had brought them up more carefully, the circumstances of the Mamluke state made the reign of a child impossible.

(5) Yet in spite of these adverse conditions, none but the descendants of Al-Nasir were considered for the throne. In a community which attached so little importance to heredity, this is a remarkable tribute to the glory which still clung to Muhammad, the victorious king.

AL-MALIK-AL-MUDHAFFAR HAJJI

Hajji was fifteen years old when he succeeded his brother, Shaaban, in September 1346. He was called Hajji, because he had been born on the pilgrimage to Mecca. Soon after his accession, the rebel Ameer Yalbugha al Yahyawi was defeated and killed in Damascus.

Hajji spent the day in the palace playing with his pet pigeons, yet orders for the arrest of ameers continued to emanate from the palace in his name. One year and three months after his accession, a group of ameers rebelled, a little battle was fought outside the Citadel and Hajji was killed. He was a handsome boy, reputed to be brave, but given to arrogance and violence. The ameers decided to appoint his brother, Hasan, who was only twelve years old.

AL-MALIK-AL-NASIR HASAN
(First Reign)

Hasan became sultan on 26th July, 1347. Soon after his accession, plague broke out in Egypt. Before long, between a thousand and fifteen hundred people were alleged to be dying daily in Cairo alone.[6]

[6] According to Maqrizi. Ibn Iyas gives much higher figures.

On one disastrous day, twenty thousand deaths were alleged to have occurred, but such figures are extremely unreliable. The victims were hastily buried in large pits, thirty or forty together. From Egypt, the epidemic went on to Palestine, twenty-two thousand people dying in the Gaza area in one month.

The plague of 1347 is alleged by contemporary writers to have been the worst which Egypt had ever experienced, though plague had been known for many centuries. The whole epidemic was said to have cost nine hundred thousand deaths in Cairo and the surrounding district. All who could do so fled the city and a great part of the Delta lay fallow for want of cultivators. From Egypt the plague passed on to Europe where it became famous as the Black Death.

Malik-al-Nasir Hasan "reigned" for four years, playing little part in public affairs. At the age of sixteen, he showed signs of wishing to intervene in matters of state. On 11th August, 1351, the Ameer Taz al Mansoori, with a group of supporters, rode up to the Citadel, pronounced Hasan dethroned and placed him under house-arrest in his mother's apartments in the palace.

AL-MALIK-AL-SALIH SALIH

Salih was not quite fourteen when he became sultan on 12th August, 1351. His mother had been a daughter of Ameer Tinkiz, the famous Viceroy of Damascus.[7] Taz al Mansoori, who had led the revolt, became dictator, suppressing an attempted revolt by two other ameers. News then came that Baybugha Aroos, Viceroy of Aleppo, was in revolt, in alliance with the Viceroy of Tarablus,[8] and had taken and looted Damascus. The Ameer Taz left for Damascus with the army and accompanied by the boy-sultan, the khalif and the four chief qadhis.

Baybugha Aroos fled to the Turkmans in the north, the revolt was suppressed and the army returned to Cairo. Qaraja ibn Dulqadir, the Turkman Prince of Albistan, was arrested and brought to Cairo and executed, for having assisted Baybugha Aroos. The Dulqadir family were to give the Mamlukes endless trouble for a hundred and sixty years. As usual, the latter handled them with violence, instead of winning their loyalty.

The empire was ruled for three years by Taz al Mansoori as dictator. In October 1354, Taz left for the Buhaira on a shooting

[7] Page 223.
[8] The former Frankish port of Tripoli will henceforward be referred to as Tarablus, a Mamluke province.

trip. In his absence, the Ameer Shaikhu al Amri seized Sultan Salih and placed him under house-arrest in the female apartments. He had reigned for three years and a little more than two months. According to Ibn Iyas,[9] Salih would have made an excellent sultan. He was religious, of good morals, well-meaning, and was deeply concerned with the well-being of the people, who loved him and were contented with his rule. The revolt of Ameer Shaikhu was, of course, not against the sultan, but against the dictator, Taz.

AL-MALIK-AL-NASIR HASAN
(Second Reign)

After consultation, the ameers decided to reinstate Malik-al-Nasir Hasan, whom Taz had dethroned in order to make himself dictator. Hasan was accordingly fetched from his mother's apartments and became sultan for the second time on 23rd October, 1354. Meanwhile the Ameer Taz had hurried back from his shooting party. His mamlukes skirmished with those of Shaikhu in the streets of Cairo for forty-eight hours.

The two rival dictators then effected a reconciliation, at which Shaikhu is reported to have wept copiously, an unexpected psychological reaction between two contending dictators. Taz was invested by Sultan Hasan with a robe of honour and left Cairo on 28th October, 1354, to be Viceroy of Aleppo. In the manner with which we are today familiar, the new administration instituted enquiries into the actions of its predecessor, thereby finding pretexts to imprison, fine or torture its political rivals.

Hasan had passed much of his three years under house-arrest in prayer and religious studies. Both Hasan and Salih seem to have been kind, pleasant and conscientious boys. The struggle for power was, of course, not between the brothers, but between Taz and Shaikhu, the rival dictators.

*　　*　　*

The Ameer Shaikhu, who was busy liquidating his political rivals, was actively engaged in the erection, near the mosque of Ibn Tulun in Cairo, of a large block of buildings including a mosque, a school and a monastery. It is interesting to note that Mamlukes were often sincerely pious in their own way. They were, however, in most cases, not converted to Islam until they were brought to

[9] Muhammad ibn Iyas, *Bidoya al Zuhoor fi Waqaia al Duhoor.*

Egypt, at about the age of twelve. But children absorb a great deal before twelve, and the boys must already have acquired much of the ruthlessness of the steppes. Their harsh cruelties must be attributed to the savagery of the steppes rather than to Islam. The Muslim rulers who had preceded them—the Arab khalifs and the Ayoubids for example—had been tolerant rather than cruel.

The mixed culture acquired by the Mamlukes, as a result, caused them to deal savagely with their enemies in the manner of the nomads of the steppes, but simultaneously to seek to propitiate the Muslim God by lavishing their material wealth on the erection of mosques, schools and monasteries. At least they thereby bequeathed to us an amazing heritage of splendid buildings, not to mention marbles, mosaics, furniture, jewellery, filigree work and objets d'art.

It is surprising how frequently men perform actions in the name of their religion, completely contrary to the precepts of that same religion. Thus the Mamlukes constructed wonderful mosques, though Muhammad was indifferent to buildings. His first mosque in Medina was a mud hut, roofed with palm-fronds. In the same manner, so-called Christians fought and tortured one another in the name of religion, though their Master called peacemakers the children of God and told his followers to love those who persecuted them. "If your conception of God is radically false," wrote Archbishop William Temple, "the more devout you are, the worse it will be for you."[10]

In 1355, the sons of Qaraja ibn Dulqadir of Albistan, who had been executed for helping Baybugha Aroos, came to Cairo with a propitiatory gift. In 1336, Hasan Buzurg al Jalairi died and was succeeded as ruler of Iraq by his son Uwais.

In the Mediterranean, Frankish privateers continued to harass Muslim shipping. In 1356, they raided Tarablus and Sidon from the sea. Our historians omit to tell us what kind of Franks, but they may have been based on the Lusignan Kingdom of Cyprus.

On 28th July, 1357, while sitting with the sultan in the Hall of Justice to hear complaints, Shaikhu was attacked with a sword by a Royal Mamluke. He was carried out alive, but died later at his home. The murderer was nailed to a plank and paraded through the streets on a camel. The motive of the crime is not known. Shaikhu was the first Mamluke to bear the title of Grand Ameer. He was succeeded in power by Sarghatmish al Nasiri.

It is of passing interest that Sarghatmish repaired Amman and moved the capital of the district there, it having previously been at

[10] William Temple, *Christian Faith and Life*.

Hesban, the biblical Heshbon. The Ammonites are frequently mentioned in the Old Testament, their citadel still dominates the town and Bronze Age forts surround it. Under Alexander the Great it received a new Greek name—Philadelphia—but the local people still called it Amman, as they do today.

About this time begin the complaints concerning the devaluation of the currency. Dating from the early days of Islam, the standard coin had always been the gold dinar, which was divided into twenty silver dirhems, like the old English pounds and shillings. The devaluation began by mixing copper with the silver dirhem, the percentage of copper varying and, therefore, the intrinsic value of the dirhem doing the same. The number of dirhems to the gold dinar went up and down accordingly. Then pure copper dirhems were minted, their value being at one time fixed at twenty-four copper to one silver dirhem. So many copper dirhems were needed for even a modest purchase that they were exchanged by weight and not by count.

*   *   *

Sultan Hasan was now twenty-three and old enough to rule. On 27th August, 1358, Sarghatmish was arrested, sent to Alexandria and later executed. He was an example of a new type of Mamluke ameer, for he wrote a good hand and was an expert in Muslim law. He also spoke Arabic and, for some time, controlled the civil administration in person. After the fall of Sarghatmish the sultan promoted a number of his own intimate mamlukes.

In November 1359, the Viceroy of Aleppo again invaded Cilicia and took Adana, Tarsus and Massissa,[11] which were annexed. Mamluke garrisons were placed there and governors appointed. The Armenian kingdom was now on its last legs, and was reduced to a small mountain area around Sis.

In 1361, the Egyptian wazeer, the head of the civil administration, was arrested. Fakhr-al-Deen Majid ibn Khaseeb had maintained great state in Cairo, kept open house, and had seven hundred slave girls as servants. When he passed through Cairo, he liked to ride on his horse, while his escort and the civil officials walked on foot. After his arrest, he was made to pay a large sum of money to the treasury, and was banished to Jerusalem.

This, and other similar incidents, draw our attention to two factors. Firstly, that the career open to the talents was available for Syrians and Egyptians, as well as for Mamlukes, though in a civil

[11] Map 22, page 177.

capacity. Majid ibn Khaseeb had begun his career as a minor clerk. Secondly, it is surprising how many, when they reached the highest rank, indulged in vain display, which perhaps provoked the jealousy, or the cupidity, of the sultan, for grandeur was a prerogative of the military class. We may also conclude that, for one Egyptian who displayed such grandeur as did Majid ibn Khaseeb, hundreds more were rich but more discreet.

It is noticeable that not all the great Egyptians were *nouveaux riches*. We find the same family names repeated in high offices, generation after generation, revealing the existence of important families who supplied administrators or judges over long periods. Two such family names, at random, might be Ibn Jumaa and Al Bulqini. The sums often mulcted from senior officials were not necessarily punishments, but when a small clerk like Majid ibn Khaseeb became immensely rich, it was assumed that he had acquired his money from the nation, and it was reasonable that he give some of it back on his retirement!

* * *

On 15th March, 1361, when camped beneath the Pyramids, Sultan Hasan received information that the Ameer Yalbugha al Umari al Khassaki was coming to kill him, wearing armour beneath his clothes. With the fatal credulity and haste so common among Mamlukes, he caused Yalbugha to be sent for and stripped naked. When no armour was found, the sultan apologised, but Yalbugha went out, filled with bitter resentment at this humiliation.

Three days later, Yalbugha armed and mounted with his mamlukes. The sultan did the same and the two troops faced one another till sunset, when the sultan withdrew. Many of his mamlukes left him, seeing him afraid of one of his own ameers. During the night, Sultan Hasan returned to the Citadel and gave orders for all the mamlukes to arm and saddle, but was told that, the sultan being in camp west of the Nile, all the horses had been sent out to grass. Thereupon Hasan seems to have panicked and left the Citadel alone and on foot.

Next morning, Yalbugha arrived and found that the sultan had gone, but discovered him hiding in the Husainiya suburb. Having seized him, Yalbugha brought out Muhammad, the son of Hajji, and caused him to be proclaimed sultan. Sultan Hasan was never seen again, and was presumably murdered by Yalbugha.

According to Maqrizi, Hasan was one of the best Mamluke sultans. He never drank alcohol or indulged in sexual licence, though he was very devoted to his wives. He was a sincerely pious Muslim and might have ruled successfully for many years, had it not been for his credulity and his youthful impetuosity in publicly humiliating Yalbugha. Hasan's second reign had lasted for six years and six months. He was under thirty when he died.

AL-MALIK-AL-MANSOOR MUHAMMAD, the son of AL-MALIK-AL-MUDHAFFAR HAJJI

Muhammad was the first grandson of Malik-al-Nasir to mount the throne. The surviving sons of the great sultan were now men and dictators found a young ruler more convenient. The inauguration took place on 17th March, 1361. The Ameer Yalbugha took over sole control of the government, the sultan exercising no influence whatever.

The Viceroy of Damascus, the Ameer Baidamur, rose in revolt, ostensibly out of loyalty to Sultan Hasan. Yalbugha, taking the sultan with him, marched on Damascus and the rebellion collapsed.

In December 1362, the plague reappeared in Cairo and later spread to Syria. The epidemic lasted three months. On 31st May, 1363, Yalbugha decided to dethrone the sultan, who was now eighteen years old. After consultation with the ameers, he announced the dethronement on the grounds that Sultan Muhammad was mentally unbalanced. He had been nominal sultan for two years and three months, but Yalbugha had never spoken to him of public affairs, nor did he allow any outside persons to speak to him alone. It is probable that he was dethroned because he was growing up and beginning to ask questions.

Muhammad remained the rest of his life in the women's apartments, where, perhaps from frustration, he took to drink. He maintained a troop of ten singing girls, who sang and played to him morning and evening. He lived thus for thirty-five years, dying in 1398 at the age of fifty-three.

Yalbugha had meanwhile decided that a child would be more convenient and chose Shaaban, the son of Husain, the son of Sultan Al-Nasir, who was only ten years old. His father, the Ameer Husain, had conveniently died three months earlier.

AL-MALIK-AL-ASHRAF SHAABAN, the son of HUSAIN

On 10th October, 1365, news came that a fleet from Cyprus had landed at Alexandria. It consisted of twenty-four Venetian ships, two Genoese, ten belonging to the Knights of St. John of Rhodes, five French and about forty from Cyprus, a total of some eighty sail. The force was commanded by Peter I de Lusignan, King of Cyprus.

Peter I was an old-fashioned Crusader. His plan was to seize Alexandria and then offer to return it to the sultan in exchange for Jerusalem. He had spent the previous three years touring the courts of Europe, collecting support, money and men for his Crusade. In October 1363, he had crossed to England and had been entertained by King Edward III and Queen Philippa. The Mayor of London invited him to a great banquet in the city at which were present also Edward III, John, King of France, David, King of Scots and Edward, Prince of Wales. After dinner, the mayor was tactless enough to win fifty marks from King Peter at dice. The king was annoyed—he had come to raise money not to lose it. Fortunately, however, the mayor returned the money. On these journeys, Peter I had collected a force of volunteers from all over Europe, most of them adventurers, more interested in loot than in religion.

The force seized Alexandria by surprise on 10th October, 1367, and held it for several days. The city held a virtual monopoly of the Oriental trade and was one of the richest commercial harbours in the world. The adventurers disregarded King Peter's orders, stripped the city of all its wealth which they loaded into their ships, killed a great many people and sailed away. Yalbugha gave orders for the immediate arrest of all Franks in the Mamluke Empire.

This act of piracy was a disaster for all. It put an end to the Oriental trade on which much of the wealth of Egypt depended. It did immense harm to the maritime cities of Marseilles, Genoa, and Venice and ultimately resulted in the destruction of the Kingdom of Cyprus.

While these alarms were distracting Cairo, civil war had broken out in Nubia, where the tribes were of mixed ethnic origin, Arab, Berber and Black African. On 9th December, 1365, a force of three thousand Mamluke cavalry left Cairo and reached Aswan, where the boats were unloaded and dragged up the cataract. The boats were then reloaded and the column proceeded. Eventually the force returned to Cairo, dragging with it many tribal chiefs in chains, and great numbers of women, children, sheep and other loot. The Mamluke intervention seems to have been purely negative, a mere pretext to plunder.

Yalbugha had ordered the construction of a great fleet to attack Cyprus. Shipbuilding yards were constructed on Urwa, the Middle

Island.[12] Mamlukes would only fight as cavalry, so crews were recruited from Algerians, Turkmans and Egyptians. Genoa and other cities sent embassies to beg in vain for peace. On 16th October, 1366, a delegation came from a petty Turkman ameer of Asia Minor, Orkhan ibn Othman, offering to send ships. This little known ameerate was to grow into the mighty Ottoman Empire.

A fleet of one hundred ships was now ready and Yalbugha, with the boy-sultan, went to inspect it on Urwa Island. The bands played, the flags flew and the crews stood to action stations. After the review, the royal party landed at Jiza, on the west bank.

Power had made Yalbugha increasingly autocratic and irascible. His mamlukes complained to other ameers, who interceded with Yalbugha. The Grand Ameer was furious and vowed vengeance on his own mamlukes. On 9th December, 1366, his mamlukes tried to kill him but he escaped. His mamlukes then swore allegiance to Sultan Shaaban.

A domestic revolt in Yalbugha's household now became a contest between him and the boy-sultan. The Grand Ameer ordered the khalif to pronounce the deposition of the sultan, but he demurred. On 11th December, fighting continued all day on Urwa Island. In Cairo, the sultan, returning to the east bank, received a popular ovation.

On 14th December, 1366, Yalbugha gave up and retired to his house, where he was arrested and imprisoned in the Citadel. His personal mamlukes, however, broke into the prison and killed him. The bands played all night to celebrate the event.

* * *

But, in the autumn of 1367, Yalbugha's mamlukes were still out of control. Having killed their master, they decided to kill the sultan also. Eventually, however, both the other mamlukes and the public turned on them. Some were imprisoned, some killed, some drowned in the Nile and some exiled to Kerak, including a certain Barqooq, of whom we shall hear more.

On 6th August, 1370, a delegation of Franks came to discuss peace. Unfortunately, the Arab historians do not specify what Franks. In December 1370, the last of the Muslim prisoners taken at Alexandria were returned and peace was concluded. We may guess that the Franks concerned were Genoese or Venetians, anxious to renew trade relations. The Church of the Holy Sepulchre in Jerusalem had been closed as a reprisal for the attack on Alexandria. This was a regular

[12] Map 14, page 72.

form of reprisal against the Christian West, just as the seizure of the oilfields has been in recent years.

At the end of 1372, the sultan received a present from the Viceroy of Damascus, consisting of two lions, a hyena, forty-eight salukis or greyhounds, forty mares, fifty rolls of best quality textiles and three pairs of gold clogs, two of them set with jewels, for the royal ladies. Horses, hounds and female luxuries were the presents most valued by the Mamlukes.

The Nile failed to rise in 1373 and food prices began to soar. Many citizens, with their wives and children, went out barefoot to the desert plain by the Dome of Victory, weeping and imploring God to let the Nile rise. Every ameer of one hundred was allotted a hundred poor to feed, and other ameers, merchants and officials in proportion.

On 23rd April, 1375, Sis, the capital of the Armenian Kingdom of Cilicia, was taken after a siege of two months. The kingdom ceased to exist and its territory was annexed to the Mamluke Empire. The Armenian royal family had intermarried with the Lusignans of Cyprus, and the last Cilician king, Leo VI, died in Paris in 1393.

*　　　*　　　*

In March 1377, the sultan left on the pilgrimage. On 17th March, however, when camped at Aqaba, his mamlukes mutinied, many of them being former mamlukes of Yalbugha. The sultan escaped and rode back post-haste to Cairo, where he found that a similar mutiny had occurred, and he was captured and strangled.

Malik-al-Ashraf Shaaban was born in 1353, became sultan at the age of ten and reigned for fourteen years. He was a man of quiet and pleasant manners, who greeted everyone affably. His reign was a period of peace. He was sincerely religious and felt for the people's interests. There was no ostensible reason for his murder.

The entire Mamluke system, however, had been deeply shaken by the murder of Yalbugha by his own mamlukes, for the whole régime was built on the devotion of every mamluke to his patron. Perhaps Yalbugha was at least partly to blame, for he maltreated his mamlukes when he should, according to tradition, have treated them as his comrades. This mutual code of honour had never before been trampled under foot. After the outrage had been committed, the Yalbughawis—the former mamlukes of Yalbugha—remained a nucleus of intrigue and instability, and the Mamluke system never recovered.

In view of the fact that he was only ten years old when he came to the throne and was constantly surrounded by insubordinate, arrogant and seditious mamlukes, it is remarkable that Shaaban succeeded in giving his country fourteen years of peace.

- -

AL-MALIK-AL-MANSOOR ALI IBN SHAABAN

- -

Ali was proclaimed sultan by the rebels on 15th March, actually before his father was strangled. The reign of Shaaban, as we have seen, had been successful, but the power-greedy ameers preferred a child sultan, and Ali was only seven years old.

It is interesting to compare these Mamluke coups d'état with those with which we have recently become familiar in Asia and Africa. The coup today may be carried out with tanks instead of galloping mamlukes, but the principles are the same.

Senior appointments were now given to upstart mamlukes who, by mutiny and murder, had risen from being private soldiers to be the lords of the land. The principal engineer of these intrigues was Barqooq al Othmani, who had played a part in the murder of Yalbugha, his former patron. In a few days, Barqooq rose from a private soldier to be an ameer of drums. The commander-in-chief was disposed of in a chemical coup d'état, planned by Barqooq. Having been drugged at dinner, he fell asleep and woke up in prison in Alexandria. Cairo was in revolutionary chaos. Barqooq was made an ameer of one hundred and became virtually the dictator.

NOTABLE EVENTS

Plunder of Alexandria by Peter I, King of Cyprus	10th October, 1365
Peace concluded, probably with the Italian cities but not with Cyprus	December, 1370

VICISSITUDES OF THE DESCENDANTS OF AL-NASIR MUHAMMAD

Name	Age	Reign	Remarks
Abu Bekr May–July 1341	20	3 months	Was dethroned owing to rivalry between Tajar and Qusoon. Exiled to Qus and strangled.
Kuchuk August 1341– March 1342	7	5 months	Returned to his mother.
Ahmad April–June 1342	21(?)	72 days	Ahmad was mad. His father had warned the ameers not to elevate him.

Name	Age	Reign	Remarks
Ismail July 1342–July 1345	18(?)	3 years	An extremely promising young ruler. Died of illness.
Shaaban July 1345– September 1346	17(?)	1 year and 2 months	Imprisoned his brothers, possibly due to rivalry between their mothers. Was dethroned and strangled by ameers.
Hajji September 1346– July 1347	15	10 months	Killed by rebel ameers. Never exercised authority.
Hasan July 1347– August 1351 (First Reign)	12	4 years	A nice boy, but never exercised any authority. Dethroned by Taz, who wanted to be dictator.
Salih August 1351– October 1354	13	3 years and 2 months	Dethroned by Ameer Shaikhu, who was a rival of Taz. A very promising potential ruler.
Hasan October 1354– March 1361 (Second Reign)	19	6 years and 6 months	Was kept under by Shaikhu but in August 1358, assumed power himself. Killed in clash with Yalbugha. A good sultan.
Muhammad, son of Hajji, grandson of Al-Nasir March 1361– May 1363	16	2 years and 3 months	Allowed no influence at all by Yalbugha. After dethronement took to drink and lived on in privacy in the palace.
Shaaban son of Husain and grandson of Al-Nasir May 1363– March 1377	10	14 years	Quiet, popular, pious, a good sultan. Was murdered owing to collapse of discipline in connection with mamlukes of Yalbugha.
Ali, son of Shaaban March 1377– May 1381	7	4 years	Too young to play any part. Probably done to death.

It is not possible simply to say, in a sweeping generalisation, that Al-Nasir's descendants were failures. Of the eleven sultans mentioned, analysis reveals the following facts:

Ismail is described as an extremely promising ruler, who died of illness.

Hasan was a good sultan, though unable to deal with an old dictator like Yalbugha.

Shaaban, son of Husain, reigned successfully for fourteen years.

Salih was a promising young ruler, who was a victim of the rivalry between dictators Taz and Shaikhu.

Abu Bekr
Kuchuk
Hajji
Muhammad, son of Hajji
Ali, son of Shaaban

} Were none of them allowed to exercise any influence at all.

Shaaban quarrelled violently with his brothers, but was only about seventeen years old. Possibly violent by nature.
Ahmad was actually insane.

Of these eleven, therefore, four were potentially quite good material, five were never allowed any power, Shaaban, the son of Al-Nasir, was possibly of a violent nature and only Ahmad was definitely insane.

XIII

A New Race of Rulers

Barquq, who made his fellow-Circassians the ruling caste in the Mamluk Kingdom, brought about one of . . . the greatest racial transformations ever witnessed in that state . . . This transformation led to far-reaching changes in the organisation of the state.

D. AYALON, *The Circassians in the Mamluk Kingdom*

When the feeble descendants of en-Nasir, after enduring rather than enjoying a mock sovereignty for forty years under the tyranny of a series of powerful emirs . . . gave way to the usurpation of the emir Barkuk in 1382, the change made little difference in the government of Egypt . . . The new line was known as the Burgy Mamluks. They are also called the "Circassian Sultans", from their common race, for none of them were Turks. The mamluk guard of each king formed a distinct party . . . and after his death or deposition they remained a separate factor in politics and contributed to the bloodshed, confusion and intrigues.

The sultans could scarcely restrain their own soldiery, much less these formidable relics of their predecessors. The character of the rulers was much the same as before, but everything was on a meaner scale. There was hardly a warrior king among them . . . The Circassians were not soldiers but schemers.

STANLEY LANE-POOLE, *The Story of Cairo*

WE left Barqooq an ameer of one hundred, while the sultan, Malik-al-Mansoor Ali, the son of Shaaban, was a boy of seven years. One more step, and Barqooq was promoted commander-in-chief. A few months before, he had been a soldier in the ranks. Ever since the commencement of the Mamluke régime, sultans had frequently risen and fallen, but these struggles had followed the ancient rules. They were personal contests between senior ameers as to who should become sultan. But following the murder of Yalbugha, a social revolution had occurred. Men who were still in the rank and file had risen to the highest positions, and mamlukes had killed their patrons, to whose service they were bound by the Mamluke code of honour. Further to strengthen his hold, Barqooq promoted his brother, Baraka, to be Master of the Horse, a high position at court.

In October 1379, Barqooq went one day for a ride for a distance of three miles across the desert plain north of Cairo. A number of ameers seized the opportunity to revolt. Barqooq had to return at the gallop and only recovered control after a fight.

Barqooq now began to practise the arts of diplomacy and to gain popular favour by affability. His brother Baraka, however, behaved with a haughty ruthlessness which hampered Barqooq's efforts. The brothers quarrelled and Baraka was sent to prison in Alexandria. A new list of dismissals and promotions was issued after this tussle, in which all the senior appointments were seen to have been filled by Circassians. The rule of the Bahris, or Qipchaq Turks, was at an end.

On 20th May, 1381, the child-sultan, Malik-al-Mansoor Ali died in the Citadel and was buried secretly at night. Murder was suspected. He had been nominal sultan for four years and was now eleven, but had never taken any part in public affairs.

- -
AL-MALIK-AL-SALIH HAJJI IBN SHAABAN
(First Reign)
- -

Barqooq, though now sole dictator, hesitated to grasp at the sultanate. An eleven-year-old brother of Ali, called Hajji, was made sultan with the name of Malik-al-Salih. But the situation remained tense, the tribes in the Western desert rebelled and Cairo was seething with rumours.

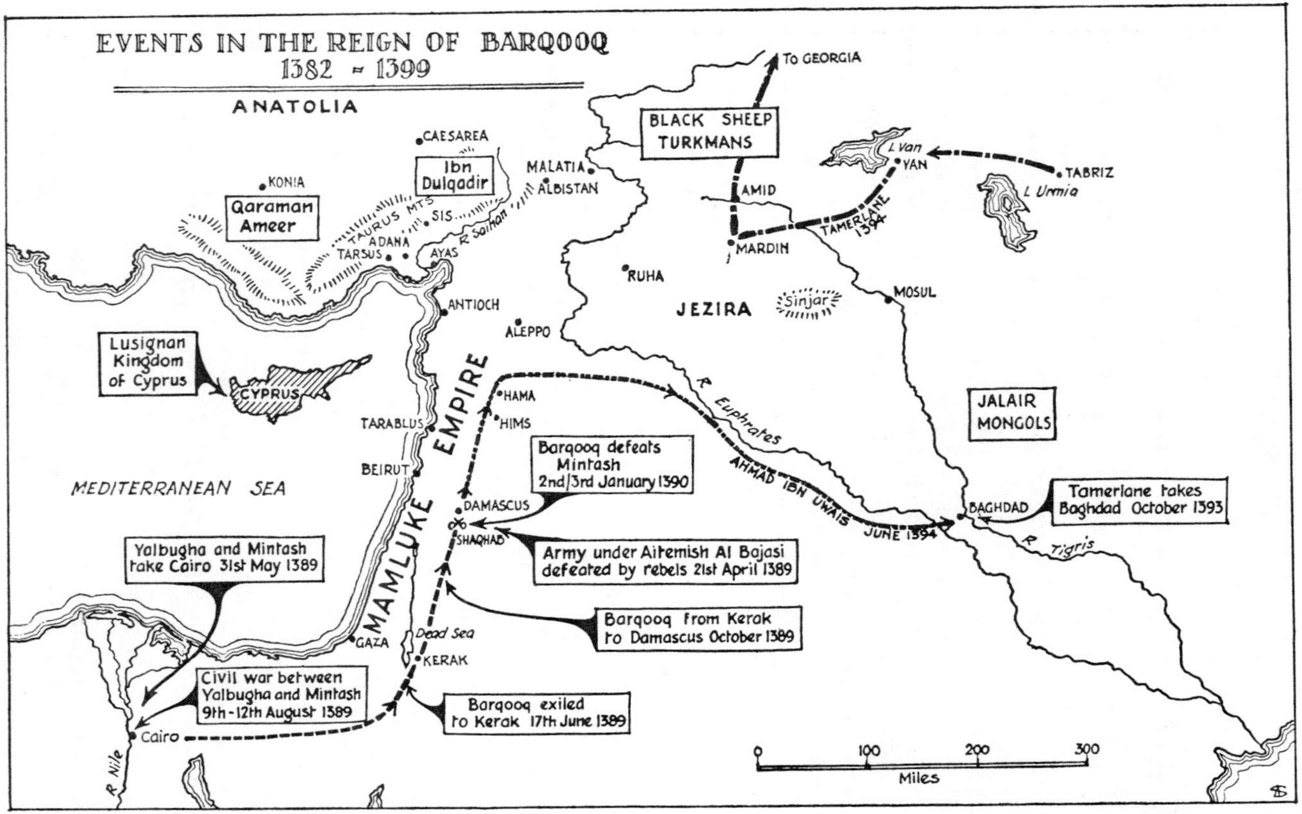

EVENTS IN THE REIGN OF BARQOOQ
1382 - 1399

ANATOLIA

BLACK SHEEP TURKMANS

To GEORGIA

L. Van

L. Urmia

TABRIZ

VAN

TAMERLANE 1394

AMID

MARDIN

Sinjar

MOSUL

JEZIRA

RUHA

R. Euphrates

AHMAD IBN UWAIS JUNE 1394

JALAIR MONGOLS

BAGHDAD

Tamerlane takes Baghdad October 1393

R. Tigris

CAESAREA

Ibn Dulqadir

MALATIA

ALBISTAN

SIS

TAURUS MTS.

ADANA

ANTIOCH

ALEPPO

HAMA

HIMS

DAMASCUS

SHAGHAB

Barqooq defeats Mintash 2nd/3rd January 1390

Army under Aitemish Al Bajasi defeated by rebels 21st April 1389

Barqooq from Kerak to Damascus October 1389

Konia

Qaraman Ameer

TARSUS

AYAS

TARABLUS

BEIRUT

MAMLUKE EMPIRE

Dead Sea

KERAK

GAZA

Barqooq exiled to Kerak 17th June 1389

CYPRUS

Lusignan Kingdom of Cyprus

MEDITERRANEAN SEA

Yalbugha and Mintash take Cairo 31st May 1389

Civil war between Yalbugha and Mintash 9th-12th August 1389

Cairo

R. Nile

0   100   200   300
Miles

MAP 24

As a result, Barqooq summoned a council, attended by the khalif, the four qadhis and the senior ameers. The confidential secretary addressed the meeting, emphasising the universal confusion and the general spread of disaffection. The only cure, he claimed, was to end the custom of choosing child-sultans, and to appoint a strong experienced man, who could pull the country together. The council passed a resolution dethroning Malik-al-Salih Hajji and raising Barqooq to the throne. Hajji had "reigned" for a year and six months and now returned to the nursery.

AL-MALIK-AL-DHAHIR BARQOOQ AL YALBUGHAWI AL OTHMANI
(First Reign)

Barqooq was a Circassian, not a Turk, and had been sold into Egypt by a merchant called Othman ibn Musafir and bought by Yalbugha al Umari al Khassiki. He plotted against Yalbugha and was one of those who incited his comrades to murder his patron. He then remained for a long time in prison and was subsequently employed by Sultan Shaaban in Cairo. In 1376, he, with other Yalbughawis, rose against Shaaban and killed him.

As a result of these two mutinies against their masters, many Yalbughawis rose to power, among them Barqooq. When Hajji was dethroned on 26th November, 1382, Barqooq was proclaimed sultan. The ameers, the qadhis and the notables took the oath on 4th December, 1382.

We may note that, at this time, the senior ameers and officials who formed the sultan's council were as follows:

Mamluke ameers
Grand Ameer, the Commander-in-Chief
Ameer of the Council
Ameer of the Horse
Grand Chamberlain
Ameer of Arms
Viceroy of Egypt
Executive Secretary
Chief of Guards

Civilians (Egyptians)

Wazeer, Head of the Administration

Controller of the Army (Pay and Administration)
Controller of the Royal Domains.[1]

In January 1383, Altunbugha al Sultani, the Governor of Albistan, deserted to the Tatars, saying that he would not serve under a Circassian. The Viceroy of Aleppo, however, Yalbugha al Nasiri, kissed the ground before Barqooq, though he had been an ameer of one hundred when Barqooq was still a private soldier.

In February 1386, a number of Royal Mamlukes were flogged, paraded on camels and then cut in half at the waist. Barqooq, who as a mamluke had freely plotted against his chief and against successive sultans, declared his determination to restore discipline. In November 1387, Timurbugha al Ashrafi, more commonly called Mintash, the Governor of Malatia, declared himself in revolt.

Yalbugha al Nasiri had already sworn loyalty in Cairo, but Barqooq had made the capital error of arresting and then releasing him, and sending him back to his viceroyalty of Aleppo. The revolt of Mintash in Malatia was growing and he had been joined by Kara Muhammad, the Black Sheep Turkman chief, and by many Ashrafis,[2] his barrack-comrades.

In August 1388, Altunbugha al Jubani, Viceroy of Damascus, was reported to be in revolt, but immediately rode to Cairo to prove his innocence. Nevertheless, he was arrested and imprisoned in Alexandria, although he was a Yalbughawi. The Viceroy of Tarablus and twenty other ameers in Syria were arrested. Barqooq was obviously extremely nervous.

In the autumn of 1388, a letter came from the Turkman chief, Kara Muhammad, saying that he had taken Tabriz and begging to be appointed the sultan's viceroy there. This would be an immense increase of territory, if it could be held. The Black Sheep were a Turkman tribe in the Van district, who had risen to prominence since the fall of the Il-Khan Empire.

Tension in Aleppo was increased by friction between the Viceroy, Yalbugha al Nasiri, and the Commander of the Citadel, Sudoon al Mudhaffari.[3] It will be remembered that citadel commanders were not under command of their viceroys. Barqooq wrote to Sudoon, suggesting the possibility of murdering Yalbugha, but the latter learned the contents of the letter and had Sudoon murdered first.

[1] These were the appointments the holders of which constituted the sultan's council. The "electoral body", which chose a new sultan, consisted of all the ameers of one hundred in Cairo. The presence of the khalif and the four qadhis was also necessary to legitimise a new sultan.
[2] Former mamlukes of Malik-al-Ashraf Shaaban.
[3] Former mamluke of Malik-al-Mudhaffar Hajji.

Yalbugha had been loyal to Barqooq, who had twice tried to get rid of him. Now, however, he joined Mintash in his rebellion. Yalbugha was the leader of the turbulent Yalbughawis,[4] while Mintash was head of the Ashrafis. Between them, they had a large following.

On 22nd February, 1389, news reached Cairo that the ameers of Damascus, Hims and Hama had declared for the rebels. In March, the bedouins of the Syrian desert joined the revolt, as did also Ibn Dulqadir, the Turkman chief of Albistan.[5]

The army from Egypt left Cairo on 15th March, 1389, under Aitemish al Bajási, and entered Damascus on 5th April. Barqooq remained in Cairo.

When a battle was fought on 21st April, three senior ameers went over to the rebels, and the army of Egypt was routed. The news of the defeat created chaos in Cairo, where an epidemic of plague was raging. Barqooq, a poor fighter, was in despair and his demoralisation unnerved his supporters. He ordered that barricades be erected in the streets of Cairo, showing that he did not mean to go out and fight. Yalbugha and Mintash reached Gaza unopposed and many deserters left Cairo to join the rebels. Barqooq's only action was to try to gain supporters by handing out money. His tearful panic was so pathetic that the public felt pity for him. On 29th May, Yalbugha and Mintash camped under the walls of Cairo. From the Citadel, guns fired at groups of rebels.

This is the first mention of artillery in Mamluke history. Flamethrowers had long been in use, and when guns firing cannonballs were introduced the word for projectors was used for them. It is, therefore, sometimes difficult to know whether flame-throwers or cannon are meant. For two hundred years, the Mamlukes were probably the world's finest cavalry with bow, lance, sword and mace. Eventually they admitted reluctantly that guns could be used in siege warfare but they themselves insisted on fighting only on horseback.[6]

On 30th May, a group of Barqooq's men made a sortie from the Citadel, Taghri Birdi, the father of the historian, taking part in the action. The same afternoon, Barqooq sent his surrender to Yalbugha, who advised him to go underground till the crisis was over. After dark, the sultan, in disguise, slipped out of the royal stables alone and was lost in the night.

The day of 31st May passed in a nightmare. The troops looted the

---

[4] Yalbugha al Nasiri had been a mamluke of Yalbugha al Umari al Khassiki.

[5] Map 24, page 256.

[6] The subject is discussed in David Ayalon, *Gunpowder and Firearms in the Mamluke Kingdom.*

city, assisted by bandits and convicts, who had broken out of the
prisons. Not until evening was order restored, the good people of
Cairo having spent the day cowering in their houses. Yalbugha had
now arrived with sixty thousand men. At a council held on 1st June,
1389, the khalif, the qadhis and the ameers pressed Yalbugha to
become sultan, but he resolutely refused. At length it was decided to
restore Malik-al-Salih Hajji, changing his throne-name to Malik-al-
Mansoor, the Victorious King.

Barqooq had ruled the Mamluke Empire for five years as Grand
Ameer, and then for more than six years as sultan. At the time of his
fall, he had two thousand purchased mamlukes. He had been
thought to be courageous until his pathetic collapse before the
advance of Yalbugha. He had reduced a number of vexatious taxes
and executed some public works, including a bridge over the River
Jordan. Maqrizi alleges that it was in his time that bribery became
general to secure government appointments, but Ibn Taghri Birdi
denies the charge.

AL-MALIK-AL-MANSOOR HAJJI
(Second Reign)

The return of Hajji was proposed by Yalbugha al Nasiri, who
became commander-in-chief and regent, as the sultan was still a
child. A large number of ameers who had supported Barqooq were
imprisoned. The rebel soldiers had behaved so badly in the city that
the people were praying for Barqooq. The saying became common
that "Barqooq and his gazelles have gone, Al Nasiri and his bulls
have come."

Then Barqooq was arrested. At a conference of Yalbugha's party,
the majority favoured his imprisonment, only Mintash demanding
his execution. Yalbugha eventually carried a resolution to exile him
to Kerak. He left Cairo secretly at night on 17th June, 1389, and was
lodged in the castle of Kerak. The governor was a former mamluke
of Yalbugha al Umari al Khassiki, and thus a barrack-comrade of
both Barqooq and Yalbugha al Nasiri, who instructed him to treat
Barqooq well.

Yalbugha was now dictator of the empire. The auxiliaries, or
riffraff, who had come with him from Syria, tribesmen, Turkmans or
bedouins, were sent home. Twenty-four ameers of one hundred were
appointed or confirmed, the original establishment under Baybars
and Qalaoon. Proclamation was made in Cairo, "Let anyone who

has been wronged within the last twenty years, come to Grand Ameer Yalbugha al Nasiri to receive justice."[7]

But rarely indeed could two Mamluke ameers share power. Relations grew strained between Yalbugha and his ally, Mintash. On 9th August, 1389, ten weeks after the capture of Cairo, Mintash feigned sickness. Yalbugha sent a deputation of ameers to express his sympathy, but no sooner were they inside the house than they were set upon, one even being killed. Mounting their horses, Mintash and his mamlukes tried to surprise the Citadel. Being repulsed, they occupied the mosque of Sultan Hasan, a massive building on the opposite side of the Roumaila, facing the Citadel. Mintash soon was joined by his own barrack-comrades, the Ashrafis, and by Barqooq's mamlukes, who were unemployed. The former mamlukes of Yalbugha al Khassiki joined their barrack-comrade, Yalbugha al Nasiri.

All day long cannonballs, rocks from mangonels, javelins and arrows flew back and forth between the Citadel and the Sultan Hasan mosque. Mintash, a natural demagogue, made inflammatory speeches in the streets and scattered handfuls of gold. His following increased, while Yalbugha's men began to desert. Yalbugha sent the Khalif Mutawakkil to mediate but Mintash refused to negotiate. In Syria, he claimed, Yalbugha had promised to share equally with him, but now he had taken all power to himself. "By God, I shall not stop until either I kill him or he kills me," Mintash shouted.

Yalbugha then collected his men and went down into the streets to fight but was hampered by crowds of roughs supporting Mintash and throwing stones. On the evening of 11th August, Yalbugha slipped away and vanished.

Next morning, 12th August, 1389, Mintash entered the Citadel and waited on the little sultan. He himself and his closest supporters, he said, were Ashrafis, mamlukes of the sultan's father, Malik-al-Ashraf Shaaban. Protesting that he was the slave of the royal family, he offered his loyal service. Sultan Hajji, in return, appointed him regent and commander-in-chief. Those who had helped Yalbugha were imprisoned in the usual manner, as also were the friends of Barqooq. Yalbugha himself was then captured and imprisoned in fetters. But news was received that the Viceroy of Damascus, Buzlar al Nasiri, being a barrack-comrade of Yalbugha al Nasiri,[8] had rebelled against Mintash.

On 2nd October, 1389, four ameers were arrested, nailed to stakes and halved at the waist, on the grounds that they had been friends of

[7] W. Popper, *A History of Egypt.*
[8] Both had been mamlukes of Malik-al-Nasir Hasan.

Barqooq. Mintash promoted his followers wildly, ordinary mamlukes being made directly into ameers of one hundred, an unprecedented action calculated to ruin the army. He then sent an ameer to
Kerak with secret orders to kill Barqooq. But the people of Kerak
heard of the plan, seized and killed Mintash's emissary and, releasing
Barqooq from captivity, hastened to bring him weapons, horses and
supplies. News then came hot-foot that the Viceroy of Aleppo refused
to recognise Mintash. He too was a Yalbughawi, a barrack-comrade
of Yalbugha al Nasiri.

On 13th October, 1389, Barqooq left Kerak with a number of his
old mamlukes, and some local Arab tribesmen. On the old battlefield of Shaqhab, a fierce battle was fought between Barqooq and the
garrison of Damascus, Barqooq proving victorious. Damascus closed
its gates, but the Viceroy of Aleppo arrived to assist Barqooq.

Consternation prevailed in Cairo. The treasury was empty, but
Mintash robbed orphanages and religious institutions, and squeezed
money from Jews, Christians, merchants, civil officials and ameers
who had opposed him. On 11th December, 1389, Mintash set out
with the advanced guard for Syria, the sultan, the khalif, the qadhis
and the main body following. The army reached Gaza on 27th
December. Barqooq, meanwhile, had been joined by the Turkmans,
the Druzes, and some Arab tribes and was growing stronger. He
awaited Mintash on the old battleground of Shaqhab.

The battle was fought on 2nd January, 1390. Mintash's army outnumbered that of Barqooq and was able to defeat him on both wings.
Believing the battle to be won, he rode in hot pursuit till he reached
Damascus. But Barqooq and the centre stood fast. When the dust
cleared, he saw before him the sultan, the khalif, the staff, and the
baggage of the army of Egypt. Advancing with the centre of his
army, he greeted the sultan and the khalif and took his stand beneath
the royal banners. Taghri Birdi, the father of our historian, was with
Barqooq's mamlukes.

Next morning, Mintash returned and a second battle was fought.
Barqooq, with the sultan and khalif, was now facing north, while
Mintash advanced southwards. The battle lasted all day, but in the
evening a heavy storm blew up from the south into the faces of
Mintash's men, who, unable to see, became confused and then
broke. There was no pursuit. Barqooq's army was prostrate with
exhaustion.

On 1st February, 1390, Barqooq and his army camped outside
Cairo, where successive deputations came out to greet him. Although
many had opposed him during his first reign, the disturbances, street
battles and looting which had occurred in his absence had now made

him a popular hero. Ameers, shaikhs, sufis, dervishes, mamlukes, a Jewish procession bearing the Torah, the Christians carrying the Gospels—all gave evidence of their joy, calling upon God to bless the sultan, who, dismissing his guards, mixed affably with the crowd.

Malik-al-Mansoor Hajji returned to the female apartments, his abdication was announced and Barqooq re-ascended the throne. The Khalif Mutawakkil, a Muslim Vicar of Bray, invested Barqooq with the sultanate.

AL-MALIK-AL-DHAHIR BARQOOQ AL YALBUGHAWI AL OTHMANI
(Second Reign)

Yalbugha al Nasiri was brought from prison with seventeen ameers who had helped him to overthrow Barqooq, but the latter greeted them amicably and ordered their release. Malik-al-Mansoor Hajji continued to occupy his apartment in the palace. Barqooq often invited him to social occasions and treated him as an equal. Hajji would get drunk and Barqooq would then smilingly say to the attendants, "Take the ameer home now."

The frustration of his hopes made Hajji an alcoholic and a sadist, who enjoyed whipping his slave girls. When Barqooq heard the screams of the victim, he would send someone to knock on the door and the whipping would cease. Hajji sometimes ordered his troupe of female musicians to play their flutes and beat their tambourines to drown the cries, but the girls sent word of this ruse to Barqooq, who thereafter would send someone to knock as soon as the tambourines were heard. The ex-sultan must have been a trying neighbour in the next flat. Such was the last descendant of the great Sultan Malik-al-Nasir Muhammad.

Meanwhile Mintash had established himself in Damascus. Barqooq sent Yalbugha al Nasiri to fight Mintash, thereby accepting a risk. If Yalbugha defeated Mintash, he might turn against Barqooq a second time. He did indeed capture Damascus, and Mintash vanished into Asia Minor.

If Barqooq had learned wisdom, he had not learned pity, and many ameers were arrested and halved at the waist. On 4th June, 1391, Mintash reappeared in Damascus but, after several days' fighting, he vanished again. Barqooq decided to go to Syria himself. Thirty-seven ameers were executed before his departure, to ensure against trouble in his absence. Six hundred mamlukes were left in the Citadel, under Taghri Birdi. Barqooq left Cairo on 29th July,

1391, and reached Damascus on 24th August. On 22nd September, he went on to Aleppo.

Mintash was reported to be in Mardin, but when a column was sent to arrest him, he fled to Sinjar.[9] Barqooq grew suspicious of Yalbugha's loyalty and caused him to be arrested and executed, a disappointing result, for Barqooq had seemed to be more liberal. The sultan was back in Cairo on 15th December, 1391, where he made Taghri Birdi an ameer of one hundred. Mintash was captured and executed in July 1393.

As we have seen, the position of a new sultan was always insecure until he could promote his own mamlukes to a majority of the key appointments. Barqooq had hitherto been in this insecure position. Those who had actively supported Yalbugha or Mintash could be executed or imprisoned. But many ameers tried to avoid these political struggles and to continue their military duties. Such people could not be arrested, yet they were not heart and soul behind the sultan. By 1393, however, the Viceroy of Damascus was Tanam al Dhahiri, and the Viceroys of Aleppo, Hama, Tarablus and Gaza were all former mamlukes of Malik-al-Dahir Barqooq.

*   *   *

It is extremely difficult to define all the causes which resulted in the replacement of the Turks by the Circassians as the rulers of the Mamluke Empire. There are indications that the numbers of Qipchaq boys and girls imported into Egypt had been falling off. Perhaps, while the Qipchaq Sultans governed Egypt, too many children had been taken, and the population had been depleted. Tamerlane also devastated the Qipchaq area, killing great numbers of people, but the reduction of Qipchaq immigrants had begun before Tamerlane.

Circassian boys had been imported even under Malik-al-Salih Ayoub, but they seem to have been a minority until after Malik-al-Nasir Muhammad. Baybars the Jashnekeer is thought to have been a Circassian, and Qipchaq-Circassian rivalry began to appear from his time onwards. The power struggle developed after the death of Al-Nasir Muhammad. During the reign of Hasan, Circassians were reduced, but under Hajji they increased. The Qipchaq régime had deliberately suppressed racial rivalries, but the Circassians made use of racial affinities to help one another.

There seems to be no doubt that the Circassians were inferior to the Qipchaqs as soldiers. The latter were dedicated to the army,

[9] Map 24, page 256.

promotion under them was by merit alone and there was no race prejudice and little or no nepotism. Circassians, on the other hand, were intriguers, and always promoted one another. In addition, they often brought over their adult relatives from the Caucasus and made them ameers in the army without the long years of discipline and training as boys which were the basis of the Turkish Mamluke system. Ibn Taghri Birdi alleges that, in Circassian times, a hundred old Mamlukes, who were veterans from Qipchaq days, could defeat a thousand young Royal Mamlukes. The Circassians took little interest in military training, and the period of instruction for young mamlukes was seriously curtailed.

It seems possible that the rebellion of Yalbugha and Mintash was, partly at least, a revolt of the Turks against the Circassian predominance established by Barqooq. If the two leaders had not turned against one another, the Turks might have regained their predominance and the Circassians have been suppressed.

*   *   *

Scarcely were the disorders finished and Barqooq once again firmly in power, than Tamerlane appeared. One of the world's greatest conquerors, Tamerlane was born on 8th April, 1336, at Kish, south of Samarqand. The times provided his opportunity. The Il-Khanate had fallen in 1334. The Mamluke Empire was in a confusion of child-sultans, after the death of Al-Nasir Muhammad in 1341; the Seljuqs had already collapsed in 1300. The East was in anarchy.

In 1381, Tamerlane set out to conquer and ravage Persia. Imitating Jenghis Khan, he deliberately exterminated the inhabitants of every town he captured, man, woman and child. In October 1393, he took Baghdad, the Jalair ruler, Ahmad ibn Uwais, taking refuge with Barqooq in Egypt. The Jalair were Mongols, descended, through the sister of Il-Khan Ghazan, from the family of Hulagu. Thence Tamerlane occupied Tabriz, previously held by the Turkman tribe known as the Black Sheep.

In February 1394, a long despatch, full of boastful threats, reached Cairo from Tamerlane, and a reply was returned to him in the same style. On 25th February, 1394, Barqooq left Cairo with the army, accompanied by Ahmad ibn Uwais. The Mamluke army was equipped with traditional splendour in silk, satin, silver and gold, and was followed by much baggage, including five hundredweight of ivory and ebony chess sets. This amount was needed because, wherever the sultan played chess, his opponent was, by tradition, allowed to keep the set as a souvenir.

Barqooq entered Damascus on 23rd March, 1394. Tamerlane had crossed the Tigris at the beginning of March and had taken Mardin. Another of those great pitched battles, similar to those against the Mongol Il-Khans, seemed to be imminent. But from Mardin Tamerlane turned northwards and destroyed the Christian Kingdom of Georgia, south of the Caucasus. In April 1395, he passed the Derbend Gates to fight the Golden Horde, destroying their cities of Astrakhan and Sarai on the Volga.[10] Early in 1396, he returned to Samarqand, which he had made his capital.

Ahmad ibn Uwais set out on 13th June, 1394, to resume his rule in Baghdad, having been lavishly re-equipped by Barqooq. These incidents added immensely to the prestige of the sultan. When the Mamluke army appeared in Syria, Tamerlane, only a few miles away, had vanished to the north without offering battle. After forty years of chaos and declining prestige, the Mamlukes seemed to be again the arbiters of the Middle East, as they had been under Al-Nasir Muhammad.

As a result of this triumph, Barqooq received embassies from Toqtamish, Khan of the Golden Horde, and from Bayazid, Sultan of the new Ottoman Empire, of which the capital was at Adrianople in Thrace. Early in September 1394, Barqooq led the army up to Aleppo, of which he appointed Taghri Birdi as viceroy. When it was known that Tamerlane had finally disappeared, the sultan left Aleppo and made a triumphal entry into Cairo on 13th December, amid wild popular rejoicing.

A deputation had arrived from the Yemen bringing a royal gift which included ten white eunuchs, some black African slaves and six slave girls. It would be of interest to know where the ten white eunuchs came from. The remainder of the royal gift included ornaments of silver, pearls and cornelian, and quantities of perfumes, musk, civet, ambergris, frankincense and sandalwood.

Barqooq abolished many ancient ceremonies which had been observed by the Bahri sultans, and were mostly derived from the Fatimid or Abbasid khalifs. It will be remembered, for example, that Baybars the Bunduqdari went to play polo preceded by a brass band and followed by a state procession. Such ceremonies, often performed by accident for the first time, became well-loved traditions, like the Trooping of the Colour on the Horse Guards Parade in London on the Sovereign's birthday.

Ibn Taghri Birdi gives a description of the celebration of the Prophet's birthday in Cairo. An immense tent was pitched, in which the sultan sat at the head. On his right and left sat the Shaikh al

[10] Map 9, page 52.

Islam, the Chief Qadhi, the qadhis and religious teachers. The Mamluke ameers sat below the religious teachers. Obsessed, as we are, with the idea of race, we are surprised to see the men of religion, Syrians and Egyptians, sitting above the Mamluke ameers. To these people, race was not the supreme issue. We cannot consider the Mamluke régime as a military despotism over a conquered people, but neither were the two groups politically equal. It was unthinkable that an Egyptian be sultan, though they held the highest civilian appointments round the sultan.

When all were seated, the readers of the Qoran read passages from the holy book. Then "the preachers to the number of twenty arose one after another and delivered sermons".[11] The patient audience, which listened reverently to twenty sermons, included those military ameers whom we so easily condemn as cruel foreign conquerors. The sermons over, a luxurious banquet was served "containing choice foods so plentiful that no one would attempt to describe them".

After the meal, the qadhis and the ameers were dismissed, and the sultan, with a few intimates, remained only with the dervishes and the sufis, or religious mystics, who continued to perform, to read and to chant until dawn. The sultan watched them, his hand filled with gold, which he poured out lavishly to the performers. The treasurer stood behind him, refilling his hand when necessary.

The dervishes lived in monasteries, each occupied by an "order". Many sultans are mentioned as resorting to the shaikhs (or we should say abbots) of these monasteries for discussions and advice. When we see that life in fourteenth-century Egypt differed from our way of life today, we assume that the people must have been discontented. Contemporary writers, however, do not refer to such dissatisfaction. Not that their ideals differed materially from our own, but their minds worked in a slightly different manner.

I learned this lesson many years ago, when, as a young British officer, I was made responsible for a desert area. Inspired by the ideals of "democracy", I collected the tribal chiefs, and invited them to govern themselves. They were far from gratified. "You are paid to govern this area," they said. "Why should we do your work for you?" It all depends on the point of view. These people were of an extremely freedom-loving temperament and completely out-spoken. They were far from subservient. They just were not interested in administration or politics.

Similarly, perhaps, the Egyptians, who disliked wars, were con-tent to allow the Mamlukes to conquer an empire for them and to keep the savage Mongols at bay. For in the fields which interested

[11] W. Popper, *A History of Egypt.*

them—religion, literature, education, commerce and finance—the Syrians and the Egyptians reigned supreme.

*   *   *

In November 1397, Taghri Birdi was recalled from the post of Viceroy of Aleppo. He and the Viceroy of Damascus had been ordered to lead a column towards Sivas, to encourage the ruler of that town who had placed himself under Mamluke protection. The Viceroy of Damascus marched to Aleppo to join the force and Taghri Birdi, the Viceroy of Aleppo, rode out to meet him. After exchanging greetings, the two ameers with their escorts rode back to Aleppo. The Viceroy of Damascus was entitled to ceremonial precedence over his fellow viceroy, although the latter was not under his orders. Consequently the Damascus escort shouted to the Aleppo party to lower their standard or to fall to the rear of the procession.

The Aleppo troop took no notice and the two escorts, with their colours flying, marched side by side. The Viceroy of Damascus complained to the sultan. The incident is not without interest, for questions of precedence were endless between the feudal lords of Europe at this time. The reader will remember that, at the siege of Acre, Richard Lionheart, King of England, ordered the banner of the Duke of Austria to be thrown down, an incident which led to his detention in an Austrian castle on his way back to England.

Recalled to Cairo, Taghri Birdi brought with him from Aleppo a magnificent present for the sultan, including five very handsome white eunuchs.

On 27th July, 1398, Barqooq provided a great public fête on the race course. Tents were pitched, great quantities of meat were prepared, and also a supply of beer and intoxicating liquors. This was an action without precedent, for, though the Bahri sultans drank in private, they took drastic measures to prevent the consumption of alcohol in public. The occasion was a polo match between a team captained by the sultan and another led by Aitemish al Bajasi, the Commander-in-Chief. Aitemish was tactfully defeated, whereupon the sultan ordered him to pay for the whole party.

On the subject of drink, the good Maqrizi comments on a subsequent occasion when Barqooq drank with the ameers and then gave permission for the public to consume what was left. "It was a most unseemly and disgraceful day. The drinking of intoxicants was permitted, and people vied with one another in abominations the like of which had never been seen before. Intelligent men felt that this was the end of authority and so it was; from that day the laws of sanctity were violated in Egypt and decency became rare."[12]

Ali Bai was an ameer of one hundred and commander of the guards. One of his mamlukes had a love affair with the girl slave of another ameer, who, discovering the intrigue, caused the mamluke to be flogged. Ali Bai complained to the sultan, who took no action, with the result that Ali Bai decided to murder the sultan—another example of the pride and the mutual jealousy of Mamluke ameers. The plot was exposed and Ali Bai was arrested and strangled.

Ibn Taghri Birdi, whose father was very near to the sultan, has an interesting comment. Barqooq, himself a Circassian, had bought a large number of Circassian mamlukes, but many of those implicated in this plot were Circassians. The sultan's wife (says Taghri Birdi, who had inside knowledge of the palace) was Turkish and had warned him of the danger of recruiting only Circassians. "Make your army of four races, Tatars, Circassians, Turkmans and Anatolians," she admonished him.[13] Barqooq was obliged to admit that she had been right.

Ibn Taghri Birdi gives the following list of senior appointments in September 1398:

Khalif, Al Mutawakkil
Sultan, Malik-al-Dhahir Barqooq
C-in-C, Aitemish al Bajasi
Ameer of Arms, Taghri Birdi al Dhahiri
Ameer of the Council, Aqbugha al Lakkash al Dhahiri
Ameer of the Horse, Nauruz al Dhahiri
Executive Secretary, Baybars, a nephew of the sultan
Viceroy of Damascus, Tanam al Dhahiri
Viceroy of Aleppo, Arghun Shah al Dhahiri
Viceroy of Tarablus, Yunis al Dhahiri
Viceroy of Hama, Aqbugha al Jamali
Viceroy of Gaza, Baikhuja al Dhahiri

It will be noticed that almost every important appointment was held by a Dhahiri, that is a personal mamluke of Malik-al-Dhahir Barqooq.

At the end of 1398, reports reached Cairo that Tamerlane had left Samarqand for India where, on 17th December, he took and destroyed Delhi. Thus the Mamluke Empire was able, for the time at least, to enjoy peace and security. In March 1399, our historian Taqi-al-Deen al Maqrizi, received a minor appointment as Inspector of the Market in Cairo.

[12] Maqrizi, *Kitab al Sulook*.   [13] Ibn Taghri Birdi, *Nujoom*.

On 10th June, 1399, Barqooq played polo, after which he had a light meal and then sat drinking with his intimates. Next morning he woke with a fever which continued to increase. On 19th June, he summoned the khalif, the chief qadhi and the principal ameers to his bedside, where all took an oath of loyalty to the sultan's eldest son, Faraj. Barqooq left a legacy of two hundred and twenty thousand dinars to support his wife and her household. As the new sultan was a boy, Grand Ameer Aitemish al Bajasi, the commander-in-chief, was made regent, with the Ameer Taghri Birdi as his deputy. Four other ameers composed, with them, the Council of Regency.

Barqooq died on 20th June, 1399, probably of pneumonia, as the result of a chill after a hot game of polo. He had ruled the empire for twenty-one years, nearly five years as Grand Ameer for Ali and Hajji, six years and eight months as his first reign, and nine years and eight months as his second reign, after the defeat of Mintash. "Men's grief at his loss was widespread," says Ibn Taghri Birdi. He is generally regarded as the first Circassian sultan, though Baybars the Jashnekeer may have been of that race.

"He was a great ruler," writes Ibn Taghri Birdi, "strong, courageous, vigorous, sagacious and expert in dealing with troubles, conflicts and battles."[14] In early life, as a mamluke of Yalbugha al Umari, he had been an intriguer and an agitator, who had joined in the murder of his patron. In office, he was, on the whole, skilful, vigorous but cautious. Thus does the youthful revolutionary change into the prudent conservative. Yet he acted with undue haste in arresting the innocent Yalbugha al Nasiri, and then in returning him to be Viceroy of Aleppo. Sometimes Barqooq seemed cruel.

His taxation was less oppressive than that of many sultans, and in a year of famine he gave away eight thousand loaves of bread to the poor daily. He, like many sultans, built a college mosque in Cairo and undertook many useful public works, including an aqueduct at Arroob, between Hebron and Bethlehem.

He fought hardly any foreign wars and was fortunate that the Il-Khan Empire had vanished and Persia and Iraq were torn by civil wars. As the only stable monarch, he was at various times recognised as their suzerain by such distant cities as Tabriz, Baghdad, Mosul, Mardin and Sivas, but he was too prudent to embark on military adventures. Some of his qualities seem paradoxical. As a young mamluke, he might almost be described as a revolutionary, who undermined the Mamluke code of honour of loyalty to his patron. Resolute in many troubles, he was seized with panic in the rebellion of Yalbugha and Mintash. Professedly pious, he encouraged

---

[14] Ibn Taghri Birdi, *Nujoom*. Eng. trans. Popper.

the public consumption of alcohol. His reign inaugurated the replacement of the Turks by Circassian sultans.

*   *   *

Historians in the Middle Ages were chiefly concerned with kings, politicians and conspirators, and their records are our only contemporary source. Here, however, are a few brief notices of other persons who lived in the reign of Barqooq.

"Bedr-al-Deen Mahmoud was a professional government official, who was confidential secretary to the sultans in Cairo for twenty-seven years. An expert at drafting official documents, he was also a man of letters, with a wide knowledge of law. He came from the Fadhlullah family, who had been for several generations confidential secretaries of the government in Damascus." There were many such civil servants, who had long professional careers.

There were also Mamluke ameers, who rendered honourable services in the army. The Ameer Sudoon al Shaikhuni rose to be Viceroy of Egypt. He was honoured by successive sultans and respected in official circles. When he grew old, he retired from the service and died peacefully in Cairo in 1396.

Yet another personality of Barqooq's reign was a female saint, known as Al Baghdadiya, head of the Baghdadiya Hospice in Cairo. "Her constancy in prayer and worship were extraordinary. Men had great faith in her and she became an object of pilgrimage." She died in 1394.

Finally, here is a little light relief. We have seen that Christians were the most efficient civil servants and often achieved wealth and influence, which were envied by the Muslims, as is shown in this verse by Shihab-al-Deen Ahmad, known as Ibn al Attár.

> When they said, "You behold how the Copts with good luck
> Are richly supplied and like sultans they rule—
> They rule all the Turks," I replied unto them,
> "The food of the dog is supplied by the fool."[15]

Or something more romantic by Ameen-al-Deen Muhammad, confidential secretary of Damascus:

> Mine eyelids, red as blood, no sleep can know,
> Their streams of tears for ever overflow.
> Be I the ransom for the eyes of one

[15] English translation Popper.

Whose love is of mine eyes' sweet sleep the foe.
If she but glance at me, my heart is pierced,
By flights of arrows which her glances throw.
Those lips of hers brought healing to my heart,
But healing did but make its torments grow.
And he who of her mouth would drink to live
Will die of parching thirst from passion's glow.

"History", where principally occupied with politics, intrigues and war, does little to assist us in understanding the life of the people in a past age. For the great majority of persons in every age are absorbed in their own affairs, their business, their loves or their prayers, anxious only to avoid involvement in the violent contests of those who wish to achieve for themselves positions of importance.

NOTABLE EVENTS

Death of Malik-al-Mansoor Ali } Elevation of Malik-al-Salih Hajji }	20th May, 1381
Dethronement of Sultan Hajji } Elevation of Barqooq }	26th November, 1382
Rebellion of Timurbugha al Ashrafi, called Mintash	November, 1387
Ameers of Damascus, Aleppo, Hims and Hama, join the rebellion	February, 1389
Rebels defeat Aitemish al Bajasi near Damascus	21st April, 1389
Rebels take Cairo	31st May, 1389
Elevation of Hajji (Second Reign)	1st June, 1389
Barqooq exiled to Kerak	17th June, 1389
Battle between Yalbugha and Mintash in Cairo	9th–12th August, 1389
Barqooq leaves Kerak for Damascus	13th October, 1389
Battle of Shaqhab } Mintash defeated by Barqooq }	2nd–3rd January, 1390
Barqooq retakes Cairo } Hajji dethroned } Barqooq reinstated }	1st–3rd February, 1390
Execution of Mintash	July, 1393
Capture of Tabriz by Tamerlane	Autumn, 1393
"Confrontation" of Barqooq and Tamerlane	March, 1394

Ahmad ibn Uwais returns to Baghdad   June, 1394
Tamerlane passes the Derbend Gates   April, 1395
Death of Barqooq   20th June, 1399

PERSONALITIES

Mamluke Sultans
Malik-al-Mansoor Ali
Malik-al-Salih Hajji
Malik-al-Dhahir Barqooq

Other Mamlukes
Yalbugha al Nasiri, rebel and Viceroy of Aleppo
Timurbugha al Ashrafi, commonly called Mintash
Aitemish al Bajasi, Commander-in-Chief

Turkman Chiefs
Kara Muhammad. Captured Tabriz
Ibn Dulqadir, Chief of Albistan
Tamerlane, the great conqueror

XIV

Tragedy of Adolescence

Mamluk Egypt began its history under proud and triumphant rulers . . . By the end of the period, however, with its military oligarchy, factions . . . debased coinage, high taxation, insecurity of life and property . . . both Egypt and its dependency Syria were all but ruined.

Ophthalmology was practised on a more scientific basis in Syria and Egypt throughout the twelfth and thirteenth centuries than anywhere else in the world. In the social sciences, the main contribution under the Mamluks was biography . . . Not only in biography but in the general field of history the Mamluk age was moderately rich.

The most pleasant surprise of the Mamluk period . . . is the extraordinary architectural and artistic productiveness of a scale and quality that find no parallel . . . The Mamluk school of architecture received fresh Syro-Mesopotamian influences when Egypt became a haven for Moslem artists who fled before the Mongol invasions.

PHILIP HITTI, *History of the Arabs*

XIV

- -

AL-MALIK-AL-NASIR FARAJ IBN BARQOOQ
(First Reign)

- -

FARAJ was nine years old when he became sultan on 20th June, 1399, on the death of his father, Barqooq. He received the throne-name of Malik-al-Nasir, the Victorious King. All the senior appointments in the Council and all the viceroyships in Syria were held by Dhahiris, the purchased mamlukes of his father. We have seen, however, that a mamluke was supposed to be devoted to his patron, but not necessarily to his descendants.

Aitemish al Bajasi had been named as regent by Barqooq but the Ameer Sudoon, a relative of Barqooq, refused to allow Aitemish to live in the Citadel. When the ameers waited upon the boy-sultan, Sudoon refused to attend. He was arrested and sent to prison in Alexandria. No sooner was the hand of their late master removed, than all the ameers began to eye one another with suspicion.

On 26th June, 1399, Faraj held a levée, at which he gave robes of honour to Aitemish al Bajasi, to Taghri Birdi, the Ameer of Arms, and to various officials and qadhis. No sooner had the sultan left the hall than his young mamlukes burst in and arrested a number of senior ameers—some of whom had just received robes of honour—bundled them into a ship on the Nile and sent them to prison in Alexandria. As a result, the ameers of one hundred refused any more to go up to the Citadel and the government was left to the nine-year-old sultan and his young mamlukes.

Faraj listened only to his young companions and rejected all the experienced advisers on whom his father had relied. Eventually, however, the two sides compromised and swore mutual loyalty.

Meanwhile, Tanam al Dhahiri, the Viceroy of Damascus, was in revolt, and had written to all the other viceroys in Syria to report to him and not to Cairo. The truce between the ameers in Cairo and the sultan's young mamlukes had broken down. On 6th November, the sultan was told by his intimates to inform the ameers that he was now of age and would rule alone, although he was only just ten. The Regent, Aitemish al Bajasi, who seemed to be demoralised, merely replied, "As you order." A document was then drawn up, declaring

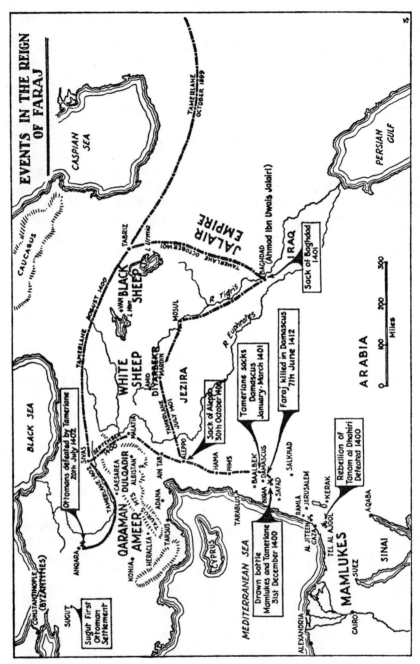

EVENTS IN THE REIGN OF FARAJ

MAP 25

the sultan to be of age. As already stated, there seemed to be no agreed laws defining when a sultan could come of age.

The ten-year-old sultan was completely dominated by his young mamlukes, who were presumably under or just over twenty, an age which easily dominates younger boys. One Yashbak al Shaabani had made himself their leader. Eventually the ameers left in a body for Damascus to join Tanam. In Cairo, the mob looted the shops and the convicts broke out of the prisons. The empire was in chaos.

Although the young mamlukes were united in their desire to drive out all senior officers, they began to quarrel among themselves. Disorders having broken out in southern Egypt, troops were detailed to go and restore order, but all refused to march. A spirit of mutiny was abroad. On 15th March, 1400, an action took place at Tel al Ajool, outside Gaza, between the army of Egypt and the advanced guard of the rebels, at which the Viceroys of Aleppo, Safad and Hama went over to the sultan. Mamluke civil wars provided an element of "glorious uncertainty", in England commonly attributed to cricket.

Tanam was in Ramla, where he assumed the ceremonial of a sultan. He declared his loyalty to Faraj, but stated that the sultan's young companions must be dismissed. An action was fought at Al Jiteen, between Ramla and Gaza. Early in the battle, however, Tanam fell from his horse and was captured by the sultan's army and later strangled. As a result, the rebellion collapsed. Aitemish al Bajasi and Taghri Birdi retired to Syria. On 29th March, 1400, Faraj and his army entered Damascus.

On 10th April, Aitemish al Bajasi, the Regent and Commander-in-Chief, was executed by the young mamlukes, and his head sent to Cairo to be nailed up over the Zuwaila Gate. He was a man, now in old age, known for his honesty and his gentleness.

When Taghri Birdi had been imported from Asia Minor as a boy, his sister Shirin had come with him and had been bought as a slave girl by Barqooq, who became fond of her. She became the mother of Faraj, who was now sultan. As a result, Taghri Birdi was the uncle of Faraj. His life was spared, but he was sent to live in retirement in Jerusalem.

On 21st May, 1400, Al-Nasir Faraj made a triumphal entry into Cairo, Tanam's rebellion having been suppressed. Almost all the ameers executed had been the most trusted advisers of Barqooq. All these troubles were the result of the ambition of Faraj's boon companions, a theme frequently repeated in history.

*　　　*　　　*

In 1221, a hundred and eighty years before the period which we have now reached, a small tribe of Turkmans from Persia had fled to Asia Minor, to escape Jenghis Khan. Under their leader, Othman, who was converted to Islam, they settled at Sugut, on the border between the Seljuq sultanate of Konia, and the Byzantine Empire.[1] The Byzantines were decadent, torn by endless civil wars among themselves. The followers of Othman extended their territory at the expense of the Byzantines. These new Turkman invaders were called Othmanlis, after their leader Othman, a name corrupted in the West to Ottoman.

In 1345, the Othmanlis crossed at Gallipoli into Europe and in 1366, they moved their capital to Adrianople. In 1385, they took Sofia and on 15th June, 1389, they defeated the Serbs at Kossovo, though the Ottoman Sultan Murad was killed. His son Bayazid consolidated his rule over Thrace, Serbia and Bulgaria, then turned east and annexed the whole of Asia Minor as far as Siyas. In 1400, therefore, three military empires met in eastern Anatolia,[2] those of Tamerlane, the Mamlukes and the Ottomans.[3]

*　　*　　*

One other item of retrospective history is necessary in order fully to explain the situation in 1400. After the final collapse of the Il-Khans in 1336, another tribe of Turkmans called the Black Sheep —in Turkish the Kara Koyounlu—established themselves in eastern Anatolia with their capital at Van. We have already seen that their chief, Kara Muhammad, had taken Tabriz in 1388. Now, in 1400, Kara Muhammad had been succeeded by his son, Kara Yusuf, or Black Joseph. Baghdad, as we have seen, was ruled by Ahmad ibn Uwais, of the Jalair Mongols.

*　　*　　*

We have already told how Tamerlane, in March 1394, had taken Mardin but, when Barqooq reached Damascus, had turned back. He had then attacked the Golden Horde, after which he had invaded India, capturing Delhi in December 1398. On his return to Samarqand in 1399, Tamerlane was informed of the death of Barqooq and of the elevation of a nine-year-old boy to be Mamluke sultan. As a result, Tamerlane moved to Tabriz, again chasing out the Black Sheep Turkmans. In August 1400, Tamerlane took

---

[1] Map 25, page 278.　　[2] In future Asia Minor will be called Anatolia.
[3] Map 25, page 278.

Sivas, a city claimed by the Ottoman Sultan Bayazid. A few days later, an embassy reached Cairo from Bayazid, proposing an alliance against Tamerlane, who was threatening Mamlukes and Ottomans alike. In addition, Kara Yusuf and Ahmad ibn Uwais, with seven thousand cavalry, wished to assist the Mamlukes in opposing Tamerlane.

But the sultan's young companions were politicians, engrossed only in their party intrigues. They rejected Bayazid's advances and made no preparations to defend Syria. On 16th September, however, reports reached Cairo that Tamerlane had invaded Mamluke territory and was at Ain Tab, eighty miles north of Aleppo. A meeting of ameers and qadhis was called at which the ameers demanded the seizure of religious bequests to finance a war, but the qadhis refused. After a heated debate, no action was decided.

Panic swept Syria, the city-dwellers commencing to abandon their homes. On 29th September, a delegate brought a letter from Tamerlane to Damascus, stating that he was marching on Egypt. The viceroy caused the messenger to be halved at the waist. The Mamluke ameers in Syria agreed to try and defend the country, abandoning hope of Cairo, where they knew that there was no leader and that every ameer was intriguing against his colleagues.

On 28th October, 1400, Tamerlane's army camped outside Aleppo. The next day, the Mamluke garrison marched out and gave battle. After a sharp but short fight, the Mamlukes collapsed and fled, Tamerlane's men entering the city with the fugitives, killing and plundering. The Tatars killed all the men and the children they could catch, but rounded up the women, who were all publicly violated before large crowds. All the women were then roped together and driven off. The killing of the men and the children lasted for three days. Aleppo was completely destroyed and all its buildings levelled with the ground. Plunder and rape continued for a month.

Miran Shah, the son of Tamerlane, went on to Hama, where he persuaded the people to open the gates by a promise of security and peace. Then, two of his men having been killed by shots from the citadel, he gave leave to his troops to kill, rape and plunder till the city was razed to the ground.

When news of the destruction of Aleppo reached Damascus, the people tried to flee in panic, but the ameers closed the gates and mounted mangonels, catapults and guns on the walls. Messengers came from Tamerlane demanding the surrender of Damascus, where the streets were filled with weeping women. Then suddenly news came that the sultan and the army of Egypt were coming.

Although Tamerlane had taken Aleppo on 30th October, no

action was taken in Cairo until 15th November, when two ameers were sent to Syria to report, and mobilisation was ordered, six weeks too late. The sultan's army reached Gaza on 8th December. Thence the sultan summoned his uncle Taghri Birdi, who, it will be remembered, was unemployed in Jerusalem, and made him Viceroy of Damascus. According to his son the historian, Taghri Birdi advised against a pitched battle. Damascus, he said, could stand a siege, and Tamerlane would run out of supplies during the winter months. But the sultan's young intimates contradicted everything the old ameer proposed. As a result, Taghri Birdi rode on ahead of the army and slipped into Damascus before the arrival of Tamerlane.

The army from Egypt left Gaza on 14th December. The sultan entered Damascus, but then returned to the army which was camped outside. Reports arrived that Tamerlane's army was completely demoralised and that half of it would desert to the sultan. It was some time later discovered that Tamerlane himself had spread these reports. Shortly afterwards, the Tatar army arrived in great numbers, filling the whole countryside.

Probably on 30th or 31st December, 1400, a general battle took place. The Mamluke left was put to flight, but their right wing forced the Tatars back, inch by inch, into their camp. The result was a draw and both sides held their positions. We are surprised to see the chaotic rivalries which divided the ameers and yet to find that the Mamlukes could still fight and win a "soldiers' battle". Tamerlane's army had never before suffered such a check.

He now sent a message asking for a truce, which the Mamlukes rejected. We cannot now know whether he really wanted a truce or whether this was one of those tricks which he was constantly devising. The young ameers, says Ibn Taghri Birdi, spent their time quarrelling over fiefs and appointments, "as though Tamerlane did not exist". When the conqueror heard of their bickerings, his hopes revived.

Suddenly a number of ameers vanished from the camp. A rumour spread that they were going to Cairo to bring about a coup d'état. The sultan's intimates were much alarmed, for they were more concerned about their personal interests than about the war. On or about 8th January, 1401, the leading ameers and the little sultan disappeared also. They rode post-haste for Cairo, leaving Damascus to its fate—"the most beautiful and flourishing city in the world" writes Ibn Taghri Birdi. They did not nominate anyone to command the army—the sultan and his ameers had just deserted.

Finding themselves without commanders, many mamlukes deserted also. A number of junior ameers left for Cairo. In brief, the

Mamluke army, which a few days before had nearly defeated Tamerlane, now disintegrated—surely one of the most extraordinary phenomena in the history of war.

On 8th January, 1401, the people of Damascus, thus abandoned, closed their gates and manned the walls. Tamerlane tried to take the city by assault, but suffered a costly reverse. Seeing that a siege would be prolonged, he sent a herald to cry to those on the wall, "The Ameer desires an armistice. Send a wise man to discuss terms." The Damascenes chose one of their principal qadhis, Ibrahim ibn Mifleh.

Tamerlane, a professing Muslim, assumed his pious manner. Telling his beads and murmuring prayers, he said that Damascus was the city of the Companions of the Prophet. "I give it its freedom for the sake of the Messenger of God (blessing and peace be upon him)," he murmured piously. The good qadhi was completely deceived. Hurrying back to the city, he praised the sincere religious faith of the conqueror and urged the citizens to abandon resistance. A heated debate ensued, but eventually all were persuaded to lay down their arms. The commander of the citadel, however, refused to surrender.

The qadhi, Ibn Mifleh, returned to the Tatar camp with a party of notables, who spent the night as guests of the pious conqueror. Next morning, they returned happily to the city, bringing a document, signed by Tamerlane, promising security for the inhabitants. A party of Tatar troops under an ameer were then admitted to the city, while the qadhi raised a fund of a million gold dinars as a gift for the kind conqueror. But Tamerlane had changed. He contemptuously rejected the million dinars and made the qadhi sign a bond for ten million.

The city was now packed with Tatar troops, and an ameer was appointed as its governor. The citadel resisted with great gallantry for twenty-nine days and only gave in when the garrison was almost exterminated. The Tatars took over all the weapons in the citadel and the citizens were obliged to surrender all private weapons. With the city entirely at his mercy, Tamerlane threw off the mask of piety, and the troops were told that they could do as they wished.

Men were subjected to fearful tortures, flogged, crushed in presses, burned alive, hung head downwards, but not allowed to die. When almost dead, the victim would be revived, and allowed an interval to recover, so that the torture could be renewed. While the father of a family was being tortured, his wife and daughters were brought out, stripped, and repeatedly raped beneath his eyes. Most of this occurred in the open air, in the streets and squares of the city, before crowds of soldiers.

At length, Tamerlane summoned his officers and asked if they had finished. They agreed that there was nothing more to do. Surviving men were roped together and dragged away as slaves. All the women were collected and driven off in flocks to the camp. Children under five and babies were left unattended in the city, where they all died within a few days.

The city was then set on fire. Warehouses, dwellings, mosques and palaces collapsed in a raging furnace. The great Umaiyid mosque, six hundred years old and one of the world's most beautiful buildings, was reduced to a few charred walls. On 19th March, 1401, Tamerlane marched away. He had spent eighty days in one of the oldest and most beautiful cities in the world, which he left as a heap of smoking ruins and a few fragments of blackened walls.

*　　*　　*

Sultan Faraj had arrived back in Cairo on 20th January, 1401, accompanied by a group of ameers and a few hundred soldiers. He appointed Yalbugha[4] al Salimi to direct the government and to raise another army. The first step was to collect money and Yalbugha set to work with the usual seizures, sequestrations, taxes and forced contributions. Perhaps the public protested less than usual, for all were terrified that Tamerlane might come to Cairo. Fugitives from the army continued to straggle into the city, barefoot, emaciated and ragged.

The usual intrigues persisted between the ameers. Yalbugha was suddenly arrested and a rival group seized office. In spite of these political activities, a new army was mobilising outside Cairo by the beginning of March. One day, the Ameer Shaikh al Mahmoodi. arrived in Cairo, having been taken prisoner by Tamerlane and escaped. He reported that Tamerlane had left Damascus to go home. Ameers were hastily sent to set up the administration, including Taghri Birdi, reappointed Viceroy of Damascus.

*　　*　　*

When we consider the political intrigues which tore the Mamluke Empire during the minority of Sultan Faraj, we can draw some alarming conclusions. The impotence of the sultan gave free rein to rival politicians to compete for power. In the heat of these political rivalries, they neglected to provide for the interests of their country. The methods used by the Mamlukes seem on the surface completely

[4] This is the fourth ameer of that name whom we have met.

different from our own. Yet with us also politicians are free to compete for power, a system in which indeed we take pride. Yet we may well deduce from these events a principle which applies to the western democracies today, as much as it did to the Mamlukes. The principle is that, when political power is open to free competition, politicians are almost irresistibly tempted to devote more efforts to obtaining office than to serving the interests of their country.

Perhaps we can deduce a second principle, endlessly illustrated in history. Before the rise of Tamerlane, the Mamlukes were perhaps the greatest military power in the world, and were not threatened by any immediate enemy. The preservation of the defensive power of the country—the first consideration under Baybars and Qalaoon—no longer received much thought. But when Tamerlane suddenly appeared on the scene, the army could not be quickly reconstructed. Yet even so, while Barqooq was in control, Tamerlane kept away. It was the absorption of the young intimates in politics and money-making, which tempted the foreign conqueror to come. Are we justified in submitting another principle? "*Never* start a war, but be *always* ready to defend yourself, for the world still contains predatory forces, ready to take advantage of weakness."

*　　*　　*

After leaving Damascus, Tamerlane marched through Aleppo and Mardin to Baghdad, to which Ahmad ibn Uwais had returned. Tamerlane's repeated treacheries had resulted in no city accepting his promises any longer. Baghdad refused to open its gates but was taken by assault in September, 1401, after desperate fighting. More than a hundred thousand severed heads were built into towers to commemorate this Tatar triumph.

A year later, on 20th July, 1402, Tamerlane utterly defeated Bayazid, the Ottoman Sultan outside Anqara.[5] The Othmanlis seemed to have been completely destroyed.

Tamerlane died on 19th February, 1405, in his tent on the steppes. He was on his way to conquer China. He left a world in ruins. The Ottoman Empire lay shattered, the Mamluke Empire was in anarchy, northern India was devastated.

*　　*　　*

No sooner had the conqueror marched away than the ameers in Cairo returned to their party politics. Yashbak al Shaabani, who had

[5] Map 25, page 278.

dominated the little sultan for two years, was overthrown and sent to
Alexandria. Nauruz al Hafidhi seized power, assisted by an Ameer
Jakam. Several hundred thousand dinars were mulcted from the
public to reward the mamlukes who had supported Nauruz. Little
Faraj was a helpless spectator of these struggles for power.

The new party sent to arrest Taghri Birdi, who had been made
Viceroy of Damascus by Yashbak al Shaabani, but he and the
Viceroy of Aleppo fled to Khalil ibn Dulqadir, the Turkman Prince
of Albistan. On 5th May, 1402, however, Yasahbak al Shabani
returned to power in another coup d'état. Taghri Birdi was called to
Cairo and received a magnificent robe of honour.

The Ameer Inal Bai had married the sultan's sister and replaced
Yashbak's influence over the sultan. On 10th August, 1404, Yashbak
seized the Sultan Hasan mosque and bombarded the Citadel, which
was held by Inal Bai. On 14th August, Yashbak fled to Damascus.

In May, 1405, Yashbak, Jakam and a prominent ameer called
Shaikh[6] al Mahmoodi marched from Damascus on Cairo, but
subsequently turned back. In Cairo, the Circassians demanded an
all-Circassian government. The basis of the Mamluke system had
been the loyalty of each mamluke to his patron. With the whole
system apparently on the verge of dissolution, racial and other groups
now appeared, threatening complete anarchy.

If any man ever suffered an unhappy adolescence, it was the young
Sultan Faraj. To Taghri Birdi he once cried, "I wish I could be anything else, if *only* I did not have to be a sultan." Taghri Birdi's
sister, it will be remembered, was Shirin, the mother of Faraj. Now
the latter married Taghri Birdi's daughter, the sister of our historian.[7]

But Taghri Birdi was an Anatolian, and the Circassians demanded
his arrest. On 14th September, 1405, to save the sultan embarrass-
ment, Taghri Birdi escaped from Cairo with a hundred personal
mamlukes and rode to Jerusalem. The next day, however, Faraj,
now seventeen years old, himself vanished. The ameers sent for the
khalif and the qadhis, and proclaimed his younger brother, Abdul
Azeez, to be sultan.

AL-MALIK-AL-MANSOOR
ABDUL AZEEZ IBN BARQOOQ

Abdul Azeez was proclaimed sultan on 21st September, 1405. In

------

[6] Shaikh was his personal name, not a title.
[7] The marriage of first cousins is legitimate in Islam.

Cairo, business was at a standstill owing to public insecurity. Syria was torn by civil wars between rival ameers, of whom Shaikh al Mahmoodi seemed to be the most prominent.

Faraj, meanwhile, was lying hidden in the house of an Egyptian qadhi in Cairo, Saad-al-Deen ibn Ghurab. On the night of 28th November, 1405, Faraj suddenly reappeared in the streets, where he was quickly surrounded by a crowd of ameers and citizens, and walked up to the Citadel unopposed. Abdul Azeez was sent back to his mother and Faraj became sultan once again. Abdul Azeez had been nominal sultan for two months and seven days.

AL-MALIK-AL-NASIR FARAJ
(Second Reign)

Yashbak al Shaabani returned to power in Cairo, Shaikh al Mahmoodi became Viceroy of Damascus and Jakam Viceroy of Aleppo. The Khalif Mutawakkil died and was succeeded by his son with the title of Al Mustaeen.

But the turbulent Jakam rebelled and seized Damascus on 17th June, 1406, Shaikh escaping to Egypt. On 23rd July, Sultan Faraj set out for Damascus with the army and Jakam withdrew across the Euphrates. The sultan remained six weeks in Aleppo, returning to Damascus on 17th November. The day after he left Aleppo, it was reoccupied by Jakam. On 22nd December, 1406, Faraj was back in Cairo and the rebels reoccupied Damascus. The sultan's campaign had achieved nothing. The explanation of this negative result seems to have been that the Mamlukes and the public were disgusted with fighting. The sultan or Jakam could come or go as they wished, no one opposed them or supported them.

It is to be noticed also that the obituaries for these years mention both ameers, officials and men of religion, who served under successive sultans and retired at an honourable old age. Many are described as modest, generous, courageous and pious. The continued survival of the Mamluke Empire must have been due to the loyal, routine services of such officers. Indifferent to the marches and counter-marches of the contestants for power, these modest, permanent officials must have enabled the life of the people to continue.

*   *   *

Faraj was now eighteen years old, having lived for nine years surrounded by fear, intrigue, greed and treachery. Now he could bear it no longer and sought oblivion in drink. On one occasion, he had been so drunk that his mamlukes threw him into the palace pool. Before he had reached maturity he was an alcoholic.

Anarchy reigned in Syria. The rebel Nauruz held Damascus, while Shaikh was in Safad. On 21st March, 1407, Jakam was proclaimed sultan in Aleppo and was recognised all over Syria, except only in Safad, where Shaikh still recognised Faraj. On 25th April, 1407, however, Jakam fought a battle against the Turkmans near Amid in which he was killed. Shaikh, by a swift march from Safad, defeated the rebels who had seized Gaza. Suddenly, the sultan's cause seemed to be victorious.

On 9th July, 1407, Faraj left Cairo, accompanied by his original protector, Yashbak, by Taghri Birdi and others. Shaikh, by a swift march, seized Damascus for the sultan and welcomed him on his arrival on 27th July. But the sultan ordered the immediate arrest of Shaikh, the only ameer in Syria loyal to him. Yashbak also was arrested and both ameers were confined in the citadel, whence they escaped. Shaikh went underground in Damascus, but Yashbak was overtaken and killed. The only explanation seems to be that Faraj was now determined to be his own master and to liquidate the senior officers *on his own side* who liked to tell him what to do. On 10th September, 1407, Faraj left for Egypt with eighteen ameers loaded with chains.

Such were the extraordinary vicissitudes of ameers in this chaotic reign. One day living in luxury in a palace, the next crouching in the poor tent of some nomadic Turkman, or lying, chained hand and foot, in a dank prison. Historians do not tell us what became of their families, their wives and girl slaves and children.

*   *   *

When Faraj returned to Cairo, Shaikh emerged from hiding and seized Damascus in the sultan's name, but Faraj rejected his professions of loyalty and announced that he was coming to fight him. At times, it is difficult to avoid the impression that Faraj was mad. On 29th April, he again left Egypt for Syria.

The Dhahiris, the old mamlukes of his father Barqooq, were now seething with disloyalty. They complained that Faraj continued to buy young mamlukes, to whom he immediately gave precedence over his father's veterans. It was rumoured that the Royal Mamlukes intended to murder the sultan. Faraj entered Damascus on 20th June, 1409. Shaikh, hitherto the only loyal ameer in Syria, but whom

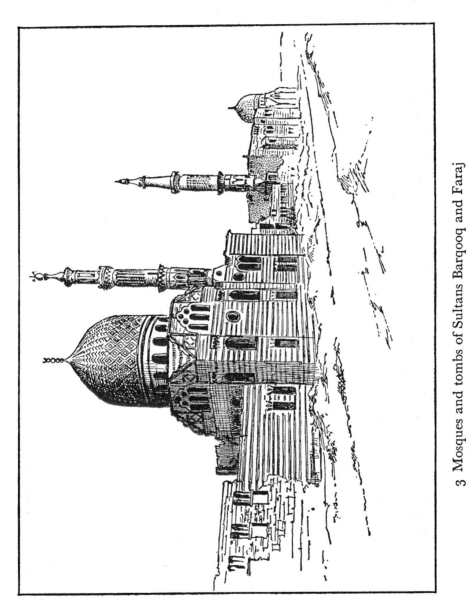

3 Mosques and tombs of Sultans Barqooq and Faraj

Faraj designated as his principal enemy, retired to Salkhad.[8]

The sultan marched after Shaikh to Salkhad, part of his army deserting on the way. Shaikh shut himself up in the castle. After a siege of several days, Taghri Birdi mediated a compromise and Shaikh again swore loyalty.

Faraj had lost the loyalty of the army, most of the ameers preferring Shaikh, a mild character who had tried to be loyal. Presumably Faraj, who since the age of nine had been exploited by ameers professing to be loyal to him, believed Shaikh to be such another would-be protector.

Shaikh sent a gift to the sultan who made him Governor of Tarablus. Faraj returned to Damascus and was back in Cairo on 21st September, where he made a triumphal march through the city, Taghri Birdi holding the royal parasol over his head. But no sooner had Faraj gone, than the "barons' wars" between rival ameers in Syria recommenced. Many persons were killed, business was at a standstill and farmers were afraid to plough.

For the sixth time, Faraj set out for Syria, entering Damascus on 31st July, 1410, accompanied by Taghri Birdi, now commander-in-chief. On 8th August, the sultan left for Aleppo, whence he proceeded to Albistan, where he remained until 1st October. Syria was ruined. The endless fines and extortions imposed by rival armies had impoverished the cities and the roads were infested with robbers.

When the sultan returned to Gaza, the two principal rebels, Shaikh and Nauruz marched to Cairo, which they entered on 5th January, 1411. Next day, however, the sultan's army arrived and the rebels beat a hasty retreat, crossing Sinai to Kerak. The sultan in person had remained in Damascus, and the army, as we have seen, were not anxious to catch Shaikh.

Hearing that Shaikh was in Kerak, Faraj hastened there by forced marches. Once again Taghri Birdi mediated. It was agreed that Shaikh would be Viceroy of Aleppo and Taghri Birdi of Damascus. Peace seemed to have been established for which the Damascenes returned fervent thanks to God. Not only had they suffered endless wars since the virtual destruction of their city by Tamerlane in 1401, but both Egypt and Syria had been visited by an epidemic of plague.

Back in Cairo, Faraj continued to make arrests and order executions. He was suffering from a persecution complex, not without some excuse, and saw conspiracies everywhere. In November 1411, more than a hundred mamlukes were halved at the waist, mostly middle-aged Dhahiris who had loyally served his father, Barqooq. Faraj seemed to be insane.

[8] Map 25, page 278.

On 25th March, 1412, Faraj left Cairo for his last campaign. The army set out in its traditional splendour. The horses bore saddles of gold, some set with precious stones, their saddlecloths were of satin, their hindquarters covered with silk cloths embroidered with gold. The bits were covered with gold and silver, and their bridles with pearls and ostrich feathers. The sultan had a boys' fife-and-drum band, dressed in yellow caps and cloaks. Behind the troops came the royal ladies, carried in litters covered with satin in bright colours. The senior wife was the sister of Ibn Taghri Birdi, our historian, and was Grand Princess and Mistress of the Court.

When the advanced guard of the sultan's army reached Damascus, it marched straight on to Aleppo and joined Shaikh. Scarcely a man was loyal to the sultan in the magnificent army which he led. In Damascus, Taghri Birdi, the prudent old Councillor, was on his deathbed. Reaching Damascus on 12th April, Faraj visited the dying Taghri Birdi, who begged him to be kind and generous to his mamlukes and to win their loyalty. But the sultan brushed aside the old man's advice, saying that all he wanted was to make the rebels stand and fight.

Suddenly showing signs of humanity, Faraj told the Grand Princess to stay and nurse her dying father. He then asked to see Taghri Birdi's other children, of whom our historian was one. "I have committed my children to God, the Exalted, and I implore His help for them," murmured the dying man, whose mamlukes were propping him up on his pillows.

The sultan marched to Hims but, hearing that the rebels had passed him in the Buqaa,[9] he pursued them. Shaikh still proclaimed his resolve never to fight the sultan, but Faraj with only a small escort pursued him at breakneck speed. He overtook the rebels in the afternoon and galloped straight at them, sword in hand. Deserted by his escort, Faraj found himself alone among the rebels and covered with wounds. Wheeling his horse, he rode back at full speed for Damascus, where he arrived with only three followers, on 25th April, 1412.

The rebels followed and, on 27th April, laid siege to Damascus. Next day, Taghri Birdi died. For a week, the rebels exchanged a bombardment with the defenders of the city. The Khalif Mustaeen was taken prisoner by the insurgents, and many qadhis had gone over to them. A herald was sent through the rebel camp, announcing that the khalif had deposed Sultan Faraj. The khalif was alarmed at finding himself thus committed, but the rebels persuaded him willy-nilly to accept the sultanate for himself, on the principle that in for a

[9] Map 25, page 278.

penny was in for a pound. Setting up an improvised throne, the rebel ameers kissed the ground before Mustaeen, on 7th May, 1412.

Meanwhile, Faraj was conducting the defence with his usual fearless courage, but on 2nd June, 1412, he gave up and walked out of the gate of the citadel with his women and children. He was imprisoned in a cell. On 7th June, 1412, five men entered his cell and stabbed him to death. His body was thrown out on a garbage heap— an indication of the lack of chivalry among the people, says Ibn Taghri Birdi indignantly. In the rebel camp, all kissed the ground before the Khalif Mustaeen.

Malik-al-Nasir Faraj was twenty-two years old when he died, having reigned for thirteen years. For the first two-thirds of his reign, he was the helpless victim of the rivalries of greedy and ambitious ameers. As a result, his character was warped, he trusted no man, inflicted savage punishments, and tried to forget his sufferings in drink. He was of medium stature with fair hair being, of course, a Circassian from the Caucasus.

Ibn Taghri Birdi, his brother-in-law, takes a more lenient view of Faraj than does Maqrizi, who says that "by bad government he brought ruin on Egypt and Syria". Not only was the country ruined by endless civil wars, but neglect of the administration caused the irrigation works to silt up. The plague also raged in Cairo for several successive years. Maqrizi charges Faraj with being dissolute, drunken and impious. This is true of his last three or four years, but we must remember that for most of his reign he was an unhappy frightened child. His life was a human tragedy, for which most of the blame rests on the unscrupulous lust for power of the ameers.

NOTABLE EVENTS

Accession of Malik-al-Nasir Faraj, at the age of nine	20th June, 1399
Faraj claims to be of age ⎫ Yashbak al Shaabani the sultan's ⎬ favourite ⎭	6th November, 1399
Battle of Al Jiteen ⎫ Tanam's rebellion defeated ⎭	March, 1400
Execution of Aitemish al Bajasi	10th April, 1400
Capture of Ain Tab by Tamerlane	September, 1400
Destruction of Aleppo by Tamerlane	30th October, 1400
Drawn battle outside Damascus between Tamerlane and the Mamlukes	31st December, 1400

The sultan and the ameers desert the army and return to Cairo	8th January, 1401
Destruction of Damascus by Tamerlane	January to March, 1401
Disappearance of Faraj	15th September, 1405
Elevation of Abdul Azeez	21st September, 1405
Return of Faraj to the throne	28th November, 1405
Rebels besiege Faraj in Damascus	27th April, 1412
Surrender of Faraj	2nd June, 1412
Murder of Faraj	7th June, 1412

PERSONALITIES

Mamluke Sultan
Sultan Malik-al-Nasir Faraj

Mamluke Ameers
Yashbak al Shaabani, favourite of Faraj
Aitemish al Bajasi, Regent
Taghri Birdi, maternal uncle of Faraj
Tanam, rebel Viceroy of Damascus
Nauruz al Hafidhi ⎫
Ameer Jakam ⎬ Rebels
Shaikh al Mahmoodi ⎭

Foreign Rulers
Tamerlane, World Conqueror
Bayazid, Ottoman Sultan

XV

The Royal Paternalist

He that can have patience can have what he will.
FRANKLIN

Peace hath her victories
No less renowned than war.
JOHN MILTON

Among the strange anomalies of Oriental history none perhaps is
more surprising than the combination of extreme corruption and
savage cruelty with exquisite refinement in material civilization
and an admirable devotion to art which we see in the Mamluk
sultans. The Circassians were not inferior to their Turkish fore-
runners as architects. Personally some of the second line of
sultans were men of considerable culture ... They were also
good Moslems, fasted ... abstained from wine, made pilgrimages and insured their place in the next world by building
mosques, colleges, hospitals ... El-Muayyad (Shaikh), for
example, was personally a devout man and a learned, a good
musician, poet, and orator ... very simple and unpretentious
in his mode of life.

STANLEY LANE-POOLE, *The Story of Cairo*

XV

IT will be remembered that, when besieging Sultan Faraj in Damascus, the rebel ameers had declared the Khalif Mustaeen to be sultan. This action was primarily intended to win over the army and the public from the party of Faraj. But, secondly, it was directed to preserving the peace between the two rebel leaders, Shaikh al Mahmoodi and Nauruz al Hafidhi. A temporary *modus vivendi* was reached, according to which the two ameers would proceed together to Cairo in the train of the new sultan, Mustaeen.[1] In Cairo, the two ameers would hold exactly equal rank. So delicate a balance of power could not last.

Eventually, however, it was agreed that Shaikh be made commander-in-chief in Cairo and that Nauruz should return to Syria, not as Viceroy of Damascus, but as Governor of all Syria from Gaza to the Euphrates. He was granted authority to nominate and dismiss governors and officers, and to allot fiefs. No previous sultan had ever delegated such powers, which virtually divided the empire into two.

On 12th July, 1412, the Sultan-and-Khalif Mustaeen made a state entry into Cairo, after which he took up his residence in the Citadel. Shaikh, as commander-in-chief, arrested or promoted ameers as he wished. Seeing that the real power rested with him, the army and the public resorted only to him, and the khalif found himself alone in his palace, with neither staff nor duties. Shaikh had appointed one of his own men to be the khalif's private secretary, and to report on his actions.

The position of Mustaeen was indeed impossible. A man of religion and peace was unlikely to be able to dominate a half-barbarian military caste. His nomination as sultan when the rebels were outside Damascus had been a short-term political expedient to detach the Damascenes from Faraj. The Prophet's family had indeed provided sultan-khalifs for two hundred and twenty-nine years (632–861), men who had ruled as autocrats and commanded armies. But that was five hundred and fifty years before. Dead political forms cannot be revived, and again command the loyalty of men.

Al-Mustaeen Billah means "he who seeks help from God".

4 Mamluke tombs and mosques outside Cairo

On 6th November, 1412, a council of ameers, qadhis and officials was convened. The confidential secretary made a brief speech, stating that the duties of sultan and khalif were incompatible. It was decided unanimously that Shaikh be sultan and the khalif be dethroned. He had been nominal sultan for five months.

* * *

MALIK-AL-MUAIYAD SHAIKH AL MAHMOODI

Shaikh had been brought to Egypt by a slave merchant called Mahmood Shah al Yezdi. Hence the new sultan's surname of Mahmoodi. He had been bought by Barqooq, when the latter was still commander-in-chief. Shaikh was then about twelve years old. When Barqooq became sultan, he manumitted the boy, made him his cupbearer, then one of his intimates, then ameer of ten, and then of forty. He was made an ameer of one hundred immediately after the death of Barqooq. After the rebellion of Tanam, Shaikh was made Viceroy of Damascus.

A former mamluke of Barqooq, his principal associates were his old barrack-comrades, the Dhahiris, against whom Faraj developed an increasing hatred, as already described. Yet, for the sake of Barqooq who had brought him up, Shaikh always refused to fight against Faraj. When the ameers in Damascus voted for the death of Faraj, Shaikh alone had demanded that his life be spared, indicating a feeling of loyalty to Barqooq.

When Shaikh was made sultan in Cairo, Nauruz al Hafidhi in Damascus prepared for war, and the sultan prepared to march against him. On 29th April, 1414, Shaikh and his army reached Damascus. Throughout the march from Egypt, Shaikh dictated letters to the secretaries of his principal ameers, ostensibly from their masters, informing Nauruz of their wish to desert to him when they reached Damascus. Deceived by this trick, Nauruz waited confidently in Damascus, expecting Shaikh's army to come over to him.

When approaching the city, Shaikh sent a venerable qadhi, in his own name, to ask Nauruz for a truce. The latter, taking the request as a sign of weakness, refused, and marched out to fight. The sultan's army, however, did not desert but inflicted a sharp defeat on Nauruz, who took refuge in the citadel, and sent a message to Shaikh, asking for peace. Terms were quickly arranged, the sultan agreeing to spare Nauruz, who sent some of his supporters to witness Shaikh's oath to

the terms. Before a large gathering of judges the oath was administered by Qadhi Nasir-al-Deen al Bárizi, who read out the text.

The judges were, of course, all Egyptians and Syrians, but Nauruz
had sent Mamlukes as his witnesses. Classical and legal Arabic is a
complicated language, in which a mispronunciation or a false
quantity can change the meaning. The agreement, as read out by the
good qadhi, was gibberish, but Nauruz's Mamluke witnesses, whose
knowledge of Arabic was slight, expressed themselves perfectly
satisfied.

Accordingly, on 10th July, 1414, Nauruz came out of the citadel
on foot and was received by the sultan before a large gathering of
ameers and qadhis. In an obviously rehearsed act, some of the qadhis
exclaimed piously, "O blessed day, which brings an end of bloodshed
between the Muslims." To this Qadhi Nasir-al-Deen replied, "A
blessed day indeed, if this be accomplished." "Why should it not be
accomplished?" enquired the sultan innocently. Nasir-al-Deen,
turning to the assembled qadhis, asked, "O Qadhis, is the sultan's
oath valid?" "No, by God," they replied in unison. Nauruz was
immediately shackled and that night was beheaded.

Ibn Taghri Birdi has an interesting comment. He states that, at
this time, a number of "Turks"[2] aspired to become lawyers and
studied under local qadhis until they could read a thesis before some
learned Egyptian or Syrian jurist. After which, they would claim to
be intellectuals, although in fact their knowledge of Arabic, the
language of science and law, was scanty. "They even utter faulty
opinions concerning scientific subjects other than jurisprudence, and
that is ignorance itself,"[3] says Ibn Taghri Birdi severely.

This passage is significant. The savage Mamlukes are developing
a taste for culture so earnest that they seek lessons from the Egyptians
and the Syrians, and boast of their academic successes. The Mamlukes had, at this time, ruled their empire for a hundred and sixty-
five years. The Crusaders, in a similar period, had been transformed
from coarse European warriors into an Eastern Mediterranean
community. Yet the Crusaders had lived, from generation to generation, in the Middle East. It was precisely to avoid this "decadence"
that the Mamlukes insisted that every man of their community must
be born on the steppes, and that those born in Egypt were not
recognised as true Mamlukes. The intellectual "Turks" condemned
by our historian were probably first generation born in Egypt or
Syria, who thereby were debarred from the army. But the signifi-

---

[2] The Syrians and Egyptians always called the Mamlukes Turks, including even
Circassians.

[3] "A little learning is a dangerous thing", Pope, *Essay on Criticism*.

cance lies in the fact that, with all the precautions regarding birth on the steppes, the Mamluke community, as a whole, was becoming middle Easternised.

The next factor to notice is that this stage of intellectualism has, in every nation, been the precursor of collapse, for it produces an antipathy to war and to military service. This development may well be hailed as an improvement, for war is hateful and brutal. But it is a development which always results in the destruction of the civilisation concerned, because some other community, still in the military stage of development, seizes the opportunity to invade and conquer the people which has neglected its own defence. Every civilisation thus carries within it the seeds of its own destruction. As soon as it rises to the level of hatred of war, it is destroyed by a more warlike group.

But this is only half the story, for the period of civilisation also produces security, wealth and luxury, leading to materialism, a loss of the sense of obligation to the community and an individualistic outlook of unrestricted greed. Whether this takes the form of commercial competition or the lust for power, it destroys the cohesion of the community. As a result, many civilisations seem first to collapse internally, by increasingly bitter rivalries, party politics, military coups d'état or civil wars, which are caused by material greed and an abandonment of the sense of duty. These bitter and selfish rivalries so weaken the community that a more cohesive and disciplined people find it easy to conquer the country.

These peculiarities are not primarily fit objects for praise or blame —they are just the way of the world. As a young man may be headstrong, foolish but energetic, whereas an old man may be physically weak, perhaps cynical, but experienced and wise, so young civilisations are aggressive but disciplined and ready for sacrifice, whereas old ones are pacific, cultured but materialistic. These are the effects of youth and age. We cannot blame the young for hastiness or the old for feebleness—these are the effects, on states or on individuals, of the passage of time. Yet it would be a great human achievement to discover such methods as would prevent new states from attacking the old, and to enable the old to retain the idealism, the sense of duty and the discipline which distinguished them in the early stages of their rise to greatness.

*   *   *

Shaikh was now the undisputed ruler of the empire. Marching north, he visited Aleppo, Albistan and Malatia, restoring order and

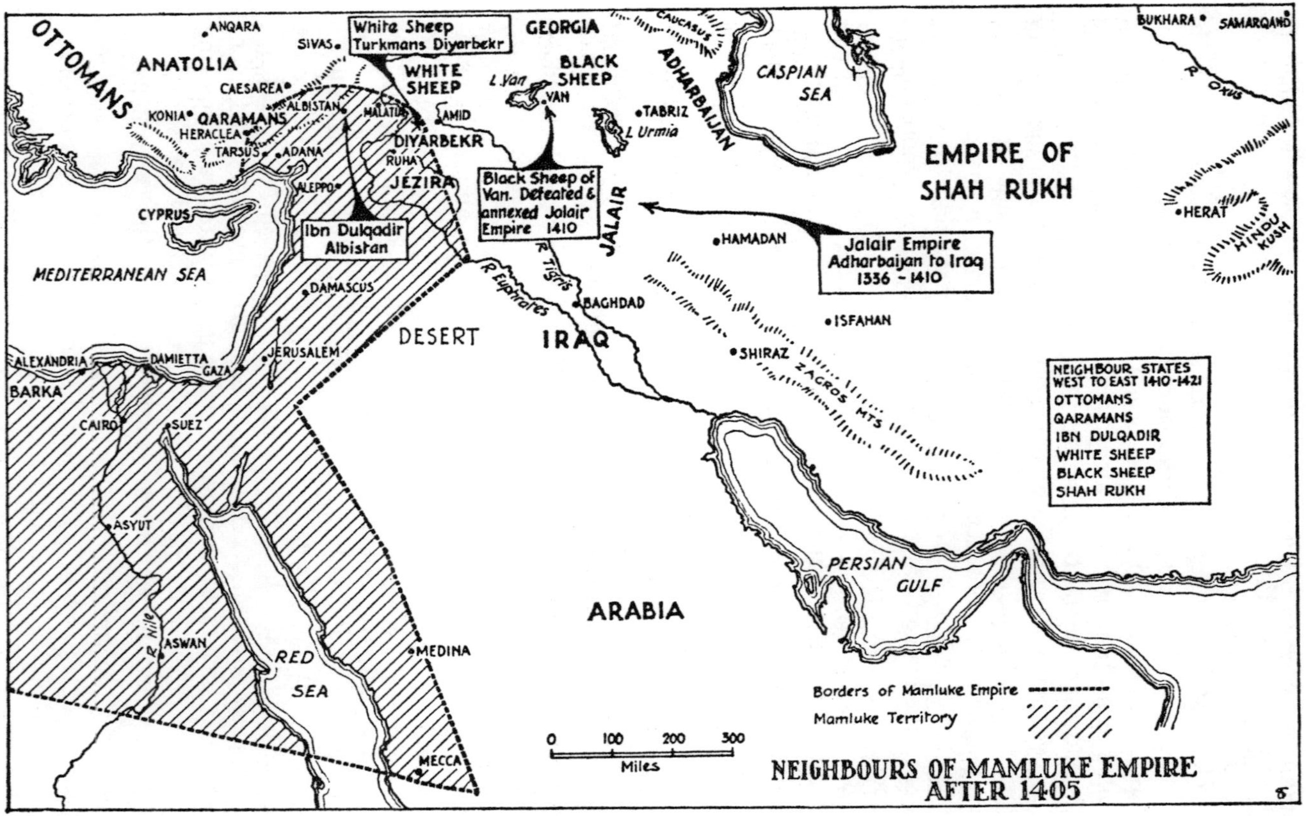

EMPIRE OF SHAH RUKH

•BUKHARA •SAMARQAND

R. Oxus

•HERAT

KUHI NUH

CASPIAN SEA

ADHARBAIJAN

GEORGIA

•TABRIZ
L. Urmia

CAUCASUS

BLACK SHEEP

L. Van
•VAN

•HAMADAN

•ISFAHAN

•SHIRAZ

ZAGROS MTS.

Jalair Empire
Adharbaijam to Iraq
1356 - 1410

PERSIAN GULF

JALAIR

BAGHDAD

R. Tigris

R. Euphrates

Black Sheep of
Van. Defeated &
annexed Jalair
Empire 1410

WHITE SHEEP

White Sheep
Turkmans Diyarbekr

•AMID

DIYARBEKR
•RUHA
JEZIRA

ANATOLIA

•ANQARA

•SIVAS

•CAESAREA

QARAMANS

•KONIA
HERACLEA
•ADANA
•TAPSUS
•ALBISTAN
•MILITENE

•ALEPPO

Ibn Dulqadir
Albistan

•DAMASCUS

•JERUSALEM

•GAZA

DESERT

IRAQ

ARABIA

OTTOMANS

CYPRUS

MEDITERRANEAN SEA

•ALEXANDRIA
BARKA
•DAMIETTA

•SUEZ

•CAIRO

•ASYUT

•ASWAN

R. Nile

RED SEA

•MEDINA

•MECCA

NEIGHBOUR STATES
WEST TO EAST 1410-1421
OTTOMANS
QARAMANS
IBN DULQADIR
WHITE SHEEP
BLACK SHEEP
SHAH RUKH

Borders of Mamluke Empire ------

Mamluke Territory ////

NEIGHBOURS OF MAMLUKE EMPIRE
AFTER 1405

0   100   200   300
Miles

MAP 26

stable administration. On 15th December, 1414, he returned to Cairo.

* * *

Four years of confusion had followed the death of Tamerlane in 1405. Thereafter, Shah Rukh, the fourth son of Tamerlane, became sultan and ruled from 1409 until 1447. His capital was in Herat, while his son, Ulugh Beg, ruled in Samarqand.[4] Both father and son were men of peace, and encouraged scientists, poets and men of learning.

It will be remembered that, after the collapse of the Il-Khans, the most prominent dynasty in the east had been the Jalair Mongols, the descendants of Hasan Buzurg, who ruled from Tabriz to Baghdad. But Ahmad ibn Uwais had been driven out by Tamerlane and had taken refuge in Egypt with Barqooq. In 1410, he recovered Baghdad, but in trying also to recover Tabriz, he was defeated by the Black Sheep Turkmans, who drove him out of Iraq also, and put an end to the Jalair dynasty.

The Black Sheep and the White Sheep Turkmans had also arisen from the ruins of the Il-Khan Empire, the Black Sheep around Van, the White Sheep in Diyarbekr. The Black Sheep had opposed Tamerlane and been driven out by him, the White Sheep had fought under his banner. In 1405, after the death of Tamerlane, the Black Sheep recovered their power and at first fought against Shah Rukh, but in 1415 peace was made, and Gauhar Shad, the sister of Qara Yusuf, was married to Shah Rukh. Shaikh was worried by this apparent reconciliation, for he felt safer when his eastern neighbours were fighting one another. The White Sheep, at this period, were weaker than the Black Sheep. Their capital was at Amid.[5]

In Cairo, Shaikh quietly pursued the normal procedure of removing ameers associated with other factions and promoting his own barrack-comrades or personal mamlukes. In August 1415, however, the inevitable revolt threatened. The Viceroys of Damascus and Aleppo prepared to rebel, but finding inadequate support, retired on Antioch. The sultan and the army reached Damascus on 11th October and marched on to Aleppo. The rebel viceroys fled to Qara Yusuf, chief of the Black Sheep Turkmans, who, by destroying the Jalair Mongol dynasty of Baghdad, had now become the ruler of an empire extending from Tabriz to Iraq. The sultan appointed one of his own mamlukes to Aleppo and was back in Egypt on 13th February, 1416.

[4] Map 26, opposite.   [5] Map 26.

Shaikh had been passing through the inevitable period of uncertainty which faced every new sultan, when the senior ameers were
all people appointed by his predecessor. No sultan was safe till these
ameers had been disposed of and replaced by his own personal
mamlukes.

Two days after his return, Malik-al-Muaiyad Shaikh made a
triumphal march through Cairo, the streets of which had been
lavishly decorated. He then devoted himself to the economic situation. The price of food had risen rapidly, owing to a succession of low
Niles, epidemics of plague and the civil wars of Faraj. He attempted
to fix the price of food, which produced a slight improvement. Perhaps more important, the morale of the public rose at the sight of a
sultan who was anxious to improve matters. He distributed four
thousand dinars to the very poor, who were really hungry. The
importation of wheat from southern Egypt was subsidised. Shaikh
devoted himself personally to the welfare of his subjects, and "the
breath of life returned to men".

At Friday prayers in the mosques, the names of God and the
Prophet were spoken by the preacher in the pulpit. As a sign of
humility, Shaikh ordered that, when his name was mentioned in the
prayers for the sultan, the preacher should descend one step from the
level on which he had spoken the name of God.

On 23rd March, 1417, the sultan again set out for Syria with an
army. There was no war or rebellion, but he thought it an advisable
precaution to show the flag. ("Show force so as not to have to use it"
was the motto of the French Marshal Lyautey in Morocco during the
First World War.)

The sultan seems again to have visited Aleppo. The Ottoman
Empire was gradually recovering from its disastrous defeat by
Tamerlane and had defeated the Qaraman Ameer, whose capital
was at Konia. The belt of country extending from Tarsus to Malatia
was mountainous and was mostly held by Turkman tribes, who
henceforward formed little buffer states between the Mamluke and
the Ottoman Empires. On the present occasion a Mamluke column
besieged and took Tarsus, which had previously been held by the
Qaraman ameerate.[6]

On 26th August, 1417, Shaikh returned to Aleppo after visiting
Albistan. Deputations came from Qara Yusuf, and from the local
rulers of Ruha and Diyarbekr. The sultan suffered pains in his feet,
possibly gout, and was carried in a litter. On 12th October, 1417, he
was back in Damascus. On 15th November, he made a pilgrimage to
Jerusalem, prayed in the Aqsa mosque and sat there for a long time,

[6] Map 26, page 302.

while the Traditions of the Prophet[7] were read out before a large gathering. On 25th November he was back in Cairo, where he made a state entry, his son Ibrahim holding the royal parasol over his head. The city was gaily decorated, candles and lamps burned in all the shops, and groups of singing girls sat in the windows and on the roofs, singing and beating their tambourines. The khalif, the qadhis and the civil officials, all in splendid robes, took part in the procession. Altogether it was a notable day of genuine public rejoicing, long remembered by all who took part.

The sultan showed great activity in visiting the neighbouring districts and in calling upon ameers and officials in Cairo. From one of these social occasions, he returned to the Citadel in a reprehensible state of intoxication, according to Ibn Taghri Birdi. In September 1418, reports stated that Qara Yusuf, the Black Sheep Turkman chief, was approaching the Euphrates east of Aleppo. Mobilisation was ordered, but Qara Yusuf withdrew after apologising to the Viceroy of Aleppo.

The incident reminds us once again that a strong sultan and an efficient army were of immense benefit to the peoples of Egypt and Syria, whose neighbours for two hundred and fifty years were savage Turks and Mongols. The cruelties of the Mamlukes were, in most cases, practised on one another. It is an extraordinary example of human folly that this handful of foreigners, governing a considerable empire, spent most of their efforts fighting one another, in spite of the tortures, the long years in prison, the stranglings and the halvings-at-the-waist which were the fate of the unsuccessful.

The increase of corruption since the reign of Barqooq gave a clear index of the slow decadence of the empire. One of the principal abuses was the practice of entering the same man as a royal and also as an ameer's mamluke, thereby drawing two salaries or holding two fiefs. But, on mobilisation, only one man paraded, where two men were on the nominal rolls. Shaikh ordered a general review, at which such pluralists could be identified. The offenders excused themselves on the grounds that, owing to the rise in the cost of living, a single salary was insufficient. The sultan tried to give adequate fiefs to Royal Mamlukes, but pluralism was never eradicated and continued to reduce the strength of the army.

Another dangerous abuse had crept in—namely the sale of their fiefs by mamlukes. The principle of the whole system was that all the land belonged to the government, which allotted a fief to a soldier to provide him with a livelihood in lieu of pay. If the man were killed or retired, the fief was transferred by the Army Office to another soldier.

[7] Bukhari, Al Sahih.

But if the soldier were allowed to sell his fief for cash and leave the army, he often sold it to a civilian who was not capable of military service. Incredible as it may appear, this practice was sanctioned at various times, merely, it would seem, because the government took a fee on the transaction, although thereby it permanently lost a soldier.

No importance, as we have seen, was attached to nationality or race. Yet we may suspect that the fact that Mamlukes were now of many different ethnic origins may have increased disunity. For the first century and a half, they had been nearly all Qipchaq Turks, and the empire had been confident, strong and wealthy. Now they might be Tatars, Turkmans, Circassians, Turks, Armenians or even Greeks. Yet any differences in loyalties must have been unconscious, for the historians make no mention of racial motivations, except in the case of Circassians.

The point is of some topical interest owing to the great increase of different racial elements in the West. Do foreign immigrants into the United States, to take one example, immediately make loyal citizens?

*　　*　　*

In March 1419, the plague reappeared in Cairo. A three-day fast was proclaimed, and many people continued to fast three days a week until the epidemic ended. On Thursday, 11th May, 1419, the sultan, dressed only in a white woollen garment like a sufi or monk, rode out to the plain outside Cairo. The chief qadhi went out on foot, accompanied by great crowds of qadhis, religious teachers, dervishes and nearly all the notables from Old and New Cairo.

The sultan dismounted and, standing among the men of religion, offered up a fervent prayer to God, weeping and lamenting the sins of the people, for which the plague was seen as a divine punishment. After the prayers, the sultan remounted and rode to the tomb-mosque of Barqooq, which was on the plain near by. Here a meal was prepared, the sultan himself assisted in the slaughter of a great many animals. It is curious for how long the idea of appeasing God by killing animals has survived. The meat of the animals sacrificed was distributed to the poor, who also received eight hundred and twenty thousand loaves of bread. According to Ibn Taghri Birdi, the plague from that day began to decrease.

When the prayers and distribution of charity were completed, Shaikh rode back to the city, still dressed as a monk, without weapons or escort. The immense crowds pressed in upon him from every side, holding the bridle of his horse and his stirrups, and rubbing against its flanks.

This scene also obliges us to modify our estimate of the Mamlukes as military tyrants. We witness their lives in many different ways mingling with the lives of the people. As in all life, we see that these human relationships were extremely complicated. Men cannot be divided into heroes and villains. Sweeping generalisations, the daily bread of politics, are never true.

It is sad to pass from this scene of the sultan surrounded by his affectionate subjects, to discuss his next objective—the humiliation of Jews and Christians. It is doubtless gratifying to human nature to feel that we can humiliate persons of whom we are jealous and at the same time please God by doing so. The Muslims have not been alone in indulging this practice, of which neither professing Christians nor Jews have been innocent.

On 2nd June, 1419, the sultan summoned the qadhis to an assembly before which the Christian Patriarch of Egypt was arraigned. The sultan abused him for the humiliations allegedly inflicted on the Muslims in Abyssinia. The Egyptian Christians were of the Coptic rite, distinct from the church in Abyssinia, and the Emperor of Abyssinia was an independent monarch. Shaikh Ahmad ibn al Ajami then went up to the patriarch and "let him hear some ugly words".[8] This was probably a popularity winning exercise, such as those with which our own politics have made us familiar. After a long consultation between the sultan and the qadhis, it was decided that no Christians should in future fill any post in the offices of the sultan or the ameers—a decision often taken before.

It is necessary, once again, to avoid comparing the actions of the fifteenth-century Muslims with conditions in Western Europe or North America today. The fifteenth century was a time of religious fanaticism everywhere. Seventy-three years later, Ferdinand and Isabella, the Catholic sovereigns, secured the surrender of Granada, the last Muslim capital in Spain. The terms of surrender included a pledge that "the Muslims were guaranteed the safety of their lives and possessions and freedom to practise their religion under their own laws". Seven years after the surrender, a campaign of forced conversions to Christianity began, under the control of the Inquisition. In the century following the pledge of religious toleration given by Ferdinand and Isabella, some three million Spanish Muslims are believed to have been executed or banished.

Today, it is true, we no longer torture members of other religions, because our fanaticisms are concerned with other things, such as

---

[8] Ibn Taghri Birdi, *Nujoom*.

communism, democracy or racialism. But to show our superiority in these directions our generation has massacred innocent victims in gas chambers, caused millions to perish in concentration camps, dropped atomic bombs on Japan, or used napalm to burn alive the peasants of Viet Nam and Palestine. When expressing our horror of fifteenth-century cruelty, are we sure that we are not just the pot calling the kettle black?

It may, perhaps, also be noticed that the periodical purges carried out against the Christians took the form of humiliation, rather than of physical persecution, as practised by the Inquisition in Spain. Yet Ibn Taghri Birdi, a moderate and reasonable historian, is enthusi-astic for the humiliation of Christians. He trusts that God will forgive Sultan Shaikh his sins, in view of his activity in the humiliation of Christians and Jews.

*   *   *

Meanwhile, a Mamluke army, under the nominal command of the sultan's son, Ibrahim, was continuing operations in the north. Caesarea in Anatolia was taken from the Qaraman Ameer. Heraclea, Tarsus and Adana were strongly garrisoned.[9] The Mamluke Empire had never been so extensive or seemed so dominant. In October 1419, Ibrahim returned to Cairo, but on 27th June, 1420, he died.

At a service in the Muaiyad mosque, which the sultan had just built, the preacher spoke of the Prophet's son, who also died young and whose name was Ibrahim. The sultan wept unrestrainedly throughout the sermon and many of the congregation did the same.

Shaikh was again immobilised by the pains in his feet and was carried everywhere in a litter. Ibn Taghri Birdi mentions that he gave up alcohol owing to this trouble, which suggests that he may have had gout, and that it was thought to be due to excessive drinking. Everything was quiet and peaceful throughout the empire, and the sultan was universally regarded with veneration.

Early in July 1420, anxiety was caused by the failure of the Nile to rise. An open-air meeting was again called on the plain outside Cairo and vast crowds assembled to pray. The sultan arrived alone on horseback, dressed as a monk, without arms or escort. The chief qadhi led the prayers and preached a sermon from an improvised pulpit, during which the sultan sat on the dusty ground near by.

Unable to stand, he was lifted on to his horse by the crowd. As he rode away, the people crowded round, calling down blessings on his name. Next day, the Nile rose twelve inches and, three days later, a further thirty inches.

[9] Map 26, page 302.

In August 1420, a campaign against Qara Yusuf, the chief of the Black Sheep Turkmans, seemed to be imminent. Qara Yusuf had made himself ruler of Tabriz and Baghdad, but his followers were wild tribesmen who had completed the ruin of Baghdad, begun by Hulagu in 1258 and continued by Tamerlane in 1401. Once the richest, most learned and most splendid city in the world, it was now little more than mounds of rubble and a few sordid hovels.

On the death of his confidential secretary, Qadhi Nasir-al-Deen, the sultan demanded the surrender of all his wealth, but his son swore that he did not know where his money was hidden. Later, finding a horde of seventy thousand dinars, he told the sultan, who took it all for the treasury. We have already seen that the Mamluke custom was not to collect estate duty, but to seize all the wealth of officers or officials who had grown rich in government service. Shaikh, however, did not torture anyone to find out where the money was.

On 28th November, 1420, the sultan had a severe attack of diarrhoea, in addition to the pains in his feet which prevented him from walking. He took an occasional boat trip on the Nile for fresh air. On 17th December, however, he took to his bed, from which he was not again to rise. His mind was clear, but he could not stand.

In Cairo, all was confusion. Shaikh had nominated his eldest surviving son, Ahmad, to succeed him, but he was only one year and eight months old. The sultan's intimates were alarmed. If an outsider ameer were to seize the throne, his first action would be to liquidate Shaikh's mamlukes and intimates. The Ameer Tatar[10] had been a mamluke of Barqooq, and was thus a barrack-comrade of the Dhahiris, whom Shaikh had promoted. Tatar also persuaded the Muaiyadis, the purchased mamlukes of Shaikh, that he would retain them in their offices if he came to power.

The rival faction was headed by Qujdar al Qardami, whose supporters were mostly of Tatar origin. Once again, with the decline of the Mamluke system, we see racial affinities beginning to appear. This factor may well be common to all empires in decline. In the period of imperial glory, all are proud to be citizens of the empire, but when decline sets in, every man remembers his own true or alleged racial origin. It is confusing, in the present case, that the leader of one party was called Tatar by name, but was not so by race, but the members of the opposing faction were Tatars by origin. In this uncertain situation, which filled the public with foreboding, Malik-al-Muaiyad Shaikh died on 13th January, 1421.

Shaikh was only fifty years old when he died. No important

[10] This was his name, not his race.

personalities attended his funeral, for all were on tenterhooks as to what would happen. It was with difficulty that a towel, a shroud and other essentials could be found. A few hours before, all kissed the ground in his presence, now scarcely a servant or a slave could be found to assist in his burial.

Shaikh had ruled for eight years. All agree that he was brave, extremely astute and a strong supporter of the established religion. He enjoyed the company of men of religion and it was alleged that he sometimes rose at night to pray. Maqrizi accuses him of parsimony, but Ibn Taghri Birdi defends him. The latter was, of course, a first generation descendant of the Mamluke class, while Maqrizi was a Syrio-Egyptian.

We are bound to notice some unusual qualities in Shaikh. His refusal to fight Malik-al-Nasir Faraj, the son of his former master, Barqooq, is most noteworthy, in view of the way in which Faraj behaved to him.

He maintained good discipline among his mamlukes and was more moderate than most sultans in imprisoning or executing his opponents. Though himself a Circassian, he did not give them precedence either in his purchases of mamlukes, or in promotions. His sole aim was to produce an efficient army by advancing the best soldiers. Ibn Taghri Birdi reports that he was emotional, enjoyed poetry and good music and was at times quite witty. He was not superior to somewhat dishonest tricks, as in the case of Nauruz al Hafidhi. His social drink-parties in Cairo show him as a convivial companion. He was, on the whole, one of the best of the Mamluke sultans and, before his death, had become the patriarch of his people.

NOTABLE EVENTS

Sultanate of Khalif	
Mustaeen	2nd June–6th November, 1412
Elevation of Malik-al-Muaiyad	
Shaikh al Mahmoodi	6th November, 1412
Defeat and execution of Nauruz al	
Hafidhi	10th July, 1414
Abortive rebellion of the Viceroys	
of Damascus and Aleppo	August, 1415
Epidemic of plague	March to May, 1419
Annexation of Heraclea, Tarsus and	
Adana	Summer, 1419
Death of Malik-al-Muaiyad Shaikh	13th January, 1421

PERSONALITIES

Sultan-and-Khalif Al-Mustaeen Billah

Al-Malik-al-Muaiyad Shaikh al Mahmoodi

Nauruz al Hafidhi, rebel Viceroy of Aleppo

Shah Rukh, fourth son of Tamerlane, Ruler of Herat

Ahmad ibn Uwais, Jalair ruler of Iraq, defeated by Qara
Yusuf

Qara Yusuf, chief of the Black Sheep Turkmans, who
made himself ruler of an empire extending from
Adharbaijan to Iraq

XVI

The Collapse of Discipline

The essential qualities of national greatness are moral, not material.

LECKY, *History of England*

Weakness, not vice, is the opposite of virtue.

PIETRO SODERINI (Florence, 1502)

It is good for a man that he bear the yoke in his youth.

Lamentations III, 27

A rapacious and licentious soldiery.

EDMUND BURKE

Party is the madness of many for the gain of a few.

JONATHAN SWIFT

There is a limit at which forbearance ceases to be a virtue.

EDMUND BURKE, *Thoughts on the Present Discontents*

AL-MALIK-AL-MUDHAFFAR
AHMAD IBN SHAIKH

AHMAD, the son of Shaikh, was made sultan on 13th January, 1421, when still a baby in arms. He cried loudly throughout the ceremony and was then carried back to the nursery. The Ameer Tatar immediately seized and imprisoned his rival, Qujqar al Qardumi. The latter had been an ameer's mamluke, and so did not have many barrack-comrades, as did former Royal Mamlukes. Tatar was then made regent and guardian. A handsome donative was given to the Royal Mamlukes. Tatar had had a legal education and himself sat in court and heard cases. It is remarkable that, as the sultans became more educated, the empire declined.

Early in February 1421, the Viceroy of Damascus declared his rejection of the authority of Tatar. An army sent by Shaikh against the Qaraman Ameer was still in Syria under the commander-in-chief, Grand Ameer Altunbugha, whose loyalty was unknown. An army accordingly set out from Cairo, accompanied by the baby-sultan in his mother's arms in a litter. Fortunately, however, Altunbugha had meanwhile defeated the rebel viceroy and now kissed the ground before the baby-sultan. When the news reached Cairo, the city was gaily decorated and the bands played for ten days.

Our historian, Ibn Taghri Birdi, was now grown up and a witness of the scenes which he describes. "The Ameer Altunbugha", he writes, "was one of the ornaments of the time in intelligence, modesty, leadership, dignity and generosity, coupled with leniency, deference and humility." Such qualities would scarcely have earned such praise in the days of Baybars the Bunduqdari. Tatar, nevertheless, caused Altunbugha to be arrested and strangled. The Grand Ameer was too popular and had too many barrack-comrades. The baby-sultan and Tatar moved on to Damascus and then to Aleppo, where they arrived in July 1421. Tatar further strengthened his position by marrying the sultan's mother, the widow of Shaikh.

Tatar could count on the wholehearted support of his barrack-comrades, the Dhahiris, the mamlukes of Barqooq. In order to gain power, he had also conciliated the Muaiyadis, the former mamlukes of Shaikh. Now, in one swoop in Damascus, he suddenly destroyed the Muaiyidis. Seven ameers of one hundred and many more ameers of drums and of ten, were arrested in one surprise purge. Then, on 29th August, 1421, when Shaikh's old mamlukes had been made powerless, the baby-sultan was deposed. Tatar, thereupon, divorced the sultan's mother, whom he had married two months before to allay the suspicions of the Muaiyadis, whom he wished to arrest. The baby-sultan was sent to Alexandria, where he died eleven years later.

AL-MALIK-AL-DHAHIR TATAR

Tatar became sultan on 29th August, 1421, and rode through the streets of Damascus with the emblems of royalty. He was the thirtieth sultan since Spray-of-Pearls. He had been brought up by a merchant, who taught him jurisprudence, and sold him to Barqooq. Tatar was thus literally a barrack-room lawyer, and had been prominent in the intrigues and revolts which characterised the stormy reign of Faraj. He had been with the party of ameers which deserted the army of Faraj, which was facing Tamerlane, though he himself was then only a young mamluke.

Before leaving Damascus, he promoted a number of his old barrack-comrades, former mamlukes of Barqooq, to replace the Muaiyadis (former mamlukes of Shaikh), whom he had arrested. On 20th October, 1421, Tatar fell ill and stayed in bed for a week. Then he recovered, the bands played and the citizens perfumed themselves with saffron, a popular way of showing joy. Tatar seemed to be a just and capable ruler—his arbitrary acts had been directed solely against potential Mamluke rivals. In any case, anything was better than more insecurity and civil wars. On 6th November, however, he was ill again and grew worse.

Cairo was in intense anxiety, rich men began to hide their valuables and everyone prepared for a breakdown of law and order. On 28th November, the sultan sent for the khalif, the qadhis and the ameers and nominated his son Muhammad as his heir. Tatar died on the morning of 30th November, 1421, at the probable age of fifty years. He had ruled the empire for eleven months, eight as regent and three as sultan.

During his brief reign, he had proved capable, generous and a skilful handler of men. When Shaikh died, his mamlukes, the Muaiyadis, were extremely powerful. In a few months, Tatar had dismantled their power without bloodshed. His character had been affected by his study of law and the Qoran, and he was a supporter of official religion. A clever politician, he was not above using deceit. He was kind and affable to his servants, and was interested in law, science, art, music and literature.

AL-MALIK-AL-SALIH MUHAMMAD IBN TATAR

Tatar's son, Muhammad, was proclaimed sultan on 30th November, 1421, at the age of ten. Grand Ameer Janibek al Suff, the commander-in-chief, assumed control of the government. The Ameer Barsbai al Duqmaqi became guardian of the boy-sultan. Beneath the surface, however, the ameers were discussing various candidates, of whom the two principal were Janibek al Suff and Barsbai al Duqmaqi.

The Feast of Sacrifice, the principal feast of the Muslim year, fell on 5th December, 1421, a day on which every Muslim went to prayers in the mosque. Janibek was arming his supporters to attack Barsbai. One of his men quoted an Arabic proverb, "Pray and then ride and you will not be thrown." But Janibek, according to Ibn Taghri Birdi, knew no Arabic and did not understand. He merely said, "Get armed quickly and we will attack first." "So", comments the pious historian, "Janibek rode but did not pray and so was defeated."

Barsbai sent a delegation to Janibek to ask why he was arming and to invite him to come to a house in the city, where they could sit and talk. The Grand Ameer was simple enough to agree. No sooner, however, did he enter the house, than the doors were shut and bolted, and he found himself in fetters. The same day, he was escorted to prison in Alexandria.

Barsbai now found himself at the head of the government. In his contest with Janibek, he had been much helped by the Ameer Tarabai, who was his equal in rank, and who was now promoted to commander-in-chief. Such was the jealous and violent character of ambitious Mamluke ameers, that a clash between the two soon appeared to be inevitable.

Barsbai decided to take the initiative. On 26th February, 1422, a levée was to be held in the palace and Tarabai rode up to the Citadel with a large suite. The levée was held in the presence of the ten-year-old sultan, petitions were read out and annotated. Then the usual formal lunch was served. Barsbai then rose and made a brief speech. "The country is in confusion," he said, "because authority is divided. Public business is at a standstill, because men have not agreed on a leader. A single leader is essential for the proper conduct of business."

One of the Ameer Barsbai's supporters, with whom of course the scene had been rehearsed, immediately replied, "You are our leader. Command us as you wish." Pointing to Grand Ameer Tarabai, Barsbai instantly said, "Arrest that man."

Tarabai and his friends were taken by surprise. Before they could draw their swords, Tarabai was seized and dragged off to prison. Seeing that the contest was over, his followers hastily acclaimed Barsbai. Next day, Tarabai was transferred to the fortress of Alexandria. A softening of manners may here be noted. In the "good old days", a defeated claimant was immediately hacked to pieces, or strangled the same night with a bowstring. Tarabai now joined Janibek, whom he himself had helped to kidnap a few weeks before.

There remained only one of Barsbai's friends of whom he was still afraid. He was the Ameer Tanbek, whom Barsbai had sent as Viceroy of Damascus. Rebellions had so frequently begun with some Viceroy of Damascus that Barsbai was afraid to declare himself sultan without first making sure of Tanbek, whom he accordingly invited to Cairo. The two friends had a long private talk. Barsbai expatiated on the country's need for a single ruler, concluding with the statement that Tanbek must be the man, for he was the senior in the service and the older in years. "May God forbid," cried Tanbek, rising from his seat and kissing the ground before Barsbai.

The last obstacle having been thus removed, the dethronement of Malik-al-Salih Muhammad was agreed and Barsbai was acclaimed sultan with the throne-name of Al-Malik-al-Ashraf.[1]

The removal of boy-sultans was now almost a matter of routine, but Barsbai must be credited with an innovation. The young Sultan Muhammad was not imprisoned but continued to live in the palace. After a year or two, he was in the habit of going out riding alone or of strolling down into the city like a private person. He became a close friend of Barsbai's own son, also called Muhammad, and the two young men were often to be seen in public together. Barsbai later arranged for his marriage to the daughter of the commander-in-chief, but he died of the plague in his early twenties. He was a pleasant cheerful youth, free from ostentation or ambition.

*   *   *

After the death of his father, our historian Ibn Taghri Birdi was brought up by his elder sister, who was married to the Shaikh-al-

[1] The Most Noble King.

Islam, Abdul Rahman, the son of a former Shaikh-al-Islam, Umar al Bulqini. The title Shaikh-al-Islam was equivalent to Chief Qadhi. Thus we see here an exception to the principle that Mamlukes did not marry Egyptians or Syrians. This fortunate circumstance resulted in our historian receiving a good Arabic education, and taking up the study of history and literature.

AL-MALIK-AL-ASHRAF BARSBAI

Malik-al-Ashraf Barsbai took his seat on the throne on 1st April, 1422. A notable feature of his accession was that no donation was made to the troops, as had become the custom, nor did the Royal Mamlukes demand one.

Barsbai had been brought from the Caucasus by a merchant who sold him to the Ameer Duqmaq, the Governor of Malatia, who sent him as a present to Barqooq. After the death of his master, Barsbai went with the rebel ameers, Shaikh and Nauruz, and remained with them until the death of Sultan Faraj.

When Shaikh became sultan, he made Barsbai first an ameer of ten, then of drums and finally an ameer of one hundred. When Tatar was raised to the throne, he made Barsbai executive secretary, an official who was virtually in control of the administration. On his death, he appointed him guardian of his son. As we have seen, Barsbai disposed of Janibek and of Tarabai, both equal to him in seniority, and exiled them to Alexandria. Barsbai did not rise by treachery and intrigue as Barqooq had done. Until he found himself at the top, he had been loyal to his superiors.

On 16th July, 1423, Janibek al Sufi escaped from Alexandria. Fear of Janibek, a man much respected, was to haunt Barsbai almost to the end of his life. In former times, unsuccessful rivals were almost always killed. Barsbai's clemency was to poison his reign. Another of his liberal reforms was to abolish kissing the ground. It is not certain whether the custom was really abandoned, for it is referred to again in later reigns. It is interesting to note the accumulating signs of decadence, the increase in bribery, the relaxation of army discipline, the absorption of leaders in internal politics, the neglect of the armed forces and the increasing public consumption of alcohol. Yet these signs of decline were accompanied by an increase in learning and culture, a softening of manners and a mitigation of punishments.

The empire was at peace from external enemies, but Barsbai had the Viceroy of Damascus put to death. No reasons are stated, but reliance on spies has always been a feature of Middle East governments.

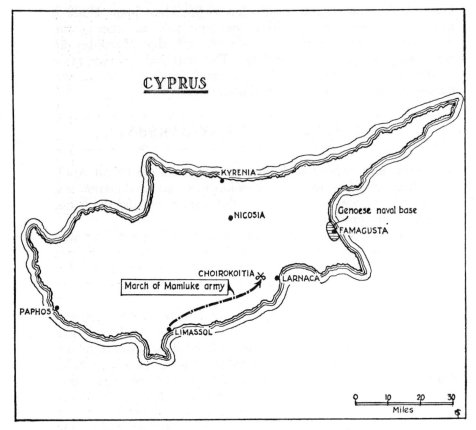

MAP 27

Meanwhile, the activities of Frankish pirates were on the increase. In August 1422, they even seized a laden ship from the harbour of Alexandria and sailed away with it. In May 1424, they captured two Muslim vessels off Damietta, both laden with valuable cargoes. In reprisal the sultan ordered the confiscation of all the property of Frankish merchants in Alexandria, Damietta and Damascus. It is interesting to know that there were European business communities in these cities, though our authorities do not specify their nations.

A naval war now began to build up, for which the Muslim writers blame the Franks. The charge is probably true, for there were several seafaring nations in the West, while the Mamlukes never took to the sea.[2] Barsbai was a pioneer in the arming of ships. In July

[2] Sir Harry Luke in his book, *Cyprus*, states of the King of Cyprus, "The imprudent Janus now embarked on hostilities against Barsbay, Mamluk Sultan of Egypt."

1424, two vessels from Egypt and several more from Tarablus sailed to search for Frankish privateers. They raided Limassol in Cyprus, returning to Cairo with loot and prisoners. In December 1424, work began in earnest on the building of a battle fleet.

In January 1425, the sultan ordered the occupation of Jidda.[3] The Mamlukes had long claimed Medina and Mecca for religious reasons, and had sent troops there. But they had avoided the sea, using the land route across Sinai. The wealth of Egypt depended largely on the Oriental trade, up the Red Sea and over to Alexandria. Originally the ships called at Aden, but the Yemeni kings demanded very high transit dues. As a result, some ships' captains passed Aden and made their first landfall at Jidda, where there was no organised government and no customs. Barsbai hoped to collect customs at Jidda for the Mamluke government.

In June 1425, eight galleys built at Bulaq, the port of Cairo on the Nile, sailed to Tarablus, where they joined a flotilla of forty ships, half of them galleys propelled by oars and carrying troops, the other half barges loaded with horses. The fleet was not designed to fight at sea but to ferry troops to Cyprus. It was manned by mixed volunteers, some Mamlukes, some Arab tribesmen, some Syrians.

The expedition landed south of Famagusta,[4] and raided inland, looting, burning and taking prisoners, until all the ships were heavily laden. The flotilla then sailed back to Tarablus. On 8th September, 1425, the force returned to Cairo and passed in a triumphal procession through the city. Immense crowds had collected, some standing on the ground, others at windows, in shops or on the roofs. The loot, consisting chiefly of cloth, wool, metal utensils and weapons, was carried on forty mules, ten camels, and a hundred and seventy porters. The prisoners also walked in the procession.

The operation was on a small scale, but created great jubilation owing to the previous exasperation caused by Frankish piracy. In a hundred and seventy-five years of empire, it was the first successful Mamluke naval expedition. The loot was auctioned, the prisoners sold as slaves. Barsbai gave orders that children should not be sold separately from their parents, nor near relatives from one another— one more indication of a gradual softening of manners.

It is interesting to note that prospective buyers were admitted to the auction by classes, ameers, qadhis, lawyers, merchants and then the general public—presumably the order of precedence in Cairo.

*   *   *

[3] Map 23, page 213.   [4] Map 27, opposite.

In June 1425, the sultan released Tarabai from confinement, gave him a thousand dinars, and permission to live in retirement in Jerusalem. This clemency evoked surprise, for Tarabai had been a great ameer and might again become a dangerous rival.

But Barsbai was still haunted by fear of Janibek al Sufi. On 8th March, 1426, a large force searched the Jandariya quarter of Cairo. It was later revealed that the house was searched in which Janibek was actually hiding under a rug. It seems that he was an attractive personality. Perhaps some men in the army did not wish to find him.

*   *   *

Early in 1426, great enthusiasm was devoted to the preparation of another expedition against Cyprus. On 10th May, 1426, a fleet of over a hundred vessels sailed down the Nile. Four ameers of one hundred led the expedition, which consisted of Mamlukes, tribesmen and volunteers. The fleet arrived off Limassol early in July, and captured and destroyed the town. The land troops then marched up the coast with the cavalry, while the ships moved parallel with the army, keeping close inshore.[5]

Suddenly the land column found itself facing the army of Cyprus, commanded by King Janus in person. The Muslims charged impetuously and swept the enemy from the field, taking two thousand prisoners, including King Janus himself. The battle was fought early in July 1426, at Choirokoitia, three or four miles south-west of Larnaca. Shortly afterwards, about 18th July, the force re-embarked for Egypt, after first burning Nicosia, the capital, and taking with them King Janus and several thousand prisoners.

Barsbai and the Muslims were amazed at the completeness of their victory. Richard I, Cœur-de-Lion, had given Cyprus to Guy de Lusignan on 5th May, 1192, and the family had ruled the island ever since. Surrounded by the sea, Cyprus had never been threatened by the great land armies of the Ayoubids, the Mamlukes, the Mongols or Tamerlane, and had perhaps neglected land warfare, though active at sea. But Cyprus had been crippled by the Genoese who, in 1374, had ravaged the island, imposed a crushing tribute and occupied Famagusta as a Genoese naval base. But, although the Republic of Genoa dealt with Cyprus with extreme harshness, it took no steps to assist in her defence.

On 12th August, 1426, the Cyprus expedition made a victory march through Cairo, through dense crowds. The cheering was deafening, the men keeping up a continuous chant of "God is Most

[5] Map 27, page 320.

Great! There is no god but God", while the women maintained their continuous, trilling cries of joy. Everyone in Cairo seemed to have perfumed himself with saffron.

The procession was headed by the Mamluke cavalry, followed by the foot soldiers, Arabs, bedouins, Syrians and volunteers. The booty, including the gold crown of Cyprus, was carried on a long line of pack animals, followed by the Cypriot banners, dragged along in the dust. At the end came King Janus, bareheaded and riding a mule.

When the procession reached the Citadel, the king, dishevelled and in fetters, was made to walk through dense crowds and between lines of troops. Once he fell in a faint but was revived. Barsbai was seated on an elevated couch in a pavilion, surrounded by a brilliant gathering of ameers, diplomats and notables. Janus was made to approach slowly, exhausted and bedraggled. At intervals his escort made him stop, kiss the ground and rub his nose in the dust.

"This was a great and glorious day, such as had not occurred in past ages," writes Ibn Taghri Birdi. "One on which God the Exalted glorified the religion of Islam." Yet how sadly does the humiliation of King Janus contrast with the chivalrous courtesy of Saladin.

Next morning, Barsbai sent to Janus to enquire what ransom he would pay for his release, but the king replied hopelessly that he had no money. Stunned by the disaster he had suffered, he made no attempt to retain his dignity.

The sultan sent for the consuls of the Frankish nations, and told them that he required five hundred thousand gold dinars for the king's ransom. Eventually, after some bargaining, two hundred thousand dinars was the figure accepted, a hundred thousand in cash before the king's release, and another hundred thousand dinars after his return home. The king also agreed to pay twenty thousand dinars a year tribute and to become the sultan's vassal.

When the financial agreement was signed, the king's fetters were removed and Barsbai sent him two suits of clothes from his own wardrobe. In March 1427, an ambassador of the Knights of St. John in Rhodes came to Cairo and kissed the ground before the sultan and asked for his protection, fearing the fate of Cyprus. The Mamluke victory had greatly increased their prestige. In April 1427, Janus was released and set sail for Cyprus.

*   *   *

A further relaxation of the ancient Mamluke discipline was the habit indulged by the sultans of riding out—even through Cairo—in casual dress. The Bahri sultans never left the Citadel except in full dress, with an armed escort and usually a band. Faraj was the first to ride out in casual clothes. The subject is of some interest nowadays. It may be argued that a man could be as loyal and as efficient in any old clothes as in a stiff uniform. Yet history warns us that slovenly dress indicates an undisciplined nation and is one of the signs of decadence.

In 1429, in a council of ameers, the commander-in-chief, Grand Ameer Jar Qutlu, advised the sultan to take drastic action to improve discipline among the young purchased mamlukes. The Royal Mamlukes, it will be remembered, consisted partly of men who had been mamlukes of other sultans or ameers, before being engaged under the ruling sultan. These old soldiers were normally disciplined and loyal. The remainder were young mamlukes purchased by the sultan and were adolescents. The ameers present at the council were asked by the sultan not to repeat what had been said, but the news leaked out. The young mamlukes determined to revenge themselves on the commander-in-chief for the advice he had offered.

A few days later, the young mamlukes mutinied, marched to the city, and attacked the commander-in-chief's house, which was defended by his personal mamlukes. The young mamlukes, supposed to be the corps d'élite of the army, had received so little military training, that they could not take the Grand Ameer's house, but spent two days rioting in the city. They demanded that the commander-in-chief's mamlukes be handed over to them for punishment. They eventually agreed to a compromise, under which the sultan had the Grand Ameer's mamlukes flogged. No penalty was imposed on the mutinous young mamlukes. The incident has a modern ring, the rioters being appeased, the loyal penalised. A week before, the young mamlukes had plundered the house of the wazeer, as a protest against delay in the issue of their rations. On 17th June, 1429, the sultan's young mamlukes demanded an increase of pay. The government yielded to their defiance.

The White Sheep Turkmans of Amid having occupied Ruha (Edessa), a force was sent against them from Cairo. The Viceroys of Damascus and Aleppo, who were in command of the Mamluke column, swore that, if the city surrendered, none of its defenders would suffer harm. When, however, Ruha opened its gates, the Royal Mamlukes refused to obey their commanders and began to rape, kill and loot All the men in Ruha were killed and the women and children driven off as slaves. The town was then burnt down. "What they did was as bad as what Tamerlane did in Syria," writes Ibn Taghri Birdi indignantly. Maqrizi calls the incident "a shameful abomination".

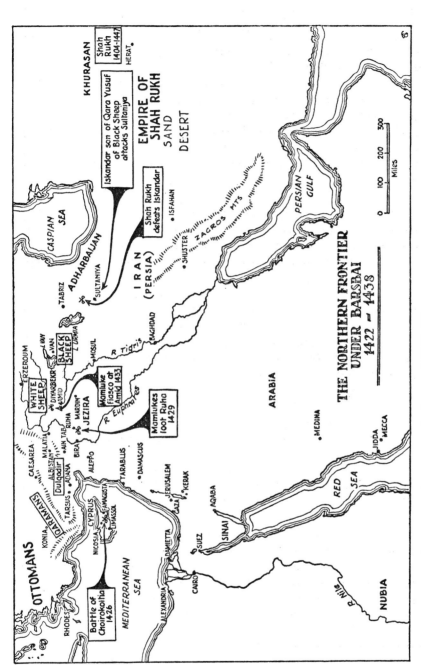

THE NORTHERN FRONTIER
UNDER BARSBAI
1422 — 1438

MAP 28

Iskandar, the son of Qara Yusuf, chief of the Black Sheep Turk-mans, at this time the ruler of Tabriz, attacked the city of Sultaniya, the property of Shah Rukh, the son of Tamerlane, whose capital was in Herat.[6] Normally a man of peace, Shah Rukh could not over-look the plundering of Sultaniya, but marched against Iskandar with a large army. Iskandar was defeated and Shah Rukh's army, mostly Mongols, laid waste Adharbaijan, killing, looting and raping, as their ancestors had done under Jenghis Khan. The ruin and despair of these eastern lands left the Mamlukes without an enemy, and enabled them to live in safety, although their army had lost its discipline and its efficiency.

In October 1429, an ambassador reached Cairo from Shah Rukh, asking for a commentary on Bukhari's *Traditions*,[7] and a copy of Maqrizi's *Sulook*, from which much of the present narrative has been compiled. He also expressed a pious wish to send a covering to drape the Kaaba, the holy place in the great mosque of Mecca. The pro-vision of the covering of the Kaaba was a jealously guarded Egyptian privilege, but the other requests were both harmless and pious. Barsbai, however, curtly rejected them all.

In December 1429, the plague reappeared in Egypt and Syria, many thousands dying daily. Normal life ceased, shops and markets closed and everyone resigned himself to die.

Ibn Taghri Birdi tells how he accompanied some of his family servants to bury their seven-year-old son. Dense crowds had been waiting for hours for their turn to reach the burial ground. During this time, another party took up the dead boy in error and buried him, leaving another child of the same age. Our historian, noticing what had happened, carefully covered the corpse left behind, and the parents buried the strange child without knowing what had occurred. "To talk about it", adds our author pathetically, "would only have added to their grief."

After an almost complete cessation of work, and of government activity, life began slowly to return in April 1430. The young mam-lukes had been among the worst sufferers. Many ameers having died also, the army virtually ceased to be operational.

For reasons unknown to us, epidemics of plague came to Egypt more frequently and more violently after 1400, than in the first one hundred and fifty years of the Mamluke Empire. Between 1417 and 1517, there were fourteen outbreaks.[8]

The principal losses in all plague epidemics occurred among young mamlukes, children, black slaves, slave girls and foreigners in general.

---

[6] Map 28, page 325.   [7] Bukhari, *Al Sahih*.
[8] David Ayalon, *The Plague and its effects on the Mamluke Army*.

Presumably the native population of Egypt had acquired a considerable measure of immunity, or at least of resistance.

In general, the young offered much less resistance than the old. Young mamlukes, newly imported, suffered a much higher proportion of deaths than did older mamlukes, who had lived for a number of years in Egypt. The sultan's purchased mamlukes, still under training and probably under twenty years old, seem, on some occasions, to have lost more than half their numbers in a single epidemic. The resulting difficulties in recruiting and training can easily be appreciated. When we read that the sultan sent only five hundred Royal Mamlukes to resist a threat of invasion, the small numbers may well have been due to losses in a recent plague epidemic.

The paucity of mamlukes surviving an epidemic may also have been one of the reasons for the acquisition of military fiefs by Egyptian civilians. All in all, the plague was an important factor in weakening the Mamluke army.

*   *   *

To the east, violence and bloodshed continued. Qara Yuluk,[9] the chief of the White Sheep of Diyarbekr, had assisted Shah Rukh against Iskandar, the son of Qara Yusuf of the Black Sheep. Iskandar fled to Georgia and the White Sheep now dominated the Jezira, though a brother of Iskandar still held Baghdad for the Black Sheep, but was too weak to leave the walls of the city. "The very word civilisation was no longer applied to Baghdad," writes Ibn Taghri Birdi gloomily. Iraq and north-west Persia up to the Caucasus were a welter of pillage and slaughter.

In October 1430, Qara Yuluk attacked the Mamluke town of Malatia.[10] A force of five hundred Royal Mamlukes, under Grand Ameer Jar Qutlu, was sent to support the Viceroys of Aleppo and Damascus, so weak had the army become. But Qara Yuluk retired, and Jar Qutlu's force was recalled.

The ameers and mamlukes of the army were obliged to supply their own horses, weapons and equipment. As a result, all received a cash allotment before a campaign to enable them to buy what they needed for the war. Jar Qutlu's men had received the usual advances, but as the column returned without fighting a battle, the treasury demanded the repayment of their advances. The troops, probably truthfully, claimed that the money had all been spent. The incident yet further undermined the loyalty of the army.

---

[9] His full name was the Ameer Othman ibn Tur Ali.   [10] Map 28, page 325.

*   *   *

Amid the general signs of decline, there is a modern touch in the problems arising from the depreciation of the currency. This was done, as already mentioned, by mixing copper with the silver dirhem, and then by minting plain copper dirhems. In November 1430, the gold dinar was, by proclamation, valued at two hundred and thirty-five copper dirhems, while the "Frankish" ducat was declared to be worth two hundred and thirty. The ducat was the coin used in Italy, Venice, Hungary and Bohemia and, after 1559, by Germany, but its value differed in each country. Commerce was hampered by the fact that every nation mixed a different amount of copper in its currency. Under Barsbai, an attempt was made to mint pure silver dirhems, as had been done in the old days, but the attempt failed, and chaos returned. Thenceforward, till the ultimate collapse of the empire, exchange rates, devaluation and the high cost of living are endlessly discussed.

*   *   *

In October 1431, a crowd of young purchased sultan's mamlukes rioted in Cairo and plundered the house of the wazeer, Kareem-al-Deen Kátib al Manákh. No disciplinary action was taken.

An interesting note in Ibn Taghri Birdi's *Nujoom* reports the arrival of two Chinese ships in Aden, laden with china, silk, musk and other articles of luxury. As the Kingdom of the Yemen was in disorder, the captains sailed on to Jidda to discharge their wares.

In June 1432, Janus, King of Cyprus, died in Nicosia and was succeeded by his son, John II. Barsbai sent a deputation to Cyprus to exact an oath of allegiance from John II and twenty-four thousand gold dinars in arrears of tribute. The king admitted himself to be the sultan's mamluke and paid fourteen thousand dinars. Heralds then announced in Nicosia that Malik-al-Ashraf Barsbai had appointed John II as his Viceroy of Cyprus.

The general softening of manners in these years is reflected in the greater familiarity between the Mamlukes, the Egyptians and the Syrians. Barsbai often rode into Cairo, not to visit some great ameer, but a wealthy Egyptian. Referring to Muhammad Al Barizi, a Syrian who held the post of confidential secretary, Maqrizi says, "Men were very happy at his excellent conduct of the office, his efficiency, his attractive manners, his generosity and his great modesty." Maqrizi was a Syrian resident in Egypt, but Ibn Taghri

Birdi, the son of a Mamluke, quotes this passage and adds, "He was as Maqrizi says and more. I do not know nowadays anyone who approaches him in his many merits." This is not the language of a military despotism, speaking of a subject race.

Yet all this softening of manners is accompanied by a continuous reduction in the strength of the army. Baybars the Bunduqdari could lead twenty thousand men to Syria, Barsbai sent only five hundred Royal Mamlukes. The army had not only dwindled in numbers, but its discipline was undermined. We are faced with the recurrent phenomenon of history. When a nation becomes cultured and civilised, it reduces its armed forces and despises the military profession. Soon another nation arrives, still in the military stage of its life, destroys the civilised state and the whole process recommences.

* * *

For several years, Qara Yuluk, the White Sheep ruler of Mardin, Amid, Erzeroum and the Diyarbekr region had inflicted many troubles on the rulers of the Jezira. Although not himself courageous in battle, he spent his life in local wars, making use of treachery and persistence. For several years, he had threatened the Mamluke frontiers and even Aleppo itself. Barsbai, a man averse to wars, finally left Cairo with an army on 12th March, 1433. Maqrizi says he took two thousand seven hundred Royal Mamlukes, but Ibn Taghri Birdi, who himself went with the expedition, thinks that the number was greater. Each mamluke had received a gratuity of a hundred dinars. The commander-in-chief, Grand Ameer Sudoon, had received a grant of three thousand dinars, ameers of a hundred were given two thousand dinars, ameers of drums five hundred and ameers of ten two hundred dinars.

The sultan reached Aleppo on 26th April, 1433, and made a state entry into the city. On 28th May, 1433, the army reached Amid, Qara Yuluk's capital. Ibn Taghri Birdi, who was present, describes the advance of the army across the plain to Amid, the modern town of Diyarbekr.[11]

"The people of Amid were awestricken at the number of troops ... such as had seldom been seen ... Large units advanced with drums beating and trumpets sounding. The number of the ameers' regiments was unusually large, because of the extent to which they

[11] In the fifteenth century, Diyarbekr was the name of a district, of which Amid was the capital town. Since then the name of Amid has disappeared and the name Diyarbekr is now used of the town.

had been gathered for the sultan, by the Egyptian and Syrian armies, the Viceroys of Syria and the ameers of the Turkmans and the Arabs. The number of bands of drums and flutes exceeded one hundred."[12]

This stirring picture drawn by an eye-witness is unfortunately devoid of figures. Nor do we know how many of these troops were trained soldiers, or how many were undisciplined Arab or Turkish tribesmen. We are not told the strength of the ameers' contingents. We have seen that, in the days of the Bahri sultans, an ameer of one hundred commanded a thousand men in war, the additional nine hundred being from the *halaqa*, or first-line reserve. But we have seen that, after Al-Nasir Muhammad, the *halaqa* had been almost abolished.

A hundred bands is perhaps not excessive, as every first class and second class ameer had one, and the Turkman chiefs also had drums.

"When the sultan advanced, all the drums of these ameers were beaten simultaneously", continues Ibn Taghri Birdi, "and the trumpets gave one blast together, so that the plain was covered with drums and flutes sounding for battle . . . The armies extended as far as the eye could see . . . The people of Amid were astounded by the sight of these forces . . . the great splendour of their trappings, furnishings, horses and weapons."[13]

The Mamluke army may still have appeared as splendid as a hundred years before but a profound change had occurred in it. Since the disappearance of the Il-Khans in 1336, the Mamlukes had no serious enemies and had lost their martial spirit. Internal political rivalries monopolised their thoughts. The army now advanced to the city moat with colours flying and then halted. No orders had been issued and no one knew what to do. For several days, they sat inactive. No bombardment was opened and no trenches dug. The sultan hoped to bluff the enemy into surrender.

Then Barsbai suddenly ordered a general assault, but no breaches had been made in the walls and the attack failed. The sultan abused officers and men for their cowardice. Baybars the Bunduqdari, in similar circumstances, had gone forward with the sappers and hacked at the walls himself with a hammer and chisel. The sultan's military inefficiency alienated the loyalty of the troops. Alarmed by their murmurs, his resolution faltered.

Qara Yuluk was camped not far away, but hesitated to offer battle. The sultan sent a small force against him, of which Ibn Taghri Birdi was a member, but it was repulsed. Why Barsbai did not send a force strong enough to defeat him is not known. Only at

[12] Ibn Taghri Birdi, *Nujoom*. Eng. trans. Popper.   [13] Ibid.

this stage did he order guns and mangonels to be mounted to bombard the walls.

After thirty-five days, peace was concluded on the condition that Qara Yuluk kiss the ground and insert the sultan's name in the Friday prayers. Qadhi Sharaf-al-Deen al Ashqar, father-in-law of Ibn Taghri Birdi, was sent to Qara Yuluk with a robe of honour, which the latter gave to his servant to wear.

The army was only anxious to go home. "The troops", writes Ibn Taghri Birdi, "had become used to the safety and comfort of their homes, and were unwilling to endure the hardships of war." After midnight on the night of 2nd July, 1433, the sultan and the Royal Mamlukes suddenly marched away. No warning had been issued to the army, and no order of march, route or destination. When the ameers heard that the sultan had gone, they packed up as best they could. As the army had left in the dark without orders, many units lost their way. The troops left Amid like a defeated army in flight.

The sultan arrived back in Cairo on 6th August. The campaign had only revealed to the world the military incapacity of the sultan and the lack of training or discipline of the Mamluke army. The economic condition of Egypt was almost as bad as the military. Whereas, forty years before, fourteen thousand looms had been weaving silk, now only eight hundred were left. Ibn Taghri Birdi alleges that the number of villages in Egypt had decreased in a hundred years from ten thousand to two thousand one hundred and seventy. Our historian attributes the decline to bad administration, but the virulent epidemics of plague must also have greatly reduced the population.

*   *   *

On 2nd September, 1434, a further ambassador came from Shah Rukh, saying that the latter had vowed to cover the Kaaba and asking the sultan's help. A contemptuous reply was returned.

On 20th September, 1434, the sultan's young mamlukes rioted in Cairo, because their pay was in arrears. They looted the houses of the wazeer and the controller of the army (the civilian paymaster). Barsbai exiled the controller to Alexandria but took no action against the troops. Qadhi Saad-al-Deen Ibrahim was appointed wazeer, but refused. The sultan ordered that he be flogged, but he still refused. Eventually Qadhi Jamal-al-Deen Yusuf was forced to be wazeer. Ibn Qutara, a Christian, was obliged to be controller. Barsbai's fear of his own soldiers reduced the civil administration to chaos.

Suddenly, in May 1435, Janibek al Sufi appeared in Anatolia and wrote to the Qaraman Ameer, to Ibn Dulqadir of Albistan and to Shah Rukh. The latter sent back robes of honour and urged all concerned to invade Syria.[14] Janibek thereupon besieged Malatia.

Just when the situation looked ominous, Iskandar, the son of Qara Yusuf of the Black Sheep, defeated and killed Qara Yuluk of the White Sheep, and sent his head to Barsbai, who caused it to be nailed up on the Zuwaila Gate. The débâcle of Amid was avenged. The situation now stood as follows: the Black Sheep were friends of Barsbai. Shah Rukh was urging on the Qaramans, Ibn Dulqadir, and Janibek al Sufi to invade Syria.

On 21st January, 1436, an ambassador from Shah Rukh, at a court levée in Cairo, ordered Barsbai to insert the name of his master in the Friday prayers, and tried to invest Barsbai with a robe as a provincial governor under Shah Rukh. The ambassador, however, received a painful beating and was ducked in the horse-pond in the royal stables.

Ibn Taghri Birdi was present and was delighted. "By my life," he cries, "this performance of Malik-al-Ashraf Barsbai was one of his best actions, one by which the honour of the Egyptian armies will last till the day of Resurrection ... God, the Almighty and the Glorious gave him success in this action, and thanks be to God."

On 9th July, 1436, Janibek with some twelve thousand men was defeated near Ain Tab, north of Aleppo, and in October 1437 he was killed. His death, the defeat of Qara Yuluk and the humiliation of Shah Rukh's ambassador, did much to restore Mamluke prestige.

*   *   *

On 15th January, 1438, Barsbai fell ill but recovered. On 29th April, however, he fell ill again. He was carried into the palace courtyard, in the presence of the khalif, the qadhis and the ameers. All the royal mamlukes were on parade. The sultan nominated his son Yusuf as his heir, and the commander-in-chief, Ameer Jaqmaq al Alai, as regent.

Addressing the mamlukes from his bed, Barsbai told them that their indiscipline had angered him, but that now he was dying and forgave them. He begged them to be loyal to his son and to maintain discipline. Many of these rough, violent men sobbed aloud, all fell on their knees, kissed the ground and called out fervent prayers for his recovery. Ibn Taghri Birdi claims that he witnessed the scene. Barsbai died on 7th June, 1438, after a reign of seventeen years.

[14] Map 28, page 325.

*   *   *

The reign of Barsbai passed, on the whole, in peace and fair prosperity. His greatest victory had been the conquest of Cyprus. The most alarming feature of his reign had been the increasing indiscipline of the Royal Mamlukes. His armies successfully defended the northern frontier, but only against Turkman tribes.

"He was a great sultan, efficient, intelligent, and sagacious," writes Ibn Taghri Birdi, who was a member of his court. "He displayed great magnificence in the matter of mamlukes and horses. He was fair in complexion, tall, slender, graceful, with glistening white hair and of handsome appearance. He did not curse or use foul language but was good-natured and gentle . . . He did not partake of intoxicants and did not like any of his mamlukes or servants to do so."[15]

Maqrizi's estimate is slightly less favourable. He accuses him of parsimony and of employing Christian revenue officials. Their influence, however, was partly offset by the qadhi, Mahmood al Aini, who used to read history to the sultan. Al Aini never mixed in politics but limited his work to the reading and exposition of history, thereby contributing greatly to the sultan's enlightenment.

NOTABLE EVENTS

Elevation of Ahmad, son of Shaikh	13th January, 1421
Dethronement of Ahmad	
Elevation of Malik-al-Dhahir Tatar	29th August, 1421
Death of Tatar	
Elevation of Muhammad, son of Tatar	30th November, 1421
Arrest of Janibek al Sufi	5th December, 1421
Arrest of Grand Ameer Tarabai	26th February, 1422
Elevation of Malik-al-Ashraf Barsbai	1st April, 1422
Escape of Janibek al Sufi	16th July, 1423
Mamluke occupation of Jidda	January, 1425
First raid on Cyprus	June, 1425
Battle of Choirokoitia Conquest of Cyprus	July, 1426

[15] Ibn Taghri Birdi, *Nujoom*. Eng. trans. Popper.

Riots by Royal Mamlukes	1429
Looting of Ruha	1429
Mamluke fiasco at the siege of Amid	June, 1433
Ducking of Shah Rukh's ambassador	January, 1436
Death of Janibek al Sufi	October, 1437
Death of Barsbai	7th June, 1438

PERSONALITIES

Mamluke Sultans
Malik-al-Mudhaffar Ahmad, son of Shaikh
Malik-al-Dhahir Tatar
Malik-al-Salih Muhammad, son of Tatar
Malik-al-Ashraf Barsbai

Other Mamlukes
Ameer Janibek al Sufi
Ameer Tarabai
Grand Ameer Jar Qutlu

Turkmans
Qara Yusuf, Chief of the Black Sheep
Iskandar, his son
Qara Yuluk, Chief of the White Sheep
Shah Rukh, son of Tamerlane, Ruler of Persia

XVII

Gentleman Jaqmaq

The Mamluk school of architecture, whose origins go back to Nurid and Ayoubid models, received fresh ... influences ... Domes were constructed that defy rivalry for lightness, beauty of outline and richness of decoration ... Happily the finest examples of Mamluk structures have survived ... Extant specimens of ornate bronze mosque doors, bronze chandeliers in delicate Arabesque designs ... exquisite mosaics in niches and intricate woodwork in pulpits and lecterns testify to their flourishing state ... Among these minor arts none is more individual and characteristic than the illumination of manuscripts ... Various articles of luxury—cups, bowls, trays, incense-burners testifying to the fidelity of the picture of high life depicted by contemporary chroniclers—have come down to us. Royal princesses bedecked themselves with anklets, ear-rings, necklaces, bracelets ... Of the Burji Mamluks Jaqmaq (1438–1453) expended 3,000,000 dinars in three years.

PHILIP HITTI, *History of the Arabs*

Neither will it be, that a people overlaid with taxes should ever become valiant and martial.

FRANCIS BACON

AL-MALIK-AL-AZEEZ YUSUF, son of BARSBAI

YUSUF, the son of Sultan Barsbai, was raised to the throne on 7th June, 1438, at the age of fourteen. A donative of one hundred dinars was made to every man of the Royal Mamlukes. After a period of suspense, the shops reopened and business was resumed.

A week later, quarrels began to appear between rival ameers, whom only the fear of a master could compel to co-operate. On the occasion of the accession of a new sultan, however, the mamlukes of his predecessor were always the principal threat to stability. In the present instance, the ameers, the older mamlukes and the public were equally incensed against the young purchased mamlukes of Barsbai, who had committed so many outrages.

On 7th August, 1438, Grand Ameer Jaqmaq rode up to the Citadel, to reduce the young Ashrafis to discipline. Jaqmaq was a Dhahiri, a former mamluke of Barqooq, and was supported by all the ameers and the older mamlukes. The young Ashrafis blockaded themselves in the Citadel, but ultimately surrendered on 10th August. They numbered fifteen hundred men.

On 10th September, 1438, the ameers passed a resolution deposing Malik-al-Azeez Yusuf, and raising Grand Ameer Jaqmaq to the sultanate. Yusuf had been nominal sultan for ninety-four days, during which he had scarcely ever opened his mouth. He remained with his family, living in the Citadel.

*   *   *

As far as foreign affairs were concerned, in September 1438, Shah Rukh was the ruler of Persia, from Adharbaijan to Khurasan. Iskandar, the son of Qara Yusuf of the Black Sheep, was the nominal ruler of Tabriz, but was in flight from Shah Rukh. Isbahan, another son of Qara Yusuf of the Black Sheep, was still ruler of Baghdad and Iraq.

The sons of Qara Yuluk of the White Sheep owned Amid, Mardin and Erzeroum. The greatest monarch of the Balkan Peninsula and

Anatolia was the Ottoman Sultan, Murad II. The Byzantine Emperor, John VIII, still held Constantinople and a small territory outside the walls of the city.

On the northern border of the Mamluke Empire, Ibrahim ibn Qaraman was the ruler of Konia.

AL-MALIK-AL-DHAHIR JAQMAQ AL ALAI

Jaqmaq had been brought to Egypt from the Caucasus and sold to the then commander-in-chief, Inal al Yusufi, and was presumably freed by his son, Ali ibn Inal, since he assumed the name of Alai. Barqooq took him from Ali and made him an intimate. Under Faraj, he was a cupbearer and then an ameer of ten. Shaikh made him an ameer of drums. Under Barsbai, he was Ameer of the Horse and later commander-in-chief.

Two weeks after his accession, the young mamlukes of Barsbai staged another revolt, but two hours sufficed to disperse them, which Barsbai should have done ten years before. This abortive uprising gave the sultan the opportunity to arrest sixty and to disperse the remainder.

In February 1439, the Viceroy of Damascus revolted, ostensibly out of loyalty to the boy-sultan, Yusuf. The Viceroy of Aleppo, himself a Turkman, raised the tribes on his own account. A new sultan could not rule until he had shown his mastery in action. In the various stages of these revolts, it is noticeable that hardly anyone fought seriously. Many of the ameers corresponded with both sides, waiting to see which seemed to be the most probable winner. At this moment, the fourteen-year-old sultan, Malik-al-Azeez Yusuf, escaped from his apartment in the palace. Men's hearts were filled with fear of more civil wars.

The increasing reluctance of the Mamluke ameers to fight is interesting, for these were the world's most famous soldiers, and indeed they had few other accomplishments. None of them had been born in Egypt, so their decline in military qualities cannot be attributed, as in other empires, to several generations born in luxury, wealth and power.

This is the most intriguing aspect in Mamluke history. Although every man was born under the hard conditions of the steppes, yet the system became decadent, just as if they had been the descendants of persons living in luxury for two hundred years. Their unwillingness to fight, however, may also have been due to the fact that these civil wars had become mere political musical chairs, in which one ameer seized the throne and others tried to replace him—not unlike our democratic politics today. No great moral principle was at stake.

The escape of Malik-al-Azeez Yusuf had been contrived by an Indian eunuch called Sandal, a freedman of his mother, Princess Julban, and with the support of Barsbai's pampered young mamlukes. Houses all over Cairo were cordoned and searched and acute tension prevailed. On 12th April, 1439, Cairo breathed again—the boy-sultan had been arrested. He was sent to detention in Alexandria, where, however, he was given comfortable apartments.

Meanwhile, on 28th March, 1439, an expeditionary force had left Cairo to fight the rebel Viceroy of Damascus. On 16th April, a battle was fought, the viceroy was defeated, taken prisoner and executed. He had been an honest administrator and had greatly endeared himself to the Damascenes, who openly lamented his fall. Once again we see that some Mamlukes were honest rulers and good men. It was their mutual rivalries which inflicted harm on the empire.

The paucity of troops in this campaign is striking. The sultan sent only six hundred and fifty-two Royal Mamlukes, and perhaps a similar number of personal mamlukes accompanied the ameers, giving a total of twelve hundred. They were assisted by an unspecified number of Arab irregulars. The army of Damascus is said by Ibn Taghri Birdi to have consisted of only a thousand Arab and Turkman tribesmen. These figures give some idea of the extraordinary reductions in the army.

The reduced strength of the Mamluke army gave increased influence to the local population. The rival armies in the Damascus revolt consisted, as we have seen, largely of Arabs and Turkmans.

The force sent from Cairo went on to Aleppo, where it defeated the rebel ameer, took him prisoner and executed him. While the Damascenes had not hesitated publicly to show their devotion for their rebel viceroy, the people of Aleppo hated their Turkman governor. When he was brought in as a prisoner, the public turned out in large numbers to shout at him their hatred and defiance. The Syrians were no cowed and subject race.

When Jaqmaq became sultan, the principal danger to his power lay in the Ashrafis, the young mamlukes of Malik-al-Ashraf Barsbai. Jaqmaq's strength rested on his own barrack-comrades, the Dhahiris (Barqooq) and on the Muaiyadis (Shaikh), who were obviously older men. When Barsbai became sultan, his mamlukes had ousted the Muaiyadis, who were now burning for revenge.

Unfortunately, these vicissitudes, peculiar to the Mamluke system, occupy much of the narratives of the historians, including, willy-nilly, my own. To assess the importance of these disturbances, it is

useful to examine their chronology. Jaqmaq became sultan on 10th
September, 1438, but the ensuing turmoil ended with the capture of
the Viceroy of Aleppo on 15th May, 1439. The state of insecurity,
therefore, lasted eight months, but the ensuing reign of Jaqmaq
continued for fourteen and a half years. Often the tussle which followed the elevation of a new sultan played only a small part in
Mamluke history. It was also a test of the new ruler's capacity. If he
failed, a more efficient candidate could take over.

In March 1440, Muhammad ibn Dulqadir, the Turkman chief of
Albistan, kissed the ground in Cairo. He had been in rebellion against
Barsbai but had been attracted by Jaqmaq's reputation for leniency
and courtesy. He was treated with high honour and the sultan
married his daughter. The visit cost Jaqmaq thirty thousand dinars.
In May 1440, the sultan appointed Khalil al Sakhawi, a merchant
of Jerusalem, as administrator of that city and Hebron, another
indication of the direction in which affairs were moving.

On 24th September, 1440, an embassy arrived from Shah Rukh,
whom Ibn Taghri Birdi calls the King of the East. The city was
decorated and vast crowds watched the procession. Four days later,
at a formal levée, the ambassador presented a letter congratulating
Jaqmaq on his accession. The embassy remained in Cairo until 18th
October, when the ambassador was summoned to the palace and
invested with a "robe of departure" of exceptional splendour. It was
of velvet with two faces, red and green, with brocaded gold sleeves
worth five hundred dinars. He also received a horse with a gold
saddle and silk housing and a royal gift of silk, swords inlaid with
gold and other treasures, worth some seven thousand dinars.

Thus were friendly relations re-established between the two
empires, after almost leading to war through the irritability of
Barsbai. How often in history has war been avoided by tactful
diplomacy. Nowadays, unfortunately, the greatest nations constantly
give the lie to one another in public in the most offensive manner,
thus greatly increasing the danger of war, of which they profess to be
afraid.

*   *   *

Jaqmaq gained much respect by his piety. He detested intoxicants,
and alcohol was unknown at court. In 1441, the Khalif Mutadhid
died and was succeeded by his brother, who assumed the throne-
name of Al Mustakfi Billah.[1]

A naval expedition had been sent against Rhodes in the hope of

[1] He to whom God is sufficient.

emulating Barsbai's conquest of Cyprus, but it returned without success. A stronger force was sent in the spring of 1442, but it also was repulsed. Finally, in July 1444, a third flotilla carrying no less than a thousand Royal Mamlukes and many volunteers landed on the island, the whole of which was ransacked and its inhabitants made prisoners. The Muslims, however, again failed to take the fortress held by the Knights of St. John, and returned to Egypt at the end of the summer.

*   *   *

Meanwhile, on 25th June, 1442, the young mamlukes bought by Jaqmaq followed the example of those of Barsbai. They rioted in their citadel barracks, ascended to the roof and shot at any officers who approached. The sultan conciliated them and they returned to duty. No disciplinary action was taken.

The administration was also deteriorating, and many senior officials obtained their posts by cash payments to the treasury. Some sultans (with a sense of humour) accepted the cash and appointed the official, but dismissed him soon afterwards on the grounds of inefficiency, before he could recoup his expenses. These officials were, of course, normally Egyptians or Syrians, but the competition between them was intense. Ibn Taghri Birdi was particularly outraged by the case of a Christian Copt who secured his appointment as major-domo of the palace, an office which carried the honorary title of ameer. The man, however, continued to wear civilian clothing and could not even speak Turkish. "His appointment was one of the errors of the age", snorts our indignant historian, with a good deal of exaggeration.

In November 1444, a large deputation came from Shah Rukh, with the embroidered covering with which he had vowed to cover the Kaaba. The ameers, mamlukes and the public were angry, and preferred Barsbai's horse-pond methods to Jaqmaq's courtesy. On 21st December, 1444, the ambassador and his entourage went up to the palace, carrying the Kaaba covering and was received in state.

As the ambassador returned to his house, he was greeted by the crowd with curses and stones. No sooner had he re-entered his house, than it was attacked by three hundred of the sultan's young mamlukes, assisted by the mob, who looted everything the ambassador possessed. Eventually a party of old mamlukes arrived, charged the crowd and dispersed it. The sultan made large financial gifts to the members of the embassy before he could soothe their ruffled feelings. The public, though afraid of war, had done their best to provoke it, a phenomenon not uncommon in history.

Ibn Taghri Birdi, discussing Sultan Jaqmaq, has an interesting dissertation on "the simplemindedness of thoughtless Turks". Their frankness of speech, he says, made them easy victims of the subtle Egyptians and Syrians, who now wielded increasing influence. The pages of our historians are no longer filled with battles, marches and victories, nor even with armed revolts by jealous ameers. The intrigues of rival Egyptian politicians now occupy the records.

A certain Abu-al-Khair al Nahhás, a worker in the copper-smith's bazaar, attracted the sultan's notice and ingratiated himself into his favour. Soon he became the sultan's trusted adviser. We have seen a similar phenomenon in the case of Neshu and Al-Nasir Muhammad, the son of Qalaoon.[2] These simple northerners were always dupes.

One day a large crowd, assisted by the sultan's young mamlukes, waylaid Abu-al-Khair in the street, beat him and stripped him naked, until he was rescued by the governor of the city. From being a manual worker and a coppersmith, he had become rich and powerful, but with the change of fortune he grew insolent and arrogant. Eventually, as in the case of Neshu and the great Sultan Al-Nasir Muhammad, Jaqmaq realised that Abu-al-Khair had made a fool of him, and he was flogged and exiled to Tarsus.

Jaqmaq, from 1450 onwards, appears increasingly as a kind and pious old man, finding it difficult to discipline his young mamlukes or to vitalise the decadent régime. On 8th February, 1451, the Khalif Mustakfi died and was succeeded by his brother, who took the throne-name of Al Qaim.

In March 1451, an embassy arrived from Shah Jahan, the son of Qara Yusuf, the Black Sheep ruler of Tabriz. The sultan entertained the party to a banquet, but dismissed it after four days. On 17th May, 1451, the sultan sent an embassy to congratulate the new Ottoman Sultan Muhammad II on his accession. Known to history as Muhammad the Conqueror, he was to take Constantinople in 1453 and finally to extinguish the Byzantine Empire, which had endured for more than a thousand years.

On 20th September, 1451, the annual clothing-money was issued to the Royal Mamlukes, each man receiving a thousand dirhems. The soldiers, however, refused to accept that amount, demanding an increase. Jaqmaq was angry but was obliged to negotiate. The great Al-Nasir, it will be remembered, had reduced all other forces and had added to the numbers of the Royal Mamlukes, hoping

[2] Page 215.

thereby to increase his own autocratic power. But now the wheel had gone full circle, and it was the Royal Mamlukes who dominated the sultan. Jaqmaq was obliged to give way and each mamluke received two thousand dirhems. Al-Nasir had, indeed, been doubly responsible for the indiscipline of the young mamlukes, for it was he also who had introduced the custom of pampering the boys, instead of keeping them under strict discipline.

The Khalif Mutasim (832–842) had built up a great army of Turkish mercenaries, who rose against and killed his son. Saladin had used mamlukes, who killed his great-grand-nephew Turan Shah in 1250, and made themselves sultans. Now the Mamluke sultans were themselves threatened by their own mamlukes. Later the Ottoman sultans in the same manner were to be constantly dominated by the Janissaries.

Throughout this period, Ibn Taghri Birdi continues to complain of the appointment of unsuitable men to high office, in return for money payments to the treasury, not as private bribes. He shows resentment against Al Jamali, the Controller of the Privy Purse, who, he states, wielded great power over the government. Once again, it seems, an Egyptian had established his influence over the sultan.

Jaqmaq was old and ailing and anxious for peace. He did not need money for private pleasures, but the country was in chronic financial trouble, having been ruined by bad administration since the reign of Faraj (1399–1412). Everyone complained of the cost of living. The government was always bedevilled by inflation and efforts to fix the price of gold. The mamlukes were constantly on strike, claiming more pay to meet the increased cost of living.

In January 1453, Ibn Taghri records lists of all senior office holders of the time, giving us an outline of the government.

Khalif—Al Qaim
Sultan—Malik-al-Dhahir Jaqmaq
Four Chief Qadhis for the four Muslim schools, Shafii, Hanafi,
    Maliki and Hanbali.

It is to be noticed that our historian places the khalif first in order of precedence, the sultan second, and the four qadhis in the third place, before the Mamluke ameers.

The Council of Ameers
Commander-in-Chief—Grand Ameer Inal al Nasiri (Faraj)[3]

[3] As there were so many sultans bearing the throne-names of Nasir, Dhahir and others, the personal name of the sultan is inserted in brackets.

Ameer of Arms—Jarbash al Karimi al Dhahiri (Barqooq)
Ameer of the Council—Tanam al Muaiyadi (Shaikh)
Ameer of the Horse—Qani Bai al Sherkasi
Head of Guards—Asanbugha al Nasiri (Faraj)
Executive Secretary—Daulat Bai al Muaiyadi (Shaikh)
Grand Chamberlain—Khushqadam al Muaiyadi (Shaikh)

It will be noted that most of these officers were middle-aged or old men, dating from Barqooq, Faraj or Shaikh. None of the mamlukes of Jaqmaq's predecessor, Barsbai, the Ashrafis, were included. All the members of the council were ameers of one hundred. There were also three others in Cairo, without office, of whom one was a Dhahiri (Barqooq) and two were Nasiris (Faraj).

The following were the principal officials in the government:

Confidential Secretary—Qadhi Muhammad ibn al Ashqar
Controller of the Army and of the Privy Purse—Jamal-al-Deen
  Yusuf (the man denounced by Ibn Taghri Birdi)
Wazeer—Ibrahim ibn al Haisan
Major-Domo—Yahya al Ashqar

The four civilians were, of course, Egyptians or Syrians. It will be noted that the wazeer, once the prime minister at the head of the administration, is now just one of the office holders. It was against these civilian officials that the young mamlukes so often rioted.

The provincial viceroys outside of Egypt, all Mamluke ameers, were the following:

Damascus
Aleppo
Tarablus
Hama
Safad
Gaza
Kerak

These seven viceroys reported direct to Cairo.

In January, 1453, Jaqmaq was in poor health. On 20th January, he held a levée, walking unaided to his seat, and signing documents. Ibn Taghri Birdi says he saw no signs of early death in his face.

On 31st January, however, he sent for the khalif, the four qadhis and the ameers and, saying that he had abdicated, asked them to choose a successor. The khalif immediately swore allegiance to the sultan's son, Othman. Those present followed his example. The name of Malik-al-Mansoor, the Victorious King, was bestowed upon him. Jaqmaq retired to his bed and died on 14th February, 1453. He was about eighty years old and had reigned for fourteen and a half years. He was the first sultan who, after coming to the throne, never led an army on a campaign. Indeed, no wars were fought in his reign, except the brief action against the Viceroy of Damascus, soon after his accession.

We may reckon it among the benefits conferred by the Mamlukes that the empire had enjoyed comparative peace in the long period since the collapse of the Il-Khans in 1336. During this time, Persia, Iraq and Anatolia had been devastated again and again by Mongols, Turkmans and Ottomans, until most of the cities were ruined and the irrigation works destroyed.

A novelty in the reign of Jaqmaq was that he allowed Khalil, the son of Faraj and the grandson of Barqooq, to come to Cairo in liberty and to perform the pilgrimage to Mecca.

Jaqmaq was deeply religious, kind and generous. He was well read and intelligent, a good horseman and brave in battle. His moral character was high, he never touched alcohol and was said never to have had illicit relations with a woman. He had had six wives, two of whom he divorced, and one died of plague. Muslims are permitted four wives, but no more, at any one time. The Mamlukes as a community were distinguished for magnificent robes of silk, satin and gold lace, but Jaqmaq was always plainly dressed.

He was generous to a fault with money, and left the treasury almost empty. He sometimes lost his temper, but almost always in connection with public affairs, not as a result of his private vanity. Like so many Mamlukes, he was of extreme simplicity of mind and tended to believe what the first man he saw told him. This simplicity, endearing in a kind old gentleman, was dangerous in a sultan, who was pious, gentle and benevolent. These qualities, alas, were to hasten the ruin of the empire and of Syria and Egypt.

Sultan Jaqmaq had begun his reign with firmness, at the age of sixty-five, riding up to the Citadel and suppressing Barsbai's insubordinate young mamlukes. Yet, a few years later, the young men whom he himself had bought became as mutinous as those of Barsbai had been. This weakness may perhaps be attributed to his age, yet the fact remains that, until the ultimate collapse of the Mamluke Empire, the adolescent mamlukes were constantly in revolt. Their numbers were small and they could easily have been suppressed, but the art of rule, or the courage to act, had somehow been lost.

*   *   *

AL-MALIK-AL-MANSOOR OTHMAN

Othman was eighteen years old when he came to the throne, while his father was still alive. The first problem seemed to be the emptiness of the treasury as left by Jaqmaq, for a new accession necessitated a donative to the Royal Mamlukes. But soon another problem proved to be more urgent.

It has been seen that the senior ameers under Jaqmaq had been Dhahiris (Barqooq), Nasiris (Faraj) and Muaiyadis (Shaikh). These were old men, whose surviving barrack-comrades were few. The Ashrafis (Barsbai), on the other hand, were still numerous, but had been suppressed and scattered by Jaqmaq. Young men rarely work happily with their fathers' old advisers and one of Othman's first actions was to dismiss all the Muaiyadis (Shaikh). As a result, the Muaiyadis allied themselves with the Ashrafis, both being out of favour.

The boy-sultan, having scraped together some money, proposed to distribute a donative to the Royal Mamlukes on 12th March, 1453. But that morning a large number of Muaiyadis, Ashrafis and Saifis[4] assembled outside the Citadel. When the ameers rode up to attend the sultan's levée, the mamlukes seized them and took them all to the house of Grand Ameer Inal al Alai, the commander-in-chief, whom they also arrested.

The large gathering of mamlukes thus assembled then renounced their allegiance to Malik-al-Mansoor Othman and demanded the elevation of the commander-in-chief, Inal Al Alai, who, however, refused—at least that was what he said. However the insurgent mamlukes now seized the mosque of Sultan Hasan, which faced the walls of the Citadel. Guns came into action, arrows flew through the air, and Cairo was in chaos.

The next morning, the executive secretary, an ameer of one hundred, went over to the rebels, and throughout the day more Royal Mamlukes did so. The khalif now began to speak against Othman, although it was he who had taken the lead in swearing loyalty to him. On the fifth day of the bombardment, the controller of the privy purse went over to Grand Ameer Inal. The guns had now been shooting for four days and many cannonballs had hit private houses or killed civilians in the streets.

---

[4] Saifis were unemployed mamlukes, formerly the personal mamlukes of ameers.

On 16th March, the khalif and the qadhis held a consultation in the house where Inal had set up his headquarters, and passed a resolution dethroning Malik-al-Mansoor Othman, after a reign of forty-three days. Inal al Alai was then chosen by acclamation. Fighting began again on the morning of the seventh day, but later in the morning the besiegers broke into the Citadel and its defenders fled. One more stop-gap boy-sultan had been dethroned. It was proved once again that this fierce and jealous community could not be controlled by a boy, but only by an experienced member of their own group. Why dying sultans still named their children as their heirs is difficult to understand.

On 9th April, 1453, Malik-al-Mansoor Othman was placed in a boat on the Nile and escorted to Alexandria to prison. He was given comfortable accommodation, which allowed his mother, his girl slaves and his children to live with him.

NOTABLE EVENTS

Elevation of Malik-al-Azeez Yusuf	7th June, 1438
Dethronement of Yusuf	
Elevation of Malik-al-Dhahir Jaqmaq	10th September, 1438
Escape and re-arrest of Malik-al-Azeez Yusuf	March–April, 1439
Defeat of revolt in Damascus	16th April, 1439
Abortive attacks on Rhodes	1441–1444
Plundering of the embassy from Shah Rukh	December, 1444
Elevation of Malik-al-Mansoor Othman	31st January, 1453
Death of Malik-al-Dhahir Jaqmaq	14th February, 1453
Dethronement of Malik-al-Mansoor Othman	16th March, 1453

THE GREAT SULTANS[5]

(omitting children and short-term adventurers)

Aibek and Spray-of-Pearls	1250–1257
Qutuz	1259–1260
Baybars the Bunduqdari	1260–1277

[5] This list is inserted, in view of the great numbers of sultans, to remind the reader of the outstanding personalities of Mamluke history.

Qalaoon	1279–1290
Al-Nasir Muhammad (Third Reign)	1309–1341
(Twelve sons and grandsons of Al-Nasir)	(1341–1382)
Barqooq	1382–1399
Faraj	1399–1412
Shaikh	1412–1421
Barsbai	1422–1438
Jaqmaq	1438–1453

XVIII

More Mutinous Mamlukes

We set ourselves to bite the hand that feeds us.

EDMUND BURKE

Do you know what is more hard to bear than the reverses of fortune? It is the baseness, the hideous ingratitude of men.

NAPOLEON BONAPARTE

History is indeed little more than the register of the crimes, follies and misfortunes of mankind.

EDWARD GIBBON, *Decline and Fall of the Roman Empire*

The condition upon which God hath given liberty to man is eternal vigilance, which condition if he break, servitude is at once the consequence of his crime and the punishment of his guilt.

J. P. CURRAN, *Speech on the Election of the Lord Mayor of Dublin, 1790*

Confusion now hath made his masterpiece.

SHAKESPEARE, *Macbeth*

XVIII

AL-MALIK-AL-ASHRAF INAL

ON 19th March, 1453, the Citadel having been captured the day before, the new sultan Inal donned the black Abbasid robe and rode in state to the palace inside the Citadel, with all the insignia of royalty. He took his seat on the throne, the ameers kissed the ground and the normal ceremonial was carried out.

Inal was a Circassian and had been brought to Cairo as a boy by a merchant and sold to Barqooq, probably in 1397. When the latter died, however, Inal was still a boy under training, and was only freed by Malik-al-Nasir Faraj, thereby acquiring the name of al Nasiri. In 1421, Faraj made him an ameer of ten, while, in 1422, Barsbai promoted him to be an ameer of drums. In 1427, he became Viceroy of Gaza, whence he accompanied Barsbai on the abortive Amid campaign in 1432. At the end of the campaign, he unwillingly accepted the post of Governor of Ruha (Edessa).[1]

Next year, he was made an ameer of one hundred. Sultan Jaqmaq made him executive secretary and a member of his council. In 1445, he became commander-in-chief, and was holding this post when Jaqmaq died and Othman succeeded him, as already related.

On his accession, Inal distributed a donative of one hundred dinars to every Royal Mamluke. They had hoped for two hundred, but there was, in fact, no money in the treasury. A number of Ashrafis (Barsbai) were given good posts. As we have seen, they had been suppressed under Jaqmaq.

In October 1453, an ambassador came from the Ottoman Sultan Muhammad II to congratulate Inal on his accession and to inform him of the capture of Constantinople[2] and of the extinction of the Byzantine Empire. Cairo was decorated for several days and the bands played

In December 1455, the young mamlukes purchased by Inal commenced their outrages. They went down from the Citadel and looted the house of Nasir-al-Deen ibn Ali al Faraj, the civilian controller of the army. At this point, Ibn Taghri Birdi inserts a tirade against the low-class holders of the once-mighty post of wazeer. He describes

---

[1] Map 28, page 325. [2] Hereafter Constantinople will be referred to as Istanbul.

them as "low Coptic clerks", perhaps with some religious spite. Nevertheless, the post was no longer one to be coveted. On 20th March, 1455, Sultan Inal was at his wits' end to maintain the administration, the young mamlukes being on the verge of mutiny. Hoping to find a better wazeer, he sent for three possible candidates, Ibn al Najjár, Ibn al Haisam and Ibn al Nahhál. But when he called for Ibn al Najjár, he was told that he had gone into hiding. Ibn al Haisam's relations reported that he was dead.

Ibn al Nahhál was eventually brought in, but positively refused to be wazeer, pointing out that the bankruptcy of the treasury and the endless mutinies of the young mamlukes made government impossible. Inal was so furious at these candid remarks that he ordered that Ibn al Nahhál be flogged, presumably *"pour encourager les autres"*.[3]

Meanwhile the mutinous mamlukes molested the chief secretary, who escaped only with great difficulty. Next day, the Dhahiris (Jaqmaq), who had been dismissed by Inal, joined the latter's young mamlukes, and obliged the Khalif Al Qaim to declare for the insurrection. At this stage, however, Inal's young mamlukes returned to obedience. They had mutinied to compel Inal to raise their pay, but they did not want him overthrown, or they would lose their own position. The Dhahiris, left alone, were dispersed and the khalif taken prisoner and sent to detention in Alexandria, his brother being appointed in his place. The unworthy intrigues of the khalifs greatly reduced their prestige.

These incidents illustrate the chaos into which the Mamluke régime had fallen. The root of the trouble lay in the collapse of discipline among the Royal Mamlukes, who, since the virtual abolition of the *halaqa*, were the only regular army. The administration had always been staffed by Syrians and Egyptians, who, under the Bahri sultans, had enjoyed great prestige. Mutinous young mamlukes, however, enjoyed assaulting these officials, with the result that no one would accept office.

The ordinary Egyptians took no part in the struggles for power between the ameers, or between the sultans and their mamlukes. In the two hundred and sixty-seven years of the Mamluke Empire, there was never any question of a Syrian or Egyptian national rising. But the public suffered from the decline in administrative efficiency, the bankruptcy of the treasury, the neglect of the irrigation and public works, and the general insecurity paralysing trade.

The civilian population had been wealthy and prosperous under

---

[3] To encourage the others. The remark was made by Voltaire, when the English Admiral Byng was shot for not defeating the French.

the great sultans like Baybars the Bunduqdari, Qalaoon and Al-Nasir Muhammad, under whom Egyptians were able to maintain an efficient administration and who enjoyed both wealth and prestige in return. Trade and agriculture flourished and local business men grew rich. The cultivators, it is true, were oppressed but so they had been before under the khalifs and continued to be afterwards under the Ottomans.

In December 1456, the young mamlukes again rioted, demanding more pay. When the sultan himself appeared, he was greeted with a volley of stones by his own mamlukes. Eventually he gave way and granted the pay increases demanded. No one was punished.

In June 1457, an expedition was sent against the Qaraman Ameer of Konia, who had raided Mamluke territory near Tarsus. The Qaramans ruled from Konia to Caesarea, and formed a buffer state between the Mamlukes and the Ottomans.

As we have seen, one of the principal problems produced by these —the normal—signs of decadence was "inflation", the decline in the value of the currency, which in the case of the Mamlukes, took the form of the increasing adulteration of the silver dirhem with copper. In January 1457, a reform of the currency was attempted. A new silver dirhem was minted, with the result that merchants holding large amounts of adulterated dirhems lost one-third of their capital with the fall in the value of the old corrupt dirhems. To counteract their complaints, the sultan ordered the reduction of the price of food and clothing by one-third.

These crude methods were, of course, unsuccessful, though our own politicians today seem little more skilful than the Mamlukes in handling inflation. Such problems, which have attacked nearly every great nation in history, are due to the loss of a sense of duty to the community, resulting in the break-up of the nation into separate groups, each seeking only its private advantage. Inflation is, therefore, not an economic but a moral problem. The chaos resulting from the struggles of these groups causes a loss of confidence in the survival of the state.

In April 1458, an embassy came from the Qaraman Ameer soliciting peace, and a treaty was concluded. The King of Cyprus died in the summer of 1458, and the throne passed to his daughter, Carlotta. He also had an illegitimate son of the name of James, who arrived in Cairo to solicit the support of Sultan Inal, the suzerain of the island. On 5th August, 1458, the sultan received the prince at a formal reception in the palace, invested him with a robe of honour and promised to support his claim to the throne. Orders were issued for the construction of a fleet to invade the island.

The excesses of the young mamlukes had now seriously affected the administration of justice. Anyone with a complaint against an opponent no longer bothered to go to court. It was easier to complain to the young mamlukes, who would willingly accompany the plaintiff, break into the house of the defendant and seize the amount of the alleged debt, together with a handsome commission for themselves.

The winter of 1459 to 1460 was a time of fear and misery in Cairo. The young mamlukes inspired a reign of terror in the city and no man ventured out of doors after dark. Then, in February 1460, the plague appeared. Before long, four thousand people a day were said to be dying in Cairo. Ibn Taghri Birdi himself caught it but recovered, a rare occurrence, for most of the victims died. One thousand four hundred Royal Mamlukes died.

In the spring of 1460, two rival delegations from Cyprus were in Cairo, one representing Queen Carlotta, and the other Prince James. On 25th May, 1460, the sultan received both delegations, after which he announced his intention to maintain the queen on the throne. Her ambassadors left the palace in procession, wearing their robes of honour. No sooner were they outside the palace, however, than they were attacked and stripped of their robes by the young mamlukes, who announced their decision to make James king. A violent riot ensued, which was only ended when the sultan gave way, reversed his policy and proclaimed James to be king. Rarely, if ever, in history has so disgraceful an action been forced on any ruler by his own troops.

Orders were then issued for the despatch of a fleet to place James on the throne. It sailed on 5th August, 1460, with a military force on board, including some six hundred and fifty Royal Mamlukes. The fleet was unsuccessful but it left James with a force of Mamlukes on the island.

On 3rd February, 1461, Malik-al-Ashraf Inal was suddenly taken ill and went to bed. On 25th February, the khalif, the qadhis and the ameers were called to the bedside, and the sultan's eldest son, Ahmad, was proclaimed his successor. The next morning, 26th February, 1461, Sultan Inal died. He was eighty years of age and had reigned for eight years less one month.

Inal was by birth a Circassian, tall, lean, and with a very small white beard. His appearance was unprepossessing and he was never popular. As an army officer, he had shown bravery before he came to the throne. As sultan, he was patient, prudent, quiet and soft-spoken —so much so, indeed, that he was sometimes accused of cowardice. He scarcely ever imprisoned anyone, nor did he arrest any ameers belonging to other factions, as was normally done. Perhaps his advanced age made him anxious to avoid trouble.

Mamluke ameers were, in general, more educated than in former times. It is, therefore, surprising to learn that Inal could neither read nor write. Perhaps he was naturally lacking in intelligence though, as a result of his long period of military service and his many campaigns, he was well acquainted with the topography and the inhabitants of the empire and of its neighbours.

These, however, were minor factors. The outstanding characteristic of his reign was the collapse of law and order due to the sultan's inability to discipline his own purchased mamlukes. This failure was not due to lack of power. There were in the country great numbers of older mamlukes still trained and disciplined. Indeed so hated were the young mamlukes, that the whole country would have risen against them. But Inal took no action, even when they pelted him with stones.

The outrages committed by the young mamlukes encouraged thieves and bandits to follow their example. Lawlessness spread from the city to the open country, where the roads were infested by robber gangs. We have little detailed information about Syria, where conditions may have been much better. There were, on the other hand, no rebellions and no foreign invasions during the reign.

In the East, Uzun Hasan, the son of Qara Yuluk of Amid, the White Sheep ruler, and Shah Jahan, the son of Qara Yusuf of Tabriz, of the Black Sheep, continued to fight one another, and neither fell foul of the Mamluke Empire.

Taxation became increasingly onerous. Indeed the taxes were so high that the economic situation continued to deteriorate and business was at a low ebb. On the whole, in spite of the fact that Sultan Inal scarcely ever did anyone any harm, he was a totally incapable ruler and his reign, in Egypt at least, was a period of misery.

*   *   *

AL-MALIK-AL-MUAIYAD AHMAD

Ahmad, the son of Inal, succeeded to the throne on his father's death on 26th February, 1461. He was extremely tall, fair-haired and handsome, and his appearance in his black Abbasid robes at his inauguration excited general admiration. Unlike the child-sultans who had so often succeeded their fathers, Ahmad was thirty years old and had gained considerable administrative experience under his father. The Ameer Khushqadam al Nasiri was made commander-in-chief.

In Egypt, the death of the feeble old Sultan Inal and the elevation of his handsome son caused a revival of confidence, especially as he disciplined a number of his father's young mamlukes, who had committed so many outrages against the public. But soon the rivalries between different groups of mamlukes destroyed these hopes.

The Ashrafis (Barsbai) and the Dhahiris (Jaqmaq) had formerly been jealous of one another. The Viceroy of Damascus, Janim al Ashrafi, aspired to be sultan and sent his son to Cairo, where he succeeded in winning over the Dhahiris.

Meanwhile, trouble was brewing in Cairo. There were disorders among the tribes in the Buhaira, and a detachment of Royal Mamlukes were detailed to suppress it. Only the older mamlukes were ordered to go, no young purchased mamlukes were warned to prepare. This order angered everybody. The older men complained that they did all the work, the younger were insulted that the sultan did not trust them. Finally those detailed for duty refused to go.

The sultan, though he was thirty years old, was not intimate with the senior ameers, who were in their fifties or sixties. He lacked competent advisers. When the mamlukes refused to march, he remained hesitant. His obvious vacillation lost him respect.

On the morning of 27th June, 1461, several groups of ameers including the Nasiris (Faraj), the Muaiyadis (Shaikh), the Ashrafis (Barsbai) and the Dhahiris (Jaqmaq), with their followings and other ameers and senior civil officials, assembled in the house of Khushqadam, the commander-in-chief, though the latter had not joined in the plot. The principal personality present was Janibek al Dhahiri, who commanded the universal support of the Dhahiris (Jaqmaq). The leader of the Ashrafis (Barsbai) was still in Damascus.

Janibek al Dhahiri, in a forcible speech, said that they must remove Sultan Ahmad that very day, but that a sultan could only be removed in the name of another sultan. Janim al Ashrafi was still in Damascus, and they could not await his arrival. He suggested the immediate elevation of Khushqadam, the commander-in-chief, on the grounds that he was a native of Anatolia, not a Circassian, and consequently had few friends. He was also a Muaiyadi (Shaikh), who were few in number, Shaikh having been already dead for forty years. Consequently, he said, Khushqadam could easily be removed when desirable.

The Ashrafis (Barsbai) accepted Khushqadam, on the grounds

that he would do to get rid of Ahmad, and that they would remove him again when Janim al Ashrafi came from Damascus. The Dhahiris, on the other hand, accepted Khushqadam in order to get a sultan before Janim al Ashrafi could come, for the Dhahiris (Jaqmaq) were determined not to be subjected to the Ashrafis. As a result, Khushqadam was elected by acclamation.

Skirmishers moved off immediately to attack Sultan Ahmad in the Citadel. The latter found that his only supporters were a thousand of his father's young mamlukes, the same who had maintained a reign of terror in Cairo during the lifetime of Inal. During the night, most of these deserted the Citadel and scattered. On the morning of 28th June, 1461, Sultan Ahmad retired to his mother's apartments in the palace, leaving the Citadel gates open. Two days later Malik-al-Muaiyad Ahmad was sent to prison in Alexandria, after a reign of four months.

These incidents show that the groups of mamlukes of former sultans had now virtually become political parties contending for office. The most powerful groups were naturally those of the two most recent sultans, who had enjoyed long enough reigns to build up large bodies of mamlukes, in this case Barsbai (sixteen years reign) and Jaqmaq (fifteen years). Faraj and Shaikh had died too long ago and only a few old ameers survived from their mamlukes. Inal had reigned for eight years, but having only just died, his mamlukes were still too young.

Thus the Ashrafis (Barsbai) and the Dhahiris (Jaqmaq) were the two parties contending for office. Both, as in all decadent régimes, put party before country. Ahmad seems to have been a capable young man, who might have made an excellent sultan. A good administrator, he was no politician, but relied on his own efficiency. His mistake was that he did not take the senior ameers into his confidence. Had he identified himself with either the Dhahiris or the Ashrafis, he might have survived by using one party against the other.

More generally, the Mamluke system was breaking down. It had been founded on two firm bases—the complete loyalty of every mamluke to his patron and, of course, of the Royal Mamlukes to their sultan—and secondly, of every mamluke to his barrack-comrades. Loyalty to the sultan, that is to the country, had vanished, and the Royal Mamlukes were the most undisciplined of all. In the absence of a respected sultan representing a united country, loyalty to barrack-comrades had become a means of grouping the Mamlukes into rival political parties, each indifferent to the empire and contending only for the fruits of office.

* * *

AL-MALIK-AL-DHAHIR KHUSHQADAM

Khushqadam al Muaiyadi (Shaikh) became sultan on 28th June, 1461. As we have seen, he had not plotted, or even hoped to obtain the post. All the historians agree that Khushqadam was a *Roumi*, a word normally translated Greek. The country of Roum (Rome) was a name applied to Anatolia, which had been so called by the Arabs for seven hundred years or more. It was a purely geographical term, and had no clear ethnic significance. Anatolia had actually been occupied by Turks for some four hundred years.

Khushqadam had been brought as a boy from Anatolia in 1412 or 1413 and sold to Sultan Shaikh, who subsequently freed him and made him a Royal Mamluke. Jaqmaq at first made him a cupbearer and then an ameer of ten. In 1446, we find him an ameer of one hundred in Damascus. In 1450, Jaqmaq made him Chamberlain of the Palace. Inal made him Ameer of Arms and a member of the Council. He commanded the force sent by Sultan Inal against the Qaraman Ameer, as already reported. Sultan Ahmad, the son of Inal, made Khushqadam Grand Ameer and Commander-in-Chief.

When Khushqadam was settled on the throne, Janibek al Dhahiri, who had proposed his elevation, was rewarded with the position of Grand Executive Secretary of the government. On 3rd July, 1461, five days after the elevation of Khushqadam, Janim al Ashrafi, the Viceroy of Damascus, arrived outside Cairo with an armed force. It will be remembered that he had sent his son ahead of him to secure promises of support from the Ashrafis and the Dhahiris. The situation remained tense for a few days, but as no movement in his favour took place in Cairo, he marched back to Damascus.

Khushqadam set himself to win popularity among the ameers, many of whom were promoted and given fiefs. Land for more fiefs was obtained by many expedients, some even from the royal domains. The chief obstacle to his policy of pleasing everybody was that the treasury was empty as a result of the chaotic reign of Inal. Only a limited donative could be made to the mamlukes for this reason.

There were now three deposed sultans in prison in Alexandria, all sons of former sultans. The first was Yusuf, the son of Malik-al-Ashraf Barsbai, the second was Othman, the son of Malik-al-Dhahir

Jaqmaq. Orders were given for their release from actual prison, and they were allotted comfortable apartments, though still inside the Citadel. Ahmad, the son of Inal, whom Khushqadam had replaced, was to remain in prison, but his fetters were removed. The release of the sons of Barsbai and Jaqmaq was intended to placate the Ashrafis and the Dhahiris, their fathers' mamlukes.

In October, 1461, however, the Ashrafis staged an abortive revolt, quickly suppressed. The offenders were officially pardoned, but the sultan gradually dispersed them and Ashrafi power was broken. A number were sent to Cyprus, where the civil war was still dragging on, the Mamlukes assisting James. In December 1461, Janim al Ashrafi, who had attempted to make himself sultan earlier in the year, fled from Damascus to the ruler of Amid, Uzun Hasan, the son of Qara Yuluk, of the White Sheep.

On 7th July, 1462, a report was received to the effect that Janim al Ashrafi, with a party of mamlukes, was marching on Aleppo, supported by a Turkman force sent by Uzun Hasan. Orders were issued for the despatch of a force of six hundred mamlukes (note the small numbers of mamlukes who could now be made available). A week later the order was cancelled. Janim had quarrelled with the men sent by Uzun Hasan of the White Sheep, and the whole force had returned to the Jezira. Six months later, Janim was murdered in Ruha (Edessa). In September 1462, Uzun Hasan, the son of Qara Yuluk, took Hisn Kaifa, and finally exterminated its ruling house, the last petty Ayoubid dynasty still in existence.

We may note here also, the death of a daughter of the sultan's wife by a former marriage to the Ameer Abrak al Jakami. This daughter had been married to the Chief Qadhi Bedr-al-Deen al Aini. This is another example of the marriage of a Mamluke lady to a distinguished Egyptian. Mamlukes and Egyptians did not normally intermarry, but these occasional examples prove that such marriages were not unknown, even in the highest circles.

In August 1463, Janibek al Dhahiri, the executive secretary of the government, the man originally responsible for the elevation of Khushqadam, was murdered by a party of young mamlukes purchased by the sultan. Immediately afterwards, six other Dhahiri ameers were arrested. Janibek, supported by his barrack-comrades, the Dhahiris, had attained a position of great power, especially since the liquidation of the Ashrafis. His murder and the arrest of his friends seems, therefore, to have been a coup d'état by the sultan. Having disposed of the Ashrafis, he desired also to scatter the Dhahiris and reign in his own right.

A few days later, however, Khushqadam received a report that some of Inal's former young mamlukes had formed a plot to kill him. It will be remembered that Inal's purchased mamlukes had been the most mutinous of any such group in the past. Khushqadam had made the mistake of allowing some of them to remain in the Royal Mamlukes. Whether the reports were true or not, Khushqadam was alarmed. Having alienated the Dhahiris, he had no solid body of older men to rely on. He suddenly reversed his coup d'état, released the Dhahiri ameers arrested, and heaped them with favours. For the moment, the young mamlukes relapsed into quiescence.

Apparently immediately after this fiasco, the sultan summoned the qadhis and drew up a proclamation prohibiting the employment of Christians or Jews in government offices. It is amusing to note the manner in which this routine popularity-winning device was produced whenever a sultan felt insecure. Within a year, they were all back in their offices, as the sultan well knew, but it was a useful, if somewhat stale, political subterfuge.

In October 1463, the sultan ordered two young mamlukes to be halved at the waist, possibly the instigators of the plot to murder him.

Ever since the reign of Inal, civil war had been dragging on in Cyprus, the sultan—though somewhat feebly—supporting James against Queen Carlotta. On 9th December, 1463, the force of Mamlukes fighting for James returned to Cairo without the sultan's permission, an illustration of the extraordinary laxity of army discipline. Khushqadam was secretly annoyed, but dared not take action, owing to his doubts of the loyalty of the Royal Mamlukes. He accordingly concealed his anger, and invested the commanders with robes of honour.

James had occupied Nicosia soon after he had landed in Cyprus in 1460, and the queen had shut herself up in the fortress of Kyrenia.[4] James, however, was a young man of courage and energy, and succeeded in driving the hated Genoese from Famagusta, thereby becoming a national hero. In 1464, he took Kyrenia and was proclaimed King James II of Cyprus. Carlotta surrendered her rights to a relative, the Duke of Savoy. As a result, the Kings of Italy claimed the titles of King of Jerusalem, Cyprus and Armenia, until the abdication of the dynasty in 1946.[5]

James II married a Venetian, Katharine Cornaro. This was a somewhat unscrupulous plot by the Serene Republic who, like her rival Genoa, coveted Cyprus as a naval base. When James II died in 1473, Venice succeeded in taking control of the island, and any shadowy Mamluke rights disappeared.

[4] Map 27, page 320.   [5] Sir Harry Luke, *Cyprus*.

*   *   *

In 1465, the young mamlukes taken over by Khushqadam from Inal began once again to commit outrages, going down to the city of Cairo and robbing merchants and private citizens. In December 1466, they mutinied in the Citadel, demanding more pay, clothing and forage for their horses. The government showed itself weak, and negotiated a compromise.

In August 1467, a report reached Cairo that Shah Suwar ibn Dulqadir, the ruler of Albistan, had denounced his—no more than nominal—allegiance to the sultan and was marching on Aleppo. A few days later, it was announced that the pilgrim caravan returning from Mecca had been robbed by the Beni Uqba Arabs near Aqaba. In October, the tribes on the Upper Nile revolted and defeated the Mamluke governor of the province.

Khushqadam was suffering from dysentery and was too weak to leave the palace. Reports of his failing health may indeed have been the cause of the sudden outbreak of these disorders.

On 10th October, 1467, the sultan growing weaker, the senior ameers held a meeting at which they decided that Grand Ameer Yalbai, the commander-in-chief, should be the next sultan. He was a Muaiyadi, a barrack-comrade of Khushqadam. On the same day, Malik-al-Dhahir Khushqadam breathed his last.

He was believed to be sixty-five years old, and had reigned for six years and four months. He was of medium height, of slender build, with fair hair and a reddish beard, turning grey. He had been a good horseman and polo-player when he was young. He was intelligent, well educated, respected men of learning, and spoke Arabic fluently, though with a slight foreign accent. He had been, on the whole, a wise ruler and a competent politician. He was haunted by the mutinous spirit of Inal's former mamlukes, though he kept order better than Inal had done. His reign was an interval of relative security in the disintegrating empire.

*   *   *

AL-MALIK-AL-DHAHIR YALBAI
AL MUAIYADI

Yalbai at first refused to accept the sultanate to which he had been elected on the morning of the death of Khushqadam. Finally he accepted, assuming the name of Al-Malik-al-Dhahir. A Circassian by birth, he had been bought in 1416 by Shaikh, who also manumitted him. Under Barsbai he became an intimate mamluke, and under Jaqmaq an ameer of ten and then of drums. Inal made him an ameer of one hundred. Under Khushqadam he became successively Chamberlain, Ameer of the Horse and then Commander-in-Chief.

A few days after his accession, reports arrived that Shah Suwar ibn Dulqadir had defeated the Mamluke forces in Syria. The Turkmans had plundered Damascus, Aleppo and all northern Syria. In this crisis, the new sultan gave evidence of weakness and hesitation. The customary donative to the Royal Mamlukes was distributed in a disorderly manner, some men snatching more than their share, others obtaining nothing.

Opinion veered sharply against Yalbai, who appeared completely incompetent. It seems almost incredible that he was illiterate, for this was not an age of barbarism, but rather of effete civilisation. The Syrians and Egyptians were highly cultured, as witness their extensive literary and historical output, which is still in our hands. It was an age of magnificent architecture, many monuments of which are still to be seen. Skilful and beautiful works of art were in great demand and the richer classes, Mamluke ameers, Syrian and Egyptian officials and business men lived in luxury, and were dressed in silk and satin, gold and jewels.

It appeared now that Shah Suwar's victory in Syria had been largely due to the treachery of Bardbek, the Viceroy of Damascus, who had a grudge against Khushqadam, and had consequently assisted the Turkmans. After the death of Khushqadam, Bardbek came to Cairo. Yalbai ordered him to live in retirement in Jerusalem. No disciplinary action was taken against him, although he had betrayed his country.

By mid-November 1467, six weeks after his accession, it was evident that Yalbai was incapable of being sultan, and the usual intrigues, secret meetings and alliances became active. The young mamlukes were in a state of half-mutiny. Yalbai was one of the Muaiyadis, a small group of old men, afraid of a coup by the powerful Dhahiris (Jaqmaq). The surviving Muaiyadis, therefore, allied themselves with the Ashrafis. There were old and young Ashrafis, the old being the former mamlukes of Barsbai, the young those of Inal, for these two sultans had both been Malik-al-Ashraf. Opposing the combined Muaiyadis (Shaikh) and Ashrafis, were the powerful Dhahiris (Jaqmaq), who allied themselves to the semi-mutinous young mamlukes.

On the evening of 2nd December, 1467, the Dhahiris went up to the Citadel in a body, seeing which, the Ashrafis, Muaiyadis and many of the public gathered in the city. If Yalbai had slipped out and joined his supporters in the city, the Dhahiris would probably have been defeated. But he vacillated, and was taken prisoner by the Dhahiris. Fighting continued for some twenty-four hours, but when it was known that Yalbai was in the hands of the Dhahiris, the Ashrafis gave up the struggle. On 5th December, Yalbai was pronounced deposed and Timurbugha al Dhahiri was proclaimed sultan.

Yalbai had been sultan for two months, during which everything had gone wrong, the young mamlukes were out of hand, the Turkmans had overrun Syria and southern Egypt was in rebellion. It is not only surprising that a man like Yalbai could become sultan, but that he could rise to the rank of commander-in-chief through a successful official career. The explanation seems to be that Mamluke party politics now controlled the country. The Muaiyadis and the Ashrafis wanted to keep the Dhahiris out of office, and Yalbai was their figurehead. As in so many declining nations, in our own times as in the past, party politics was now more important to the contenders for power than were the interests of the country.

* * *

MALIK-AL-DHAHIR TIMURBUGHA
AL DHAHIRI

The Ameer Timurbugha became sultan on 5th December, 1467, and assumed the title of Al-Malik-al-Dhahir. The number of sultans who had used this throne-name was confusing. An ameer who was a Dhahiri could have been a former mamluke of either Jaqmaq, Khushqadam, Yalbai or Timurbugha. The Ameer Qaitbai al Mahmoodi al Dhahiri was made commander-in-chief.

Unlike Yalbai, Timurbugha was well educated, with a good knowledge of law, history, literature and poetry. His conversation was intelligent and affable, and he was reputed to be a good soldier. He seemed eminently fitted to be sultan and his accession was greeted with pleasure.

He released Ahmad, the son of Inal, and Othman, the son of Jaqmaq, both former boy-sultans, from prison in Alexandria, and allowed them to live as ordinary citizens in that city. Timurbugha had been a mamluke of Jaqmaq, and Othman was thus the son of his former master. Other political prisoners were also released. These acts of generosity, combined with the new sultan's pleasant manners, gave rise to optimism.

Timurbugha seems to have been an Albanian by origin. He had been bought by Jaqmaq, who, when he became sultan, made him an intimate mamluke. In 1442, he became an ameer of ten and then second executive secretary, a post which he filled with distinction. On the death of Jaqmaq and the succession of his son Othman, Timurbugha became first executive secretary. When Othman was dethroned, Timurbugha, one of his close friends, was imprisoned for six years by Inal, but under Khushqadam he became an ameer of one hundred, and then Ameer of the Council. When Yalbai was made sultan, Timurbugha was made commander-in-chief.

The accession of Timurbugha was marked by the promotion of Dhahiris, his barrack-comrades, to many senior positions. However, he gave no donative to the Royal Mamlukes. Yalbai had reigned so short a time that the distribution of his donative was not yet complete. As a result, Timurbugha contented himself with completing the payment of Yalbai's donative. Moreover, as usual, the treasury was empty.

In December 1467, a stir was created in the East by the defeat and death of Shah Jahan of the Black Sheep Turkmans, whose capital was in Tabriz. He was killed by Uzun Hasan, of the White Sheep Turkmans, who thereby became the strongest power in the area extending from the Caucasus to the Jezira and northern Persia. Thereafter, the Black Sheep Turkmans of Tabriz fade out of history. Venice, who was afraid of the rising power of the Ottoman Sultan, Muhammad II the Conqueror, concluded an alliance with Uzun Hasan, and an exchange of embassies took place.

On 31st January, 1468, certain Royal Mamlukes in the Citadel mutinied, seized the person of the sultan and nine other Dhahiri ameers and locked them in a dungeon. They then proclaimed Khairbek, one of their number, to be sultan.

When news of this outbreak reached the commander-in-chief, Qaitbai, he collected a force and attacked the Chain Gate of the Citadel, to rescue the sultan. The mutineers fled before this concerted attack, and Qaitbai, at the head of the column which he had organised, broke into the Citadel. As he moved forward followed by his troops, one of the ameers shouted, "Long live the Victorious King, Qaitbai". The latter reproved the speaker, but others took up the call and some of the ameers kissed the ground.

After at least a show of refusal, Qaitbai consented to be sultan, and a message to this effect was sent to Timurbugha, who had returned to the palace. He received the news calmly. On 3rd February, Qaitbai greeted Timurbugha in the palace and began to make excuses for what had happened, but Timurbugha cut him short, requesting only that he be allowed to reside in Damietta, to which Qaitbai readily agreed. The two men were close friends and had been barrack-comrades in the days of Jaqmaq, thirty years before.

Timurbugha, having spent two days in prison in the Citadel, was indeed deeply relieved that Qaitbai was the next sultan. He would probably have been killed if Qaitbai had not rescued him. The latter does not appear to have captured the Citadel to make himself sultan but to rescue Timurbugha. The acclamation which he received seems to have been spontaneous.

Timurbugha and Qaitbai talked to one another in private for a long time. Then they came out together, embraced one another, both shedding tears, and bade each other an affectionate farewell. Timurbugha rode down to the Nile with his family and accompanied by a number of Dhahiri ameers, who had come to see him off. He embarked without an escort and sailed down the Nile to Damietta without a guard, like a private citizen.

Thus ended what must certainly have been one of the most remarkable coups d'état in history. For it was carried out by mistake, by a loyal officer who had come to rescue his sultan, but who accidentally finished up by replacing him.

NOTABLE EVENTS

Accession of Malik-al-Ashraf Inal	19th March, 1453
Capture of Constantinople by Muhammad II, the Conqueror	29th May, 1453
Young mamlukes attack the embassy of the Queen of Cyprus	25th May, 1460
Fleet sails for Cyprus with Prince James	5th August, 1460
Death of Sultan Inal Elevation of his son Ahmad	26th February, 1461
Dethronement of Sultan Ahmad	28th June, 1461
Elevation of Al-Malik-al-Dhahir Khushqadam	28th June, 1461
Return of Mamluke force from Cyprus	9th December, 1463
James II crowned King of Cyprus	1464
Conquest of Syria by Shah Suwar ibn Dulqadir	1467

Death of Sultan Khushqadam	
Elevation of Malik-al-Dhahir Yalbai	10th October, 1467
Dethronement of Sultan Yalbai	
Elevation of Malik-al-Dhahir Timurbugha	5th December, 1467
Defeat and death of Shah Jahan of Black Sheep by Uzun Hasan of White Sheep	December, 1467
Dethronement of Sultan Timurbugha	
Elevation of Qaitbai	31st January, 1468

PERSONALITIES

Mamluke Sultans

Al-Malik-al-Ashraf Inal	1453–1461
Al-Malik-al-Muaiyad Ahmad	1461
Al-Malik-al-Dhahir Khushqadam	1461–1467
Al-Malik-al-Dhahir Yalbai	1467
Al-Malik-al-Dhahir Timurbugha	1467–1468

Ottoman Sultan
Muhammad II, the Conqueror

Turkmans
Shah Jahan, Ruler of the Black Sheep
Uzun Hasan, Ruler of the White Sheep
Shah Suwar ibn Dulqadir, Ruler of Albistan

XIX

Grand Old Man

Our patience will achieve more than our force.

EDMUND BURKE, *Thoughts on the Present Discontents*

From hence let fierce contending nations know
What dire effects from civil discord flow.

ADDISON, *Cato*

The shameful dilapidation into which a great empire must fall by mean reparations on mighty ruins.

EDMUND BURKE, *Thoughts on the Present Discontents*

We find no evidence in Mamluk sources of the military prowess of the Circassians, as we do with reference to the ruling race in the early Mamluk Period.

DAVID AYALON, *The Circassians in the Mamluk Kingdom*

XIX

AL-MALIK-AL-ASHRAF QAITBAI AL DHAHIRI

QAITBAI was the forty-first Mamluke sultan to rule over Egypt and Syria. The usual ceremonies of inauguration were carried out on 1st February, 1468, while Timurbugha was still living in the palace.

A Circassian by race, Qaitbai was imported into Egypt in 1435 and was bought by Barsbai. However he completed his training under Malik-al-Dhahir Jaqmaq, and consequently became a Dhahiri. Jaqmaq made him a junior secretary and an intimate mamluke, where he was a colleague of Timurbugha. Inal made him an ameer of ten, and he became an ameer of drums and then of one hundred under Khushqadam. When Timurbugha became sultan, Qaitbai was made commander-in-chief.

A considerable number of examples have now been given of the careers of ameers who ultimately became sultans. It will be noted that, in the days of the Bahri sultans, ameers were military officers, who spent their days with their men, shooting arrows from horseback or wielding sword and lance. Even the sultans often exercised in arms with the troops. But under the Circassians, the road to promotion became increasingly through admission to the sultan's intimate mamlukes or to appointment to secretarial posts. At the end of a palace career, such officers found themselves suddenly made commander-in-chief with little experience in the field.

In the same way, the Royal Mamlukes, who had been intended by Malik-al-Nasir Muhammad to be the corps d'élite of the army, had become the worst type of Praetorian Guard. They underwent a minimum of military training, but were engrossed in politics, bullied the civilian population, aspired to make and unmake sultans and were ever ready to mutiny for more pay.

With the beginning of the reign of Qaitbai, we take leave of our philosopher and friend, Abu al Mahasin ibn Taghri Birdi. The last entry in his book, *Al Nujoom al Dhahira*, is in 1468, the year of Qaitbai's accession, and he died on 5th June, 1470. Henceforward our principal guide will be Muhammad ibn Iyas. His book, *Al Mashhoor bi Bidaya al Zuhoor*, has indeed been with us since the

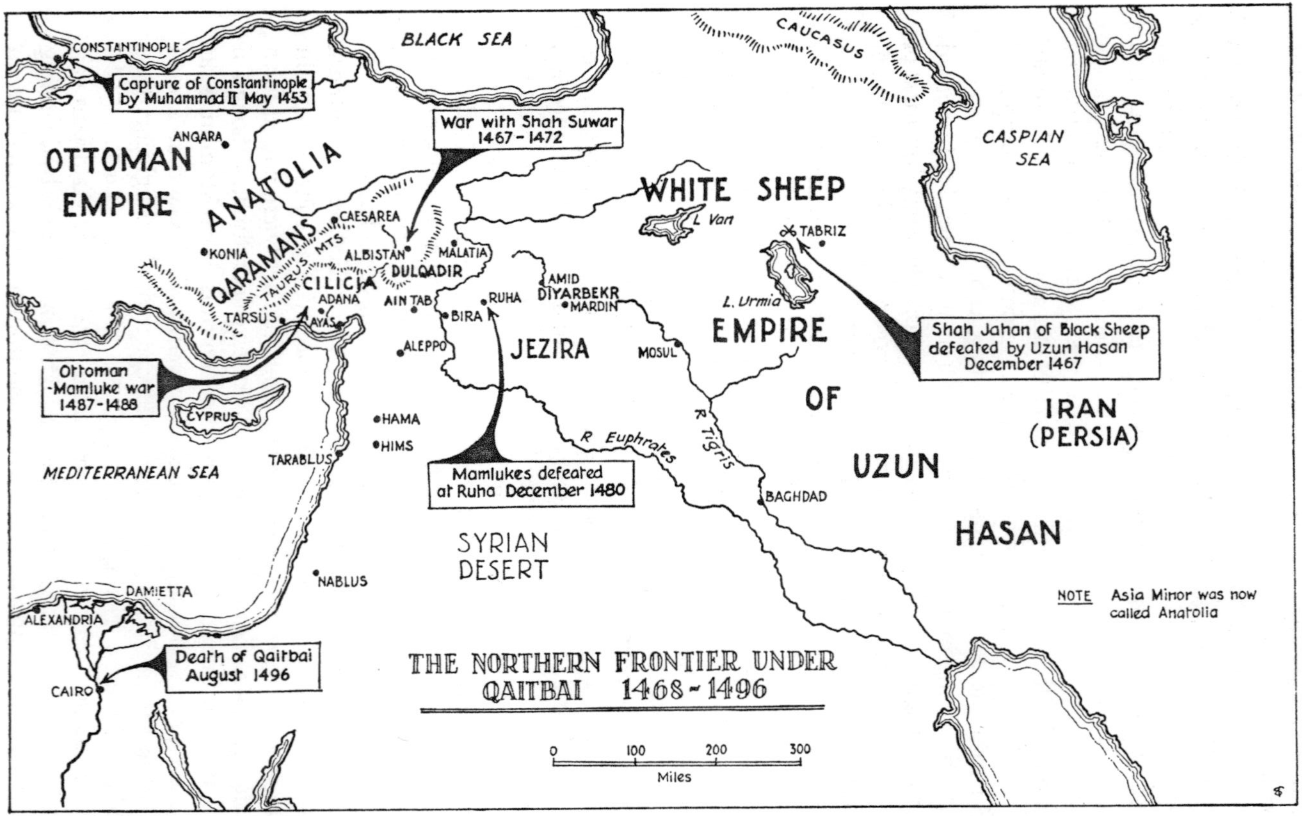

MAP 29

THE NORTHERN FRONTIER UNDER QAITBAI 1468~1496

NOTE Asia Minor was now called Anatolia

Shah Jahan of Black Sheep defeated by Uzun Hasan December 1467

EMPIRE OF UZUN HASAN

IRAN (PERSIA)

WHITE SHEEP

CASPIAN SEA

CAUCASUS

L. Van

L. Urmia

TABRIZ

BAGHDAD

R Tigris

R Euphrates

MOSUL

JEZIRA

AMID
DIYARBEKR
MARDIN

RUHA
BIRA

Mamlukes defeated at Ruha December 1480

SYRIAN DESERT

War with Shah Suwar 1467-1472

BLACK SEA

ANGARA

CONSTANTINOPLE

Capture of Constantinople by Muhammad II May 1453

OTTOMAN EMPIRE

ANATOLIA

KONIA

CAESAREA

TAURUS MTS

DULGADIR

MALATIA

ALBISTAN

AIN TAB

ALEPPO

HAMA

HIMS

KARAMANS

ADANA

TARSUS

CILICIA

AYAS

CYPRUS

Ottoman-Mamluke war 1487-1488

MEDITERRANEAN SEA

TARABLUS

NABLUS

DAMIETTA

ALEXANDRIA

CAIRO

Death of Qaitbai August 1496

Miles
0   100   200   300

beginning, but henceforward he is almost our only source for the next forty-five years.

A campaign was ordered immediately against Shah Suwar ibn Dulqadir. It is interesting that many *aulad al nas* were ordered to report for military service. These, the sons of "nice" people,[1] were presumably a kind of relic of the *halaqa*, descendants of mamlukes, who held military fiefs, but were rarely called up for service. Every Royal Mamluke detailed for the campaign received a hundred dinars. The force consisted of one thousand mamlukes and twenty ameers. The Bahri sultans, it will be remembered, regularly employed eight to ten thousand mamlukes.

On 1st June, 1468, however, the force was completely routed north of Aleppo by Shah Suwar ibn Dulqadir. The army lost most of its horses and weapons, and the commander-in-chief was taken prisoner.

Great efforts were made by Qaitbai to raise a fresh army, but no money was available and the qadhis refused to allow money to be taken from religious bequests. All *aulad al nas* fiefholders were made to report. Each was invited to draw a bow. If he drew it and shot an arrow, he was taken for the army, or was allowed to pay one hundred dinars for his exemption. If he was unable to draw a bow, he was deprived of his fief.

This account reveals that many fiefs were in the possession of persons who had no military training and had never been called up. These fiefs were, of course, intended for soldiers, who were bound to present themselves when needed for war. The small number of mamlukes which could be raised in an emergency was, doubtless, due to the fact that the fiefs which should have paid for soldiers were held by civilians. As in our own days, the public was afraid of war, but grumbled when asked to contribute money for defence.

A column was also sent to suppress the rebellion in southern Egypt, which was done with the usual brutality. The column brought back four hundred women captives. Though they were cowed for a time, the hostility of the tribes was thereby increased, although if well treated, they might have provided recruits. The Mamlukes, as we have seen, behaved well to city Egyptians, who offered no armed threat to them. But to the tribes who were capable of fighting, they used only violent repression.

The White Sheep ruler, Uzun Hasan (the Arabic historians call him Hasan al Taweel) had conquered all northern Persia by defeating and killing Abu Saeed, the great-great-grandson of Tamerlane, in 1467. Uzun Hasan, who had thereby become a power capable of

[1] Page 137.

threatening the Mamlukes or the Ottomans, sent a flattering embassy to Qaitbai. This conciliatory attitude seems, judging by subsequent events, to have been only a ruse.

In addition to all these disasters, an intense outbreak of plague attacked Cairo, great numbers of mamlukes dying while the army was mobilising for the campaign against Shah Suwar. Even after the army had moved off, soldiers continued to die daily during the march to Syria. The morale of all ranks was accordingly low. A sum of a hundred thousand dinars was sent to the Nablus area of northern Palestine, in the hope of raising tribesmen to accompany the army. In June 1469, a report was received that Shah Suwar had been repulsed in an action and his brother killed. Soon, however, another battle was fought north of Aleppo in which the Mamlukes were defeated with heavy losses. In Cairo, Shah Suwar was feared almost as much as Tamerlane had been. Fugitives arrived in Cairo barefoot and in rags.

However, soon afterwards, the Ameer of Malatia unaided defeated Shah Suwar as also did Ibn Ramadhan, a Turkman chief of Cilicia, who was loyal to Egypt. It appeared that it was the Cairo army and the Royal Mamlukes who were always defeated, although the Turkman tribes were able to stand up to Shah Suwar. The war dragged on, while Uzun Hasan returned to Amid, after defeating the descendants of Tamerlane. In Cairo, fears were entertained that the pitiable inefficiency of the Mamluke army might tempt Uzun Hasan to attack Aleppo.

In March 1471, a new army was at last mobilised in Cairo and left for Syria with great pomp and ceremony. In July 1471, the Ameer Yashbak al Duwadar, with this new Mamluke army, retook Ain Tab, Adana and Tarsus.[2] Then a pitched battle was fought on the Sayhan River, in which Shah Suwar suffered a heavy defeat. Abandoned by most of his troops, Suwar asked for terms of peace.

At last, in June 1472, the rebel gave himself up. On 24th August, 1472, the army returned to Cairo in triumph. The city had been lavishly decorated and high prices had been paid for seats in shops or in windows or on the roofs all along Grand Avenue up which the procession was to pass. Everyone was passionately anxious to catch a glimpse of the famous Shah Suwar, who rode in the parade mounted on a fine charger, and dressed in a robe of honour with a large turban. But, beneath this regal display, he was fastened by a chain under his robes, the other end being attached to an ameer of ten, who rode beside him. Twenty brothers and notables of his court rode before him.

[2] Map 29, page 370.

Behind the princely captive rode the Ameer Yashbak, who had commanded the Mamluke army in the campaign. No one in Cairo could remember so glorious a day.

The procession passed through the city amid wild cheering, singing and shouting and everyone was drunk with enthusiasm. But after the victory march, Shah Suwar and his courtiers were stripped of their finery, nailed to wooden planks on the backs of camels, and paraded through the streets in the barbarous Mamluke manner. Before them a herald cried, "This is the fate of those who disobey the sultan." The ghastly torture was continued until all the prisoners were dead with the exception of one boy, on whom the Ameer Yashbak had mercy. The corpses were hung for twenty-four hours on the Zuwaila and Nusr Gates before burial.

But in spite of all the shouting, the five-year war against Shah Suwar had done irreparable damage to the military prestige of the Mamluke Empire. The fact that a petty Turkman prince could defy the empire for so long, and inflict on it numerous defeats, revealed to the world the decadence of the Mamlukes. Not only Uzun Hasan and the White Sheep Turkmans, or the Ottoman sultan, but the Arab tribes of Egypt and Sinai ceased to respect the government. Even the serfs who cultivated their fiefs no longer treated the Mamluke ameers with the same respect as before.

Suwar is described as a handsome man, with a round face, a white skin and blue eyes. Of middle height and thickset build, he was in his forties, of a commanding personality and of great bravery. He was the most famous of the Dulqadir family, the rulers of Albistan. The Turkmans were, of course, small, sallow men, but the inhabitants of Anatolia were of very mixed ethnical origin, and it is impossible to know from what racial stocks Shah Suwar was descended.

*   *   *

Scarcely was the affair of Shah Suwar concluded, than Uzun Hasan—Hasan al Taweel—mobilised an army to invade Syria. Unlike the petty chieftain Shah Suwar, Hasan was a great conqueror, who had defeated the descendants of the mighty Tamerlane. Once again mobilisation was ordered. In December 1472, two thousand Royal Mamlukes set out, under the command of Yashbak Al Duwadar, the conqueror of Suwar. The young mamlukes in the Citadel chose the moment to riot.

Two rival military alliances seemed to be taking shape. Venice, who held colonies and trading stations in the Aegean, was alarmed at the rapidly expanding power of the Ottomans, and sent an embassy to Uzun Hasan, to urge him to attack the Ottomans. Thus an embryo alliance between Venice and Uzun Hasan threatened the two Muslim empires, the Ottomans and the Mamlukes. In 1472, Uzun Hasan invaded Anatolia but his troops were repulsed.

Meanwhile, the Mamluke army commander, the Ameer Yashbak, on the northern frontier, received a letter from the Ottomans, offering military aid against Uzun Hasan and the White Sheep. Yashbak replied by sending a friendly delegation to the Ottomans. Yashbak also defeated a Turkman force sent by Hasan to besiege Bira.[3] An Ottoman ambassador arrived in Cairo to concert measures against the White Sheep. In May 1473, Frankish ships appeared off the Nile Delta, perhaps as allies of Uzun Hasan. Ottoman troops moved eastwards as if to attack Uzun Hasan. A state of acute tension remained between the four powers—the Ottomans, the Mamlukes, Uzun Hasan and Venice.

In November 1473, with the situation in this precarious condition, the young mamlukes again mutinied. Going into the city, they plundered the shops and private houses. In May 1474, a partial détente occurred in the international situation, when an embassy came from Uzun Hasan apologising for his provocative actions, doubtless owing to fear of the Ottomans, who had sent a delegation to Cairo to seek an alliance against the White Sheep.

In the same month, the young mamlukes again rioted. Cairo was in chaos, all the shops being shut.

*   *   *

A perhaps significant event took place in the year 1474. The sultan's wife returned from the pilgrimage and was met at Birkat al Haj[4] outside Cairo by all the ameers and the religious shaikhs, all of whom dismounted to do her honour. Carried in a litter, she was escorted to the palace in a triumphal procession, even the royal parasol being carried over her. When she reached the palace, she gave a reception to the ameers, the senior officials and the notables. A constant increase in the power and influence of women has often, rightly or wrongly, been accepted as a sign of the decadence of any régime.

*   *   *

In 1475, Grand Ameer Uzbek Tatah al Dhahiri began the construction of the Uzbekiya in the centre of Cairo. It had been a piece

³ Map 29, page 370.   ⁴ Map 20, page 151.

of salty land with a few acacias and tamarinth bushes on it. Uzbek spent more than a hundred thousand dinars on it, reclaiming the land and making a lake, round which wealthy families came and built fine houses.

Plague broke out again in December 1476, and increased in intensity in January. Emphasis is again laid on the high rate of mortality among young mamlukes and foreigners. The 1477 epidemic was of a peculiarly virulent type, causing death in twenty-four hours. By March 1477, about two thousand Royal Mamlukes had died. Twenty-five palace eunuchs were also among the dead, leaving the female apartments almost without male servants.

In the middle of this terrible plague, the Ameer Yashbak al Duwadar was one morning out riding at dawn and met an old countryman carrying a basket. The Ameer enquired kindly where the old man was going and was told that he was going into town to sell his eggs, for he had a wife, a son and three daughters to support. Yashbak found twenty eggs in the basket and bought them for one dinar each, thereby providing enough money to support the old peasant's family for several months. Such kindly incidents, scattered through the books of the Arab historians, provide many human touches, and often reveal Mamluke ameers as benevolent and pious old gentlemen.

A pleasant modern touch is supplied by a statement in Ibn Iyas that much discussion was provoked in 1477 by the government's wish to widen the streets, a project involving the demolition of many buildings.

In October 1477, Qaitbai left unexpectedly for Syria with an escort of only forty mamlukes, and a number of officers and officials. All the senior ameers and the army remained in Cairo, Grand Ameer Uzbek Tatah being viceroy. This confident departure for Syria without an army speaks well for the internal stability of the empire.

Early in January 1478, the sultan was back in Cairo. He had visited Aleppo and reached the Euphrates. Cairo had been magnificently decorated and the royal procession passed through the city with great pomp. Qaitbai had been away for four months, had met great numbers of people and his prestige had been vastly increased.

Nevertheless the known military weakness of the empire had lost the government the respect of the tribes, whom the Mamlukes had always treated with brutality when the army was strong. The Huwwára tribe in southern Egypt, an arabicised Berber group, rebelled, but were driven into Nubia. Seven members of the chief's family, taken prisoners, were nailed on camels and paraded through the streets of Cairo. Ibn Iyas, a cultured Egyptian, comments that the people felt pity for them.

On 6th January, 1478, Uzun Hasan died. He had made himself ruler of a vast area extending from Diyarbekr and eastern Anatolia and including nearly all Persia and Iraq, but after his death his empire disintegrated. The Mamlukes were greatly relieved at the death of this stormy petrel.

In April 1479, the Khalif Mustanjid died. He was the thirteenth Abbasid khalif in Egypt, had held the position for twenty-five years, and had invested five sultans.

This year also died the Princess Zainab,[5] the widow of Malik-al-Ashraf Inal. She had been his only wife and had never remarried. There was never again to be a princess like her, comments Ibn Iyas, a woman of great personality, universally respected. Women, as we have seen, played a considerable rôle among the Mamlukes. In 1479, the sultan went on pilgrimage to Mecca. The two great ameers of his reign, Yashbak al Duwadar and the Grand Ameer Uzbek Tatah, were left in Cairo.

In the year 1480, Saif, the shaikh of the bedouin Fadhl tribe in the Syrian desert, rebelled and defeated and killed the Viceroy of Hama. In May, a punitive force set out, under Yashbak al Duwadar, and including five hundred Royal Mamlukes. Saif had taken refuge in Ruha, the ancient Edessa, now called Urfa, a town held by a garrison of White Sheep from Yaqoub, the son of Uzun Hasan.[6]

Yashbak marched against Ruha, but the Turkman garrison came out and gave battle, and in December 1480 completely defeated the Mamluke army. Yashbak, its commander, was captured and beheaded. The Viceroys of Damascus and Aleppo, also taken prisoners with great numbers of their troops, were paraded through the White Sheep dominions, dressed in rags and loaded with chains, together with great quantities of horses, weapons and loot.

Ibn Iyas calls this the most disgraceful defeat ever suffered by a Mamluke army. When we remember that these Mamlukes defeated the great Mongol conquerors from Hulagu onwards, we are astounded to see their army almost annihilated by the garrison of a small town, in what Ibn Iyas calls "one short hour". These repeated defeats can only be attributed to the lack of discipline and training. In a constant state of mutiny demanding more pay and privileges, the mamlukes no longer felt either a sense of duty or military pride.

Yashbak al Duwadar had enjoyed a brilliant career; widely respected, wealthy, generous and public spirited, he was one of the

---

[5] The wives of sultans were called princesses, not sultanas.
[6] Map 29, page 370.

new type of ameers, the courtly gentleman rather than the fighting soldier.

The disaster at Ruha caused consternation in Cairo. It was feared that the triumphant Turkmans might attack Aleppo. Orders were issued to raise a new army to be commanded by Grand Ameer Uzbek Tatah.

In March 1481, however, a despatch was received from Uzbek, who had gone on ahead to Aleppo. He reported that he had exchanged embassies with Yaqoub ibn Uzun Hasan of Tabriz. Yaqoub apologised for the "regrettable incident" at Ruha and sent back the Mamluke prisoners.

On 3rd May, 1481, died the Ottoman sultan, Muhammad II, the Conqueror. He had ruled for thirty-one years and had raised the Ottoman Empire to a new pinnacle of greatness and power. His eldest son, Bayazid, was, at the time, the governor of Amasia, while his second son, Jem, was the governor of Qaraman, which had been annexed by the Ottomans. It seems that Muhammad wished his second son, Jem, to inherit the throne, but the Janissaries mutinied in Istanbul (Constantinople) and made Bayazid sultan. On this occasion, for the first time, the Janissaries insisted on a donative on the occasion of the accession.

The career of the Corps of Janissaries was closely to resemble that of the mamlukes. They were a corps raised probably by Orkhan, the Ottoman ruler (1326–1359). Until then, the Ottoman forces had been of a feudal character and displayed the usual unreliable qualities of feudal levies. It was decided to form a full-time regular paid infantry to stiffen them. The recruits, like the mamlukes, were young boys, but they were taken by force from Christian families and converted to Islam. Thenceforward, soldiering became their whole lives. For two hundred or more years, the Janissaries were the world's finest infantry, as the Mamlukes had been the best cavalry. But from the sixteenth century onwards, they followed the same course as the mamlukes, interfering in politics and frequently in a state of mutiny.

Jem, the unsuccessful claimant to the Ottoman throne, arrived in Aleppo, and Qaitbai, ill-advisedly, invited him to Cairo. In 1482, at his own request, he returned to Ottoman territory in order to fight his brother, but was defeated. Endeavouring to escape by sea, he was captured by the Franks. From our point of view, the significance of the incident was that Qaitbai's reception of Jem was regarded by the Ottoman Sultan Bayazid as an unfriendly act.

*   *   *

In Cairo, the young mamlukes were now constantly in a state of revolt. In June 1483, for example, they rioted in Cairo, burned down houses and looted the shops. No disciplinary action was taken. These constant riots provided the opportunity for common thieves and bandits to rob and assault. Crimes of violence continued to increase all over Egypt. Meat was scarce in Cairo, because farmers were afraid to bring sheep into the city for sale, as the young mamlukes seized them without paying for them.

In July 1483, Ali Daulat ibn Dulqadir, the ruling prince or Albistan, laid siege to Malatia. It was reported that he had been subsidised by the Ottoman sultan, Bayazid, as revenge for Qaitbai's support of Jem. A force was sent from Cairo, including some five hundred Royal Mamlukes, but was defeated by Ali Daulat, who was the younger brother of Shah Suwar, the former Dulqadir rebel. In October 1484, the Viceroy of Aleppo was killed. Shortly afterwards, however, on the arrival of reinforcements from Cairo, Ali Daulat suffered a defeat and a number of Ottoman soldiers and several regimental colours were captured, fighting on the side of the Turkmans. Thenceforward real hostility grew between the Ottomans and the Mamlukes. The question of relations with the Ottomans was discussed by the sultan in the council. It was decided to placate Sultan Bayazid II by sending an embassy with gifts.

A further cause of Ottoman resentment was that an Indian ruler had sent a royal gift to Sultan Bayazid, but it had been seized by the customs office in Jidda. The articles were eventually released but Qaitbai kept a dagger, set with gold and jewels.

A new army was sent against Ali Daulat in 1485 and efforts were made to raise further troops. Retired mamlukes, formerly in the personal service of ameers, were sought out. The *aulad al nas*, descendants of mamlukes who held fiefs, were combed through once more. Mamlukes detailed to go on active service seized mules and horses from civilians without payment. In November 1486, a new force of three thousand mamlukes left Cairo for the north. In further engagements in the north, Ottoman army officers were taken prisoners. The embassy sent to Istanbul was coldly received by the Ottomans.

This year, 1486, the sultan's horse one day reared and fell back on him, breaking his thigh. Qaitbai was laid up for three months, after which the fracture seemed to have healed. Cairo was decorated and the sultan's recovery was the cause of genuine popular rejoicing.

At this crisis on the northern frontier, the army sent from Cairo mutinied in Aleppo. The sultan sent fifty dinars for each man, and the men resumed duty. Cairo, however, was in anarchy owing to particularly savage riots by the young mamlukes in protest against the high cost of living. For several days, all shops were shut, dwelling-houses barred and shuttered and the streets deserted. Eventually all young mamlukes were given fifty dinars each and the riot subsided. The cost of living, however, continued to increase, and soon the troops were again demanding more pay.

Reports of Ottoman troop concentrations continuing, the sultan ordered the merchants of Cairo to produce forty thousand dinars for the army. After much haggling, they produced twelve thousand. The Jews and the Christians were also told to raise funds. The small-ness of the sums raised, in spite of all these efforts, is remarkable. The whole empire seemed to have shrunk. Where once ten thousand Royal Mamlukes could be sent at short notice, now infinite trouble was needed to raise one thousand men. In earlier times, four hundred thousand dinars or more were spent to equip an expedition, now painful efforts were needed to produce twelve thousand dinars. The reduction in the sums available was made more catastrophic by the fact that the value of money had been greatly reduced.

In March 1487, reports reached Cairo that the Ottomans had now openly invaded the plain of Cilicia and reached Adana.[7] In April, the invaders reached Ayas on the Gulf of Alexandretta. The very survival of the empire seemed to be at stake. In this crisis, a supreme effort was made. Grand Ameer Uzbek Tatah raised four thousand mamlukes for a new army. Officers were sent to raise the tribes in the Nablus area. A total of a hundred thousand dinars was collected for the cost of the campaign.

The mamlukes leaving for the front seized all mules and camels without payment, causing great hardship. Even water for drinking was scarce in Cairo, as it was normally carried down the streets on the backs of camels or mules. An Ottoman army was sent by sea to land on the Syrian coast, but most fortunately it was wrecked by a storm, and the seaborne operation ended in disaster.

At last, on 18th August, 1488, the Ottomans were defeated by the new army raised by Grand Ameer Uzbek Tatah. An Ottoman force was besieged in Adana, and, after three months of resistance, sur-rendered on terms. Bands played in Cairo for seven days to celebrate the victory.

In 1489, the young mamlukes were again making trouble, demand-ing a donative of a hundred dinars per man for expenses. Qaitbai summoned the qadhis and the ameers and told them there was no money to give the mamlukes and that he was abdicating. He stood up and began to take off his robes, asking those present to choose

[7] Map 29, page 370.

another sultan. The qadhis prevented him from disrobing, while the ameers went to negotiate with the young mamlukes, who eventually agreed to settle for fifty dinars, forty in cash and ten to follow. As the sultan had already abdicated, the khalif had to be called in to reinstate him. The cost of living, however, continued to rise.

Urgent demands having been received for reinforcements for Aleppo, the old struggle to squeeze more money and raise more men was resumed. In the autumn of 1489, however, a letter was received from the wazeer of the Ottoman sultan suggesting peace, but then nothing more was heard.

In February 1490, as a result of intelligence reports of Ottoman military preparations, orders were given to raise a new army. Once again the *aulad al nas* fiefholders were summoned and were ordered to learn to shoot handguns or muskets. They were given thirty dinars per man and a camel between two. The Janissaries, the infantry backbone of the Ottoman armies, were already armed with a personal firearm, and were full-time regular soldiers, who spent their days training. The casual way in which the *aulad al nas* were told verbally to learn to shoot was absurd. However, a number of them were sent with the army. Four thousand Royal Mamlukes were drafted into the expedition under Grand Ameer Uzbek Tatah. The Mamluke column reached Caesarea in Anatolia.[8] The sultan again begged to be allowed to abdicate and retire to Mecca.

Grand Ameer Uzbek returned to Cairo at the end of November 1490. He had marched the army round the frontiers during the summer without opposition. In January 1491, the young mamlukes again mutinied, demanding more money to set off the still-increasing cost of living. The sultan threatened to escape by night and go to live in Mecca. Money was squeezed from hospitals and orphanages and the pensions of crippled old soldiers were cut, to satisfy the young mamlukes. In the spring of 1491, however, an embassy came from the Ottomans to discuss peace and prisoners of war were released.

Iraq and Persia were in chaos owing to internal feuds between the sons of Uzun Hasan. One of the sons, Yaqoub, killed his brother. The Ottomans seemed inclined to leave the Mamlukes and invade the dominions of the Turkmans in eastern Anatolia.

In May 1491, a virulent epidemic of plague fell upon Cairo. Ibn Iyas states that there had been no plague for sixteen years, but that, during that period, sexual immorality and drunkenness had greatly increased. The Prophet, he claimed, had said that any nation in which adultery increased would be overtaken by disaster.

[8] Map 29, page 370.

The year 1495 was passed in relative peace on the northern frontiers. It should not be imagined, however, that the Mamlukes had defeated the Ottoman Empire. The ethos of the Ottoman state, since the days of Othman, its founder, had been that of Muslim holy war against Christian Europe. During the reign of Bayazid II (1481–1512), the Ottoman Empire had been at war with Venice, Hungary and Poland and had been constantly troubled by the conditions of anarchy which prevailed in eastern Anatolia, in the former territory of Uzun Hasan. Thus to the Ottomans, the fighting in Albistan and Cilicia had been only a minor sideshow although, as we have seen, the Mamlukes had been obliged to strain every nerve to hold their own.

In the summer of 1495, Grand Ameer Uzbek was obliged to flee from Cairo in disguise and to take refuge in Mecca. He had been commander-in-chief for seventeen years and had won the two campaigns which had freed the northern borders from Ottoman invasion. But in 1495 he was unlucky enough to incur the displeasure of the young mamlukes, and was obliged to abandon his office of commander-in-chief and to flee for his life.

It must be realised that the young mamlukes, who played so important a part in the destruction of the Mamluke Empire, were adolescent recruits still under instruction. Legally they were still slaves. It is impossible to avoid a comparison between their endless riots and mutinies, and the frequent strikes, protests and riots by students in our own times. Theoretically, the young mamlukes, like the students in modern states, were hopelessly weak. Yet it seems as if, in an old and decadent society, responsible men of mature age fall under the domination of the young.

In this year, the ruler of Samarqand, Mahmood ibn abi Saeed, was assassinated. He was Mahmood ibn abi Saeed ibn Ahmad ibn Mirza Shah ibn Tamerlane, and was the last ruler of Tamerlane's family. But Baber, the son of Umar Shaikh Mirza, another son of Abu Saeed, had appeared in northern Khurasan and Ferghana. In 1503, Baber seized Kabul. Two years later, he invaded India and founded the Moghul (Mongol) dynasty, which was to rule till the arrival of the British.

*   *   *

In the summer of 1496, the sultan ordered a general parade at which every officer and man was required to renew his oath of loyalty. He then gave a donative of a hundred dinars each to the young Royal Mamlukes, fifty dinars to employed mamlukes formerly with ameers, and twenty or thirty dinars each to *aulad al nas*, who were fit for military service. Some old mamlukes, however, received a hundred or fifty dinars.

We are inclined to visualise Mamluke ameers as greedy and tyrannical, but they may also have been in acute difficulties due to the high cost of living. Ibn Iyas mentions a number of such officers who asked the sultan for grants of money, fiefs or favours and who, when refused, committed suicide.

In August 1496, the sultan fell ill and took to his bed with acute dysentery. After the flight of Uzbek Tatah, the Ameer Timraz al Shemsi was made commander-in-chief. As the sultan appeared to be dying, Timraz took Muhammad, the son of Qaitbai, to the Chain Gate, preparatory to making him sultan. But the Ameer Qansuh Khamsmiya suddenly seized Timraz and sent him under escort to prison in Alexandria.

On 7th August, Qansuh Khamsmiya summoned the khalif, the qadhis and the ameers to the chamber above the Chain Gate. Qaitbai was declared deposed and Muhammad was made sultan. The sultan died the next day.

*   *   *

Qaitbai was about eighty-six years old and had reigned for twenty-eight years, the longest reign in all Mamluke history, except Al-Nasir Muhammad. All his life he had been respected. He had never been imprisoned or exiled throughout all his career. There was something about him which inspired reverence, his appearance was venerable and he looked the picture of a sultan. Tall in stature, of a rather dark complexion, he was slender and had a grey beard. In his youth he had been a fine horseman, especially adept with the lance.

He was broadminded and wise, and was thoroughly conversant with the affairs of the empire. He was never hasty in his decisions and gave every problem careful thought, with the result that he was never taken unawares by events. Ibn Iyas says that he would have been the best of all sultans, had he not been parsimonious. Ibn Iyas is not always reasonable on this subject, for he reports the bankruptcy of the treasury, but bitterly criticises the action taken by the sultan to raise money.

Yet even Ibn Iyas says that he might be excused, because he was forced to fight Shah Suwar ibn Dulqadir, Uzun Hasan and the Ottomans, all of whom were the aggressors. He is alleged to have raised 7,065,000 dinars to pay for military campaigns which were forced upon him. At various times he bought eight thousand mam-

5 Mosque of Qaitbai

lukes, though many of these died in epidemics of plague. All subsequent sultans until the end of the empire had been his mamlukes.

Qaitbai was personally abstemious, never touched alcohol or used drugs. He was fond of learning, was well read and himself wrote a number of literary pieces. He was considerate of the poor and had a social gift which enabled him to talk freely with all classes and to make them feel at ease. He was hospitable, gave generously to charity and was deeply religious.

He married only one wife, who remained with him till he died, and who gave him only one son, Muhammad, who succeeded him.

He was a great builder, especially of schools and mosques. He built schools in Mecca, Medina, Jerusalem, Damascus, Gaza, Damietta and Alexandria. In Egypt, the mosques and schools which he built are too numerous to enumerate. He also opened new roads, repaired the irrigation dykes and executed other useful and beautiful works.

Qaitbai would have been a great ruler in any age and in any country.

NOTABLE EVENTS

Accession of Al-Malik-al-Ashraf Qaitbai	1st February, 1468
Mamlukes defeated by Shah Suwar ibn Dulqadir	1st June, 1468
Death of Abu-al-Mahasin ibn Taghri Birdi	5th June, 1470
Surrender of Shah Suwar	June, 1472
Threat of war with Uzun Hasan	1472–1474
Riots by young mamlukes	{ November, 1473 May, 1474
Death of Uzun Hasan	6th January, 1478
Defeat of the Mamluke army at Ruha (Edessa)	December, 1480
Death of Sultan Muhammad II, the Conqueror / Accession of his son, Bayazid II	3rd May, 1481
Jem, pretender to the Ottoman throne, in Cairo	1481–1482
Ottoman invasion of Cilicia	March, 1487
Ottomans defeated by Grand Ameer Uzbek	18th August, 1488
Death of Qaitbai	8th August, 1496

PERSONALITIES

Mamluke Sultan
Al-Malik-al-Ashraf Qaitbai al Dhahiri

Other Mamlukes
Ameer Yashbak al Duwadar
Grand Ameer Uzbek Tatah

Ottoman Sultans
Muhammad II, the Conqueror of Constantinople
His son, Bayazid II

Ottoman Pretender
Ameer Jem, son of Muhammad II

Turkmans
Uzun Hasan (Hasan al Taweel), chief of the White Sheep
Shah Jahan, chief of the Black Sheep, killed by Uzun
    Hasan

XX

Toman the Traitor

I am justly killed with my own treachery.

SHAKESPEARE, *Hamlet*

Hateful to me as are the gates of hell
Is he who, hiding one thing in his heart,
Utters another.

HOMER, *Iliad*

What is a king? A man condemned to bear
The public burden of the nation's care.

MATTHEW PRIOR, *Solomon*

Treason doth never prosper; what's the reason?
For if it prosper, none dare call it treason.

JOHN HARRINGTON, *Of Treason*

I charge thee, fling away ambition
By that sin fell the angels.

SHAKESPEARE, *King Henry VIII*

XX

AL-MALIK-AL-NASIR MUHAMMAD
IBN QAITBAI

AT the elevation of Muhammad, the fifteen-year-old son of
Qaitbai, the royal parasol was carried by Qansuh[1] Khams-
miya, who was made commander-in-chief in succession to
Timraz al Shemsi, whom he himself had kidnapped and sent to
Alexandria. The public was deeply distressed at the death of Qaitbai,
which was marked by a genuine outburst of popular mourning.

Muhammad was a lively, handsome boy, but it was said that
Qaitbai had not wished his son to succeed him, had not death overtaken
him before he could produce an alternative plan. The ameers and
officials swore loyalty on the Qoran, but Qansuh Khamsmiya was
not present at the ceremony. It had now almost become an established custom for the son of a deceased sultan to succeed him, the
most prominent ameer being made commander-in-chief and succeed-
ing to the throne within a year.

Qansuh spent the next six months in preparing his own accession.
His enemies were arrested, imprisoned, or executed, his supporters
were given the key posts. Suddenly, probably on 3rd February, 1497,
Qansuh summoned the khalif, qadhis and ameers to the chamber
over the Chain Gate, and persuaded them to dethrone Muhammad
and to raise himself to the sultanate. Qansuh then sent to arrest
Muhammad and to confine him to an apartment in the palace.

Quite unexpectedly, a thousand of Qaitbai's mamlukes objected,
placed the palace in a state of defence, opened the armoury, and
extracted weapons, and began shooting at Qansuh and the ameers,
who replied from the royal stables.[2] On the third day of fighting, the
mamlukes threw gunpowder and used flame-throwers against the
stables and set them on fire. Qansuh and his supporters were obliged
to retire. As Qansuh rode away, he was shot by a sniper and fell from
his horse. The mamlukes then rushed the stables, seized the khalif

---

[1] Certain names seem to have been fashionable at various times. We formerly saw
several Yalbughas in a short time, and then no more. Now we find a frequent appearance
of the name Qansuh.

[2] Map 21, page 158.

and the qadhis and robbed the ameers. The incident was notable in that there were no ameers or officers with the mamlukes.

The next morning the khalif and the qadhis went up to the palace, congratulated Sultan Muhammad and reinvested him with the sultanate. The drums were beaten to announce good news, and the palace mamlukes donned yellow favours as a sign of rejoicing. Qansuh's supporters were dismissed and his enemies promoted. Cairo was in chaos, shops and houses were looted and the public barricaded themselves in their homes. Tribesmen came in from the country and plundered the suburbs. The sultan's maternal uncle, Qansuh ibn Qansuh, was given a post in the Citadel.

On 21st February, 1497, Qansuh Khamsmiya tried to organise a new rising in Cairo, but it failed. Qansuh Khamsmiya, endeavouring to escape to Syria, was killed in a skirmish at Khan Yunis, south of Gaza. Qaitbai's mamlukes insisted that Sultan Muhammad take the name of Malik-al-Ashraf like his father, though he had received the name of Malik-al-Nasir on his elevation. The reason was that, if he remained Malik-al-Nasir, mamlukes bought by him would be Nasiris. But if he took Qaitbai's throne-name, Malik-al-Ashraf, the mamlukes he bought would be Ashrafis, indistinguishable from those of his father.

Muhammad, however, behaved like an adolescent. With his boon companions he wandered through the streets of Cairo. Aqbirdi al Duwadar, an ameer of one hundred, arrived from Syria, seemingly hoping to be commander-in-chief, but the Citadel mamlukes refused to admit him. Aqbirdi seized the Sultan Hasan mosque, and bombarded the Citadel, as in the days of Yalbugha and Mintash. After an unsuccessful siege of thirty-one days, Aqbirdi marched back to Syria with about a thousand men. For thirty-one days, shops and houses in Cairo had been barricaded and no woman had ventured in the streets.

When Aqbirdi had gone, the mamlukes cut off the head of Timraz al Shemsi, the commander-in-chief. He had been an honourable, popular and generous officer and was eighty-five years old. Cairo was in the hands of a mob of mamlukes, with no one to wield even a semblance of authority. The rioters not only robbed shops and houses, but even schools and mosques from which they stole the carpets, the lamps, the brasswork, the windows and the doors. Food prices soared and most of the harvest remained uncut. Grand Ameer Uzbek Tatah was summoned from Mecca, where he had been some two years and two months in retirement, and was reappointed commander-in-chief.

Much friction had arisen between the young sultan and the

ameers owing to the irresponsible and childish conduct of the former. One day in 1498, when the sultan was playing polo with the ameers, a certain Toman Bai took the ball from him. Al-Nasir Muhammad was so angry that he galloped after Toman Bai and struck him several times on the back with his polo stick. The incident was to have tragic results.

In February 1498, plague appeared in Cairo as it did so often in times of trouble. The mamlukes were extremely exasperated against the sultan and began to talk of replacing him by his uncle, Qansuh ibn Qansuh. In March an expedition sent in pursuit of Aqbirdi al Duwadar defeated him north of Aleppo. The immense amount of plunder acquired by ordinary mamlukes during this time of anarchy is illustrated by the case of one who died and who, according to Ibn Iyas, was found to be in possession of fifteen thousand gold dinars.

Tribes on the edge of the delta revolted in 1498 and refused to pay taxes. The sultan ordered the despatch of a punitive column, but no ameers or mamlukes consented to go, and the rebellion continued, no taxes being collected. The sultan ordered four ameers to go into exile at Mecca, but they replied openly that they would not go.

On 1st November, 1498, the sultan went out riding with two young cousins, and passed a small group of tents under the command of Toman Bai, who had been detailed to take a column to restore order among the delta tribes. Toman Bai came out of his tent and offered the sultan a bowl of yoghurt, which he began to drink sitting on his horse's back, while Toman Bai held the horse's head. At this moment, a party of Toman Bai's mamlukes came out of the tents and slashed the sultan and his attendants to death.

Malik-al-Nasir Muhammad was a handsome boy, with a white skin, a slender figure and of medium height. He was seventeen years old when he died. He was very childish in his conduct, enjoyed low company and committed many disgraceful actions. He was probably the most immoral of all the Mamluke sultans. It is extraordinary that he survived for two years and one month. His survival was probably due to the intense rivalry between Qansuh Khamsmiya and Aqbirdi al Duwadar, both of whom wished to replace him.

The reign passed in constant disturbances, crimes of violence, civil war and a disastrous epidemic of plague.

- -

AL-MALIK-AL-DHAHIR QANSUH
IBN QANSUH

- -

Malik-al-Nasir Muhammad was succeeded by his maternal uncle,

Qansuh ibn Qansuh, a former mamluke of Qaitbai, who had him trained as a clerk. He had apparently been a sultan's mamluke for some time before it was discovered that he was the brother of the sultan's wife. As a result, Qaitbai gave him horses and clothing and a post on the palace staff. When Qansuh Khamsmiya attempted his coup d'état, Qansuh ibn Qansuh was one of the leaders of the young mamlukes who defeated the attempt. As a result, the young sultan made his uncle an ameer of drums. When Aqbirdi al Duwadar was driven out, the sultan's uncle became executive secretary of the government.

When Sultan Muhammad was murdered by Toman Bai, the ameers were taken unawares. They assembled in the house of Grand Ameer Uzbek Tatah, and pressed him to be sultan, but he absolutely refused. Finally they turned to Qansuh, the uncle of the late sultan. The khalif and the qadhis were hastily summoned and Qansuh was made sultan with the throne-name of Malik-al-Dhahir. It was 3rd November, 1498, Surprisingly to us, Toman Bai, the murderer of the late sultan, was made executive secretary of the government.

The new sultan was not yet thirty years old, but his accession was popular, largely owing to the public relief at getting rid of Sultan Muhammad. The rise of Qansuh to the sultanate was unprecedented for he had only arrived in Egypt as a slave six years before.

Aqbirdi al Duwadar reappeared in the north and laid siege to Aleppo. The mobilisation of an expedition was ordered to march against him. The sultan, meanwhile, sent him a safe-conduct and offered him the post of Viceroy of Tarablus, which he accepted. But before he could take up his post, he died in Syria. Ibn Iyas praises him for his capabilities, his generosity and his popular manners. He had been a mamluke of Qaitbai and had succeeded Yashbak as chief secretary, when the latter was killed at the disgraceful defeat at Ruha (Edessa). He had remained chief secretary for sixteen years but, like so many ameers, had been ruined by his rivalry with a brother-officer. Both he and Qansuh Khamsmiya had been tempted by the succession of the boy Malik-al-Nasir Muhammad, to aspire to the throne, until their mutual jealousy destroyed them both.

Uzbek Tatah, the Grand Ameer, died in 1499. He had been a mamluke of Jaqmaq, but had before that been trained as a clerk by Barsbai. He had married two successive daughters of Jaqmaq, and filled many senior posts, until he became commander-in-chief under Qaitbai in 1468, and retained the post for thirty years. He had shown great determination in the field and won the war against the Ottomans in Cilicia.

Uzbek was highly respected, benevolent, generous and categorically refused to be sultan. The Mamluke Empire produced few

greater men, both from the angle of efficiency and of moral character. He spent large sums of his private money in the public service,
but when he died he left seven hundred thousand dinars, which were
immediately seized by the state. He would have been much richer, if
he had not spent a great part of his fortune on the army and in public
benevolence. The Uzbekiya, in the heart of Cairo, remains to this
day as his memorial.

Loyal as was the Grand Ameer Uzbek, it is interesting to notice
that the great ameers could still accumulate immense fortunes,
while the state treasury was always empty. In every crisis, the merchants, the civil officials, the Jews and the Christians were squeezed
for money, but not the great ameers.

In November 1499, the Viceroy of Damascus, the Ameer Qasruh,
declared himself in rebellion. The sultan sent an emissary to attempt
conciliation without success. A column of two thousand mamlukes
was consequently mobilised in Cairo to proceed to Damascus. At this
moment, Toman Bai, the chief secretary and the murderer of Sultan
Muhammad, the son of Qaitbai, camped at Jiza and declared himself also in rebellion. Crossing the Nile from Imbaba to Bulaq, he
established himself in the Uzbekiya. Calling a meeting of ameers, he
agreed with them to dethrone the sultan, and proceeded to lay siege
to the Citadel.

Only a thousand mamlukes remained with Sultan Qansuh. After
three days, Toman Bai captured the Chain Gate. The same night,
Qansuh, disguised as a woman, slipped out of the Citadel and went
into hiding. He had been sultan for one year and eight months. Ibn
Iyas describes him as pleasant-mannered, a good mixer, who always
agreed with the proposals of his council. His reign was a time of
reconstruction after the anarchy of Al-Nasir Muhammad's sultanate.
Tribal disturbances east and west of the delta decreased, the cost of
living fell, and there were no outrages by the Royal Mamlukes.

Although Qansuh did no one any harm, he was presumably not
strong enough to deal with such violent ameers as Toman Bai.
Moreover, his rise to the sultanate had been so rapid that he had no
solid group of barrack-comrades to support him. Qansuh was
slender, of a pale complexion and was probably some thirty years old
when he was dethroned.

- -

AL-MALIK-AL-ASHRAF JANBULAT IBN
YASHBAK AL ASHRAFI (QAITBAI)

- -

Janbulat was a Circassian, who had been bought as a boy by the

Ameer Yashbak al Duwadar, the chief secretary, who had him well educated, and taught Arabic and the Qoran. He was given by Yashbak to Qaitbai, who freed him and made him an intimate mamluke. In 1489, he became an ameer of ten and later an ameer of one hundred and chief secretary of the government. When Grand Ameer Uzbek died, in the reign of Qansuh ibn Qansuh, he was made commander-in-chief.

After the disappearance of Qansuh, Cairo remained for three days without a sultan. The murderer of Sultan Malik-al-Nasir Muhammad, and the instigator of the revolt against Qansuh had been Toman Bai, who coveted the sultanate himself. But he was junior to Janbulat, and hesitated to snatch at the throne. He decided, therefore, to allow Janbulat to be sultan and then to ensure his failure. The latter did not covet the throne, but was obliged by the ameers to accept.

He began by making a mistake, writing to Qasruh, the Viceroy of Damascus, who was in revolt, and offering him the post of commander-in-chief. But Qasruh administered a severe rebuff to the sultan by rejecting the offer.

Twenty-four days after his disappearance, Qansuh ibn Qansuh was arrested. His wife and her slave girls had been tortured to reveal his whereabouts but none of them had talked—incidentally an interesting sidelight on domestic slavery, and the relations between master, mistress and the slaves. Qansuh's hiding place was revealed by one of the *aulad al nas*. Janbulat, however, was his brother-in-law and arranged for him to be sent quietly to Alexandria.

Meanwhile, in the autumn of 1500, Toman Bai contrived to gain influence and to accumulate money and offices. Then he offered to mediate between Janbulat and the rebel viceroy, Qasruh. Janbulat was completely deceived and accepted the proposal, while in reality Qasruh's rebellion had all along been instigated by Toman Bai himself. Orders were issued for the mobilisation of a force, including a thousand Royal Mamlukes, to go and fight Qasruh, the command being entrusted to Toman Bai.

No sooner did this army reach Damascus, than Toman Bai conferred with the rebel Qasruh, and a proclamation was issued, announcing the elevation of Toman Bai to the sultanate, with the throne-name of Al-Malik-al-Aadil—the Just King. The rebel Qasruh was named as commander-in-chief, and Qansuh al Ghori, of whom we shall hear more, was appointed chief secretary. All the principal government posts were allotted by Toman Bai to his friends, while he was still in Damascus.

In Cairo, Janbulat suddenly awoke to the treachery of Toman Bai, in whom he had placed all his confidence. In the latter half of December 1500, Toman Bai left Damascus and marched on Cairo, which he entered in triumph on 2nd January, 1501, unopposed. The next day, the rebels attacked the Citadel, dug trenches, mounted guns and opened a heavy bombardment. On 9th January, Toman Bai's men captured the Chain Gate and poured into the Citadel. Janbulat was arrested and loaded with chains. At the end of January, he was transferred by boat to the fortress of Alexandria. He had been sultan for six and a half months.

Janbulat seems to have been a somewhat stupid man. Throughout his reign, he placed his entire confidence in Toman Bai, who was busily betraying him. The civil population were squeezed throughout the six months to provide money to enable the sultan to give a donative to the Royal Mamlukes. Janbulat was tall, with a white skin, a black beard and a handsome appearance. He was forty years old.

AL-MALIK-AL-AADIL TOMAN BAI AL ASHRAFI (QAITBAI)

Toman Bai was a Circassian, who had been bought by a Viceroy of Damascus, who gave him to Qaitbai. The latter had him educated as a clerk, while he was a Royal Mamluke, and then freed him, making him an intimate mamluke, and then an ameer of ten. In 1496, he became governor of Alexandria, but soon returned to Cairo as an ameer of one hundred. He became chief secretary under Malik-al-Dhahir Qansuh ibn Qansuh, while, under Janbulat, he assumed a large number of appointments at the same time.

After his own investiture, he made the rebel Viceroy of Damascus, Qasruh, commander-in-chief. The city was decorated, for Toman Bai was popular with the Egyptian public. Qasruh had been principally instrumental in raising Toman Bai to the throne, by his concerted rebellion in Damascus. Shortly after the elevation of the new sultan, Qasruh went up to the palace and dined with Toman Bai. After dinner, the sultan said to his guest, "I am afraid of you, Grand Ameer." Some mamlukes then seized the commander-in-chief and removed him to another apartment, where he was strangled.

We have seen many Mamluke treacheries, but Toman Bai far exceeded all rivals. Grand Ameer Qasruh had committed an offence which Toman Bai was unwilling to overlook—he had made himself loved and respected by all the ameers and the army. Toman Bai, who had himself betrayed three sultans, naturally suspected the intentions of his own right-hand man, with whom he had exchanged solemn oaths. Qasruh had been completely loyal to Toman Bai who, by thus betraying him, committed not only a crime but a mistake.

Qasruh, says Ibn Iyas, was a man of social virtues, who never indulged in women or drink, was generous with his money and brave in battle, though perhaps over-credulous. He was just under fifty years of age. The treachery of which he was the victim finally alienated the affection of everyone from Toman Bai. Shortly afterwards, orders were sent to strangle Janbulat in the fortress of Alexandria.

But nemesis was soon to overtake the arch traitor. Doubtless his own treacheries made him suspicious of all the ameers about him. Increasing numbers of them were arrested, while others went underground for fear of being apprehended. Even the common mamlukes were now against him. Suddenly one day, the mamlukes in the Citadel staged a mutiny, to which they had been instigated by a number of ameers.

Toman Bai went to the chamber above the Chain Gate, hoisted his standard and called upon all ameers and mamlukes to rally to the colours. But no one appeared. Meanwhile, a number of ameers who were inside the palace slipped out by another gate and vanished into the city, the last of the mamlukes following their example. As soon as it was dark, Toman Bai himself disappeared and went into hiding. The next morning was the holiday marking the end of Ramadhan, a feast which, on this occasion, marked a double cause for jubilation. Toman Bai was forty years old. He was intelligent, but amazingly cruel and treacherous.

Five years had elapsed since the death of Qaitbai, the grand old man who had reigned for twenty-eight years and had been reverenced by all his subjects. Four sultans had reigned and fallen in these five years, of whom three had been treacherously betrayed by Toman Bai, the fourth being himself.

*   *   *

Our task is nearly over. We have followed the careers of forty-eight[3] Mamluke sultans, covering a period of two hundred and fifty-one years. The first impression which we receive, in glancing superficially over these two centuries and a half is one of endless fighting and civil war. On second thoughts, however, we find it necessary to modify this impression. Wars, rebellions and assassinations are "news", and were the same in the fourteenth and fifteenth

[3] Including Spray-of-Pearls and Al-Ashraf Musa.

centuries. They therefore occupy the greater part of the historical records, whereas long periods of peace are passed over in silence.

This impression is further exaggerated by the habit of Mamluke sultans of nominating their small children as their heirs. This practice, we have seen, became almost a recognised ritual. The child was hastily elevated to the throne on the death of his father and served, for a few months, as a stop-gap, until the most powerful candidate established his influence and the child was swept away. This custom greatly lengthened the list of sultans, although many of them reigned only in name. Moreover the "interregnum" between genuine sultans, while the child was on the throne, necessarily occupies several pages of the histories and thus increases the impression of endless instability.

There is also a third point worthy of note. The races of northern Europe are more stolid than those of the Middle East. Revolutions in the north are relatively rare, and when they occur the whole nation suffers intensely. The peoples of the Middle East are more changeable, coups d'état are more frequent but are often comparatively bloodless and largely confined to the capital. After 1945, in our own times, for example, coups d'état were of frequent occurrence in Syria, with the result that that country seemed, to Western eyes, to be in continual confusion. But residents in the country scarcely noticed these changes. The process was sarcastically described as "musical chairs". The music in the capital stopped for a few seconds, a number of people lost their chairs which were occupied by different individuals, and the harmony of life was resumed. Those who did not live in the capital were scarcely aware that anything had occurred.

Nearly all the contemporary historians of the Mamluke period lived in Cairo, and were thus acutely conscious of a riot in the city. But we need not assume that the bulk of the population in the provinces—without newspapers, radio or television—were much affected by the struggle for power between rival ameers or politicians.

To enable us to estimate the length of the periods of stability and insecurity, a more detailed analysis may be of assistance. It will be seen from these tables[4] that, of the two hundred and sixty-seven years of the Mamluke Empire, two hundred and twenty-two were passed under reasonably stable sultans all of whom reigned for five years or more. Forty-five years were passed under thirty-three insecure sultans, who ruled less than five years, twenty-two of these being the children of deceased sultans, who were raised to the throne as stop-gaps. Ten were pretenders who snatched the throne, but failed to retain it.

[4] Appendix, page 459.

*   *   *

These periods of insecurity refer, of course, only to internal troubles. The Mamluke Empire underwent numerous periods of insecurity due to invasions by external enemies, notably the Mongols and the Ottomans, although the White and Black Sheep Turkmans, the Dulqadirs, the Franks and others gave them periodical trouble.

The whole world owes a debt to the Bahri Mamlukes because they saved Syria, Palestine, Egypt and the Mediterranean from the terrible devastation which the Mongols inflicted on those countries which fell under their rule. The most notable of these was Persia, which, until Jenghis Khan, was one of the world's leading nations in culture and civilisation, and which, to this day, has not recovered.

But to have saved the Mediterranean countries from the Turkmans—Black Sheep and White Sheep alike—was in itself a considerable service rendered by the Mamlukes. For these people were responsible, after the Mongols, for the repeated devastation of Iraq, north Persia and eastern Asia Minor. If any of these central Asian nomads had established themselves firmly in Syria and Egypt between 1250 and 1500, the consequences for the Mediterranean and the Western world would have been incalculable. Thus we may say that, indirectly, we owe a great debt to the Mamlukes for the development of Western civilisation during their period of empire.

Another notable feature in Mamluke history is that they did not use their military power to attack their neighbours. After the collapse of the Il-Khanate in 1336, the Mamlukes remained the most powerful military empire in the Middle East. Yet they never seriously used their strength to expand their empire, as most of their neighbours attempted to do, and as most of the great nations of Europe have tried to do from that day to this. The only exceptions were Nubia—the modern Sudan—and Cilicia, against which the Mamlukes waged campaigns of aggression on several occasions.

Their self-restraint in their northern and eastern borders was not for lack of a pretext, for, as we have seen, minor rulers in Diyarbekr, Mosul, and as far afield as Tabriz, on several occasions solicited their military intervention. It is true that their refusal to engage in military adventures was wise and in their own interest. But does not the same apply to all the military conquerors of Europe? Would not Sweden have been better off if Gustavus Adolphus and Charles XII had stayed at home? Or France without the military ambitions of Louis XIV and Napoleon? Or Germany without Frederick the Great, Kaiser Wilhelm II or Hitler? Or the United States without

Vietnam? But history shows that most nations which feel themselves in a dominating military position are tempted to use their strength against their neighbours. The Mamlukes had more common sense.

Another direction in which the Mamlukes surely deserve commendation is the manner in which they treated the conquered Egyptians and Syrians. Here also their action was entirely to their own advantage. Both Syria and Egypt were ancient, civilised and highly cultured nations. Both had skilled administrative and judicial services, and both were wealthy and commercial, with trade relations extending over the then known world. The Mamlukes were sensible enough to appreciate the value of all this, and to allow the civilian populations in general to remain in control. Thus the Mamlukes themselves resembled an army stationed in allied territory. They did not normally interfere in the administration or in the processes of justice, but neither did they submit themselves to them.

They dealt in their own arbitrary manner with military matters, with rebellion or breaches of the peace, but they did not interfere with the proceedings of the law-courts, in so far as the civil population was concerned. This, it may be said, was obviously common sense, but how few conquerors have been so sensible. The Mongols destroyed everything and no reasonable civil service was ever established in Persia during their rule. Even the Ottomans, as we shall see, gave offence in Egypt when they conquered it, by introducing their laws and customs, by appointing judges and officials from Istanbul, and by encouraging the use of Turkish in place of Arabic, a practice never followed by the Mamlukes.

When the French occupied Egypt, they introduced their own political ideas, and the British, wherever they went, brought the concepts of "Western democracy", often undesired by and ill-suited to the local populations.

It is true that the Mamlukes were brutal in their punishments, especially the barbarous custom of nailing political criminals on boards on the backs of camels and parading them through the streets of Cairo. We must, however, remember that the Mamluke Empire came to an end in 1517. Torture was, at this time, in common use all over Europe. The rack was often employed in the reign of Queen Elizabeth I (1558–1603). Some tortures were not legally abolished in England until the reign of George III and in Scotland until 1708, and certain tortures were not finally abandoned in France until 1789. Burning alive, which was regularly used in Europe for religious offences, was never a regular penalty in Middle Eastern countries. It is noticeable also that Egyptian writers mention the public revulsion felt in Cairo at the Mamluke torture of nailing on camels.

Perhaps we may summarise these comments by saying that the Mamlukes as a whole were essentially fighters—during the first half of their period, perhaps the finest fighters in the world. By their martial spirit, they directly saved Syria and Egypt and, indirectly, the Mediterranean and Europe, from the savagery of the Mongols. They made use of violence to settle most of their rivalries, as did the peoples of northern Europe during the same period.

On the other hand, having taken over Syria and Egypt from the Ayoubids, they did not attempt the conquest of their neighbours, even when they were the strongest military power in the area. They showed both restraint and wisdom in allowing the natives to remain in control of the civil service and the judicial system and in encouraging commerce, industry and agriculture, and allowing the Syrians and Egyptians to become rich, in receiving them at court, bowing to their religious control, and bestowing honours upon them. A new sultan could only be legally inaugurated by the khalif and the qadhis.

On the whole, the city populations were prosperous under the Bahri sultans, though less so under the Circassians, owing to the general imperial decline and, in Cairo, the indiscipline of the Royal Mamlukes. They always acted with violence, often with brutality, in dealing with tribal revolts, a mistake continued by the Ottomans. This policy was a political error, for many of the tribesmen were good fighters, particularly in the eastern deserts, the mountains of Nablus and Lebanon, and in southern Egypt. Had they been better treated, they might have supplied valuable military units.

*   *   *

These, however, are local peculiarities. To us, the most striking lesson from the study of the Mamluke Empire is broader. On the surface their régime is unique in history. It is the only example of which I am aware of a foreign military dictatorship, recruited solely by the importation of young boys from distant foreign countries. The fact that the boys were bought (and have thus been called slaves in the English language) is unprecedented, as was the ultimate selection of the sultan and the ameers from these "slaves", and from them alone.

It is almost incredible that this system was maintained for two hundred and sixty-seven years, without the establishment of a hereditary aristocracy. No ameer, however rich and powerful in his lifetime, was able to pass on his wealth or his influence to his descendants. No sooner had the great ameer died, than all his wealth was

seized by the treasury and his fiefs redistributed by the Controller of
the Army to other ameers. The most for which his sons could hope
was to be accepted as *aulad al nas*. But the great men of the next
generation must rise from the ranks of the imported "slave" boys.
These, and many similar peculiarities, make the Mamluke Empire
an historical prodigy, a unique curiosity among civilised states.

But by far the most amazing factor in this extraordinary story is
that all these unique peculiarities made no difference at all to the
rise and fall of their empire. The regular rise and fall of empires may
be called an historical platitude. The early period of disorders, the
rise of monarchy, the age of courage, enterprise and pioneers, the
years of military conquest, the consequent increase of wealth,
commercialism and luxury. Then the habit of riches and of power
breed the loss of a sense of duty to the state, the belief that the ruling
race is *entitled* to be rich and powerful for ever, without any continuing effort to deserve their pre-eminence. On the contrary, the
appearance of a captious spirit, when authority is no longer respected, and when nothing satisfies these pampered critics; the age
of protests, strikes, mutinies, increasing crimes of violence, and the
refusal to undergo military service.

Even the smallest details of decadence recorded of other empires
are reported also of the Mamlukes—the negligence in dress (after
Faraj), the revolts of the teenage mamlukes (after Barsbai), the
growing influence of women, the increasing cost of living, the
depreciation of the currency, the constant increases in taxation. The
good qualities go hand-in-hand with the bad—the refinement of
manners, the spread of education, the respect for academic knowledge and the dislike of war.

These developments are visible in the Greek Empires, the Romans,
the Arabs, the Ottomans, the Spaniards, the French and the British.
But, in such cases, it was easy to believe that the imperial race had
grown decadent as a result of the effects of power and luxury,
passed on through successive generations. But in the case of the
Mamlukes this was not the case. The leaders and the soldiers of each
successive generation were not the effete descendants of an imperial
aristocracy. On the contrary, every one of them had been born and
raised under the arduous conditions of nomadic life on the steppes or
in the mountains of the Caucasus. Every one of them arrived as a
hardy little savage of ten or twelve years. Yet, within a few years,
they were exhibiting the identical symptoms of the young men of an
imperial race with eight or ten generations of empire behind
them.

Nor did the constant introduction of fresh barbarian blood even prolong the period of imperial rule. The Greek Seleucid Empire lasted from the conquests of Alexander in 332 B.C., to Pompey's settlement in 63 B.C.—a period of two hundred and sixty-nine years, whereas the Mamlukes lasted, in the same area, for two hundred and sixty-seven years. The Spanish American Empire endured for between two hundred and fifty and three hundred years,[5] within a period extending from 1500 to 1800. If we assume the British Empire to have begun in the second half of the seventeenth century and to have ended about 1930, we find a similar figure—between two hundred and thirty and three hundred years.

It would be absurd to expect arithmetical exactitude in so human a development, occurring under such diverse conditions and covering a period of thousands of years. Yet, perhaps, we may be allowed to generalise so far as to say that the rise and fall of empires do seem to follow a remarkably uniform pattern. This phenomenon can normally be explained away by the decadence produced in the imperial race by luxury and power. But in the case of the Mamlukes, we find an imperial structure of which the rulers are changed in every generation by the substitution of an entirely different group of individuals, imported from a country where they have grown up under severe hardships and in extreme poverty.

I am not striving to prove some theory which I hold dear. All I would say, when taking leave of my reader, is, "Is not that surprising? To what factors then are we to attribute this imperial decadence?"

NOTABLE EVENTS

Elevation of Al-Malik-al-Nasir Muhammad, son of Qaitbai	7th August, 1496
Rebellion of Qansuh Khamsmiya	3rd February, 1497
Death of Qansuh Khamsmiya	March, 1497
Assassination of Sultan Muhammad	1st November, 1498
Elevation of Malik-al-Dhahir Qansuh ibn Qansuh	3rd November, 1498
Deposition of Qansuh / Elevation of Janbulat	July, 1500
Capture of Cairo by Toman Bai	2nd January, 1501
Elevation of Toman Bai	January, 1501
Deposition of Toman Bai	1501

[5] Most empires do not begin and end on fixed dates. A period of conquest and a period of decline often allow a slight variation in estimating the imperial lifetime.

PERSONALITIES

Mamluke Sultans
Al-Malik-al-Nasir Muhammad, son of Qaitbai
Al-Malik-al-Dhahir Qansuh
Al-Malik-al-Ashraf Janbulat
Al-Malik-al-Aadil Toman Bai

Other Mamlukes
Qansuh Khamsmiya
Grand Ameer Uzbek Tatah

XXI

The Débâcle

Insanity in individuals is something rare—but in groups, parties, nations and epochs it is the rule.

NIETZSCHE

Selim was already on Syrian soil and arrogantly turned back the Egyptian embassy. A battle took place near Dabiq, north of Aleppo, on August 24th; since the Mamluks had entirely neglected the development of artillery, as a weapon unworthy of them, they suffered a crushing defeat.

CARL BROCKELMANN, History of the Islamic Peoples

There are few more interesting figures . . . than the old Sultan el-Ghury, called to the throne in 1501 . . . He was a man of bold decision and boundless energy. He restored order in the anarchy of Cairo, levied ten months' taxes at a stroke to replenish his treasury . . . Having restored the revenue . . . he proceeded to spend it on great public works. He was sumptuous in his court and generous to poets and musicians, whilst he mulcted the heirs of his nobles and robbed orphans of their dower. Fully alive to the importance of the Indian trade, then menaced by the Portuguese, he furnished a fleet in the Red Sea and sent it to India. Finally, but too late, he led his army into Syria to do battle with the advancing Ottomans and fell fighting at the age of seventy-six.

STANLEY LANE-POOLE, The Story of Cairo

XXI

AL-MALIK-AL-ASHRAF QANSUH
AL GHORI AL ASHRAFI

THE very evening of the disappearance of Toman Bai, the ameers met to choose a new sultan, and unanimously selected Tanibek al Jamali. The mamlukes, however, declared their intention to mutiny, with the result that the ameers changed their minds and chose the Ameer Qansuh al Ghori. The latter, however, categorically refused, but was dragged into the council chamber by his collar, even shedding tears. The khalif and the qadhis stepped forward, pronounced Toman Bai dethroned and raised Qansuh to the throne with the title of Malik-al-Ashraf.

Qansuh was a Circassian, a mamluke of Qaitbai, who had, in 1484, made him an ameer of ten. He had been Governor of Tarsus at one time and then of Malatia. Toman Bai had made him chief secretary. The Ameer Qait al Rajabi was made commander-in-chief. Qansuh was sixty years old. His elevation was the cause of much jubilation on the part of the people of Cairo, with whom he was extremely popular.

Intensive house-to-house searches were carried out to find Toman Bai. He was discovered after forty-two days and was killed trying to escape.

In July 1502, the young mamlukes threatened to mutiny, because Qansuh had not given them a donative, there being no money in the treasury. Special taxes were imposed on house property, buildings, shops, baths, orchards, ships and other objects. Thirty thousand dinars were squeezed from Jews and Christians, and pensions were reduced. Ibn Iyas denounces these measures as iniquitous, but does not suggest how else a mutiny could have been avoided. In Damascus, the viceroy was stoned by the crowd, because he tried to raise money to pay the donative.

By July 1502, the sultan's government was well established. The number of ameers of one hundred was twenty-four, the original establishment under the early Bahris. There were seventy-five ameers of drums and a hundred and eighty-five ameers of ten. The principal civil officials were the chancellor, Qadhi Bedr-al-Deen Hanefi: the Controller of the Army, Qadhi Shihab-al-Deen, and the Controller of the Treasury, Qadhi Salah-al-Deen ibn Jian.

In August 1502, the returning pilgrimage was involved in a battle between Sharifian rivals for the lordship of Mecca and the pilgrims were stripped of their possessions. On passing Aqaba, the caravan was held up by the tribe of Beni Lam and made to pay three thousand dinars.

In north-west Persia, a new Shiite leader, Ismail al Safavi, had built up an aggressive religious movement, which had drawn many enthusiastic followers and had replaced the White Sheep Turkmans. Following on a report that Ismail was about to invade Mamluke territory, the mobilisation of an expeditionary force was ordered, for which money was squeezed by hook or by crook.

In Cairo, a gang of sixty brigands broke into the city armed with bows and arrows, and openly robbed the passers-by and the shops. In September 1502, a mule was being led into the Citadel, laden with twelve thousand dinars for the pay of the troops, when it was held up by a gang and all the money taken. Acts of banditry and violence continued to increase.

In September 1504, a certain Khairbeg was appointed Viceroy of Aleppo. In November, the Ameer Sibai, the Governor of Tarablus, renounced his allegiance. In December 1504, the commander-in-chief, Qait al Rajabi, was sent to prison in Alexandria. It was rumoured, according to Ibn Iyas, that he had instigated the revolt of the governors of Aleppo and Tarablus, expecting to be sent to fight them, whereupon he proposed to join them and proclaim himself sultan—the trick played by Toman Bai.

In the spring of 1505, the rebel governors sent to beg a pardon for their revolt, perhaps owing to the arrest of Qait al Rajabi. In June 1505, Sibai, the Governor of Tarablus, arrived in Cairo, carrying his funeral winding-sheet under his arm, in the traditional manner of a penitent traitor. The sultan received him and invested him with a robe of honour.

Meanwhile, from March to June 1505, the plague again raged in Cairo, several members of the sultan's family falling victims. As usual, the majority of deaths were among young mamlukes, black slaves, foreign slave girls and children.

Three expeditions were mobilised this year. One was sent to restore order in the Hejaz, and one to Kerak to punish the tribe of Beni Lam, which had held up the pilgrimage. For the first time since the Mamluke régime was established in 1250, no pilgrimage caravan was sent this year to Mecca, owing to the widespread disturbances in the Hejaz. The force sent there restored order in the early summer of 1506, but in September of that year the column sent to Kerak was defeated with heavy losses by the Beni Lam tribes.

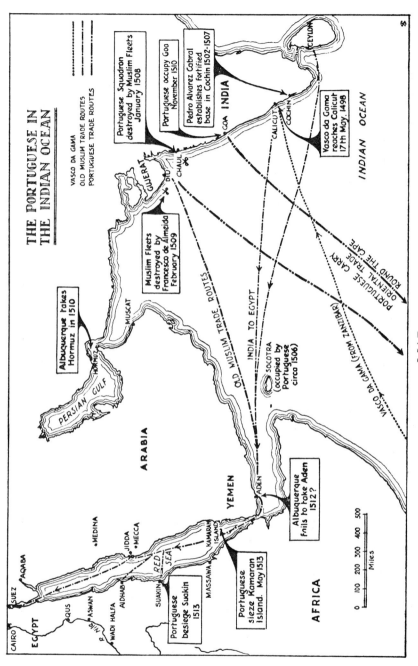

THE PORTUGUESE IN
THE INDIAN OCEAN

VASCO DA GAMA
OLD MUSLIM TRADE ROUTES
PORTUGUESE TRADE ROUTES

Portuguese Squadron
destroyed by Muslim Fleets
January 1508

Portuguese occupy Goa
November 1510

Pedro Alvarez Cabral
establishes fortified
base in Cochin 1502-1507

Vasco da Gama
reaches Calicut
17th May, 1498

Albuquerque takes
Hormuz in 1510

Muslim Fleets
destroyed by
Francesco de Almeida
February 1509

SOCOTRA
(occupied by
Portuguese
circa 1506)

Albuquerque
fails to take Aden
1512?

Portuguese
siege Kamaran
Island. May 1513

Portuguese
besiege Suakin
1513

INDIA

GOA
CALICUT
COCHIN
CEYLON

INDIAN OCEAN

GUJERAT
DIU
CHAUL

MUSCAT

HORMUZ
PERSIAN GULF

ARABIA

YEMEN
ADEN

RED SEA
KAMARAN ISLAND
MASSAWA
SUAKIN
ADHAB

MEDINA
MECCA
JIDDA

CAIRO
SUEZ
AQABA
QUS
ASWAN
WADI HALFA
NILE R.
EGYPT

AFRICA

OLD MUSLIM TRADE ROUTES

INDIA TO EGYPT

PORTUGUESE CARRY
ORIENTAL TRADE
ROUND THE CAPE

VASCO DA GAMA (FROM ZANZIBAR)

0 100 200 300 400 500
Miles

MAP 30

*   *   *

In 1498, a Portuguese flotilla under Vasco da Gama sailed round the Cape of Good Hope, reaching the western coast of India. On 17th May, 1498, he anchored off Calicut[1] with three ships. The Portuguese object was to snatch the oriental trade from Venice and Genoa, who monopolised the route across Egypt to Europe. In 1500, Pedro Alvarez Cabral arrived to command in India, establishing his base in Cochin and later seizing Socotra. He then set himself to blockade the entrances to the Red Sea and the Persian Gulf, and to load all the oriental trade into Portuguese ships and send it round the Cape of Good Hope to Lisbon.

On 5th November, 1505, a naval force commanded by Ameer Husain set out to fight the Portuguese. A few Royal Mamlukes went with it, but most of the expedition consisted of Algerians, Moroccans, black African archers and Turkmans. Real Mamlukes were unwilling to fight except as cavalry. In April 1506, the Christian patriarch was compelled to send a missive to the Christian rulers of Europe, protesting against the continual acts of piracy committed by Christians off the coasts of Egypt and Syria.

After two hundred and fifty-six years as a powerful military empire, the Mamlukes suddenly found themselves faced with naval operations, both in the Mediterranean and in the Indian Ocean—operations for which they had neither aptitude nor experience, and which every true Mamluke regarded with distaste.

Throughout 1506, the Portuguese continued their attacks on the west coast of India. Twenty Portuguese ships sailed into the Red Sea, seizing and sinking many commercial vessels plying from India to Egypt. As a result, imports from India and the Far East almost ceased, and cotton and muslin materials were virtually unobtainable. But the most serious result of this Portuguese blockade was the cessation of the transit trade from the East to Europe across Egyptian territory. The Mamluke government collected very heavy transit dues from this commerce, which was the source of a large part of their revenue. Thus within four or five years of the arrival of the Portuguese in the Indian Ocean, the Mamluke government was on the verge of bankruptcy.

*   *   *

[1] Map 30, page 409.

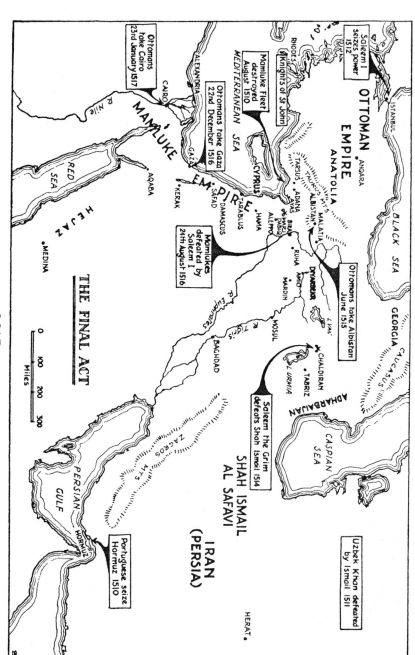

MAP 31

THE FINAL ACT

Scale:
0 100 200 300
Miles

Saleem I
seizes power
1512

Mamluke Fleet
destroyed
August 1510

Knights of St John

Ottomans take Gaza
22nd December 1516

Ottomans take Cairo
23rd January 1517

Mamlukes defeated by
Saleem I
24th August 1516

Ottomans take Albistan
June 1515

Saleem the Grim
defeats Shah Ismail 1514

Uzbek Khan defeated
by Ismail 1511

Portuguese seize
Hormuz 1510

OTTOMAN
EMPIRE

ANATOLIA

MAMLUKE
EMPIRE

HEJAZ

SHAH ISMAIL
AL SAFAVI

IRAN
(PERSIA)

ISTANBUL

BLACK SEA

GEORGIA

CAUCASUS MTS

ADHARBAIJAN

CASPIAN
SEA

MEDITERRANEAN SEA

ANGORA

RHODES

CYPRUS

ALEXANDRIA

CAIRO

R. Nile

RED
SEA

AQABA

KERAK

SAFAD

TARABLUS

DAMASCUS

HAMA

ALEPPO

BIREJIK

MARAS

PASHA

ADANA

AYAS

TARSUS

TAURUS MTS

MALATIA

ALBISTAN

RUHA

AMID

MARDIN

DIYARBAKR

MOSUL

L. VAN

CHALDIRAN

URMIA

TABRIZ

R. Tigris

R. Euphrates

BAGHDAD

ZAGROS MTS

PERSIAN
GULF

HORMUZ

MEDINA

HERAT

GAZA

98

In August 1507, a report reached Cairo that Shah Ismail the Safavi had invaded Mamluke territory near Malatia and that his troops had committed many atrocities. Orders were given to mobilise a force of one thousand five hundred mamlukes. Meanwhile Shah Ismail had passed on to the west and attacked Ali Daulat ibn Dulqadir, the Turkman Prince of Albistan. In October, however, before the Mamluke column had set out, a despatch came from Ali Daulat to the effect that he had defeated Shah Ismail's men. In witness whereof, he sent a number of severed heads and an officer prisoner, wearing a high red hat distinctive of Ismail's Shiite army, the members of which were known as *kizilbash* or redheads.

Shortly after, an embassy arrived from the Ottoman Sultan, Bayazid II, and was received by Sultan Qansuh with great ceremony. In December 1507, an embassy came from Ismail the Safavi, apologising for the Persian incursions into Mamluke territory. Ibn Iyas remarks that the Persian emissaries were badly dressed, though all wore the tall red hat. The Ottoman embassy had been much more elegantly clad.

In January 1508, a violent mutiny broke out among the young mamlukes in the Citadel, who demanded a cash-down payment of a hundred dinars to every man. The sultan was blockaded in his palace for three days, after which the mutiny died down, although no money had been paid. The sultan, however, was afraid to go out for fear of being murdered by his own troops. Crimes of violence and banditry continued to increase all over the country.

Early in January 1509, an embassy arrived from Murad Khan, Prince of Baghdad, a grandson of Uzun Hasan (Hasan al Taweel) of the White Sheep Turkmans. The ambassador complained that Shah Ismail had driven Murad Khan from Baghdad and that the latter wished to take refuge in Mamluke territory. In honour of the ambassador, the sultan held a review, at which the mamlukes gave a display of their extraordinary skill at target shooting with their bows at full gallop, but he excused himself from sending military assistance to the Prince of Iraq against Shah Ismail.

On 8th June, 1509, Prince Qurqud, the eldest son of the Ottoman Sultan Bayazid II, arrived in Cairo. It appeared that he had quarrelled with his father and hoped that Sultan Qansuh would mediate for him. Qurqud was not in rebellion, so did not present so acute a problem as had Prince Jem, Bayazid's brother, in the reign of Qaitbai. But the incident must have added to the impatience of the Ottomans at feeling that their own malcontents could always find asylum with their Mamluke neighbours.

This year, 1509, offered a remarkable example of the arrogance of the young mamlukes. One of these himself had a slave boy who escaped and took refuge in the house of an officer called Inal Bey. The mamluke arrived at the officer's house and demanded the surrender of the boy. The officer refused and slapped the mamluke in the face. The latter ran back to the barracks and returned with his comrades, who completely looted the officer's house and then burned it to the ground. No disciplinary action was taken.

*   *   *

Under the year 1510, Ibn Iyas has a pleasant interlude in this endless list of acts of war and violence. A few years before, the sultan had built a pavilion on the race course immediately below the palace. He caused five hundred camel-loads of young trees in tubs to be brought from Syria, and had them planted there. A charming garden had resulted, including apple trees, pears, quinces, cherries, vines and flowers such as white roses, lilies, iris, jasmine and many more, which loaded the air with fragrance. The sultan sat on a cushioned seat in the pavilion, screened by a climbing jasmine and fanned by a group of young mamlukes, chosen for their good looks.

On the surrounding trees hung cages of singing birds, such as bulbuls, pigeons, cooing doves, thrushes and gold finches, while the garden contained also varieties of pheasants and peacocks. Water-fowl swam on a small pool, which was kept fresh by flowing water brought by an aqueduct from the Nile. Here the sultan would pass his mornings on Fridays (the Muslim day of rest) with a few selected ameers, whom he invited.

Ibn Iyas speaks of this pavilion with emotion. He had formerly enjoyed a small state pension, which had been cut off on some occasion when the sultan was trying to raise money to give to the mutinous mamlukes. Some time later, our historian obtained an audience with the sultan in this pavilion, and presented a petition for the resumption of his pension. The sultan granted his request, in spite of the protests of some mamlukes who were present, and who wished to monopolise the sultan's bounty. Ibn Iyas, in gratitude, presented the sultan with a long poem of his own composition.

On 10th April, 1510, Qansuh al Ghori invited all twenty-four ameers of a hundred to lunch in his pavilion. A sheet was brought in full of roses, and the sultan called out each ameer by name and gave him a rose.

Soon after this idyllic scene, the young mamlukes mutinied, demanding a hundred dinars each. They attacked the house of the commander-in-chief, dragged him out, put him on his horse and

shouted, "Go and tell the sultan to give us money." Qansuh, however, refused to give money and threatened to abdicate. The mamlukes spent the next three days looting the city. Five hundred and
seventy shops were completely stripped. A fortnight later, the sultan
paraded the mutineers and invited them to swear on the Qoran to be
loyal and well-disciplined. The affair ended in this manner.

It seems curious to us that the authorities never tried to break the
tyranny of the young mamlukes, but continued to import boys from
the steppes and add them to those in the Citadel. There were thousands of mamlukes of mature age and long service in the country
who could have disciplined these boys. Alternatively, the recruits
could have been trained in other units, instead of being kept together
like schoolboys. Thus the problem was not unlike that of universities
in many countries today. But the Mamlukes in the fifteenth and sixteenth centuries had lost all initiative for change, as was witnessed by
their neglect of firearms and of their navy, as well as their timidity in
face of their violent and lawless adolescents.

*　　*　　*

Meanwhile deputations continued to arrive from Indian princes,
begging for help against the Portuguese, who had swept the Indian
Ocean of Asian ships. There was, however, no timber in Egypt for
the construction of naval vessels, and all timber had to come across
the Mediterranean from Ayas, on the Gulf of Alexandretta, travers-
ing some five hundred miles of sea infested with Christian privateers.

On 23rd August, 1510, an Egyptian fleet of eighteen sail left Ayas,
laden with timber, canvas for sails, rope and other naval stores, for a
fleet to be built in the Red Sea to fight the Portuguese. Not far from
shore, the flotilla was attacked by the ships of the Knights of St.
John from Rhodes and was completely destroyed. All the Egyptian
ships were captured and their crews killed. Qansuh was over-
whelmed by this disaster and ate nothing for two days.

A few days later, the crisis was made more alarming by the arrest
at Bira on the Euphrates, north-east of Aleppo, of messengers from
Shah Ismail to various European consuls in the Mamluke Empire,
asking them to urge their sovereigns to attack Egypt, while the
Persians would do the same from the east.

As a reprisal for the destruction of his fleet off Ayas, the sultan
ordered the arrest of all Christian merchants in Egypt and Syria,
and the imprisonment of the priests and monks of the Church of the
Holy Sepulchre in Jerusalem. The pretext for these reprisals was
that the Knights of St. John had been at peace with Egypt and thus

their naval attack was piracy.[2] The sultan demanded the return of his ships, threatening to raze the Church of the Holy Sepulchre to the ground.

The international situation was now tense. Shah Ismail was threatening both the Ottoman and Mamluke Empires in Syria and Anatolia, while the Portuguese in the Indian Ocean and European fleets in the Mediterranean, blockaded the Muslim states. Bayazid II saw the Mamlukes as his allies in this grouping and sent to Egypt a consignment of timber, iron, gunpowder and naval stores to replace the equipment lost at Ayas. The Ottoman gift reached Bulaq in January 1511, and included also three hundred muskets, thirty thousand arrows, quantities of gunpowder, two thousand oars, cables, ropes, anchors and other naval stores. Sultan Bayazid refused payment.

*　　*　　*

In March 1511, Shah Ismail defeated Uzbek Khan, the Tatar ruler, taking him prisoner and cutting off his head. The repeated aggressions of the Safavi shah kept the whole area in a state of tension. On 16th June, 1511, an ambassador from Ismail arrived in Cairo. He brought a letter from the shah and a gruesome trophy, the head of Uzbek Khan in a casket, in which were the following lines:

> The sword and dagger are to us as perfume,
> The fragrance of narcissus and myrtle.
> We rejoice to drink the blood of our enemies
> From their skulls which we use as our goblets.

The verses concealed mockery as well as menace. The pleasure taken by the sultan in his fragrant garden was ridiculed, the shah's more manly diversions being war and bloodshed.

On 24th August, 1511, the young mamlukes appeared in the Roumaila in full armour. The city panicked, all shops were closed and merchants hastened to conceal their valuables. The sultan, however, quieted the mutineers by promising them a cash donative of a hundred dinars per man.

On 29th August, the sultan rode into the city to inspect a mosque and a school, which were being built to his order. Qansuh received an enthusiastic welcome, large crowds cheering wildly, the women leaning out of the windows and showing their pleasure with the traditional treble trills, which are still used today. Essentially a man

[2] *Voyage de Jean Thenaud*, quoted by Gaston Wiet.

of peace, he was more interested in public works, bridges, mosques, colleges and gardens, than in preparation for war, to which his neighbours, the Ottomans and Safavis, devoted most of their time.

The public remained in terror of more mamluke outbreaks. The sultan, however, courageously ordered the young mamlukes to parade, all others being excluded. He then addressed them, saying that he intended to abdicate and that then they could choose their own sultan. The speech must have impressed them, for they remained quietly in their ranks. He also reduced his previous promise to pay a donative of a hundred dinars to fifty dinars. All sorts of expedients were needed to raise this sum, which was paid only to the young mutineers; older men who had not mutinied received nothing. As in our times, increases of pay are awarded only to those who make trouble.

Owing to the increasingly precarious situation with the Safavis, the Ottomans and the Portuguese, the sultan devoted more and more attention to artillery. Firing tests were held on the plain of Raidaniya.[3] At the first test, all the guns cast in Cairo blew up, but later tests were more successful. Guns were now being mounted on ships, but there was no mobile artillery on land.

* * *

A further sign of Mamluke decadence was seen in the appearance of jerry-building. The Mamlukes had always been great builders and Cairo was full of splendid edifices. The sultan himself had commissioned the erection of a mosque, but, before it was finished, one of the minarets leaned over and had to be dismantled. Then cracks appeared in the dome. It is remarkable how, when a country begins to decline, all the work done there becomes slipshod and shoddy.

* * *

On 25th March, 1512, an embassy arrived in Cairo from Louis XII, King of France, consisting of some fifty persons, two of whom, comments Ibn Iyas, were of particularly distinguished appearance, wearing velvet clothing and with gold collars round their necks. They brought valuable gifts for the sultan from the king. Jean Thenaud, who was a member of the embassy, is full of admiration for the splendid mansion in which they were lodged, which had been

[3] Map 32, page 433.

the residence of Ibn Muzhir, a member of one of those rich Egyptian families which supplied many senior civil officials.

The house, he says, contained six or seven splendid apartments paved with marble, porphyry, serpentine and other rich stones, the walls being panelled in the same manner, and painted with gold, blue and similar rich colours. The doors were inlaid with ivory, ebony and other materials. The handiwork of their ornamentation was even more astonishing than the priceless materials employed. In these rooms, and in even the lesser apartments, were fountains and baths, with hot and cold water brought in hidden pipes. "We were told," he adds, "that in Cairo there were a hundred thousand residences more magnificent than this one, some of which we actually saw." Europe was to wait another three hundred and fifty years before it acquired hot and cold running water.

"Soon after we came to Cairo," continues our French reporter, "arrived the great caravan . . . which had been to Mecca, as much for purposes of trade as of travelling. It consisted of a hundred thousand camels,[4] bringing great quantities of spices, drugs, precious stones, and perfumes." It is interesting to note that the impression he received was that the pilgrimage was a trading caravan, which perhaps explains why it was so often robbed by the tribes.

It should be remembered that Thenaud's account of the wealth and luxury of Cairo was written at a time when the country was virtually bankrupt, just before the final collapse. On 11th May, an embassy arrived from Venice. The ambassador was an old man of striking appearance with a white beard, dressed in a long cloak of cloth of gold over a yellow silk suit. It was rumoured that he had come to beg the sultan to reopen the Church of the Holy Sepulchre, closed after the naval attack off Ayas by the Knights of Rhodes.

Further tests were carried out, in May 1512, on guns cast in Cairo. It was rumoured that seventy guns had been cast, some in bronze and some in iron. Great difficulty was experienced in transporting them on carriages drawn by oxen, and they were thus quite unsuitable for use in the field. On 22nd June, further artillery tests were made at Raidaniya. Of fifty-seven guns fired, only two proved defective.

In June and July 1512, Cairo had been crowded with embassies from France, Venice, Shah Ismail, the King of Georgia, Ibn Ramadhan, chief of the Turkmans of Cilicia, the King of Tunis and the Ottoman sultan. The Safavi ambassador brought a cold and hostile letter from Ismail, to which an equally unfriendly reply was returned.

The embassy from Istanbul announced the death of Bayazid II

[4] Thenaud's numbers are somewhat picturesque.

and the elevation of his third son, Saleem. Before the old sultan died, his sons had already begun to contend for the throne. Bayazid favoured his second son Ahmad, having quarrelled with Qurqud, the eldest, as already mentioned. But the Janissaries, who were later to become as insubordinate as the Royal Mamlukes, insisted on the succession of the third son, Saleem. In April 1512, the latter appeared in arms outside Istanbul, the Janissaries rose in his support and Bayazid was forced to abdicate. He died a few days later, either of old age or poisoned by Saleem.

The new sultan was forty-seven years old, of a ruthlessly aggressive temperament, which was to earn him the nickname of Saleem the Grim. Some months later, he defeated and killed his brother Ahmad. He next determined to destroy his aggressive neighbour, Shah Ismail, who had set himself up as the religious champion of the Shiites, while the Ottoman sultan represented the Sunnis.[5] There were many Shiites in Asia Minor, who were willing to rise in support of the Shah. Saleem the Grim ordered a general massacre of Shiites in Ottoman territory, whereupon Shah Ismail advanced to rescue his co-religionists. A major clash between the Ottomans and Persia was obviously imminent.

*　　*　　*

On 9th December, 1512, the Ameer Husain, who had sailed in 1505 with a Mamluke fleet to fight the Portuguese, returned to Cairo. He had gone to the assistance of Mahmood I Begarha, King of Gujerat, one of the great rulers of Indian history. In January 1508, the combined Mamluke and Gujerat fleets destroyed a Portuguese squadron at Chaul, but, in February 1509, the Portuguese Viceroy, Francesco de Almeida, completely defeated the combined Muslim fleets off Diu. Naval command of the Indian Ocean passed into the hands of the Portuguese. The latter made use solely of naval war to seize the trade of the East. The places which they occupied on shore were purely fortified naval bases.

In November 1510, the Portuguese established themselves in Goa, whence Alfonso de Albuquerque seized naval bases at Malacca, and Hormuz, but failed to hold Aden. However, they attacked every Muslim ship in the Indian Ocean and the Red Sea, using the most ruthless cruelties. Even unarmed pilgrim ships were sunk without compunction, and the pilgrims, men, women and children, were left to drown.

[5] The Sunnis and the Shiites are the two principal divisions in Islam, similar to Catholics and Protestants in Western Christianity.

The activities of the Portuguese ruined Venice and Genoa and made Portugal rich, but they also spelt the death of the Mamluke Empire. At one time the Mamluke sultan secured one-third of the profit of the valuable pepper trade, in addition to which he took twenty per cent *ad valorem* on all articles crossing Egypt.[6]

* * *

Qansuh al Ghori was deeply alarmed at the situation. At home, the young mamlukes were again on the verge of mutiny. The treasury was empty and a large part of the income of the state had been permanently lost owing to the cessation of trade with the East. In Egypt itself, administrative neglect had reduced the revenues by omitting to repair the roads and the irrigation systems.

In the north were two powerful and aggressive military empires, the Ottoman and the Persian, on the verge of war with one another. The Portuguese sailed the Red Sea unopposed, while Christian privateers constantly coasted the shores of the eastern Mediterranean. The sultan sent a deputation to Istanbul to congratulate Sultan Saleem on his accession, but reports from Istanbul stated that Saleem the Grim had executed his two brothers, Qurqud and Ahmad, five nephews and several of his father's ministers. In May 1513, the Portuguese occupied Kamaran Island, in the mouth of the Red Sea, and laid siege to Suakin. A force was detailed to proceed to Jidda, consisting of three hundred mamlukes with artillery, musketeers, artificers, and others, but refused to set out without a financial donative.

In June 1513, the sultan was suffering acute pain in his eyes, possibly trachoma, and was almost blind. Ibn Iyas describes the old man spending all the night in prayer, crying, "O Thou, who canst not be an unjust tyrant, have mercy on thy slave, Qansuh al Ghori. O Lord, we have shown ourselves wicked, we are certainly lost unless Thou wilt forgive us, unless Thy pity descend upon us."

The sultan sent for all the ameers, causing them to renew their oaths of loyalty, placing their hands on the Qoran. Then suddenly his eyes began to improve. Summoning the mamlukes on parade, he addressed them himself. He admitted that issue of rations and forage had sometimes been delayed, owing to the many difficulties facing the country. Now he ordered all arrears to be made up, and every mamluke to receive a donative of thirty dinars. The mamlukes gave him a hearty cheer. On 11th July, donations were also made to the ameers.

[6] Sir George Dunbar, *A History of India.*

On 18th October, the sultan rode in state from the Bab al Nusr to the Zuwaila Gate. The streets had been decorated, the bands played, the troops marched and dense crowds cheered wildly. Times were not too bad for the common people. It was the sultan who had been under intense stress, from his eyes, from fears of a mutiny and from anxieties regarding the Portuguese, the Ottomans and Shah Ismail. A fresh problem arose from disturbances in rural and tribal areas, where farmers had abandoned their lands unploughed, owing to the breakdown of law and order.

In April 1514, the mamlukes again mutinied because the meat ration had ceased, the government having been unable to obtain supplies. They were also annoyed at the recruitment of a force of Turkmans, Persians and other elements to fight the Portuguese. Mamlukes did not like fighting at sea, but at the same time they were jealous of any military unit other than themselves. In June, the Ameer Husain wrote from Jidda that the Portuguese had landed on the sea coast of the Yemen.

On 6th May, 1514, an ambassador sent to the Ottoman sultan returned to Cairo, having had an amiable reception. In fact, Sultan Saleem was about to give battle to Shah Ismail, and it was in his interest to keep Qansuh friendly until he had finished with the Persians.

Meanwhile, Saleem had marched against Shah Ismail. The Ottoman army was the most efficient in the world at this time, well in advance of any in Europe. The Janissaries, armed with muskets, were still splendid infantry and Saleem alone had an efficient mobile field artillery. The Safavi army consisted solely of cavalry, perhaps sixty thousand strong.

The Battle of Chaldiran was fought on 23rd August, 1514.[7] Ismail divided his forces into two in order to turn both flanks of the Ottomans, the idea being to avoid the artillery which had been placed in the centre. Shah Ismail led the attack on the Ottoman left wing, which he drove back in confusion. But the charge against the Ottoman right wing exposed itself to the guns and was shot to pieces. After desperate fighting, the Persians broke and fled, the Shah himself being wounded. Sultan Saleem ordered the massacre of all prisoners. He sacked Tabriz but was unable to hold it, but annexed Georgia and Diyarbekr.

The bands did not play in Cairo to celebrate the Ottoman victory. The ameers were growing alarmed at the strength of the Ottoman army and feared an invasion of Mamluke territory. A force was accordingly sent to Aleppo as a precaution, but no sooner did it

[7] Map 31, page 411.

arrive there than the Royal Mamlukes behaved outrageously. They broke into houses, violated the women, robbed and looted, and defied the orders of their officers. Fighting broke out between them and the mamlukes of the viceroy. Many civilian inhabitants abandoned their homes and fled. The viceroy himself was driven from his residence. On 14th November, 1514, reports came from Aleppo that the Royal Mamlukes were in open mutiny and had driven out their officers. With the victorious Ottoman army on the northern frontier and his own troops in anarchy, the sultan called a council.

On 17th November, an Ottoman ambassador arrived in Cairo, bringing full details of the Battle of Chaldiran. No previous Ottoman sultan, he claimed, had ever won so complete and dazzling a victory. After appointing a governor of Tabriz, the Ottoman army had retired into winter quarters in Anatolia.

Officers were sent to Samaria, Damascus, Safad, Tripoli, Hama and other cities to raise special taxes to pay for a corps of infantry. The staggering success of the Janissary infantry over the Persian cavalry had taken Cairo by surprise. All over the world, trained infantry were replacing armoured horsemen, but the Ottoman army was far ahead of any other. The new taxes served only to raise a spirit of revolt. While more money was being raised, the sultan's wife went on pilgrimage in a litter which cost twenty thousand dinars, travelling in every luxury.

On 20th January, 1515, the young mamlukes in the Citadel mutinied. On 7th February, the Royal Mamlukes returned from Aleppo. They had behaved abominably, assaulted their commander-in-chief, driven out their officers, plundered shops and houses, and violated women and girls. They had also suffered severely and for a period they received no rations. Some had sold their weapons, horses and uniforms to buy food. The whole expedition had given a lamentable exhibition of incompetence and indiscipline, which probably encouraged Saleem I to attack, for he was only a few miles away.

There had been no plots, imprisonments or executions in Cairo for some years. The country was peaceful and the sultan popular, but the army was in anarchy. A peaceable nation with an inadequate army is always exposed to attack.

On 15th February, 1515, an ambassador from Sultan Saleem arrived in Cairo with a letter, saying that Ali Daulat ibn Dulqadir had ill-treated his nephew and that Saleem had promised to help the latter. Before a reply could be received, the Ottomans attacked Albistan. Early in June, they launched a column of thirty thousand men, the Dulqadir army was exterminated and Ali Daulat killed. On

7th August, 1515, an Ottoman ambassador arrived in Cairo and presented Sultan Qansuh with the heads of Ali Daulat, his son and his wazeer each in a casket. As Ali Daulat had been a subject of the Mamluke Empire, and as the Ottomans had occupied his territory, the despatch of his head to Qansuh was adding insult to injury.

On the other hand, Ali Daulat's men had harassed the flank of the Ottoman army as it advanced to Chaldiran. Sultan Saleem was also collecting a fleet in the Mediterranean, with which he was believed to intend to attack the Nile delta. At a sultan's council held in Cairo, the ameers agreed that war now seemed to be inevitable.

On 11th August, 1515, at the height of this international crisis, the young mamlukes mutinied. On 21st August, the force raised to fight the Portuguese at last set out for Suez. It consisted of 5,344 sailors, mostly Algerians (Mughrabis) and Turkmans, and 450 soldiers from the newly raised infantry unit, recruited from heterogenous sources.

On 13th September, a Mamluke ambassador sent to the Ottoman headquarters returned to Cairo. He reported that he had been despoiled and threatened with hanging, and that Saleem the Grim had spoken insultingly of Qansuh al Ghori. Several Ottoman armies were mobilising to attack Aleppo. Orders were accordingly issued for the despatch of a force to Aleppo. It set out early in October 1515.

On 3rd December, the young mamlukes mutinied again. They issued a statement demanding the abolition of extra taxes and the cessation of arbitrary confiscations, and insisting on the dismissal of the wazeer and the commandant of the Cairo police. These demands seem to reveal a political interest, new to these endless mutinies. In spite of their championing of the victims of taxation, the young mamlukes then broke into the city and spent a day and a night looting. When the sultan endeavoured to address them, he was greeted by coarse insults and a volley of stones.

Meanwhile Qansuh had ordered the interior of the palace to be stripped and all its treasures and articles of luxury to be sold. Civil officials were asked to raise a hundred thousand dinars. The money was given to the young mamlukes to call off their mutiny. Loyal mamlukes, and the older men were given nothing.

All the ameers of a hundred begged the sultan to satisfy the young mamlukes, but Qansuh would only repeat, "I never wanted to be sultan. Let me go somewhere else. Choose another sultan." The old man wept copiously and even lost consciousness. The demands of the mutineers were conceded.

*   *   *

In February 1516, the sultan was convinced that an Ottoman invasion was imminent and did all he could to conciliate the troops. The meat ration, which was months in arrears, was made up to date. Two hundred guns were sent to Alexandria where the Ottoman fleet was expected to land troops. On 15th March, a final review of the whole army was held. On 22nd April, every mamluke received a donation of a hundred dinars, four months advance of pay and the price of a camel. The fact that every man bought so much of his own equipment made mobilisation extremely slow.

On 14th May, the sultan's convoy marched out. Emerging from the Chain Gate, it crossed the Roumaila, passed through the Zuwaila Gate, up the Grand Avenue and out through the Bab al Nusr. It was in the style of the great days, extremely magnificent, the saddles of gold, robes of silk, satin and velvet and gold-mounted weapons. Camp was pitched at Raidaniya.[8] It was the last sultan's procession ever to traverse Cairo.

On 16th May, the sultan and the army left for Syria. No sultan had left for the wars in the old ceremonial style since Barsbai, eighty-seven years before, a fact showing how increasingly peaceful the Mamlukes had become. This laudable tendency to peacefulness, displayed by old empires, leads to a drastic reduction of the armed forces, which is welcomed by the citizens. But then a new aggressive power appears and easily reduces the cultured, venerable and peaceful nation to servitude. To understand the Mamluke decline, we have only to look about us today.

While Qansuh was still in camp at Raidaniya, he received a letter from Saleem, of which the following is an abbreviation. "You are my father, and I wish you well. It was with your permission that I overran the territory of Ali Daulat, who had thoroughly deserved execution. I will return to you the lands I took from Ali Daulat and we will do everything the sultan wishes." The sultan and his council were overjoyed at the prospect of peace.

Qansuh reached Damascus on 20th June, and stayed for nine days, the viceroy being the Ameer Sibay, who had once come to Qansuh with his winding sheet. A further letter received from Sultan Saleem at this stage, began, "My father, I ask your prayers on my behalf, but I beg you not to interfere to oblige me to make peace with Shah Ismail". The letter was obviously intended to suggest that the Ottomans were about to attack the Persians, and the ambassador assured Qansuh verbally that this was their objective, but intelligence reports declared that they were massing on the Syrian border.

Unfortunately at this moment, the Ottoman prince, Qasim Bey,

[8] Maps 14 and 32, pages 72 and 433.

the son of Ahmad, the elder brother of Saleem, whom the latter had killed, arrived in the Mamluke camp. He had taken refuge with Shah Ismail when his father was killed. His reception by Qansuh could be claimed by Saleem as an unfriendly act.

A Mamluke ambassador was sent to Saleem with valuable gifts, but on reaching Ain Tab, north of Aleppo, heard that a former emissary to Saleem, the Ameer Mughulbey, had been insulted and placed in irons by Saleem. The Ottoman army had already seized Malatia and was marching southwards. Saleem the Grim, his preparations complete, had thrown off the mask.

On receipt of this news, Qansuh decided that war was inevitable and left Aleppo with the army, reaching a plain called Marj Dabiq on the evening of 22nd August. On the morning of 24th August, the Mamluke army was drawn up for battle. The sultan, the khalif, the qadhis and the Ottoman prince, Qasim Bey, surmounted by the royal banners, held the centre. The right wing was commanded by the Ameer Sibay, Viceroy of Damascus, the left wing by the Ameer Khairbeg Malbai, Viceroy of Aleppo.

The battle opened with one of those desperate Mamluke cavalry charges, led by the commander-in-chief, Sudoon al Ajami, and by the Ameer Sibay, the Viceroy of Damascus. The Ottoman left was driven in and fled, abandoning seven colours and a number of guns. Even Saleem I is alleged, rightly or wrongly, to have been on the verge of flight. But both Grand Ameer Sudoon and Sibay had been killed. At this crisis, the Mamluke left wing, under Khairbeg, Viceroy of Aleppo, withdrew from the field. It later transpired that Khairbeg had been in treasonable correspondence with Sultan Saleem and had promised to betray the Mamluke cause.

Had not Khairbeg deserted, there is just a possibility that the Mamlukes might have won, if the left wing had put in an impetuous charge as the right wing did. It was their system to risk all on desperate charges. Albeit the Ottomans were a well-trained army, with field artillery and musketeers and a highly trained infantry. The Mamluke devotion to the cavalry charge was in fact out of date.

As the Mamluke army, deprived of its left wing, began to disintegrate, the old sultan shouted to the troops to stand fast, and urged the khalif and the qadhis to pray. The heat of the day was sultry and clouds of dust hung over the field. Suddenly Qansuh suffered a stroke. One side of his body was paralysed and his mouth hung open. He tried to drink some water but fell from his horse. When his officers ran to help him, he was already dead. Soon afterwards, the Ottoman army swept forward over the position. The sultan's body was never found, and was presumably lost among the heaps of dead on the field. Brockelmann[9] says that Qansuh "fell while in flight", but the narrative of Ibn Iyas, a contemporary, seems to be quite clear.

Ibn Iyas also states that almost all those killed had been veteran mamlukes. The young Royal Mamlukes had done little or no fighting.

Qansuh had been sultan for fifteen years and six months. He was about seventy-eight years old, and was tall and rather corpulent. His complexion was white, his cheeks rather fat, his voice was strong. He had a dignified manner, inspired respect, and practised great magnificence on state occasions. "Had he not committed injustice through his passion to amass riches, he would have been ... the best sovereign ever to rule Egypt," writes Ibn Iyas. We have already noticed that this historian does not seem to connect Qansuh's unjust methods of extorting money with the bankruptcy of the treasury, largely due to the interruption of the eastern trade by the Portuguese.

Business was at a standstill owing to the heavy taxes, he writes. It is true that, even without the Portuguese blockade, the Mamluke Empire was suffering from the same disease as all declining nations, high prices and a depreciated currency. Qansuh himself examined the public accounts almost daily, checking the receipts and expenditure, yet he spent unnecessary sums on magnificence. In some ways, he was rather a dilettante. He wore rings in which were mounted precious stones, loved perfumes, gardens, flowers and the singing of birds. He was himself musical and liked to attend concerts. Yet, in a situation utterly desperate, he struggled on to the end, and died sword in hand among his troops, when in his late seventies.

Stop. For thy tread is on an empire's dust,
An earthquake's spoil is sepulchred below!
Is the spot marked with no colossal bust?
Nor column trophied for triumphal show?
None; but the moral's strength tells simpler so.

And there was mounting in hot haste; the steed,
The mustering squadron, and the clattering car,
Went pouring forward with impetuous speed
And swiftly forming in the ranks of war;
And the deep thunder peal on peal afar;
And near, the beat of the alarming drum
Roused up the soldier ere the morning star;
While thronged the citizens with terror dumb,
Or whispering with white lips—"The foe. They come. They
come."

[9] Carl Brockelmann, *History of the Islamic Peoples*.

The morn the marshalling in arms,—the day
Battle's magnificently stern array!
The thunder-clouds close o'er it, which when rent
The earth is covered thick with other clay,
Which her own clay shall cover, heap'd and pent,
Rider and horse,—friend, foe,—in one red burial blent!

LORD BYRON, Childe Harold

NOTABLE EVENTS

Discovery of the Cape Route by Vasco da Gama	1498
Elevation of Malik-al-Ashraf Qansuh al Ghori	1501
Cessation of trade from the East	1506
Shah Ismail the Safavi attacks Ali Daulat ibn Dulqadir	August, 1507
Muslim fleets defeated off Gujerat by Portuguese	February, 1509
Egyptian fleet destroyed in Gulf of Alexandretta by the Knights of Rhodes	23rd August, 1510
Accession of Saleem I, the Grim	April, 1512
Battle of Chaldiran	23rd August, 1514
Royal Mamlukes mutiny in Aleppo	November, 1514
Saleem the Grim destroys Ibn Dulqadir of Albistan	June, 1515
Qansuh al Ghori leaves Cairo with the army	14th May, 1516
Battle of Marj Dabiq	24th August, 1516

PERSONALITIES

Mamlukes
Sultan Qansuh al Ghori
Ameer Sibay, Viceroy of Damascus
Khairbeg Malbai, Viceroy of Aleppo, the traitor

Shah of Persia
Ismail the Safavi

Ottomans
Sultan Bayazid II
Sultan Saleem I, the Grim

Portuguese
Vasco da Gama
Francesco de Almeida, Portuguese Viceroy in India

XXII

Saleem the Grim to Napoleon Bonaparte

> Farewell the pluméd troop and the big wars
> That make ambition virtue! O, farewell!
> Farewell the neighing steed and the shrill trump,
> The spirit-stirring drum, the ear-piercing fife,
> The royal banner and all quality,
> Pride, pomp and circumstance of glorious war!
>   SHAKESPEARE, *Othello*

In 1517 the Sultan Selim and his Turks occupied the country . . .
Egypt's status after its conquest was at first that of a pashalik, its
Turkish Governor being known merely as the Pasha. The Mamelukes, however, quickly recovered their former power . . . By the
eighteenth century the Pasha had grown to be a cipher and the
Mameluke Governor of Cairo—the Sheikh el Beled—was the
real master of the land. Disputes between rival Beys continued as
before the Turkish conquest.
                         H. WOOD JARVIS, *Pharaoh to Farouk*

At least six thousand horsemen were involved in this movement,
and it is probably true to say it was the last great cavalry charge
of the Middle Ages . . . the Mamelukes in their fluttering robes,
each man leaning forward with a sabre in his right hand . . . But
all this vanishes in a moment in clouds of dust and smoke and the
noise of the charge—the thousands of hoofs beating on the sand,
the shouts, the drums and the bugles—becomes lost in the
general uproar of cannon . . . Denon speaks of the enemy riding
right up to the mouths of the cannon before they fell . . . It was a
measure of the ferocity of the fighting and of the bravery of the
Mamelukes that only 1,000 prisoners were taken.
              ALAN MOOREHEAD, *The Blue Nile* (description of the
                                      Battle of the Pyramids)

SULTAN Saleem seized the Mamluke camp on the evening of the battle. Four days later, he occupied Aleppo without opposition. The Ottomans laid hands on countless treasures—weapons inlaid with gold, gold saddles, precious stones, works of art—such as no Ottoman sultan had ever seen. For two centuries Mamluke magnificence had been unrivalled. Saleem sent for Khairbeg, the Viceroy of Aleppo, and invested him with a robe of honour. But he did not spare his feelings for he nicknamed him Khainbeg.[1]

* * *

AL-MALIK-AL-ASHRAF TOMAN BEY

When news came of the defeat and the death of Qansuh, the ameers in Egypt agreed unanimously to elect Toman Bey Qansuh as sultan, but he categorically refused. It is interesting that, in this crisis, the ameers sent for an Egyptian religious leader to advise them, the khalif being a prisoner with the Ottomans. This man swore the ameers to loyalty and virtually made Toman Bey sultan.

The thirty-seventh and last Mamluke sultan, he had been bought by Qansuh al Ghori (who claimed him as a relative) and given to Qaitbai. It was for this reason that Toman Bey had added Qansuh to his name. When Qansuh al Ghori started on his last campaign, he had left Toman Bey as secretary of the government and viceroy in Egypt. On 12th October, 1516, Toman Bey took up his post as sultan.

On 13th October, a number of Mamluke ameers reached Cairo from Syria, including Janbirdi al Ghazali, the Governor of Hama, who had (as later transpired) been a partner of Khairbeg in his treachery. On 16th October, Toman Bey held a review of two thousand mamlukes who had been left behind by Qansuh al Ghori as a garrison for Egypt. Meanwhile Saleem had occupied Damascus, where the commandant and thirty-six Mamluke officers were beheaded.

[1] Khair means good, khain means traitor. A similar joke in English would be to change Colonel Good into Colonel Cad.

On 16th November, 1516, an Ottoman delegation of fifteen persons arrived in Cairo with letters from Sultan Saleem to Toman Bey and to many Mamluke ameers. The letter to Toman Bey began with insults and threats, but continued by saying that, if he would submit, acknowledge Ottoman suzerainty, and mint money in the name of Saleem, the latter would appoint Toman Bey as his governor of Egypt, from Gaza to the south. Syria as far as Gaza would become a province under direct Ottoman rule. "If you do not submit," the letter concluded, "I will come to Egypt and kill all the Turks,[2] and rip up the belly of every pregnant woman."

Toman Bey wished to accept these terms, but the ameers insisted on their rejection. In fact, Saleem was anxious to return to the north, where he was still at war with Shah Ismail and where the Ottoman Empire already extended far into Europe, to Hungary and Bosnia.

The mamlukes who returned from Syria were ordered by Toman Bey to rejoin the colours, but refused unless they were given a grant of one hundred and thirty dinars each. The request was not entirely unreasonable, for every man had to supply his own weapons, equipment and horse, all of which they had lost. His advisers urged Toman Bey to levy money by hook or by crook, but he refused to resort to illegal exactions. On 22nd December, 1516, the Ottomans took Gaza, killing a great many people.

Toman Bey was working frantically to manufacture guns and weapons. Two hundred artillerymen were enlisted, mostly Turkmans and Algerians, for no Mamluke would serve except in cavalry. A parade was held on the Roumaila and then marched up Grand Avenue. Dense crowds watched and applauded, and many wept, calling upon God to give victory to the sultan, for the Egyptians were whole-heartedly in support of the Mamlukes.

On 14th January, 1517, Toman Bey and all the troops concentrated at Raidaniya.[3] A long trench and breastwork had been dug from Matariya to Red Mountain, behind which the guns had been drawn up. On 18th January, reports arrived that the Ottomans had occupied Bilbeis.[4] On 21st January, they reached Pilgrims' Pool. On 22nd January, 1517, they attacked the Raidaniya line. The Mamluke guns were not mobile and thus Toman Bey was unable to manoeuvre.

The Ottoman artillery, much heavier and more efficient, quickly silenced most of the Mamluke guns, while, at the same time, their troops attacked and took Red Mountain, and appeared behind the

---

[2] It will be noted that Saleem called the Mamlukes Turks, his own subjects being Ottomans.

[3] Map 32, opposite.   [4] Map 20, page 151.

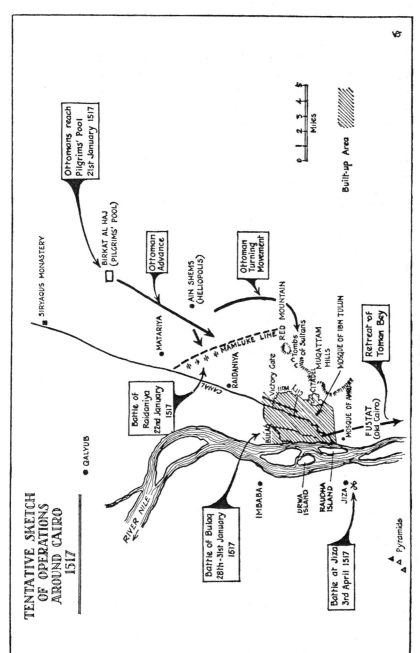

TENTATIVE SKETCH
OF OPERATIONS
AROUND CAIRO
1517

■ SIRYAQUS MONASTERY

● QALYUB

Ottomans reach
Pilgrims' Pool
21st January 1517

□ BIRKAT AL HAJ
(PILGRIMS' POOL)

Ottoman
Advance

● AIN SHEMS
(HELIOPOLIS)

● MATARIYA

Ottoman Turning
Movement

RED MOUNTAIN

✗✗✗✗✗✗ MAMLUKE LINE

CANAL

● RAIDANIYA

Battle of Raidaniya
22nd January
1517

RIVER NILE

Battle of Bulaq
28th-31st January
1517

IMBABA ●

URWA ISLAND

RAUDHA ISLAND

JIZA ●

Battle at Jiza
3rd April 1517

BULAQ

Victory Gate

CITY

IBN TULUN

CITADEL

Tombs
of Sultans

MUQATTAM
HILLS

MOSQUE OF IBN TULUN

MOSQUE OF AMR

FUSTAT
(Old Cairo)

Retreat of
Toman Bey

▲
▲ ▲ Pyramids

0 1 2 3 4 5
Miles

Built-up Area

MAP 32

Mamluke position. There seems nevertheless to have been heavy fighting and many casualties before the Mamlukes collapsed.

On 23rd January, the khalif, hitherto a prisoner with the Ottomans, returned to Cairo with Ottoman troops. Peace was announced in the streets by criers, but anyone hiding a Mamluke was threatened with death. The Ottoman soldiers, however, under pretext of searching for Mamlukes, broke into private houses, killing, plundering and raping. Every Mamluke found was instantly beheaded and many other persons also. Four thousand severed heads were hung in the Ottoman camp.

On 26th January, the Ottoman camp was moved from Raidaniya to Bulaq, and Sultan Saleem made a triumphal entry through the Victory Gate, down Grand Avenue, and then to Bulaq, with a large parade of infantry and cavalry. The Ottoman army continued to loot, but the khalif did his best to mollify the grim ruthlessness of Sultan Saleem. Cairo was, at that time, still one of the richest cities in the world and every large house was full of gold, silver, jewels, carpets, clothing and every article of beauty and luxury.

Suddenly, on 28th January, 1517, while Sultan Saleem was at Bulaq, Toman Bey appeared and attacked the Ottoman camp. The action was a complete surprise, everything was in confusion and Ottoman losses were heavy. The Mamlukes cut off the head of every Ottoman they caught, just as the latter had done to them. Toman Bey called upon the Egyptians to kill all Ottomans, who, in return, massacred the civil population indiscriminately.

Toman Bey had attacked the Ottomans on a Tuesday night and on Friday the battle still raged. The previous Friday, the Cairo mosques had prayed for Sultan Saleem but the Friday of the Bulaq battle they prayed for Sultan Toman Bey. By Saturday, however, the Mamlukes were either dead or exhausted. Toman Bey withdrew southwards through old Cairo and vanished. The streets were strewn with the dead bodies of Ottomans or Mamlukes, all without heads. The Ottomans continued their search for concealed Mamlukes, killing a further eight hundred. Sultan Saleem offered safe conduct to ameers who gave themselves up. Some forty who did so were thrown into prison and executed. All civilians south of the Zuwaila Gate were evicted from their homes, which were then occupied by the Ottoman army.

Ibn Iyas, who was intensely hostile to the Ottomans, compares their action in Cairo to Hulagu in Baghdad, an obvious exaggeration. Saleem, he says, daily ordered more executions and confiscations. "He never obeyed the principles of equity observed by the former sultans of Egypt," he complains—an interesting comment, for we are apt to think of the Mamlukes as tyrants. Ibn Iyas, now a man of middle age, was living in Cairo at the time.

Sultan Saleem had moved into the palace, where some of the finest Mamluke buildings were torn down to extract the marble, which was shipped to Istanbul. According to Ibn Iyas, the soldiers tied up their horses all over the Citadel and never swept up the dung.

Meanwhile, Toman Bey had collected a considerable force in Upper Egypt, partly Mamlukes and partly local bedouins. Early in March 1517, the sultan received a letter from Toman Bey, offering to acknowledge Ottoman suzerainty and to govern Egypt in the sultan's name. Saleem, who was anxious to return home, sent a deputation with an Ottoman escort to open negotiations. On the west bank of the Nile, however, the delegation was attacked by "Arabs", and all the Ottomans were killed. It seems unlikely that Toman Bey arranged this action, for he had always wished to accept terms, even when Saleem was still in Damascus.

A short time later, Toman Bey suddenly appeared with a mixed force near Jiza. On 30th March, 1517, Sultan Saleem crossed the Nile with his army. On 2nd or 3rd April, a savage battle was fought, in which the Mamlukes, as usual, obtained some preliminary success by a desperate charge. But the Ottomans, having survived the cavalry attack with difficulty, turned their guns on the Mamlukes and blew them to pieces.

Toman Bey escaped northwards to a village near Damanhoor. The Ottomans heard of his location, and surprised and arrested him. Loaded with chains, he was held in the sultan's camp at Imbaba for about a fortnight. He was then paraded through Cairo, dressed as a common Arab and riding a packhorse, heavily guarded by Ottoman troops.

At the Zuwaila Gate, a gallows had been erected. Toman Bey called to the large crowd to accompany him in reciting the Fatiha.[5] The crowd, led by their sultan, chanted the prayer three times. Then Toman Bey turned to the executioner and said, "Do your work." The noose was put around his neck and the rope pulled up. Loud groans and lamentations burst from the crowd. Toman Bey was forty-four years old when he died. His sultanate had lasted three and a half months.

Toman Bey had tried to govern with justice. In spite of the desperate situation, he had used no confiscations to squeeze money, but was always generous and magnanimous. He had toiled with untiring energy to raise artillery and musketeers, but it was too late to modernise the Mamluke army. Again and again he had attacked

[5] The Fatiha, the first chapter of the Qoran, is frequently used as a prayer.

the Ottoman army with improvised forces, exposing himself with reckless bravery and, in the end, calm and dignified, he died a hero's death. With him ended the Mamluke Empire. Violent, jealous, fearless, magnificent, the Mamlukes had, for two hundred and sixty-seven years, maintained perhaps the most extraordinary government the world has ever seen.

* * *

Janbirdi al Ghazali had been an ally of Khairbeg in his treachery, but had returned to Cairo after Marj Dabiq. Now, however, he was taken into favour by the sultan.

Saleem the Grim aspired to be a world conqueror on the lines of Tamerlane, though he was less brutal. Like Tamerlane, he wished to beautify his capital at the expense of the cities he conquered. Masons and artisans were employed to strip the Mamluke royal palace of its marbles and decorations. Parties were then sent, with military escorts, to strip the mosques, colleges and large private houses of Cairo. Libraries were also deprived of their manuscripts. All these materials were sent by sea to Istanbul, with groups of artisans, engineers and workers in marble.

Egyptian merchants, officials and qadhis were arrested and sent off in ships, including the Khalif al Mutawakkil. It has often been stated that the khalif surrendered his spiritual authority to Saleem I, but this story appears to have been a later invention produced by Ottoman propaganda. No such transfer in fact took place.

A thousand officials were also carried to Istanbul. The quantities of materials and artistic objects and the numbers of technicians, judges and officials removed from Egypt seem to be a tribute paid by Sultan Saleem to the superior culture of the Mamlukes.

Khairbeg, the traitor of Marj Dabiq, was appointed Governor of Egypt. Leaving a garrison of five thousand cavalry and infantry in Cairo, Sultan Saleem set out for Damascus in August 1517. "Never", says Ibn Iyas, "had Egypt had so brutal a conqueror, with the exception of Nebuchadnezzar, King of Babylon." In the past, he proudly claims, the Mamluke sultans had been the world's greatest rulers, but now all was in ruins.

The second Mamluke traitor, Janbirdi al Ghazali, accompanied the sultan to Damascus, of which he was named governor. Many Ottoman officers considered that Saleem had been too lenient with the Mamlukes, but the sultan does not seem to have been anxious to acquire so distant a province. As already mentioned, the moral basis of the Ottoman Empire had been the conquest of Europe for Islam.

It was to the conquest of Europe that all their efforts were dedicated. Saleem had been led into an Asian war by the aggressiveness of Shah Ismail. Having defeated the latter at Chaldiran without achieving peace, he probably feared to return to Istanbul, lest Ismail conclude an alliance with the Mamlukes against him.

The annexation of Syria as an Ottoman province would have separated the Mamlukes from the Persians, and rendered the occupation of Egypt unnecessary. Saleem was probably correct in these views, but the intransigence of the Mamlukes made the annexation of Egypt inevitable. The Ottoman Empire, however, was never able effectively to administer the country.

When approaching Gaza on his homeward march, Sultan Saleem was discussing the campaign with his principal wazeer, Yunis Pasha.[6] The latter was rash enough to express the view that the Mamlukes had been too leniently dealt with. Saleem the Grim was furious at this criticism of his policy, and ordered the decapitation of Yunis Pasha, who had been his principal minister throughout these campaigns. The scene of the incident has been known ever since as Khan Yunis.

*   *   *

The object of this book has been to give an account of the Mamluke Empire, which came to an end with the conquest of Egypt by Saleem I in 1517. The majority of educated persons in the West, however, have never heard of the Mamluke Empire, and know of the Mamlukes only as the opponents of Napoleon Bonaparte in 1798. The present chapter, therefore, is intended to give a brief outline of events in Syria and Egypt from the Ottoman Conquest to the arrival of the French in 1798 and the final massacre of the remaining Mamlukes by Muhammad Ali in 1811.

During this period, the Mamlukes are no longer rulers, but merely one element of the population. As a result, the history of Egypt and Syria under the Ottomans has been sketched in a summary form, with none of the detail used during the period of Mamluke rule.

*   *   *

After the sultan's departure, permission was given for Mamlukes to appear armed on horseback, a concession bitterly resented by the

[6] Pasha was a title given by the Ottoman government to senior officials and officers, somewhat similar to knighthood in Britain.

Ottoman garrison. The latter, after Saleem's departure, had become as violent and undisciplined as the young mamlukes had once been, robbing innocent civilians and kidnapping young girls, whom they carried off to their barracks. Some Mamlukes seem to have retained their fiefs, though others were reduced to extreme poverty. Two months after the departure of Saleem I, there were said to be five thousand Mamlukes in and around Cairo.

An order having been received for a number of Janissaries and Sipahis (cavalry) to march to Damascus, many deserted and scattered throughout the villages of Egypt. Eventually a thousand Sipahis and four hundred Janissaries left for Damascus, leaving only a few hundred Janissaries in the Citadel.

In May 1518, orders coming for the despatch of more of the Ottoman garrison to Aleppo, a hundred and fifty deserted and made for southern Egypt. A column of Mamlukes was sent in pursuit and every Ottoman deserter captured was beheaded—a curious reversal of fortune. Further alarms were created by the Portuguese fleet in the Red Sea, which threatened to attack Jidda. Reports having reached Sultan Saleem of the indiscipline of the Ottoman troops in Cairo, their commander, Sinan Pasha, was ordered to Istanbul where he was hanged.

On 2nd September, 1520, Saleem I died between Istanbul and Adrianople. He was a great military conqueror who, in a reign of eight years, had doubled the area of the Ottoman Empire. Hard and ruthless, he had dethroned his father, killed his brothers and made a practice of executing his wazeers. Just as the worst imprecation in Ireland was "the curse of Cromwell on you", so in the Ottoman dominions, the most vicious wish that could be expressed was "may you be the wazeer of Sultan Saleem". Yet with all these stern and autocratic qualities, the sultan was a devotee of Persian poetry, and himself composed a volume of verse in that language. This also had been a peculiarity of Tamerlane. He was succeeded without a struggle by his brilliant son, Sulaiman, known in the West as the Magnificent, but in his own country as the Lawgiver.

Soon after the death of Saleem, Janbirdi al Ghazali, the Mamluke Governor of Damascus appointed by him, rose in rebellion and declared himself sultan in Damascus. His former ally, Khairbeg, refused to join him. After some months, Janbirdi was defeated by an Ottoman army sent from Anatolia, and was beheaded.

Egypt was now a poor country. Ibn Iyas alleges that, under Baybars the Bunduqdari, the revenue of the Mamluke Empire had been twelve million dinars per year, whereas at the time of the Ottoman invasion it was one million, three hundred thousand dinars. Such figures are doubtless extremely unreliable, but they suffice to show that, in popular belief, the finances of the country were ruined. Sultan Saleem had ordered that customs dues collected in Jidda, Rosetta, Damietta and Alexandria were to be remitted direct to Instanbul. In any case, the Portuguese had cut off most of the oriental trade. In addition, Egypt had lost the revenue of Syria, now a separate Ottoman province, and the governor of Egypt was obliged to pay the expenses of the Ottoman garrison.

A source of bitter complaint on the part of Ibn Iyas is Ottoman intervention in the law courts. The Mamlukes, though exercising arbitrary power in the political sphere, normally left the law courts to the Egyptian judges. Now, states Ibn Iyas, Ottoman officials from Istanbul interfered with the rulings of the judges and even issued arbitrary decisions of their own. In June 1522, an Ottoman chief qadhi from Istanbul took over the Department of Justice, and the Egyptian qadhis of the four Muslim schools were replaced by Ottomans.

In the summer of 1522, also, the Dulqadir principality of Albistan was abolished, the prince put to death and the area incorporated into the Ottoman dominions.

On 6th October, 1522, Khairbeg died at the age of sixty. He was a capable administrator, who had ruled Egypt for five years and three months. As a Mamluke commanding Ottomans, his position was often delicate. At the end of his period of office, he became increasingly irascible and arbitrary, causing great numbers of persons to be executed. He was given to outbursts of rage when he ordered Egyptian officials to be stripped and flogged. This happened to Ahmad ibn Jian, who had the misfortune to annoy him. The Jians were an extremely distinguished family, who had supplied officials and wazeers to the Egyptian government ever since the time of Sultan Shaikh (1412–1421).

Khairbeg had been born at Samsun on the Black Sea and had been a mamluke of Qaitbai. He was tall and slender, with a short beard and a white complexion. He spoke good Arabic and was fond of music.

On 8th November, 1522, Mustafa Pasha arrived from Istanbul to replace Khairbeg. He was a man of medium height, white skin, long fair moustachios and no beard, as was the contemporary Ottoman fashion. He was married to the sultan's sister and scarcely deigned to converse with ordinary mortals. The arrival of this Ottoman grandee terminated what may be called the transition period, during which Egypt, though conquered by the Ottomans, was still governed by a Mamluke ameer.

Ibn Iyas died a short time after the arrival of Mustafa Pasha and his history comes to an end.

*   *   *

Saleem I had divided the Mamluke Empire into three provinces, Aleppo, Damascus and Egypt. To him, Aleppo was the most important, for it was at the centre of roads leading from Istanbul to Syria, Iraq and Persia, and was also at the junction of the territories of the Turkmans and the Arabs. After the revolt of Janbirdi al Ghazali, Tarablus was also made a separate province. Saleem's policy was everywhere moulded by the desire to balance different races and leaders against one another, to avoid united rebellions. The Ottoman Empire was composed of so many different nations and religions that emotional unity was impossible. Stability was sought by balancing the elements—the old principle of divide and rule. In addition to the three provinces of Aleppo, Tarablus and Damascus, Lebanon was made a semi-autonomous state under the local family of the Manis.

Just as the sultan divided the former Mamluke Empire into provinces, so he constituted the garrison of Egypt of mutually jealous elements. The units based on Cairo were six in number.

The Janissaries	Infantry
The Azban	Infantry
The Camelry	
The Musketeers	
The Circassians	Cavalry
The Mutafariqa	

It will be seen that the Circassians, or Mamlukes, were now a cavalry unit serving the Ottomans. They were not preserved for sentimental reasons, but because the Ottoman troops themselves were liable to mutiny. The Sipahis, the Ottoman cavalry, were organised on a feudal basis, and could not be posted for long periods so far from their homes. The Janissaries were compulsorily enlisted Christian boys, the Sipahis were free men.

Many mamlukes were freed by their masters and enlisted in the Circassian cavalry, where they were paid by the government, but retained their basic loyalty to their Mamluke patrons. During the period from 1524 to 1671, Egypt was constantly torn by internal rivalries and revolts, but the Ottomans were, more or less, in control. After 1671, however, the now declining Ottoman Empire lost most of its power in Egypt, and the great Mamluke houses assumed authority. Whenever one Mamluke family made itself supreme, the Ottoman governor became a nonentity. It was only by playing off the Mamlukes against one another that the pasha could exercise any influence.

* * *

Let us now return to our narrative.

Mustafa Pasha was succeeded by one Ahmad Pasha, who, finding the population extremely discontented, attempted to revolt and make himself the independent ruler of Egypt. But in 1523, Hasan Pasha was sent with a fleet, the rebellion was suppressed and Ahmad Pasha was assassinated.

In 1524, the sultan, alarmed at the chaotic state of Egypt, sent his grand wazeer, Ibrahim Pasha, to reorganise the administration. His measures consisted largely of codification of existing practice, as was Sulaiman's own codification in Istanbul. He tried to balance the power of the pasha, the Janissaries, the Mamluke ameers (henceforward known as beys) and the tribes. He fixed the annual tribute of Egypt at eight hundred thousand ducats. Ibrahim Pasha was a capable wazeer and the older portions of the Ottoman Empire at this time were comparatively well governed. Cases occurred, in both Greece and Hungary, where the Christian population preferred Ottoman rule to that of the Venetians or of the Hungarian monarchy.

Ibrahim Pasha laid down many good rules, which are praised today by those scholars who study them. But Egypt was too far from Istanbul, and few of these regulations were ultimately enforced. The Ottoman governor was, on paper, provided with a council of four advisers, on the model of the sultan's council in Istanbul, but events in Egypt were normally too violent and uncertain to enable such a constitution to operate.

Egypt, moreover, was neglected, because Sulaiman the Magnificent was engaged in a desperate struggle with the (Austrian) Empire for the domination of Europe. On 29th August, 1526, he defeated the Hungarians at Mohacs and occupied Budapest. In 1529, Sulaiman besieged Vienna. In 1534, he waged war against Persia and annexed Baghdad.

Thereafter, the struggle was transferred to the Mediterranean. In 1543-44, the Ottoman fleet wintered in Toulon, Francis I, King of France, being the ally of Sulaiman the Magnificent against the Emperor Charles V. From April to September, 1565, the Ottomans unsuccessfully besieged Malta. Engrossed in so great a war, the sultan had little time to devote to the internal administration of Egypt.

In spite of all these commitments, however, the Ottomans in 1538 sent a fleet from Suez which took Aden. In 1551, a new fleet sailed from Suez and naval operations against the Portuguese dragged on in the Red Sea, the Persian Gulf and the Indian Ocean. In 1557, the Ottomans occupied Masawa, to prevent the Portuguese landing in Abyssinia. The Ottomans never won naval command of the Red Sea or the Indian Ocean, but they prevented the Portuguese from doing so. At times, a trickle of trade from the East reached Egypt.

*   *   *

In 1566, when Sulaiman died, the Ottoman Empire was the greatest power in the world. Thereafter it declined rapidly. The Ottoman ruling dynasty had produced a succession of outstandingly capable sultans for nearly three hundred years. With the death of Sulaiman—a grand old man, wise, just and victorious—the succession of great rulers ended. His son, Saleem II (1566–1574), was a drunkard. The dynasty scarcely ever again produced a great ruler.

*   *   *

It is worth while to turn for a moment to the remarkable resemblances between the Mamlukes and the Janissaries. As we have seen, the practice of using foreign mercenaries as the backbone of their armies had been introduced by the Abbasid Khalifs of Baghdad in the eighth century and survived in Muslim states for some nine and a half centuries. The principal reasons for the employment of mercenaries were, firstly, that they would have no connection with the civil population and would not join in local rebellions and, secondly, that they would be solely dedicated to the military profession, thus constituting well disciplined and highly trained regular troops. Nearly all the other armies of the world consisted of levies, who were obliged to rally to the ruler in war, but who, in peace time, followed their own occupations. The superior training and discipline of full-time regulars made them almost irresistible.

The Mamlukes, as we have seen, were bought as boys imported from the Russian steppes. The first Janissaries were formed from young Christian lads, mostly Slavs or Albanians from the Balkans, taken from their families in the Ottoman wars of expansion. When these wars ended in the incorporation of these Christian communities in the empire, an annual tribute of boys was imposed on them. Like the boy mamlukes (who came as pagans) the Christian boys were converted to Islam, and were subjected to the severest military training. They lived in barracks, and were forbidden to marry. Every effort was made to concentrate all their minds, their enthusiasm and their pride on military glory. When they were first raised in the early fourteenth century, this Ottoman corps was called the Yeni Cheri, or New Troops, a name which Western writers transformed into Janissaries.

Just as Egyptians, Syrians and Arabs were not admitted to Mamluke units, so Muslim Ottoman subjects were not enlisted in the Janissaries. One difference, however, existed between the Mamlukes and the Janissaries. While the Janissaries, as boys, were under training, those who showed aptitude for clerical work were drafted to special palace schools where they were trained as civil administrators or palace officials. Ultimately, they could rise to be pashas, governors of provinces, wazeers and members of the Council of State. Those with the greatest physical strength, or the least aptitude for clerical work, were placed in the Janissary infantry.

Thus the Ottoman, like the Mamluke Empire, was ruled by foreigners, specially trained for the purpose. In the Ottoman Empire, this community occupied the senior positions in the civil service, but in the Mamluke Empire the civil service was staffed by native Syrians and Egyptians.

For two centuries, the Janissaries were not permitted to marry but those who attained civil service employment did so. Their children, however, were not allowed to inherit their privileged position, but disappeared into the ordinary population, just as the children of Mamluke ameers were not admitted to be Mamlukes.

In both cases, the Mamlukes or the Janissaries were, for a hundred and fifty years, the finest soldiers of their age, but, thereafter, they degenerated. In Egypt, the indiscipline of the young mamlukes caused the ruin of the empire they had created. The Janissaries also became the scourge of their country until they were finally exterminated by a general massacre in 1826.

The Janissaries did not constitute the whole Ottoman army. The cavalry was principally supplied by the Sipahis, a feudal organisation originally based on fiefs of land.

After the death of Sulaiman the Magnificent, the strict regulations governing the Janissaries were gradually relaxed. They were allowed to marry, to live out of barracks, and to obtain the enlistment of their own sons in the corps. The annual compulsory levy of Christian boys ended in 1675.

*   *   *

The Ottoman decline after the death of Sulaiman in 1566 was soon reflected in Egypt. The purchasing power of the Ottoman currency fell, but officials' salaries were not increased, and bribery resulted. In 1586, the garrison mutinied and arrested the Ottoman viceroy. Other military mutinies followed in 1589, 1591 and 1601. The Janissaries married and lived in the city, and gradually became integrated into the civil population of Egypt as a political faction.

When the garrison was disloyal, the Ottoman viceroy was obliged to lean for support on the leading Mamluke families, who were now called beys in place of ameers. In 1605, the viceroy, having tried to discipline the garrison, was murdered by the soldiers and his head nailed up on the Zuwaila Gate. In January 1609, the Sipahis mutinied, and a battle was fought outside Cairo in which they were defeated.

The Mamluke beys now virtually controlled the country. When a viceroy left Egypt, a qaimaqam, or locum tenens, was appointed until the arrival of a successor. The locum tenens was almost always a Mamluke. In 1631, the beys, the garrison and the qadhis suspended the viceroy and appointed a qaimaqam.

Egypt was dominated, from 1632 to 1656, by Ridhwan Bey al Faqari, a Mamluke who claimed descent from Barqooq and Barsbai. Ridhwan was the leader of a large faction called the Faqariya, composed of Mamlukes, Egyptians and tribal chiefs. A rival group, called the Qasimiya, opposed the Faqariya. Ridhwan Bey was always loyal to the sultan, but overshadowed the viceroys. He died in 1656.

Thereafter the Qasimiya ousted the Faqariya. The fact that the leader of the Qasimiya was one Ahmad Bey the Bosnian shows that Egypt was still the hunting ground of soldiers of fortune. On 26th July, 1662, Ahmad the Bosnian was stabbed to death. If the Mamlukes had been united, Egypt might have become independent.

From 1675 onwards, the endless schisms were increased by a feud between the units of the garrison, the Janissaries and the Azban. The Faqariya supported the Janissaries, the Qasimiya sided with the Azban.

After 1711, the Ottoman viceroys were reduced to impotence. The scene was dominated by the feud between the Qasimiya and the Faqariya. The former were in power from 1711 to 1730, after which the Faqariya returned to power. Soon they split, owing to family rivalries. The leading Mamluke bey at any time enjoyed the title of Shaikh al Beled, Chief of the Town. From 1748 to 1754, Ibrahim

Bey Kahya held the post. In 1760, Ali Bey *Bulut kapan*[7] was Shaikh al Beled.

In 1770, the Ottomans were fighting a losing war with Russia. The Russian Black Sea fleet forced the Dardanelles and appeared in the eastern Mediterranean. Ali Bey made an agreement with Russia and a Mamluke army occupied Damascus. But the endless internal jealousies of the Mamlukes frustrated Ali Bey's hopes of re-creating a Mamluke Empire.

In Cairo, Ibrahim Bey, a Mamluke, became Shaikh al Beled, sharing power with a certain Murad Bey. In July 1786, however, the sultan decided to reconquer Egypt and, in July, an Ottoman fleet reached Alexandria under Hasan Pasha. Ibrahim Bey and Murad Bey retired to southern Egypt. In 1787, Hasan Pasha left Egypt, and Ibrahim Bey and Murad Bey resumed power.

* * *

Egypt had played no part in the rivalries of the European Powers since the Ottoman Conquest in 1517. But as the Ottomans weakened, France, the expanding Great Nation of the eighteenth century, began to consider the possibility of a French occupation of that country. Both Louis XIV and Louis XV had discussed the proposal with their ministers.[8] It remained, however, for revolutionary France to put it into execution.

On 1st July, 1798, a French army of some thirty-eight thousand men landed at Alexandria, under the command of the twenty-eight-year-old General Napoleon Bonaparte. This initiative was to change world history. Thereafter, until our own times, the Middle East has remained the cockpit of the Great Powers.

The main body of the French army left Alexandria on 7th July for Cairo, marching through the desert west of the Nile and suffering much from thirst and exhaustion.[9] On 10th July, a skirmish was fought with a party of Mamlukes who, mounted on splendid horses, charged the French army. The latter, however, formed squares which the Mamluke cavalry was unable to break.

While Ibrahim Bey, the Shaikh al Beled, an old man, remained in Cairo, his younger associate, Murad Bey, assumed command of the military operations. He would, perhaps, have done better to remain on the east bank of the Nile to dispute the river crossing. But strategic plans were never a Mamluke speciality. To make straight for the

[7] Professor Holt says this nickname meant "cloud catcher", and referred to his vague ambitions.

[8] Ghorbal, *The Beginning of the Egyptian Question.*   [9] Map 33, page 446.

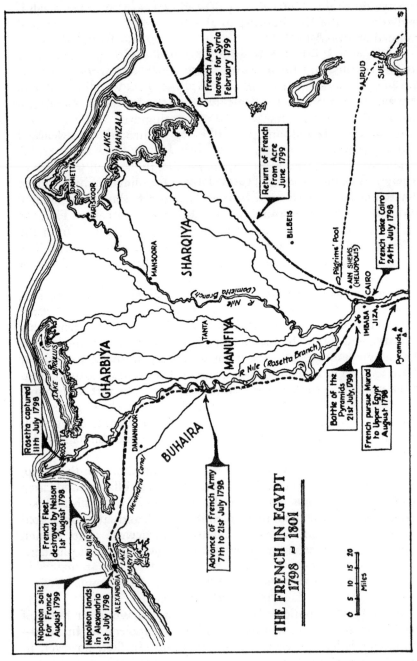

THE FRENCH IN EGYPT
1798 ~ 1801

French Army
leaves for Syria
February 1799

Return of French
From Acre
June 1799

French take Cairo
24th July 1798

Rosetta captured
11th July 1798

French Fleet
destroyed by Nelson
1st August 1798

Napoleon sails
For France
August 1799

Napoleon lands
in Alexandria
1st July 1798

Advance of French Army
7th to 21st July 1798

Battle of the
Pyramids
21st July 1798

French pursue Murad
to Upper Egypt
August 1798

LAKE MANZALA

LAKE BURULLUS

LAKE MARYUT

SHARQIYA

GHARBIYA

MANUFIYA

BUHAIRA

DAMIETTA

FARISKOOR

MANSOORA

TANTA

DAMANHOOR

ROSETTA

ABU QIR

ALEXANDRIA

Alexandria Canal

R Nile (Rosetta Branch)

R Nile (Damietta Branch)

BILBEIS

Pilgrims' Pool

AIN SHEMS (HELIOPOLIS)

CAIRO

IMBABA

JIZA

Pyramids

SUEZ

AJRUD

MAP 33

0 5 10 15 20
Miles

enemy and charge was their way of waging war. Murad Bey accordingly crossed the Nile in order to give battle on the west bank, and camped at Imbaba.

Here he established a primitive fortified camp, surrounded by rough trenches and breastworks, along which were arranged some forty guns. Incredible as it may seem, these guns were incapable of movement, exactly as they had been at the Battle of Raidaniya, when the Ottomans attacked Cairo, two hundred and eighty-one years before. The Mamlukes, like the Bourbons, had learned nothing and forgotten nothing.

The Mamluke army being thus immobile, the French were free to manœuvre as they wished. The Mamlukes may have had some eight thousand cavalry, whose only idea of warfare was the charge, a manœuvre which they could not execute inside the camp. Thus the cavalry could only fight a battle in the open, separated from the infantry and guns, which could not move out of the camp. The infantry, as always, had been despised by the Mamlukes and were a mere rabble.

On the morning of 21st July, the French infantry advanced in squares, with the artillery between. At about 2 p.m., as the French approached Imbaba, the Mamluke cavalry charged, perhaps six thousand strong. A wild mêlée ensued. The Mamlukes surged round the infantry squares, as the French cavalry were later to do at Waterloo, but were unable to break them. They rode up to the mouths of the cannon, until they were blasted to pieces. The first wild charge having failed to break the squares, there was nothing else the Mamlukes could do but ride from square to square, being shot. Eventually Murad Bey withdrew with the shattered remnants of his cavalry.

The cavalry thus disposed of, the French advanced on the camp, which they overran, the majority of the Egyptian infantry and camp followers being massacred. As in the good old days, the Mamlukes had ridden to battle in all their splendour of silk and satin robes, gold saddles, gold-inlaid weapons, money and jewels. The French soldiers were rewarded for their hardships by magnificent plunder.

* * *

In the Western nations today, many people have never heard of the Mamlukes, except as the opponents of Napoleon at Imbaba—commonly called the Battle of the Pyramids. In fact, however, in 1798, the Mamlukes had not been a government for the previous two hundred and eighty-one years. Egypt was a province of the Ottoman

Empire. The Mamlukes were a community of landowners with their clients, who, as a class, enjoyed no official position. For these two hundred and eighty-one years, they had been engaged solely in internal political struggles and had taken part in no wars.

At Marj Dabiq, in 1516, the Ottomans had made full use of field artillery, the Mamlukes of cavalry charges. At the Battle of the Pyramids in 1798, the French had field artillery, the Mamlukes used the same cavalry charges as in 1516. The absurdity of such a situation is difficult to appreciate. It was as if, in 1939, an army of Roundheads and Cavaliers, armed with muskets and pikes, had confronted the German armoured divisions invading France.

This much may be said for the Mamlukes in 1798. Three hundred years out of date in their tactics, they yet had the courage to attempt to defend their country. Had it not been for them, the French could have occupied Egypt unopposed.

*   *   *

No sooner was the result of the Battle of the Pyramids known in Cairo than the Shaikh al Beled, Ibrahim Bey, left the city with a convoy and crossed Sinai to Palestine, accompanied by the Ottoman pasha. On 24th July, 1798, Napoleon entered Cairo with a band of drums and trumpets, and took up his residence in a palace on the Uzbekiya.

French propaganda took the form of a proclamation that France, the ancient ally of the Ottomans, had come to rescue the Egyptians from their foreign oppressors, the Mamlukes. But whereas the French were nationalistic, the Egyptians were not. The Mamlukes had been in Egypt for some five hundred and fifty years and could scarcely be regarded as foreign invaders. But, above all, the Mamlukes were Muslims, while the French were not.

Meanwhile, however, on 1st August, 1798, the French fleet had been destroyed off the mouth of the Nile by Nelson. The grand French strategic plans were made impossible, including the invasion of England, for which the French fleet was needed and which Napoleon had intended to return to France to lead.

Murad Bey and a force of Mamlukes had retired to Upper Egypt. On 25th August, the French General Desaix left Jiza to pursue him, and spent the next eighteen months in guerrilla operations in Upper Egypt.

In February 1799, a French army left Egypt for Syria. Gaza fell on 24th February and Jaffa on 7th March. On 19th March, Napoleon laid siege to Acre, but was obliged to retreat on 10th May without taking the town. Plague, dysentery, short rations, the hostility of the people and the harassing attacks of the tribes had combined with the courageous defence of Acre by Ahmed al Jazzar and the British fleet under Sir Sidney Smith to put an end to the French advance. On 14th June, the remnants of the French expedition were back in Cairo. On 18th August, 1799, Napoleon embarked secretly and returned to France.

Meanwhile Britain and the Ottoman Empire had intervened and negotiations for a French evacuation were in progress. On 2nd March, 1801, a British force arrived off Alexandria. On 28th March, a battle was fought outside Alexandria in which the British General Abercrombie was killed. On 27th June, 1801, an Anglo-Ottoman-French Convention was signed in Cairo, providing for a French evacuation. The Ottomans and the Mamlukes returned to power.

The French occupation had lasted for three years, but the Mamlukes never recovered their power. Nor were the Ottomans strong enough to assume control. The situation remained chaotic, with Britain periodically suggesting solutions. The British had no wish to occupy Egypt, for all their trade was operating successfully round the Cape. The British army evacuated Egypt in March 1803.

In 1802, the Porte prohibited the export of young boys to Egypt. Until then, all through the period of Ottoman control, the Mamlukes had continued to import boys from the Caucasus.

After the French evacuation a large part of the Ottoman garrison posted to Egypt consisted of Albanian units. The Ottomans and the Mamlukes were intensely hostile to one another. By March 1804, the Albanians, under their commander, Muhammad Ali, were the most powerful element in Cairo. In July 1805, Muhammad Ali seized power. The Ottoman government, powerless to evict him, appointed him governor. The ensuing eight years were occupied by the long Napoleonic wars, while Muhammad Ali quietly consolidated his power in Egypt. Only the Mamlukes, now weak, impoverished and decadent, continued to oppose him politically. In 1811, however, he invited the Mamluke leaders to the Citadel, eliminated all who came in a general massacre, and established an Albanian dynasty which was to rule Egypt for a hundred and forty years.

Thus ended the Mamlukes, who had for two hundred and sixty-seven years controlled one of the greatest and most civilised empires of their time, from 1250 to 1517, and had remained, on and off, the virtual rulers of Egypt until 1798. With a system of government unique in history, they nevertheless ran the ordinary course of imperial rise and decay, as though they and their subjects had constituted a normal and homogeneous nation.

NOTABLE EVENTS

Elevation of Toman Bey	12th October, 1516
Battle of Raidaniya	22nd January, 1517
Entry of Saleem I into Cairo	26th January, 1517
Death of Saleem I	2nd September, 1520
Death of Khairbeg, the Traitor	6th October, 1522
Reform of administration of Egypt (in theory) by Ibrahim Pasha	1524
Death of Sulaiman the Magnificent	1566
Decline of Ottoman power	1566 onwards
Two hundred and thirty-two years of internal rivalries in Egypt	1566–1798
Landing of the French army at Alexandria	1st July, 1798
Battle of the Pyramids	21st July, 1798
Battle of the Nile	1st August, 1798
Siege of Acre	19th March–10th May, 1799
Seizure of power by Muhammad Ali	July, 1805
Final massacre of the Mamlukes	1811

Epilogue

I know of no way of judging the future but by the past.
PATRICK HENNY (1775)

For forms of government let fools contest,
Whate'er is best administered is best.
POPE, *Essay on Man*

EPILOGUE

THERE seem to be reasonable grounds for the statement that the Mamluke Empire from 1250 to 1517 was in some ways unique in recorded history. To begin with, it was one of the greatest empires in the world in its time, but it was ruled by a small group of professional soldiers who were ethnically of a race entirely different from the inhabitants. Colonies, that is countries ruled by foreigners, are as old as recorded history, but, in almost all such cases, the foreign rulers were acting for an empire based in their own country. Not only were the Mamlukes not colonial officials sent by a foreign empire, but they had no country at all. When the great Qipchaq sultans established their empire, their native country was under Mongol rule.

Situations perhaps bordering on this may have occurred elsewhere, but in all such cases the foreign rulers settled down in the country they had conquered, and made it their own. Only in the case of the Mamlukes was it laid down that the ruling class of every generation must come as boys (and sometimes girls) from their original homeland, and that their descendants, even if Turks or Circassians by both parents, were not eligible to rule. Not only so, but the rulers of the next generation were imported by purchase.

It is true that the use of the English word "slaves" is misleading, for slaves in the East were normally almost adopted into the family. To be a slave was near to being a son or a daughter—a more honourable status than that of a paid employee. But such was the custom in many eastern countries, yet no other government ever stipulated that *only* such persons could form the next generation of rulers.

An ameer's mamluke could rise to be sultan, but an ameer's natural son was not eligible to serve at all. Yet this rigid rule was abandoned in the case of the sons of sultans, owing to the problem of the succession, which the Mamlukes never solved. This is a striking example of the manner in which the mamluke system arose without planning, through a series of events which happened by accident, were dealt with by ad hoc decisions and thereby became customs.

The same remark applies to the system by which the mamluke's loyalty was to his patron (one might almost say his foster-father), and not to the army or the state. The next generation of rulers being imported as boys, some were bought by senior officers, who naturally desired to get good value from their adopted sons by insisting on their loyalty to themselves. This situation was peculiarly awkward for a new sultan, who found that every officer under him had a little private army of his own. The sultans tried to overcome this situation by juggling with the fiefs, so as to enable them to buy far more mamlukes than any of the ameers.

Any planner endeavouring to think out a constitution would have denounced such absurd customs as sheer lunacy and would have prophesied that such a state could not last for ten years. But here is the extraordinary result—by these methods the Mamlukes, complete foreigners, built probably the most powerful empire of their time. Not only so, but this empire lasted for two hundred and sixty-seven years, a period which might almost be said to be the standard lifetime of an ordinary great empire, based on the dominance of one race, operating from its native land. The British Empire did not last quite so long, if we reckon it to have begun about 1700 and ended in 1950.

Is it possible that political forms and constitutional planning are not really of great importance, if a lunatic system such as that of the Mamlukes can outlast the empire of a modern nation with its planned constitution, laws, parliaments, budgets and education? This is a materialistic age. We do not consider the spirit which inspires the people, but the gross national product, the imports and exports and the size of the country and its population. Under the Bahri or Qipchaq sultans, the Mamlukes were inspired by an unconquerable spirit, which against all conceivable odds, made them into a Great Power.

This was not done solely by fighting. For they were also practical and wise, open-minded, and encouraged commerce and agriculture. They also promoted the conquered natives to the highest appointments in those departments where they were obviously more efficient than were the Mamlukes themselves.

At the same time, their constant internal rivalries seem as insane as their absurd constitutions, yet it was their ruthless internal struggles for power which produced such men as Baybars, Qalaoon and Al-Nasir Muhammad. It may be argued that all the edifice of Mamluke greatness was due to these three men. With all our endless debates concerning laws and constitutions and political systems, we never discuss our ways of choosing our leaders. Yet the present methods of political intrigue, party politics, propaganda and election promises never produce really outstanding men as leaders, except perhaps in the stress of war and defeat.

*   *   *

A second area in which the Mamlukes have much to teach us is that of decadence. Superficially, it is easy to dismiss the Mamlukes and all their works as having no relevance for us. Every possible outward circumstance seems to be so utterly different that we could not possibly learn anything from them.

Yet in the history of the rise and decline of their empire we find many factors which are familiar to us. The golden age of wealth and power and self-confidence under the Bahri sultans bears many resemblances to the Victorian age. No one thought for a moment of accepting a military defeat. Every reverse was immediately rectified by raising more forces. Trade was booming, and many grew rich. Discipline was firmly maintained. Morality was, at least outwardly, rigidly enforced, though there was also much sincere religion, in addition to outward respectability. Everyone was confident that these happy circumstances would last for ever.

Then, after a magnificent century, the signs of Mamluke decline appear. The beginnings of financial dishonesty and bribery. The abandonment of conventions of dress in favour of casual clothing, the relaxation of efforts to enforce sexual morality, and the increase of alcoholism—these are the first pointers. Then the steady increase in crimes of violence, the depreciation of the currency, the rise in the cost of living, the excessive taxation, the great wealth of the rich, remind us of the same processes which we have seen with our own eyes. The revolt of the adolescents, who constantly resort to violence, which the authorities are too weakminded to suppress, yet which ultimately cause the national ruin. The endless mutinies of the young mamlukes, always demanding more pay, but doing less and less work and consequently becoming increasingly inefficient.

The superficial differences are due to the apparently totally different circumstances—the young mamlukes take the place of student protesters, the mutinies correspond to industrial strikes. Both are indifferent to the well-being of the nation as a whole. The young mamlukes loot the shops, the strikers of today wreck the country by withdrawing coal, electricity, transport or dock services, in order to press their claims.

Yet the young have reasons for protesting. There is inefficiency, there is bribery, some people are too rich and some too poor. Mutatis mutandis, all the ailments of the Mamluke state are with us today. Why does some paralysis seize the authorities in a decadent state, preventing them from disciplining the young? The protests of the young are frequently justified, but their youthful eagerness impels them to use violence, which only makes worse chaos. To young people, it seems too easy to dismiss the corrupt and the incapable, to appoint the loyal, the honest and the efficient to replace them, and thereby to bring in the Golden Age. But once force is used, the dream evaporates. In the confusion, it is not the idealists but the most violent and brutal who seize power. Abuses in government can only be removed by raising the moral standards of society, a slow process involving spiritual advances—but young reformers are in a hurry.

*   *   *

Then we see the Mamlukes forming themselves into political parties, the Nasiris, the Dhahiris, the Muaiyadis, constantly intriguing and manœuvring to get into power. And when they do so, all the adherents of the rival party lose their positions, and the new leaders obtain their patronage and the lucrative jobs. Might they not be equally called Socialists, Conservatives, Republicans or Democrats? At this stage in the life of a nation, internal political rivalries increase and the public receives the impression that competitors for political power are more concerned with their party interests than with the survival of their country.

*   *   *

I am no politician and it is not my intention to carry out political propaganda for any existing party or community. My object is solely to point out that all the problems which confront us have happened before. That the remedies suggested for our ills have often been tried and have failed.

The qualities which we associate with decadence are a lack of energy and will-power, resulting from descent from father to son for several generations, in wealth and leisure. Thus our cartoonists depict the heir to an old aristocratic family as being silly and feeble with no chin.

But such decadence could not overtake the Mamlukes, for the ruling class of each generation were not the descendants of their predecessors but barbarian boys from the steppes. Yet the Mamluke state became decadent by (apparently) the same stages as the modern Western Powers.

I am not advocating a policy but asking some questions, which I cannot answer. Why do nations decline and collapse and even cease to exist? Why do empires so frequently last about two hundred and fifty years? This lifespan is the same for democracies, autocracies, or any other political system. In other words, forms of government, to which in our age we attach such vast importance, make no difference. There must be other factors, which have escaped our notice, but which affect all human beings in all ages. These problems are too complicated for my understanding, but they are worthy of more thought than they seem to receive.

APPENDIX

TABLE OF MAMLUKE SULTANS

THE object of this list is (1) to record the names of all the sultans so that they can be seen at a glance, (2) to separate the successful rulers who reigned securely from the many stop-gap children and adventurers, who lasted only for short periods. The left-hand column accordingly shows those who reigned for five years or longer; the right-hand column those who were sultan for less than five years.

SECURE SULTANS (5 years and over)			INSECURE SULTANS (less than 5 years)		
Period of reign	*Name of sultan*	*Number of years reigned*	*Period of reign*	*Name of sultan*	*Number of years reigned*
1250–1257	AIBEK SPRAY-OF-PEARLS	7		AL-ASHRAF MUSA	—
			1257–1259	ALI IBN AIBEK	2¾
			1259–1260	AL-MUDHAFFAR QUTUZ	1
1260–1277	BAYBARS BUNDUQDARI	17			
			1277–1279	AL-SAEED BARAKA	2
			1279	AL-AADIL SALAMISH	¼
1279–1290	AL-MANSOOR QALAOON	11			
			1290–1293	AL-ASHRAF KHALIL	3
			1293–1294	AL-NASIR MUHAMMAD (First Reign)	1
			1294–1296	AL-AADIL KITBUGHA	2
			1296–1298	AL-MANSOOR LAJEEN	2
1298–1308	AL-NASIR MUHAMMAD (Second Reign)	10			
			1308–1309	BAYBARS JASHNEKEER	1
1309–1341	AL-NASIR MUHAMMAD (Third Reign)	32			
			1341	AL-MANSOOR ABU BEKR	¼
			1341–1342	AL-ASHRAF KUCHUK	½
			1342	AL-NASIR AHMAD	¼
			1342–1345	AL-SALIH ISMAIL	3
			1345–1346	AL-KAMIL SHAABAN	1
			1346–1347	AL-MUDHAFFAR HAJJI	1
			1347–1351	AL-NASIR HASAN (First Reign)	4
			1351–1354	AL-SALIH SALIH	3
1354–1361	AL-NASIR HASAN (Second Reign)	7			
			1361–1363	AL-MANSOOR MUHAMMAD	2
1363–1377	AL-ASHRAF SHAABAN	14			
			1377–1381	AL-MANSOOR ALI	4
			1381–1382	AL-SALIH HAJJI (First Reign)	1½
	Years of stability	98		Years of instability	35½

SECURE SULTANS (5 years and over)			INSECURE SULTANS (less than 5 years)		
Period of reign	Name of sultan	Number of years reigned	Period of reign	Name of sultan	Number of years reigned
Years of stability 98			Years of instability 35½		
1382–1389	AL-DHAHIR BARQOOQ (First Reign)	6			
			1389–1390	AL-SALIH (AL-MANSOOR) HAJJI (Second Reign)	¾
1390–1399	AL-DHAHIR BARQOOQ (Second Reign)	9			
1399–1405	AL-NASIR FARAJ (First Reign)	6			
			1405	AL-MANSOOR ABDUL AZEEZ	¼
1405–1412	AL-NASIR FARAJ (Second Reign)	7			
			1412	KHALIF MUSTAEEN	½
1412–1421	AL-MUAIYAD SHAIKH	8			
			1421	AL-MUDHAFFAR AHMAD	¾
			1421	AL-DHAHIR TATAR	¼
			1421–1422	AL-SALIH MUHAMMAD	½
1422–1438	AL-ASHRAF BARSBAI	16			
			1438	AL-AZEEZ YUSUF	¼
1438–1453	AL-DHAHIR JAQMAQ	15			
			1453	AL-MANSOOR OTHMAN	¼
1453–1461	AL-ASHRAF INAL	8			
			1461	AL-MUAIYAD AHMAD	½
1461–1467	AL-DHAHIR KHUSHQADAM	6			
			1467	AL-DHAHIR YALBAI	¼
			1467–1468	AL-DHAHIR TIMURBUGHA	¼
1468–1496	AL-ASHRAF QAITBAI	28			
			1496–1498	AL-NASIR MUHAMMAD	2¼
			1498–1500	AL-DHAHIR QANSUH	1¾
			1500–1501	AL-ASHRAF JANBULAT	½
			1501	AL-AADIL TOMAN BAI	½
1501–1516	AL-ASHRAF QANSUH	15			
			1516–1517	AL-ASHRAF TOMAN BEY	¼
Years of stability 222			Years of instability 45¼		

These figures show clearly the marked contrast between the sultans who were real rulers and the great numbers of stop-gaps and children, who scarcely or never ruled at all. The average length of reign of the real sultans was fourteen years and ten months. The average reign of the unstable sultans was one year and four months. This phenomenon was the result of the Mamluke system, which left the throne open to be won by the strongest candidate.

A SHORT BIBLIOGRAPHY FOR FURTHER READING

Abdul Dhahir, Muhi-al-Deen al   *Tashrif al Ayyam was al Usur*
Abulfeda, Al-Malik-al-Muaiyad Ismail   *Al Mukhtasar fi Tarikh al Beshir*
Anthology   *The Arab Heritage* (ed. Nabih Amin Faris)
—— *The Legacy of Islam* (Arnold and Guillaume)
Arabshah, Ahmad   *Timur The Great Prince* (Eng. trans. J. H. Sanders)
Athir, Ibn al   *Al Kamil fi al Tarikh*
Atiya, A. S.   *The Crusade in the Later Middle Ages*
—— *Crusade, Commerce and Culture*
Ayalon, D.   *Gunpowder and Firearms in the Mamluk Kingdom*
—— *Studies in the Structure of the Mamluk Army* (Bulletin of School of Oriental and African Studies, London University, Vol. 15, 1953)
—— *The Plague and its Effects on the Mamluk Army* (Journal, Royal Asiatic Society, 1946)
—— *The Circassians in the Mamluk Kingdom* (Note. David Ayalon has also written under the name of David Neustadt)
Baghdadi, Abdul Latif al   *Kitab Ifada wa al Itibar*
Batuta, Ibn   *Travels* (Eng. trans. H. A. R. Gibb)
✗ Benjamin of Tudela   *Early Travels in Palestine* (ed. T. Wright)
Brockelmann, C.   *A History of the Islamic Peoples*
Brocquière, Bertrandon de   *Early Travels in Palestine* (ed. T. Wright)
Browne   *A Literary History of Persia*
Cambridge Mediaeval History
Creasy, E. S.   *History of the Ottoman Turks*
Creswell, K. A. C.   *Muslim Architecture in Egypt*
Davis, E. J.   *The Invasion of Egypt by Louis IX*
Dhahabi, Shems-al-Deen   *Duwal al Islam*
Dunbar, Sir George   *A History of India*
Encyclopaedia of Islam
Eversley, Lord   *The Turkish Empire, its Growth and Decay*
Gaudefroye-Demombynes   *La Syrie à l'Epoque des Mamlouks*
Ghorbal, Shafiq   *The Beginning of the Egyptian Question and the Rise of Mehemet Ali*
Gibbon, E.   *Decline and Fall of the Roman Empire*
Gibbons, H. A.   *The Foundation of the Ottoman Empire*
Glubb, J. B.   *The Great Arab Conquests*
—— *The Empire of the Arabs*
—— *The Course of Empire*
—— *The Lost Centuries*
—— *A Short History of the Arab Peoples*
Grousset, René   *Histoire des Croisades*
—— *L'Empire des Steppes*

Grunebaum, Von   *Mediaeval Islam*

Harvard University   *Middle East Monographs. See* Shaw, Stanford J.

Hill, Sir George   *A History of Cyprus*

Holt, P. M.   *Egypt, Syria and the Fertile Crescent*

—— *The Exalted Lineage of Ridwan Bey* (Bulletin of School of Oriental and African Studies, London University, Vol. 22, Pt. 2, 1959)

—— *The Career of Kucuk Muhammad* (Bulletin of S.O.A.S. Vol. 26, Pt. 2, 1963)

—— *Al-Jabarti's Introduction to the History of Ottoman Egypt* (Bulletin of S.O.A.S. Vol. 25, Pt. 1, **1962**)

—— *The Beylicate in Ottoman Egypt* (Bulletin of S.O.A.S. Vol. 24, Pt. 2, 1961)

Howorth, Sir Henry   *History of the Mongols*

Hughes   *Dictionary of Islam*

Iyas, Muhammad ibn   *Al Mashhoor bi Bidaya al Zuhoor fi Waqaia al Duhoor*

Jabarti, Abdul Rahman al   *Ajaib al Athar fi al Tarajim wa al Akhbar*

Jubair, Ibn   *Travels* (Eng. trans. R. J. C. Broadhurst)

Khalliqan, Ibn   *Biographical Dictionary*

Lane, E. W.   *Manners and Customs of the Modern Egyptians (1836)*

Lane-Poole, S.   *A History of Egypt in the Middle Ages*

—— *Turkey*

—— *The Story of Cairo*

—— *Muhammadan Dynasties*

Larousse   *Encyclopaedia of Ancient and Modern History*

Lewis, Bernard   *The Arabs in History*

Maqrizi, Taqi-al-Deen Ahmad al   *Kitab al Sulook li Marifa Duwal al Mulook*

Mayer, L. A.   *Mamluk Costume*

—— *Saracenic Heraldry*

Moorehead, Alan   *The Blue Nile*

Muir, Sir William   *The Mameluke Slave Dynasty of Egypt*

Ohsson, Baron D'   *Histoire des Mongols de Perse*

Poliak, A. N.   *Feudalism in Egypt, Syria, Palestine and Lebanon*

Popper, William   *A History of Egypt 1382–1469* (Eng. trans. of Ibn Taghri Birdi)

—— *Systematic Notes on Ibn Taghri Birdi's History of Egypt*

Quatremère, M.   *Histoire des Sultans Mamlouks de l'Egypte*

—— *Histoire des Mongols de Perse*

Runciman, Steven   *A History of the Crusades*

—— *Byzantine Civilization*

—— *The Fall of Constantinople*

Setton, K. M. (Editor)   *History of the Crusades*

Shaw, Stanford J.   (Harvard University Middle East Monographs) *No. 7. Ottoman Egypt in the Eighteenth Century; No. 11. Ottoman Egypt in the Age of the French Revolution*

—— (Princeton University Press) *The Financial and Administrative Organization of the Ottoman Empire, 1517–1798*

Strange, Guy le *Palestine under the Moslems*
Sykes, P. M. *A History of Persia*
Suyuti, Jalal-al-Deen al *Tarikh al Khulafa*
—— *Hasan al Muhadhira fi Akhbar Misr wa al Qahira*
Taghri Birdi, Yusuf Abu-al-Mahasin ibn *Al Nujoom al Dhahira fi Tarikh Misr wa al Qahira*
Umari, Shihab-al-Deen al *Masalik al Absat fi Mamalik al Amsar*
Vucinich *History of the Ottoman Empire*
Wiet, Gaston *Journal d'un Bourgeois du Caire*
—— *Histoire des Mamlouks Circassiens*
Wells, H. G. *An Outline of History*
Ziadeh, Nicola *Damascus under the Mamlukes*

INDEX